G000066475

# ADVERTISING WORKS 6

# ADVERTISING WORKS 6

*Papers from the IPA Advertising Effectiveness Awards*

Institute of Practitioners in Advertising, 1990

*Edited and introduced by*

Paul Feldwick

NTC PUBLICATIONS LIMITED

First published 1991 by **NTC Publications Limited**
22-24 Bell Street, Henley-on-Thames, Oxfordshire, RG9 2BG, United Kingdom
Telephone: 0491 574671

Copyright © 1991 by NTC Publications Limited

All rights reserved. No part of this publication may be reproduced or transmitted in any form or by any means, electronic or mechanical including photocopying, recording or any information storage or retrieval system, without prior permission in writing from the publishers.

**British Library Cataloguing in Publication Data**
Advertising Works 6: papers from the IPA Advertising Effectiveness Awards 1990.
  1.  Great Britain. Advertising
  I. Feldwick, Paul     II. Institute of Practitioners in Advertising
  659.111

  ISBN 1–870562–41–0

Typeset by NTC Publications Ltd
Printed and bound in Great Britain
by The Bath Press, Avon

# Contents

CONTENTS

# IPA
# Advertising Effectiveness Awards
# 1990

This volume is a record of the IPA Advertising Effectiveness Awards scheme as it enters its second decade. The first competition in 1980 set out to do two things which would be of long-term benefit to the advertising industry. Firstly, to demonstrate through case histories that successful advertising campaigns could make a tangible contribution to business success. This may seem a modest enough ambition for an industry which even then was worth nearly £2 billion pa, but it is worth recalling that prior to 1980 there was virtually no case history material demonstrating advertising effectiveness, which was both *published* and sufficiently *rigorous* in its analysis to be convincing. Advertising had been, for many, an act of faith. And yet, as the 1970s saw increasing media costs and narrower manufacturers' margins, it became more and more important that a belief in advertising effectiveness be more than merely 'folklore'. Advertising in general was to some extent in the dock, and was (justifiably) expected to produce convincing evidence in its defence.

The same logic meant that advertising agencies had an increasingly important duty to their clients to demonstrate that advertising was working for their business in particular. Hence, the second objective of the new Awards, to stimulate more interest in the whole vexed area of how to evaluate advertising and to improve understanding and methods of measuring effectiveness throughout the industry.

The Awards were to be complementary to the many creative award schemes already in existence. None of these ever pretended to measure or reward sales effectiveness – they fulfil a different function in encouraging originality and craft skills amongst creative departments. But they could be criticised by clients as representing a value system for the advertising industry which was not necessarily that of the client.

This in itself gave rise to a widespread myth that agencies were interested in something called 'creativity' solely as a ploy to win awards, and which (by implication) was in conflict with the best interests of the client, that is, business effectiveness. The introduction of the Effectiveness Awards was a signal to the advertiser that his interests were at the heart of what agencies try to do, without denying the crucial role that creative awards do play. (The relationship between effectiveness and 'creativity' is an important subject which I shall return to a little later in this introduction).

These original objectives – to help justify the value of advertising, both in general, and in particular – have remained constant over the six biennial contests and still hold true today. At the end of the decade it seems appropriate to consider some of the changes in the advertising business that have taken place during that time, and reflect on the continued relevance of the Advertising Effectiveness Awards today and for the 1990s.

## A DECADE OF CHANGE

The decade to 1989 was a period of unprecedented growth in UK advertising expenditure – absolutely, relative to the RPI, relative to GNP, or just about any other way you care to look at it. Total display advertising at current prices went from £1,970m in 1980 to £5,517m in 1989, an increase of 180%; allowing for change in the RPI, this still represents 60% 'real' increase over the period. Looked at another way, total advertising grew from 1% of the GNP to an unprecedented 1.8% in 1989. The Advertising Association has shown that trends in advertising expenditure can be largely predicted from two other factors: consumers' expenditure and company profits. This growth then, was driven by general economic growth. It was not caused by, and certainly not reflected in, a corresponding increase in media capacity, despite the advent of some extra TV channels and press media. The result of more money chasing a limited supply of commercial TV time – to take the most striking example – was a simple escalation of the cost; 100 TVRs in 1989 cost more than 2½ times what they cost in 1980 (against retail price inflation of +70%).

This media inflation has had two effects which may be relevant to the discussion of advertising effectiveness. Firstly and rather obviously, it must focus clients' minds wonderfully on the return they are getting from their media expenditure, as it costs more in real terms.

Secondly, it seems likely that media inflation has been one of the forces leading to the increasingly negotiable nature of agency remuneration – partly because clients are under pressure to save money wherever they can, to compensate for the loss of media value in their budget, and partly because a standard commission of 15% of billings can be more easily questioned in such a volatile situation.

Whatever the reason, there is now more debate than there was ten years ago about the fairest way to pay the advertising agency, and both commission and fee systems have their advocates. Another thought which has attracted some attention recently is that some element of payment by results should be built into agency contracts. In which case the measurement of results becomes a key issue for a different reason, and I shall return to this subject too, later on.

But at the time of writing the advertising boom of the 1980s is already a fading memory in the minds of most UK advertising people. The nine 'fat' years of the 1980s are overshadowed by the lean year of 1990. The Advertising Association currently forecasts that by the year end total display advertising expenditure for the year will be down by 7%, in real terms, from 1989; and in the current mood of economic uncertainty, there seems little real comfort ahead in 1991. 7% may not sound a great deal, and an outsider might point out that we have little enough to complain of after some 17 years of continuous and substantial growth. Nevertheless, a 7% decline in agencies' income is a major devastation in agency profits unless costs reduce accordingly. In the short term costs *can* never come down as fast as income, but as the major cost in the advertising business is people, the inevitable logic is de-staffing, by redundancy or natural wastage – which we have already seen in most of the larger agencies.

Nor is this the only cloud currently hanging over the advertising business in the UK. The boom years of the 1980s were also those in which the London agency map was substantially redrawn, with the US-based multinationals giving ground to publicly quoted, UK-owned groups. For a period in the mid 1980s UK agencies were the stockmarket favourites. Shares traded at 30 times earnings, huge paper-backed acquisitions were carried out to create the expected growth. Saatchi's, and later WPP, led the way: others, like BMP, GGT, WCRS, Yellowhammer, followed in their wake. For a time it seemed as if being in advertising – or more precisely, 'marketing services' – was to possess the 'Goose that laid the Golden Eggs'.

It was all great fun while it lasted, but as the stockmarket's original enthusiasm was, with hindsight, probably unrealistic, so the collapse of the whole sector has been drastic and unforgiving. We may hope that in time, and with some pick-up in the economy, that a more realistic, balanced view can be achieved. In the meantime it all adds up to an easy conclusion for anyone in advertising – that the 1990s are going to be the reckoning for the 1980s – that the wheels have fallen off.

And it is in that context that I think the publication of this book carries an important message to all of us who work in advertising – as well as, I hope, to our clients, and perhaps even to the stockbrokers' analysts.

The message is, that *advertising still works*. The market for our product may fluctuate with the economy, as ice cream sales fluctuate with the weather, but the product itself is still as potent as ever it was. The nineties may well be difficult years. They will almost certainly see radical change in the industry, the way it is structured, the way agencies are paid for their work; they will see increasing pressure for advertising money to work harder and be accountable, which in itself is a reason for the continued relevance of these Awards. But there is no evidence that traditional media advertising has ceased to be a valuable and unsubstitutable tool of business.

In all the talk which rightly goes on about integrated communications and marketing services, it is worth reminding ourselves that this is true. Here are 20 new case histories to prove it.


## CREATIVITY AND EFFECTIVENESS


An American colleague remarked to me, 'I suppose with this recession on, you're going to have to give up this *creative stuff* and concentrate on selling.'

The relationship between 'creativity' and effectiveness is a vexed question, not helped by the difficulty of defining 'creativity' – a necessarily subjective concept. One common assumption, as above, is that creativity is a luxury which can be indulged in when times are easy, but needs to be ditched when the going gets tough.

The opposite assumption, which might be closer to what some creative directors believe, is that creativity is the essential attribute of good advertising – that impact and distinctiveness are all. A third point of view might be that there are no rules, and the concept is actually irrelevant and unhelpful.

In 1989 Paul Charman wrote an article in *Campaign*[1] in which he attempted to analyse past winners of the IPA Advertising Effectiveness Awards (1980 – 88) by their success in winning Creative Awards. His conclusion, based on the fact that only one IPA winner had taken a Gold D & AD (the most prestigious creative award) was that there was little correlation, with the implication that 'creative' ads and 'effective' ads were generally different animals.

Is this, as a general conclusion, justified? I don't think so. Charman's own analysis (which only includes first prize winners, or seconds when no firsts were awarded) looks at 28 IPA cases, of which nine – that is, almost one in three – actually received some sort of creative award as well.

There are two reasons why I think this proportion surprisingly high, rather than low, and also why the figures alone do not tell the whole story.

The first is that creative awards are extremely hard to get, and represent a fairly narrow definition of 'creativity' – whatever it is. Admittedly several of the 'undecorated' IPA winners do not fit into any plausible definition of creativity, but equally there are several which I think would be generally recognised as witty, clever, charming, original, and certainly not 'hard sell'. Campaigns like GGT's Crows for the London Dockland Corporation, Castlemaine XXXX, Clifford the Dragon for Listerine, Fry & Laurie for the Alliance & Leicester.

The second is that IPA Effectiveness Awards are, if anything, even harder to get, but for completely different reasons. Even to produce a plausible entry it is necessary to surmount a number of hurdles: firstly, the campaign must have been effective; then the data must exist to demonstrate this; then the client must give permission for the agency to enter, and this is regrettably not always granted. (Not to mention that someone must put in a lot of hard work to write the paper!).

The papers that win are chosen, *absolutely not* on 'creative' criteria, nor even on some notion of which was 'the most effective campaign', but on the essential criterion of the most convincing argument. Given these difficulties – which will necessarily screen out some of the creative award winning campaigns – and such different criteria of judgement, it is perhaps more telling that so large a number of IPA case histories demonstrate campaigns which clearly worked, not in spite of, but *because of*, their 'creativity'.

One of the striking things about the 1990 Awards is that virtually all the winning campaigns, if not actually creative award winners, represent work which I think most 'creatively minded' agency people would not be ashamed to own. Certainly I would be pleased to be associated with, for instance, the campaigns for Audi, Lil-lets, Uvistat, Choosy, Silentnight, Lanson Black Label – and I *am* pleased to be associated with some of the others.

Of course there is always the exception that proves the rule.

Radion must have been one of the most talked about campaigns of 1989, both in the industry and outside it. A throwback to the 1960s; a send-up; an insult to the intelligence, it infuriated creative departments and housewives alike. It also sold an awful lot of detergent; and if you read this paper, you will find it neatly positioned the new brand so that its sales came predominantly from Lever Brothers competitors, rather than their own Persil. Of course, it's possible that, if 'creativity' is about zigging when others zag, having the courage of your convictions and going way over the top, then Radion has it too.

Whatever the message is in all of this, it doesn't suggest to me that we have to give up creativity in a recession in order to be effective.

## REWARDS FOR 'GETTING IT RIGHT'

What the Awards also demonstrate, of course, is that spending advertising money does not automatically create a return on investment: it only does this if the agency and client between them have got it right. And sometimes that the difference between getting it right and getting it wrong is not just a matter of 5 or 10% at the margins, but between a campaign which generates extra profit and a campaign which is a complete waste of every penny spent on it.

The importance of 'getting it right' is brought home in this volume by such cases as Karvol, and particularly Uvistat, where a change of campaign achieved markedly superior results *on a reduced budget*. Clients will increasingly value agencies whose skills reduce the cost to them of effective advertising. This does not, incidentally, start with cheese-paring on production costs, or artificially inflating numbers of TVRs (at the expense of minutage) by over-use of the ubiquitous '10 second cutdown'. The case of Pirelli tyres – shortlisted but regrettably just short of a prize, so not reproduced here – was a good example of how on a small budget (average just over £1m pa) the client had the nerve to spend what it took on high production values, and never used anything less than a 60 second commercial. The result, a famous and convincingly successful campaign which belies its modest budget. The real savings are made by creating advertising which stands out, which is strategically well thought out, and which touches the hearts and minds of the consumers.

The traditional payment system to agencies of a fixed commission on billings (generally 15%) still has a lot of support in the industry. It must be said however that it offers no obvious incentive to agencies to recommend smaller media budgets! (The system was of course originally designed to stimulate media sales, the commission being nominally paid by the media owners themselves). There might be advantages to clients – and a benefit to the advertising industry itself – if a way could be found of basing some element of the agency's remuneration on the amount of business it created, not simply just how much the campaign cost to buy. This would obviously be an incentive to the agency to produce the most effective work, and might encourage more effort to be put into devising original low cost solutions to advertising problems.

To date this notion of 'payment by results' has been at the experimental stage, rather than widely adopted. One of the major problems it poses, of course, is the question of how to define and measure 'success'. To do it purely in terms of sales could be unfair to the agency, as so many other factors beyond their control could affect these; on the other hand the use of intermediate measures such as awareness or image shift could be criticised as artificial, and encourage the agency to chase high awareness scores rather than sales (there are techniques for doing this). The most likely solution would seem to be that success needs to be based on a broad understanding of various different kinds of measures, in the way that the successful papers in this book and other volumes of *Advertising Works* demonstrate. It will, even so, only work where a certain level of trust and openness exists between agency and client – but perhaps this is not too much to hope for. In developing methods of evaluation for remunerating agencies, the IPA Advertising Effectiveness Awards offer a uniquely valuable starting point. It may be that, in the future, techniques of evaluation are used to win not just awards, but *rewards*, for advertising agencies.

So far by way of putting the 1990 Awards in context; and it demonstrates, I hope, that the relevance of the Awards as a focus for the study of advertising effectiveness is as great and probably greater in 1990 than it was in 1980. We also owe a debt to the prescience of those, particularly Dr Simon Broadbent, who conceived the scheme and did so much to make it work. I for one would feel much less happy going into the advertising market of the 1990s without these six volumes behind me!

It remains to offer such commentary as may be necessary on the contents of this book; to explain, chiefly for newcomers, the rules of the competition; and to give, for the aficionados, something of a 'match report' on the 1990 entries.

## THE COMPETITION

Entries for the Awards are required to be in the form of written papers, up to 4,000 words in length not counting appendices and charts (each entry form must be countersigned by the agency's chief executive and by a competent representative of the client, by which act copyright is passed to the IPA: all papers, successful or not, are kept on file at the IPA in Belgrave Square and may be inspected on request by a member of any IPA agency).

To explain the criteria on which the judges base their decision it seems best to quote from the actual instructions which the judges were given to work to:

### *Notes for Judges*

1. The main criterion for judging is simple: how convincing is the case put? The onus is on the author to anticipate questions and counter-arguments. Many papers fail because they do not consider all the relevant facts, or present data in an obfuscatory way (on purpose or through carelessness). If the sceptical (but not necessarily 'expert') reader feels reasonably convinced that it was indeed the advertising that produced the results claimed for it, then the paper is a contender.

2. However, it is not quite so simple! In some cases it is almost absurdly easy to demonstrate the advertising effect: in other cases, the task of isolating the effect is fiendishly difficult (car campaigns are a good example). In some instances it is, perhaps, literally impossible. Clearly it would be absurd and contrary to the spirit of the Awards only to reward simple and obvious entries. We, therefore, find in practice we have to judge the arguments relative to the difficulties they have faced.

3.  Effectiveness in these Awards is defined as contribution to the business. This does not mean that measures such as awareness or brand image are irrelevant – far from it, they are often vital – but there needs to be some sort of argument which links these to business objectives, ultimately in terms of sales or profitability. We also need to be careful that we do not only reward short term paybacks – the long term competitiveness of the brand can be at least as important (this is especially true, of course, in Category 5 – Longer and Broader).

4.  Papers will obviously be less likely to convince if they are poorly written or presented. Good clear English, clarity of argument, and good presentation of data all help. We expect to see a clear exposition of the background to the campaign, the development of the strategy, and a clear statement of what was actually done and when (creative work and media plans), as well as the review of performance.

5.  The judges should not be influenced by whether they personally liked or hated the advertising, or whether it was 'creative' or not: the arguments are judged objectively. An author may as part of the case show that 'creativity' contributed to the effectiveness: that is a different matter.

6.  'Bonus points' are added for papers which add something new to our knowledge, or make an original point. They must of course conform to the basic criteria as well.

## FIVE CATEGORIES

In 1990 a total of 87 entries was received, an all-time record. It is encouraging that the number continues to grow, in view of the very considerable effort required to produce an entry: encouraging too that these entries came from 36 different agencies, including most of those in the 'Top 20' as well as entries from smaller agencies and from outside London.

This year saw the introduction of a new category, in addition to the established four. The five categories in which entries were judged are as follows:

1.  Established Goods and Services
2.  New Goods and Services
3.  Small Budgets
4.  Special (financial, public service, charity) etc
5.  Longer and Broader Effects

It is interesting to look at trends in numbers entering in each category, as 1990 saw some departure from the pattern of previous years.

| Category: | 1 | 2 | 3 | 4 | 5 | Total |
|---|---|---|---|---|---|---|
| 1984 | 27 | 11 | 12 | 9 | — | 59 |
| 1986 | 24 | 11 | 11 | 13 | — | 59 |
| 1988 | 29 | 15 | 8 | 19 | — | 71 |
| 1990 | 18 | 10 | 27 | 16 | 16 | 87 |

It was perhaps predictable that Category 5 would generate entries mainly at the expense of Category 1, 'Established Goods and Services', which in fact had the helpful effect (for the judges) of reducing the size of the field in what was traditionally an unwieldy category to judge. Less expected was the explosion in entries for Category 3. To some extent this must have been fuelled by the redefinition of 'Small Budgets' from £250,000 to £500,000: a change long overdue as the original figure was set in 1980, and on that basis still lags behind media inflation. It may also be that the disappointingly low entry in 1988 led a lot of entrants to assume this would be the easy prize to win! Whatever the reason, the quality of this category was very high, generating a large number of interesting but different case histories. In the event, eight of the papers in this category received an award of some kind, while several others came very close.

What made this category of particular interest were the number of cases which attempted ingenious and novel methods of evaluation. Choosy catfood monitored the sales effects of a poster campaign (in itself a rarity in these awards), by carrying out a special Nielsen analysis of stores within a certain radius of poster sites – the exact methodology may be open to criticism, but the author deserves the credit for innovation. And the case for Lea & Perrins took the measurement of effectiveness right into the consumer's kitchen by issuing calibrated bottles of Worcester Sauce!

## ON CONCENTRATION

The other principle demonstrated particularly well, but by no means exclusively, in the small budgets category, is the crucial importance of making strategic choices and sticking to them singlemindedly – 'concentrating your fire' as Nelson recommended. Lil-lets reversed a decline of several years by targeting exclusively at teenage girls entering the Sanpro market; Uvistat took a clear decision to return to their roots of 'protection' and so differentiate the brand from a list of competitive brands. Aberlour put their whole budget behind a single promotion, to sell hogsheads of malt whisky for delivery in the year 2000: by so doing they created more awareness for the brand on a small budget than would otherwise have been possible.

Of course the benefits of concentrating on one clearly targeted message are not confined to those on small budgets. The first prize winner in Category 2, Crown Solo, shows an equally bold decision to concentrate the entire media budget for the wide range of Crown paints behind one new product launch. The result was that not only did Crown Solo itself achieve a striking success, but that sales of the other Crown products also showed a distinct uplift, despite receiving no advertising.

The Audi case furnishes yet another parallel: the decision to concentrate singlemindedly on the fitting of catalytic converters as standard equipment. Again it seems likely that this highly focused message did more both to attract attention to the launch and to reposition the marque than a more fragmented approach could ever have done.

## LONGER AND BROADER

The easiest situation in which to demonstrate the sales effect of advertising is a dynamic one, where volume increases clearly follow the campaign; and the easiest situation in which to justify the financial investment in advertising is that where incremental profits showed an obvious short-term return. Such occasions do of course occur. But they do not represent all the situations in which it makes business sense to advertise. In fact it is doubtful whether they are even typical of the contribution advertising can make to business. The largest and most committed advertisers spend consistently year after year, not particularly in the anticipation of volume increases, and certainly not in the expectation of this year's advertising being defrayed by a corresponding increase in next year's profit. At any point the advertising could be cut and the money saved would have a major (short-term) impact on the bottom line.

Why, therefore, do they do it? They do it in the belief that advertising is one of the factors which adds value to the brand they sell. Advertising ensures that customers will continue to pay more for the brand leader than a cheaper substitute. It will help to differentiate the brand from competition so that it offers unique qualities of reassurance and satisfaction. In business terms its role is as often to provide stability and predictable long term profit, as to effect sudden change. That this is more than mere wishful thinking, is borne out by extensive analysis carried out over a number of years by the Strategic Planning Institute's PIMS programme, quoted by Alex Biel in a highly relevant article in *Admap*[2]: this shows that brands which advertise more tend to have a higher market share, higher perceived quality, and generate a higher return on investment.

All this is true. And yet by the end of the fifth IPA Effectiveness Awards in 1988, there was a growing realisation that these 'longer term' or 'indirect' results of advertising were continuing to be under represented in the papers entered for and receiving the awards. The reason was clear and understandable: it is far harder to make a convincing argument when the result of activity, year after year, is that 'things stayed more or less the same'. Far easier to pick on the dramatic sales increase, the relaunch, the quick payback. And yet if the message of the Awards is that this is all that advertising is useful for, it has dangerous implications. Simon Broadbent pointed this out in an important article in *Marketing*[3]:

'Currently, this (the Advertising Effectiveness Awards) is the cutting edge of campaign evaluation, but an edge which I believe is in danger of turning against its makers.... Nearly all published IPA papers show that the campaign studied increased sales in the weeks or months after it appeared, and did so economically. Nothing wrong with that. But as so often happens with managers who are given a new aid, they come to believe that there are no others. Once more, a particular objective, this time the achievement of short-term volume return, is seen as all there is. Perhaps the IPA should next introduce a class of entries which are about the long-term and indirect effects of advertising.... To correct the current imbalance and to extend our understanding of advertising's total effects would take us to a new era of campaign evaluation and budget-setting – and away from loose thinking about advertising'.

The criticism and the warning were so obviously well founded that the Awards Committee looked for a new initiative to try and restore the balance.

The result (after various discussions in which Simon Broadbent and others were involved) was the proposal to add a fifth category to the existing four. The name 'Longer and Broader' (for which we are indebted to Charles Channon) represents the twofold nature of the kind of papers hoped for. Firstly, those that dealt with non-dynamic situations, where consistent advertising investment over a period of years was justified by an essentially static, but profitable business; but also to look for demonstrations of the indirect, or broader effects of advertising – price premium rather than volume; retail support; enhanced effectiveness of promotion; everything which Stephen King once described as increasing the 'saleability' of a brand. The launch of the new category was supported by an IPA Publication, *The Longer and Broader Effects of Advertising* edited by Chris Baker, a selection of papers which was designed to explain more fully the background to the new category and to offer some guidelines to aspiring entrants[4].

The response to the new category, given the considerable problems of proof which it raised, and the fact that it was largely uncharted territory, can only be regarded as encouraging. A total of 16 entries was received – of those a small minority had clearly misunderstood the requirement, but most were certainly addressing the key issues of longer term evaluation.

However, it is also possible to see the effects of the new initiative outside Category 5 itself. The paper on Karvol, for instance, entered for Category 1, explicitly addresses itself to the issue of 'saleability'. And I do not think it is wishful thinking to detect in more papers than in the past, and not just those published, an explicit emphasis on the importance of price premium rather than just volume (eg Uvistat) and an awareness of the importance of retail support. There may come a time when 'Longer and Broader' as a separate category is no longer needed; when that happens it will have achieved its objective.

In the meantime the new category has provided an invaluable catalyst in reversing the trend of the Awards towards 'quick payback' scenarios, and has also given them new life in providing a new kind of challenge to the authors. The problems of demonstrating advertising's contribution over the long term, in relatively static situations, have already been referred to. Neither the committee nor the judges really knew in advance how entrants to the new category would tackle them. Any view of the strength and weaknesses of the arguments put forward in 'Longer and Broader Effects' needs to acknowledge that all the authors were breaking new ground, and working without an obvious model.

Those who expected a simple formula to emerge will not, of course, find this in the winning papers, each of which deals with a different kind of case in its own appropriate way. But it could be said that what all the winning papers do is to look at the brand's *strength*, often relative to its competitors, in many different ways: its price premium; its degree of trade support; its consumer image and awareness; blind and branded product tests; the *failure* of competition or own label to steal share; in other words, the concept of a *brand audit*.

The remaining part of the equation is to argue that the brand's 'added value' could not have been created without advertising. This structure is most explicit in the First Prize paper, PG Tips, but it is the implicit model of Croft, Lanson, and Silentnight. Where the 'traditional' IPA paper might start by demonstrating a simple sales increase, the 'Longer and Broader' papers start by demonstrating *brand strength*: as I suggested in the introduction to a previous volume, not just *Advertising Works*, but *Advertising Adds Value*.

It may be that this year's winners only represent a foundation to be built on, rather than a definitive solution to all the issues. But as they are, they represent (in my view at least) a major contribution to our understanding of how advertising and branding work. PG Tips in particular offers a published and fully detailed account of how a brand leader retains dominance in a market, in a way which I do not think has been done before. That advertising works in this way has been frequently asserted by agencies, and of course believed by many advertisers.

But to my knowledge this paper represents the first time that a coherent argument with such a wealth of factual detail has been publicly available, and as such it deserves to be widely read.

The organisation of the 1992 Awards is in the hands of the committee, but it would be my recommendation that the 'Longer and Broader' category definition be repeated. We have certainly not heard the last word on the subject. One thought that may be relevant to future entrants has been kindly pointed out to me by Simon Broadbent after he had read the Category 5 papers.

His observation was that the majority of entries for this category (and all the winners) dealt with long running and extremely consistent campaigns – but that the scope of 'Longer and Broader Effects' is not necessarily limited to campaigns which maintain executional consistency, nor indeed to advertising which runs for a long period of time (it must be said that an unpublished entry on Smirnoff would have exemplified the first point; the second may be illustrated by the published paper on Karvol). The interpretation of 'Longer and Broader' as simply meaning 'long running campaign' is perhaps understandable, but misses some of the point. Perhaps in future we will see more emphasis on 'broad' as well as 'long'.

## CONCLUSION

There has always been a danger that, as pressure for advertising 'accountability' becomes more intense, so agencies and clients fall back on dangerously simplistic solutions which misrepresent the real effects of advertising. In the sixties there was Rosser Reeves and the spurious concept of 'usage pull'; in the seventies the introduction of econometrics threw all the emphasis on to short-term fluctuations in sales rather than longer term increases in brand value. At any time various measures of awareness or recall have been used too much in isolation to equate to sales effectiveness[5]. The structure of the IPA Awards, by demanding a fully rounded and critical evaluation of all the evidence (and rejecting spurious logic) has been of incalculable value in discouraging these sorts of error.

It is gratifying to be able to report, therefore, that as we enter the new decade the IPA Advertising Effectiveness Awards are in good shape. Not only attracting more, and probably better entries than ever before, but evolving in order to continue to deepen agencies' and clients' understanding of how advertising works, and how it should be evaluated.

## REFERENCES

1. Charman, P 'Hard Sell Honours v Creative Kudos', Campaign, 19 May 1989.
2. Biel, A 'Strong brand, High spend', Admap, November 1990.
3. Broadbent, S 'Wait and Measure', Marketing, 22 September 1988.
4. Baker, C (ed) Longer and Broader Effects of Advertising, IPA 1990.
5. Feldwick, P 'What should we measure?', Admap, April 1990.

## IPA ADVERTISING EFFECTIVENESS AWARDS COMMITTEE

Michael Hockney, Managing Director, Butterfield Day Devito Hockney Ltd. (*Chairman*)

Chris Baker, Planning Director, Bainsfair Sharkey Trott

Paul Feldwick, Director and Head of Planning Department, BMP DDB Needham

Kevin Green

Tim Lefroy, Chief Executive, Young and Rubicam Ltd.

Simon Marquis, Managing Director, Burkitt Weinreich Bryant Clients & Co. Ltd.

Hamish Pringle, Director, The Leagas Delaney Partnership Ltd.

Charlie Robertson, Head of Account Planning, Bartle Bogle Hegarty Ltd.

Mark Robertson, Business Development Director, HDM Horner Collis and Kirvan Ltd.

Nigel Roby, *Marketing*

Clare Rossi, Deputy Head of Account Planning, Saatchi & Saatchi Advertising Ltd.

Mike Walsh, Chairman, Ogilvy & Mather Ltd.

## 1990 JUDGES

Sir Ronald Halstead, Deputy Chairman, British Steel (*Chairman*)

Chris Baker, Planning Director, Bainsfair Sharkey Trott

Dr Stephan Buck, Director, AGB Research

Ann Burdus, Senior Vice-President, Marketing and Communications, Olympia and York, Canary Wharf

Charles Channon, Director of Studies, Institute of Practitioners in Advertising

Ian Davis, Partner, McKinsey & Co.

Paul Feldwick, Director and Head of Planning, BMP DDB Needham

Stephen Ward, Business Development Director, Cadbury, and Chairman of Jamesons

## ACKNOWLEDGEMENTS

The success of the 1990 IPA Advertising Effectiveness Awards owes a great deal to the media who gave free advertising space:

*Campaign*
*Marketing*

Grateful thanks are due to *Marketing*, the principal sponsor of the Awards Presentation by Peter Stiles Presentation, and to the following companies whose support helped to make the presentation possible:

IPC
ITV Association
Mirror Group Newspapers
Millward Brown
Ogilvy & Mather
Olympia and York
Omnicom
Peat Marwick McLintock
J Walter Thompson
Young & Rubicam

Many people worked hard to make the Awards a success, but they owe a great debt to Michael Hockney, Chairman of the Awards Committee. Particular thanks should also be given to Hamish Pringle for the advertisements, and, for the Institute of Practitioners in Advertising, to Janet Mayhew, Secretary to the IPA Advertising Effectiveness Awards Committee, to Sarah Donegan, Public Relations Officer, and to her successor Tessa Gooding.

# Prizes

## LONGER AND BROADER EFFECTS

FIRST PRIZE AND GRAND PRIX

*How the chimps have kept PG Tips brand leader through 35 years of intense competition*
Clive Cooper, Louise Cook and Nigel Jones
   *BMP DDB Needham* for *Brooke Bond Foods*

SECOND PRIZE

*Croft Original, 'one instinctively knows when something is right'*
Melanie Haslam
   *Young & Rubicam* for *International Distillers and Vintners*

THIRD PRIZES

*The Ultimate success story – How the Hippo and the Duck advertising campaign helped to rebuild Silentnight's business in the UK bed market*
Roger Ward
   *Bowden Dyble Hayes & Partners* for *Silentnight Beds*

*Champagne Lanson – 'Why not?'*
Amelia Reynolds
   *Saatchi & Saatchi Advertising* for *J.R. Phillips*

## ESTABLISHED CONSUMER GOODS AND SERVICES

FIRST PRIZE

*Marketing sleep – The relaunch of Karvol*
Diana Redhouse
   *BMP DDB Needham* for *Crookes Healthcare*

SECOND PRIZES

*Adding volume to Vorsprung durch Technik*
Robert Poynton
   *Bartle Bogle Hegarty* for *Audi*

*Knorr Stock Cubes – How thinking local helped CPC develop advertising which toppled the brand leader*
Sarah Carter
  *BMP DDB Needham* for CPC


THIRD PRIZE

*Making Warburton's a breadwinner*
Adam Morgan
  *Still Price Lintas* for *Warburton's*


## NEW CONSUMER GOODS AND SERVICES

FIRST PRIZE

*Crown Solo – The paint which rewrites the rules*
Terry Prue
  *J Walter Thompson* Co for *Crown Berger*


SECOND PRIZE

*The case for Radion Automatic. A new brand in the Lever Portfolio*
Brent Gosling
  *Ogilvy & Mather* for *Lever Brothers*


THIRD PRIZE

*Advertised without compromise, evaluated without mercy – The new Renault 19*
Katrina Michel
  *Publicis* for *Renault UK*


## SMALL BUDGETS

FIRST PRIZE

*Uvistat – Against all odds*
Lorna Young
  *Butterfield Day Devito Hockney* for *Windsor Pharmaceuticals*


SECOND PRIZE

*Value for money in charity advertising – Advertising for Amnesty International 1988 – 1990*
John Grant
  *BMP DDB Needham* for *Amnesty International*

THIRD PRIZES

*Lil-lets brand – How a small investment safeguarded the future of a brand*
Drusilla Gabbott, Sarah King and Tara Macleod
  *Abbott Mead Vickers* for *Smith and Nephew Consumer Products*

*The relaunch of Choosy Catfood, or a dog called Tiddles*
Ruth Passmore
  *Bartle Bogle Hegarty* for *Spillers Foods*

*Hogshead revisited – How advertising helped accentuate the development of Aberlour Malt Whisky*
Ian Forth
  *BMP DDB Needham* for *Campbell Distillers*


## SPECIAL

FIRST PRIZE

*Alliance & Leicester first time buyer mortgages*
Antony Buck
  *BMP DDB Needham* for *Alliance & Leicester*


MARKETING AWARD FOR INNOVATION

*Adding a little magic to Lee & Perrins' Worcestershire Sauce*
Michael Llewellyn-Williams
  *The Creative Business* for *HP Foods*


IPC WOMEN'S WEEKLIES EFFECTIVE MAGAZINE CAMPAIGN AWARD

*Uvistat – Against all odds*
Lorna Young
  *Butterfield Day Devito Hockney* for *Windsor Pharmaceuticals*


MIRROR GROUP NEWSPAPER AWARD FOR BEST CASE HISTORY USING ON-THE-RUN COLOUR IN NEWSPAPERS

*Low cost gas central heating: how a shift in media strategy helped British Gas to consolidate its position in the market*
Alison Turner
  *Young & Rubicam* for *British Gas*


CHAIRMAN OF JUDGES PRIZE

*Vote Valley! Changing one agenda in a local government debate*
Richard Hunt
  *BMP DDB Needham* for *Charlton Athletic Supporters Club*

# Section One

*Longer and Broader Effects*

# 1

# How the Chimps Kept PG Tips Brand Leader Through 35 Years of Intense Competition

## INTRODUCTION

Our story begins in 1955, the year Brooke Bond relaunched PG Tips. Prior to 1955 it had been called 'Pre-Gestive' tea, a reference to the historical importance placed upon tea's dietary and medicinal properties.

The relaunch may have modernised PG Tips image but it didn't lead to a growth in its market share. Throughout 1955 and most of 1956, it remained number four brand.

Today, 35 years on, PG Tips is not just a player in this market, but also the dominant brand leader. How has this success been achieved and maintained?

Certainly, many things have changed over this period that might have affected the brand's performance. The nature of what the British eat and drink has changed substantially, as have fashions in the tea market and our social lives in general. Two things that haven't changed, however, are the campaign that first started in 1956 and the high level of media support given to the brand ever since.

In this paper we aim to prove that PG Tips *reached* this dominant position by 1958 because of the interest generated in the brand by the chimps advertising, then that PG Tips *maintained* its brand leadership by assimilating added value which enabled it to represent a more valued purchase to consumers, even though its absolute price has always been higher than its competitors.

After proving that added value has indeed been added, we then show that it is the chimps campaign that is primarily responsible for this addition of value.

Finally, we attempt to quantify the financial contribution of 34 years of the chimps campaign.

However, first we need to introduce them.

## THE CHIMPS CAMPAIGN

### A Unique Property

The original idea for the 'chimps' was chanced upon when a copy writer, charged with inventing the first PG Tips commercial, visited Regent's Park Zoo in 1956. The chimpanzees were enjoying a tea-party in front of a large crowd. A few months later, the first chimps commercial was shot in a stately home and featured a chimps tea-party accompanied by a voice-over by Peter Sellers.

This sixty-second commercial was designed to boost awareness of PG Tips and develop an original and inimitable property for the brand. At the time, it was believed that, on seeing the commercial, the obvious enjoyment of the crowd at the antics of the chimps in Regent's Park Zoo would be replicated in the homes of the viewers. Thus, it was hoped to establish a stronger relationship between brand, advertising and consumers.

'Stately home' first appeared on the nation's TV screens in the autumn of 1956.

### Consistency

In all honesty, nobody at that time suspected that the chimps advertising would be so effective so quickly. Within two years, the brand had toppled Typhoo from the number one slot, on the way overtaking other erstwhile giants such as Brooke Bond Dividend and Lyons (Brooke Bond).

The agency and Brooke Bond soon realised that they had a hot property on their hands. As time passed with PG Tips still retaining brand leadership, faith in the long-term potential of the chimps campaign strengthened. They quickly became so popular that Brooke Bond conducted film shows in cinemas around the country.

Consistency has been maintained ever since with similar creative executions running over the whole 34 year period. By the time of the chimps' 30th anniversary in 1986, over 100 commercials had been made.

Consistency has been maintained not only in creative style but also in media presence. PG Tips has always retained the dominant share of voice in the tea market, only varying its advertising spend (in real terms) by a relatively small proportion from year to year whereas the competitors' spends have fluctuated much more dramatically.

### Relevance

It would be tempting to believe that, having cracked a winning formula so early on, the agency's task would be solely to churn out more, very similar, chimps commercials. This of course is untrue for several reasons.

First, viewers need continually to be excited by new ideas.

Secondly, the chimps have lived through a period of exceptionally rapid social change. Making sure that they continue to reflect trends in society and do not become 'dated', has required constant change within the creative vehicle.

In the late 1960s, for example, the commercials reflected the self-expression of the times with two of them showing the chimps portraying a photographer and an artist.

# 'STATELY HOME'

Music: 'Greensleeves'
VO: The clock strikes four. In millions of English homes that means it's teatime

Teatime with its gleaming silver and tinkling teacups

What a happy time it is and how fortunate the hostess who knows that her favourite tea is also the favourite of her friends

For no matter how elegant the manners or charming the company

no guest is ever really happy without the right kind of tea

good tea, fresh tea, tea you can taste to

the last delicious drop

'He means Brooke Bond PG Tips. B-B-B-B-Brooke Bond'

Sound: Laughter from other chimps

In the 1970s, the chimps pastiched topical events such as the oil crisis and Ted Heath's preoccupation with his yacht, 'Morning Cloud'.

And of course, clearly observed sketches on the British character have always had the potential to attract enormous interest. 'Mr Shifter' who in 1972 coined the phrase 'You hum it son, I'll play it' and the 'Tour de France' cyclist with his 'Avez-vous un cuppa?' are two examples which have become part of the common vernacular.

The campaign has also adapted to take account of competitors' tactics. For example, in response to Tetley's greater emphasis on the advantages of their teabags' '2,000 perforations', the Bond series relaunched PG Tips with new 'Flavour Flow' teabags in 1981. 'Brooke Bond', a character based on James Bond, guarded the new teabags' secret.

'Ada and Dolly' formed the core campaign over the 1983 to 1985 period and were a deliberate move back to the chimps more traditional 'kitchen sink' territory, representing a retreat from the flash and spectacle of the Bond series. 'Ada' characterised the traditional packet tea user, 'Dolly' her more modern teabag-using counterpart. The appeal of old favourites still seemed to be strong however and therefore this series featured flashbacks to 'greatest hits' such as 'Mr Shifter' and 'Tour de France'. It was hoped that this would enhance the appeal of the campaign – reinforcing the campaign's and the brand's provenance.

Since then, development of the chimps has been driven by the desire to keep them in tune with ever more rapidly changing everyday life. Chimps are no longer shifting pianos but are flying on holiday to Spain, visiting health farms, doing their own DIY, making Board Room decisions and using computers.

This continual updating of the advertising has paid dividends throughout the 34 years of the campaign. As we shall show, the advertising's fame and appeal has remained consistently high.

## THE TEA MARKET: 1956 – 1989

Like many British institutions during the 1960s, tea was challenged by the new liberalisation of the times. Sales gradually went into decline as coffee became more appealing to the younger generation and consistently, albeit very slowly, since then, its growth, and that of other substitutes has eroded tea consumption.

TABLE 1:  DECLINE IN TEA

|                          | 1964 | 1974 | 1984 | 1989 |
|--------------------------|------|------|------|------|
| Tea volume (million kg)  | 156  | 140  | 130  | 110  |

Source:  Nielsen

Two major structural changes have occurred over the last 34 years – the introduction of the *teabag* and the introduction and steadily growing importance of *own label* teas.

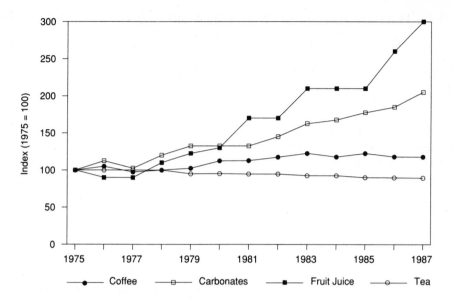

Figure 1. *Trends in drink consumption, average daily intake*
*Source:* NDS

## The Teabag

Teabags, the single most important innovation in the market, were introduced in 1963. Their arrival heralded a format change which dominates today, accounting for 80% of the market.

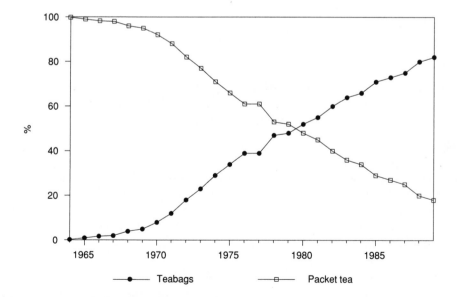

Figure 2. *The change in format, market shares of teabags and packet tea*
*Source:* Nielsen

*The Rise of Own Label*

The growth of own label and its significance in many markets is well documented. The tea market has not escaped.

It will be argued that PG Tips – the largest brand and hence the one with most to lose – has actually lost least to own label over the past 34 years.

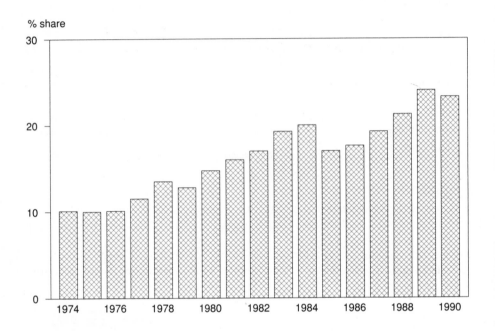

Figure 3.  *Own label's advances, share of total tea volume*
*Source:* Nielsen

## PG TIPS PERFORMANCE 1955 – 1958

*Assumption of Brand Leadership*

PG Tips became brand leader in 1958 having been number four before the chimps campaign rolled out in autumn 1956. Although we do not possess all the data from this period, we believe that PG Tips rose from about 10% volume share in early 1956, to c. 23% by the end of 1958. This represented at the time a dramatic shift in market structure. To put it in perspective, today (and remember that the market has shrunk since 1958) a gain of 13% volume share represents approximately £50 million of extra sales per annum.

*The Role of the Chimps Campaign in Achieving Brand Leadership*

It has proved impossible to trace accurate sales and other audit figures from the late 1950s. However, the following analysis eliminates other possible causes and suggests that the only causal variable for PG Tips' explosive growth in these two years was the advertising.

1. *Name Change* – Prior to 1955, Pre-Gestive was already colloquially shortened to PG by consumers, possibly because the P and the G were in bold type on the packet. Thus the name change is unlikely to have been such an important factor. Anyway, the change occurred a full year before the advertising started and share did not pick up as a result.

2. *Taste Change* – The blend was not changed at the time of the first chimps commercial.

3. *Distribution Change* – PG Tips was already in very strong distribution as the number four brand (aided by Brooke Bond Dividend's pre-eminence). As own label was not widespread at this time stocking four brands was perfectly normal.

4. *Price Change* – PG Tips was sold at the same price premium to the other brands before and after the advertising broke. So the growth was not caused by advantageous pricing.

What seems much more likely is that the advertising generated large increases in rate of sale.

Circumstantial evidence for the advertising being the root cause is also provided by the fact that this explosive volume share growth coincided with the most rapid increases in penetration of ITV and the chimps were the first TV tea advertising.

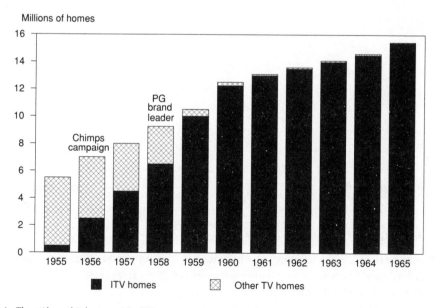

Figure 4. *The rapid growth in homes receiving ITV*
*Source:* ITV Association

Between 1956 and 1959, penetration of ITV grew fourfold, whereas between 1959 and 1962, it grew by only 35%.

Overall, although data inhibits our ability to 'prove' the claim conclusively, we believe that it is clear that it was the chimps TV advertising that thrust the brand from the number four slot to number one within the space of two years. Whilst the main theme of this paper is to demonstrate long-term advertising effects, we have also therefore shown that at one time the advertising had a very powerful and profitable short-term impact!

### PG TIPS PERFORMANCE 1959 – 1989

*Sustained Brand Leadership*

Ever since PG Tips broke through into the number one position in 1958, it has maintained brand leadership with a consistently high and stable volume share. Unfortunately, we only have accurate share data available from 1968. However, this shows the robustness of the PG Tips performance from this date onwards.

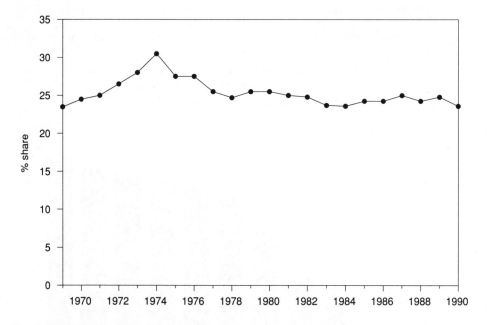

Figure 5. *PG Tips share of total tea market, year ending January*
*Source:* Nielsen, MEAL
*Note:* The unusual peak in 1974 coincided with one of the most popular ads, Mr Shifter, and with exceptional media weight

This remarkable achievement, and its rewards, should not be underestimated. The brand has faced intense competitive pressure with rival brands being relaunched (eg Quickbrew in 1986) and intermittently outspending PG Tips. In addition, every conceivable promotional weapon has been used by its rivals in an attempt to wrest away some of the PG Tips share.

The stability of the brand share over this period is evidence that these rival tactics have failed to dent PG Tips position over any significant length of time. Even when PG Tips share has dipped slightly, it has been able to bounce back shortly afterwards.

## The Concept of Added Value

PG Tips has been able to maintain such consistent and dominant share leadership because it has assimilated, over the years, an increasing amount of perceived 'added value', which supplements the functional benefits of the product. We have already noted that the brand's functional benefits are essentially generic, we now intend to demonstrate that the brand possesses added non-functional values of sufficient worth to motivate consumers to buy PG Tips even when price and other factors may mitigate against such a decision.

## Evidence of Added Value

The evidence that PG Tips has assimilated uniquely powerful added value over the past 34 years comes in many forms.

## Branded Versus Blind Tests

Consumers find it very difficult to distinguish between the major brands in blind taste tests. For example, in 1983, when asked to rate tea tastes blind (on a scale of 1 to 7), the average consumer response for the top five brands was extremely similar – varying by only 1 or 2%.

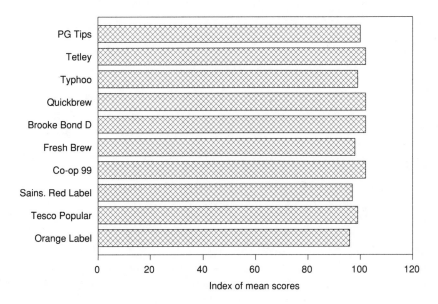

Figure 6.  *Consumers find it difficult to identify teas in blind product tests*
*Source:* Millward Brown, May 1983

This has been the case throughout the brand's history.

However, in *branded* tests, throughout the latter part of the 34 year period, PG Tips has enjoyed the greatest preference.

Even after brand size factors have been eliminated, PG Tips is perceived to be the best tasting cup of tea.

TABLE 2:  BRANDED TESTINGS

|                                               | PG Tips | Tetley | Typhoo |
| --------------------------------------------- | :-----: | :----: | :----: |
| Best tasting cup of tea (indexed against PG)  |   100   |   85   |   40   |

Source:  Millward Brown, March 1990

   This indicates that the brand has indeed attained a perceived added quality which is not justified alone by functional characteristics.

### Price Premium

Another significant measure of added value is whether the brand can justify a price premium and continue to sell in significant quantities while doing so – are consumers willing to pay more for a product that is functionally similar to its rivals? We have three pieces of evidence to suggest that PG Tips has succeeded in doing this.

   First of all, a superficial glance at pricing data suggests that PG Tips does now command a price premium over the market average, and it does so whilst maintaining its share.

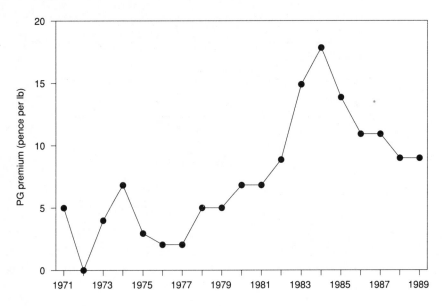

Figure 7.  *PG Tips price premium vs market average at 1985 prices*
*Source:* Nielsen

   Secondly, we have performed an econometric analysis using recent data from the teabag sector (now representing 80% of the market volume). This models PG Tips and Tetley's shares against relevant variables, details of which are given in the technical appendix.

The results show PG Tips to be much less sensitive than Tetley to price changes by both branded and own label competitors.

A 1% increase in the price of PG Tips relative to Tetley and Typhoo leads to a drop of 0.4 market share points. The effect of a similar increase in Tetley's price is much larger. A 1% increase in Tetley's price relative to PG Tips and Typhoo results in a downturn of 1.4 share points. We conclude that this is further evidence of the added value of the PG Tips brand compared with its major rivals since it implies that consumers are more likely to ignore price (in favour of other 'values') when it comes to purchasing PG Tips.

Finally, we have concrete evidence of the relative price insensitivity of the brand. In 1977, disaster struck both tea and coffee. Coffee bean and tea leaf prices rocketed. In the coffee market this provoked the introduction of cheaper, chicory based blends which grew to 30% of the market, hitting Nescafé, the brand leader, very hard.

Tea suffered too with market volume plunging by 10%. One might have expected the rapid rise in economy blends of coffee, at the expense of the brand leader, Nescafé, to be mirrored in the tea market with PG Tips. This did not happen. PG Tips retained its price premium and still held onto a 23% brand share – again demonstrating the added value justifying, even in times of crisis, a substantial price premium.

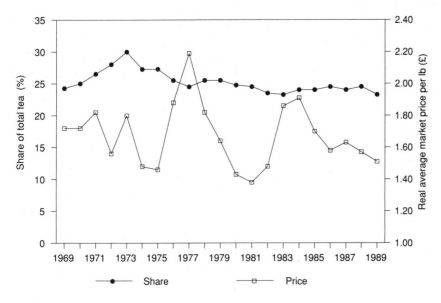

Figure 8. *PG Tips resistance to rocketing tea prices*
Source: Nielsen

### Resilience in the Face of Short-term Reductions in Media Support

If indeed the brand has assimilated added values over the past 34 years, then this would suggest that it should be less sensitive to short-term declines in the level of its advertising support.

Our econometric modelling did indeed suggest that this is the case. When less is spent behind the chimps, there is only a very small decline in share in the short-term (0.07 of a share point per 100 TVRs). Similarly, when the Tetley Teafolk are on air there is only a small impact on PG Tips share (PG lose 0.3 share points per 100 TVRs of Tetley advertising), a small proportion of what Tetley gain from spending that amount.

Tetley is far more sensitive to short-term changes in advertising weight. An increase of 100 TVRs per month gives them an extra 1.7 share points. They forfeit similarly for a reduction (see appendix for technical details of how the model was constructed. The appendix also includes data from periods when PG Tips media was withdrawn for up to four months. This confirms that significant share is not lost as a result).

Given this, it is even more impressive that PG Tips can survive off air for a few months, without suffering any significant fallback in share when we know that Tetley's advertising is capable of stealing significant share (from others).

We suggest that this is a further strong indication of the existence and potency of PG Tips added value.

Having said this, there is some downside to having such strong long-term advertising effects. Gaining short-term share from increases in the chimps media weight is relatively expensive. Certainly share is also less sensitive *on the upside* to chimps advertising than Tetley share is to Tetley advertising.

Some further evidence of relative insensitivity to short-term declines in share of voice is provided by the performance of PG Tips following the 1979 ITV strike. During this period, the only advertising available was print and radio. PG Tips share of voice fell to 12.3% compared to a more usual average of 20 – 30%. Nevertheless, its share remained static at 25% that year.

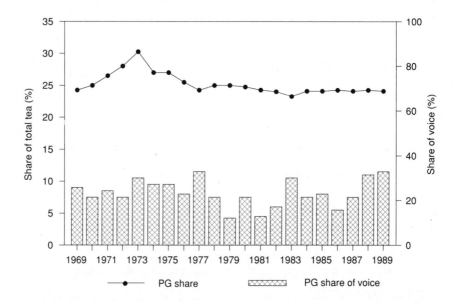

Figure 9. *PG Tips resistance to a low share of voice during the ITV strike in 1979*
*Source:* Nielsen

*Saliency and Consumer Appeal of the Brand*

PG Tips is a well known, well loved and well respected brand. All consumer audit data from the past 10 years suggests that it is consistently rated ahead of the competition on a whole raft of scores.

For example, during the whole of the 1980s, the brand has achieved higher spontaneous awareness than its nearest rivals.

TABLE 3:  SPONTANEOUS BRAND AWARENESS 1981 – 1989

|         | PG Tips | Typhoo | Tetley |
|---------|---------|--------|--------|
| Average | 100     | 91     | 58     |

Source:  Millward Brown

In terms of perceived popularity, quality and taste, the brand continually outscores the competition.

TABLE 4:  BRAND ATTRIBUTES, MARCH 1990

|                            | Average percentage agreeing | | |
|                            | PG Tips | Tetley | Typhoo |
|----------------------------|---------|--------|--------|
| Particularly popular       | 100     | 83     | 83     |
| Particularly good quality  | 100     | 54     | 76     |
| Best taste                 | 100     | 85     | 40     |

Source:  Millward Brown

*Hijacking the Teabag Sector*

The teabag arrived in 1963 as the product component of the new Tetley brand. Until then, Tetley had not existed as a tea brand at all and has never subsequently introduced 'packet-tea'.

At the time, Brooke Bond were cautious and delayed introducing a PG Tips competitive product. The reasons for this delay are now slightly obscure but three explanations seem plausible.

1.  Initial growth of the teabag sector was small. This suggested at the time that Tetley's innovation may have elicited little genuine consumer demand.
2.  The volume implications of teabags for the market were negative. When tea is brewed with loose tea, a pot is used which usually encourages waste, and of course, an extra teaspoon of tea is used 'for the pot'. When made with teabags, it is often done in a cup, with less likelihood of waste.
3.  PG Tips was already brand leader so it was not in its immediate interest to promote another sector.

Whatever the reason, PG Tips didn't introduce teabags for four years. By then, even though teabags still accounted for a relatively small share of total tea (1.4%), they had been growing by 50% year on year and it was apparent that this share would continue to grow.

Tetley, the innovator in the market, had by then established a strong brand franchise and was brand leader in the teabag sector with a share of 71%.

However, despite the strength of Tetley's position, PG Tips grew steadily and when the proliferation of teabag brands accelerated, it was Tetley not PG that lost share.

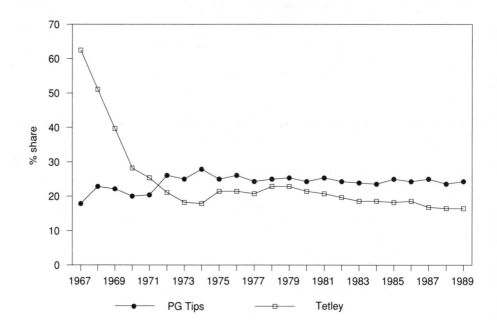

Figure 10. *Overtaking Tetley in the teabags market*
*Source:* Nielsen

We do not have media spend data for 1967 (the year of PG Tips bags launch) or 1968. However, during 1969, 1970 and 1971, Tetley bags *outspent* PG Tips bags on TV by 22%. Yet, by 1972, PG Tips had attained brand leadership.

The quality of Tetley and PG Tips teabags was equal. Distribution, if anything, favoured Tetley, as did price.

We conclude that this suggests that PG Tips already possessed significant added value compared with Tetley and that it was Tetley's lesser added values that made it the more susceptible of the two brands once competitive attack started in earnest.

Since we prove later that the brand's added value is largely due to the advertising, we can conclude that the advertising played a significant part in enabling PG Tips to hijack leadership in this sector.

The full significance of this is apparent when one considers that having grown from a meagre 1.4%, teabags now represent 80% of the market.

## *Resilience in the Face of Own Label*

Own label's share of the market has grown considerably since the early 1970s as we saw earlier.

One might have expected PG Tips to have lost share to own label in proportion to the brand's size. Maybe, one would have expected it to lose even more since its price premium over own label is higher than for other brands.

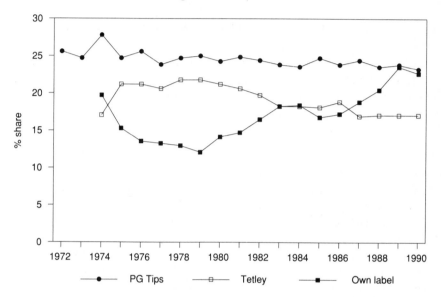

Figure 11. *The advance of own label teabags, PG Tips and Tetley vs Own label, year ending January*
Source: Nielsen

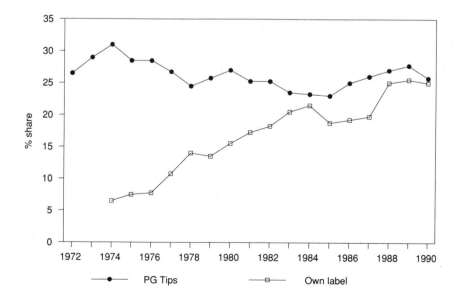

Figure 12. *The advance of own label packet tea, PG Tips vs Own label, year ending January*
Source: Nielsen

In fact, little of own label's growth has been at PG Tips expense. Instead, own label has eaten into the other brands in both packet and bags sectors.

Again, the clear conclusion is that PG Tips is more robust against price-led competition because it possesses added value compared with other branded teas. This enables the brand to offer a different, but very motivating, form of value for money to consumers.

## ISOLATING THE EFFECTS OF THE CHIMPS CAMPAIGN: 1959 – 1989

We have already shown that the chimps campaign was responsible for driving the brand to the number one position in the late 1950s. We will now show that *the chimps campaign is responsible for creating the longer term added value the brand possesses.*

There are three pieces of supporting evidence for this claim.

1.  We have examined all the other potential causal factors and they provide no plausible alternative explanation.
2.  The long-term performance of PG Tips has been compared with that of its competitors, most of whom have declined. The only factors which can explain PG Tips resilience in the face of this are differences in creative content and the level of advertising investment.
3.  Looking specifically at the chimps campaign, we have considerable 'soft' evidence showing how the advertising works. This shows direct correlations with many aspects of the brand's added values which are indirectly measurable via quantified consumer research.

### *Eliminating Other Factors*

The key point is that many elements of the brand are very similar to those of our rivals in their offering to consumers. Hence, we can conclude that these are not primary causal factors because, if they were, PG Tips would only have assimilated added value to the same extent as its competitors. The elements which are matched by our rivals are:

1.  *The Product* – PG Tips has always been an excellent product. A blend of 28 different teas, it is blended to a standard set by Brooke Bond's chief tea blender, not to a raw material price. Nonetheless, as we have seen, in blind product tests, consumers cannot tell it apart from its main competitors.
2.  *Promotions* – There is no evidence at all to suggest that PG Tips has either been more promoted than its rivals or that its promotions have carried greater value. As a consequence, even if the promotions have been more effective than the competitors, surely this is a *result* of the brand's perceived added value, not a *cause*.
3.  *Distribution* – Sterling distribution has been near universal for the major brands throughout much of the life of the chimps campaign. In March 1990, PG Tips, Tetley and Typhoo all enjoyed 90% plus sterling distribution. So we can exclude distribution gains.

4. *Price* – PG Tips has consistently maintained a 1% price premium over Tetley and Typhoo, its two closest rivals. Against own label, it has actually increased its premium over time – the brand was 57% more expensive than own label in September 1989 compared with 24% more in September 1971.

Hence, price *cannot* have been a driving factor. Indeed the data suggests the opposite – that we have been able to enjoy a consistent price premium *as a result* of our added value.

5. *Packaging* – This is a more difficult variable to eliminate completely. The very nature of packaging means that the PG Tips pack is very different from its rivals – hence, it cannot easily be dismissed as a variable that is equivalent to that of other brands. Indeed, we feel that the PG Tips packaging – the tea-picker, red and green colour coding and 'PG Tips' block branding – and its consistency have played a part in building brand recognition for the brand, and its appearance must be an important factor.

However, we also believe that the Tetley and Typhoo packaging elements are strong. It seems unlikely to us that PG Tips packaging alone could be so much more capable of adding so much value to the brand. This conclusion is circumstantially supported by the following chart which shows that claimed consumer appeal of these major brands' packs is roughly equal and certainly not significant in PG Tips favour.

TABLE 5:   CONSUMER APPEAL OF PACKS 1981 – 1989

|  | Average percentage agreeing | | |
|  | PG Tips | Typhoo | Tetley |
| --- | --- | --- | --- |
| Has an attractive pack | 100 | 94 | 114 |

Source:   Millward Brown

6. *Repeat Purchase* – It is conceivable that consistent use of the brand will reinforce positive experience and build added value which will in turn prompt further purchase – almost a self-supporting system once it has started.

This may be true. If it is, however, it is clear that advertising has played a role in this in two ways.

First, the initial consumer franchise (in 1957/58) was largely attracted through the advertising.

Secondly, we know that 'experience' of the brand in terms of all variables except advertising and packaging is matched by our rivals who have definitely not benefited in this way. Hence, if repeat purchase is a driving factor for added value then advertising is still largely responsible for this phenomenon.

Overall, this analysis leads us to believe that the only significant factors remaining which could have caused PG Tips assimilation of added value are the content of its advertising and the media weight behind it.

*Comparison With Other Brands Performance*

Many of PG Tips competitors have declined substantially over the last 20 or so years. The following table lists some of the losers.

TABLE 6:  LONG-TERM SHARE TRENDS – STANDARD TEABAGS

|                    | 1975 | 1980 | 1985 | 1990 |
|--------------------|------|------|------|------|
| Tetley             | 21.2 | 21.1 | 18.1 | 17.2 |
| Quickbrew          | 10.8 | 9.5  | 6.4  | 4.6  |
| Typhoo/<br>  Freshbrew | 11.1 | 9.0  | 6.4  | 7.1  |

Source:   Nielsen, year ending January
Note:   We only have historical data for Typhoo and Freshbrew
          combined

What is interesting, however, is that before their major decline, all of these brands were approximately equal to PG Tips in terms of their product qualities, pricing and distribution. Packaging of course was different, but not significantly lower in 'quality' or appeal.

The declining fortunes of each of these brands correlates instead with a strategy of *chopping and changing the content* of the advertising and with *lower support* for the advertising.

Hence, this offers further proof that advertising can have a very significant effect in this market. We would suggest that this makes it even more likely that PG Tips has added value precisely because of the more consistent support of its highly impactful creative vehicle and heavier media weight.

*How the Advertising Works*

Further circumstantial evidence for the part advertising has played in growing the brand's added value can be seen in analysis of how consumers react specifically to this advertising.

*Awareness and Appeal*

The chimps campaign has the highest level of awareness of all tea campaigns.

TABLE 7:  ADVERTISING RECALL INDICES 1981 – 1989

|                | PG Tips | Typhoo | Tetley |
|----------------|---------|--------|--------|
| Prompted recall | 100    | 51     | 77     |

Source:   Millward Brown

It is also the most efficient campaign in terms of generating awareness. According to Millward Brown, PG Tips advertising index is the highest in the market. (This is defined as the percentage gain in advertising awareness that would be produced by

100 TVRs in a theoretical TV region where no advertising had previously been shown).

TABLE 8: ADVERTISING RECALL INDICES 1981 – 1989

| PG Tips | Typhoo | Tetley |
|---------|--------|--------|
| 100 | 51 | 67 |

Source: Millward Brown

Combined with the heavy media weights of the past 34 years, it is hard to believe that such an impactful campaign as this had not had a significant impact on the consumer perception of the brand's value.

In addition, we know that the advertising is well loved.

TABLE 9: ATTITUDES TO THE ADVERTISING 1981 – 1989

| | Market average | Chimps |
|---|---|---|
| Amusing | 100 | 139 |
| Better than other tea ads | 100 | 146 |
| Would enjoy seeing again | 100 | 162 |

Source: Millward Brown

Given that consumers tend to talk about the chimps as part of the brand, it seems plausible that the above data suggests that the advertising is at least partly responsible for the brand's emotional appeal which in turn is surely what the added value of the brand is built on.

We also have further evidence of the advertising's inextricable role in building the brand's added value.

### Communication of specific brand benefits

The chimps advertising has always claimed in one form or another that

'There is no other tea to beat PG .... It's the taste'.

We know from consumer response to the advertising in qualitative research that the chimps campaign is 'loved'. The frame of reference for describing the campaign is always one of affection and warmth. It seems clear that the entertaining and lovable nature of the advertising enables this message of extra quality to be accepted – surely this is one direct way in which the advertising can be seen to have added value to the brand.

*Assumption of Tea Values*

Finally, in qualitative research, many consumers describe the advertising almost as 'a pick-me-up'.

'It gives me a lift after a hard day'.

This is also in fact precisely how people talk about their preferred tea. It seems that the brand and the chimps have almost become one. It is easy then to see how the appeal of the advertising which we have shown can translate into appeal for the brand.

We suggest that 34 years of such a mechanic has indeed added value, beyond functional qualities, to PG Tips.

*Summary*

We have previously shown that the brand has assimilated added value over the past 34 years.

Later we demonstrated that this *added value was primarily built and sustained by the chimps advertising*. Therefore we can conclude that the advertising has played a fundamental part in producing and maintaining PG Tips dominance in this competitive market.

## THE FINANCIAL CONTRIBUTION OF THE ADVERTISING

Since we have shown that the advertising was primarily responsible for investing the brand with the added value it now possesses, an analysis of the financial contribution should attempt to quantify financially this added value. The methodology to do this is not completely available to us. However, we can quantify three specific consequences of the power of the advertising and the added value it has generated. These instances alone suggest that the advertising has paid for itself many times over.

*Financial Benefits of Long-term Brand Leadership*

Without the short-term effectiveness of the chimps campaign from 1956 to 1958, it is unclear how PG Tips could have grown share substantially because the three brands above it at the time were all strong. Once it had achieved the number one position, we have already shown that the advertising played a primary role in maintaining that dominance.

Therefore, one way to evaluate advertising's contribution is to consider what revenue would have been lost if PG Tips had continued as the fourth brand.

From this it can be deduced that the chimps have helped the brand achieve an extra £2,000m sales over this 20 year period alone.

Brooke Bond are understandably unwilling to disclose margin data, but even on quite conservative estimates, the profit generated is much higher than the total of the amount spent on media and production over the whole 34 year period. The costs over the last 20 years at 1985 prices have been £86m (as measured by MEAL) on media and £6m on production.

### Financial Benefits of Price Premium

It is possible that the above scenario shows the campaign's profit contribution in too positive a light. Maybe the brand would have grown without advertising or with a campaign run on a much lower media spend (although we doubt this). However, another way to evaluate the chimps' contribution is to look at the revenue generated over the 32 years since the brand reached number one, by the price premium that we believe that the advertising supported. If we assume that PG Tips could only have charged average branded prices to maintain its volume without the chimps, the extra revenue is still some £125m (at 1985 prices) over the last 20 years alone.

### Financial Benefits of Hijacking the Teabag Market

Finally, we can look at the revenue generated by being able to assume brand leadership in the teabag market compared with what might have happened without the chimps.

If we assume that without the chimps, PG Tips teabags would have remained second brand to Tetley teabags with a share equivalent to the current number two brand, then PG Tips would lose £200m of revenue (at 1985 prices) which it gained because it assumed the number one position in 1972. This ignores the advertising costs of supporting the number two brand which would significantly increase this loss.

### Summary

Whichever of these methods is used, the advertising's effect over the 34 year period more than justified its cost.

## SUMMARY

Overall then there can be little doubt that PG Tips has been tremendously successful over the past 34 years. Brooke Bond has had the marketing foresight to continue to invest in rather than just milk, such a strong brand.

As a result, we have seen that PG Tips has remained brand leader over the whole of the period whilst fighting off fierce competitive challenges particularly in the form of Tetley's teabags and the growth of own label. Not only that, but it has remained price leader as well.

We have also seen that Brooke Bond have done this by investing the brand with added value that prompts consumers to continue buying even when more functional qualities of the brand suggest that other brand choices would be at least as satisfactory in purely functional terms.

This is perhaps the definition of what differentiates a true brand from a product.

And we have demonstrated that the chimps advertising has been the primary generator of this added brand value. Without it, or with advertising only as effective in the long-term as other tea brands it seems extremely unlikely that PG Tips would have been able to fight off such strong competitive activity.

Finally we have seen that quantifying the financial contribution of the advertising is difficult, but three methods have been used to show that it has generated a financial value for the brand well above its cost.

## CONCLUSION

Brooke Bond have created in PG Tips a brand that has enormous value to consumers. As a consequence, more consumers choose it compared with its rivals even though it sells at a price premium.

In addition, the brand's perceived value is so strong that it can actually *exploit* a *rival's* innovation. In a market place where technical barriers to entry are very low, this ability is vital for the brand's long-term maintenance of leadership. After all, no brand, not even PG Tips, can have a monopoly on successful innovation over a long time period.

We believe that there are two key lessons to be learnt from all this, which are inter-related:

1.  The importance of foresight. In maintaining brand leadership, a brand is going to encounter unexpected and unplanned for competitive activity. The only way to guarantee successful repulsion of these attacks is to have *already* built added values into the brand. Waiting until the threat is specifically known is costly and could be fatal.
2.  The importance of consistent advertising support. If the paper has shown nothing else, it has shown that *consistency* in a very strong creative vehicle and in high levels of media weight can ensure the brand does indeed become invested with added value and can pay back dramatically over the long-term.

Taken together, these two points suggest the critical part treating advertising as a long-term investment can play in building and maintaining a brand's strength. PG Tips is and will continue to be a testament to that.

## TECHNICAL APPENDIX

Ideally we would have wished to construct a very long run econometric model to try and test some of our hypotheses about whether, as PG Tips continued to advertise, its response to marketing variables was changing over time, eg whether it was becoming less price sensitive or less vulnerable to competitive activity. Our only available long-run of data however was annual and was not sufficient therefore in terms of the number of available data points to start constructing a complex model.

So, in order to investigate PG Tips responses, we tested our hypotheses 'cross-sectionally'. That is we constructed two models, one of PG Tips and one of

Tetley, and made comparisons of the market share responses of the two brands to the various pressures in the teabag market. From consumer data we knew that differences between the products were imperceptible and thus that any difference in terms of response to price etc was not a result of product difference.

The two models were estimated using 'ordinary least squares' on monthly Nielsen data from its start at the end of 1985 to December 1989.

For reasons of confidentiality, we do not wish to report the exact structures of the models. Both models, however, fitted the data well and performed very acceptably on a range of statistical tests. They included variables like branded competitive price, own label price, own label distribution, own and competitive advertising and the introduction of any line extensions/packaging changes.

In pricing terms, the models were similar in structure; the overall impact of price changes however differed markedly with PG Tips being much less sensitive to price than Tetley. Their response to advertising was quite different. Tetley was much more volatile, exhibiting marked short-term blips as a result of advertising but which died away quite quickly.

The following statistical tests and diagnostics for the fit and specification of both models were carried out and reported: $R^2$, standard error of the regression, sum of squared residuals, DW, Lagrange multiplier tests (portmanteau tests for higher order autocorrelation) with up to 1, 4 and 12 lags, ARCH tests for auto-regressive heteroscedasticity (1, 4 and 12 lags), the variance ratio test for homoscedasticity and the two Chow tests for post-sample predictive failure and for parameter stability and homoscedasticity respectively.

Both models have subsequently continued to predict the market well.

# 2

# Croft Original
## 'One Instinctively Knows When Something is Right'

### INTRODUCTION

Croft Original pale cream Spanish sherry was launched by IDV in 1966. As the very first light-coloured sweet sherry, it represented a challenge to both the conventions of a traditional, conservative market and the dominant brands of three, well-established sherry shippers – Domecq, Harveys and Gonzalez Byass.

However, as we aim to show in this paper, it was the Jeeves and Wooster campaign, introduced in 1977, that fully realised the potential of this challenge. In the 1977 – 81 period, Croft Original advanced from being a small brand of limited appeal to be the second largest, mainstream brand in the Spanish sherry market.

This transformation of the brand's franchise was vital to the longer term health of Croft Original. In the 1980s, the Spanish sherry market declined and own label established a strong position. Under these adverse conditions, Croft Original was the only brand to substantially increase its market share, further narrowing the gap with Harveys Bristol Cream, the brand leader. Other, less well-placed brands suffered badly.

### BUSINESS BACKGROUND

Sherries are defined by their country of origin. Only sherry imported from Jerez in Spain is permitted the designation 'Spanish sherry'. Other sherries include those from Montilla in Spain, Cyprus and South Africa. 'British' sherry is made from an imported concentrate.

Spanish sherry is of a higher quality and sold at a considerable price premium to the other sherries. Consequently, Spanish sherry is in many ways a self-contained market, operating largely independently of the other sherries.

Despite changes in the absolute size of the Spanish sherry market over the last two decades, there are three market characteristics that have remained essentially the same. They place Croft Original's performance in an appropriate perspective.

1. *Sherry Styles* – The Spanish sherry market divides into three broad sectors defined by the sweetness of the sherry. These are sweet (or cream), medium and dry; also called Oloroso, Amontillado and Fino. The volume shares of these three styles have been remarkably consistent over the last 20 years. The sweet sector accounts for 60% of the market (see Figure 1), and thus is the most important sector in terms of volume opportunity and determining a brand's and shipper's market performance.

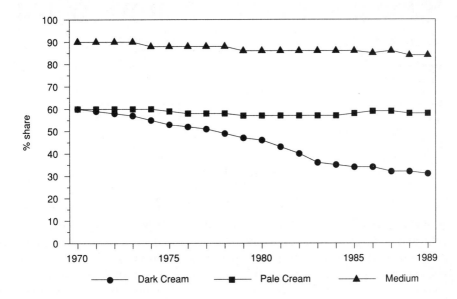

Figure 1. *Spanish sherry by style*
Source:    *Nielsen/IDV*

   In 1966, when Croft Original was launched, all sweet or cream sherries were dark in colour. As Figure 1 shows, the growth of pale cream has clearly been at the expense of dark cream sherries, not affecting the relative size of the other sectors, despite the fact that both medium and dry sherries are also pale in colour.

2. *The Importance of Christmas Volume* – Christmas is a crucial time of year for the sherry market. It brings in a large number of lighter/occasional sherry buyers who are stocking up the drinks cabinet for the festive season and buying for Christmas gifts. The occasional and less experienced consumer will tend to purchase a quality, premium brand that is a 'safe' choice in terms of brand reputation and taste. Thus, Spanish sweet sherries, particularly the bigger well-known brands, are the main beneficiaries with over one third of their annual volume accounted for by the December/January period, compared to about a quarter for other sherries (see Table 1).

3. *Premium Priced Brands* – Some brands within the Spanish sherry market, most notably Harveys Bristol Cream, have consistently been sold at a price premium to the rest of the market. This premium pricing is usually part of a quality positioning that, as just noted, is most effective in the Christmas period.

The combination of volume opportunity with improved margins means that a successful quality brand is a particularly profitable proposition.

TABLE 1:  CHRISTMAS VOLUME OPPORTUNITY

|                | 1983* | 1984* | 1985 | 1986 | 1987 | 1988 | 1989 |
|----------------|-------|-------|------|------|------|------|------|
| *% volume accounted for in December/January* | | | | | | | |
| Spanish        | 33    | 33    | 32   | 31   | 32   | 32   | 32   |
| Non-Spanish    | 23    | 23    | 27   | 23   | 24   | 24   | 24   |
| *Spanish sherry by style* | | | | | | | |
| Pale cream     | 40    | 38    | 37   | 35   | 35   | 36   | 35   |
| Dark cream     | 38    | 38    | 38   | 35   | 36   | 37   | 35   |
| Amontillado    | 26    | 26    | 26   | 24   | 26   | 26   | 27   |
| Fino           | 24    | 25    | 25   | 22   | 24   | 25   | 25   |

Source:   Nielsen
Note:   * England and Wales only

### The Spanish Sherry Shippers

Within this market framework, three major shippers have been prominent over the last 20 years: Harveys, Gonzalez Byass and Domecq. They all offer sweet, medium and dry sherries, but the relative strengths of the shippers vary by sector. Harveys has always been particularly strong in the cream sector with Harveys Bristol Cream – consistently the leading brand of Spanish sherry. Gonzalez Byass, by comparison, has maintained a stronger presence in the Fino sector with brands like Tio Pepe and Elegante. But Domecq has not had such strong brands as Tio Pepe and Harveys Bristol Cream (this ultimately made their position in the market a very vulnerable one, as will be seen later). In 1966 these three shippers had two thirds of the market, good distribution and an established consumer base.

## THE LAUNCH OF CROFT ORIGINAL

During the buoyant years of the 1960s IDV took the decision to enter the Spanish sherry market.

IDV recognised that the volume and profit opportunity lay in developing a well-known quality brand of sweet sherry. It would be aimed at mainstream sherry consumers, including the occasional, Christmas buyer. But this inevitably involved taking on the strongest brand in the marketplace – Harveys Bristol Cream. A basis for differentiating the projected brand from Harveys Bristol Cream, and other sweet sherries, was clearly desirable.

IDV speculated that there might be an opportunity to capitalise on the trend from dark to light drinks evident among young drinkers, and on the perception that dry

Note: Throughout the rest of this paper any reference to Harveys is to the shipper as a whole and Harveys Bristol Cream will be specified separately as the brand.

drinks (which tended to be light or pale) were more sophisticated than sweet ones. Their suppliers in Jerez therefore developed a product with the sweetness of taste preferred, but with an increasingly fashionable pale colour. This proposition was as yet untested in the older, more conservative sherry market.

Recognising the need to give a new sherry a brand heritage and pedigree, the decision was taken to launch the product under the Croft House name. Croft had been established as a port shipper since 1648 and had some presence in the UK, although only with a limited distribution and consumer base. Croft Original was launched in 1966. As a quality brand, it was priced at a premium to other Spanish sherry brands, but retailed at 5 – 10p less than Harveys Bristol Cream. This targeted price differential has since been maintained as far as possible. The packaging has remained substantially unchanged over the years.

## CROFT ORIGINAL: PROGRESS TO 1976

The Spanish sherry market grew strongly over this period, imports increasing 34% between 1971 and 1976. Croft Original grew ahead of the market, slowly but steadily building share so that by 1976 it held an estimated 3.6% of the market.

As Croft began to grow, other shippers also saw the opportunity and introduced their own pale cream brands. 1974 saw the launch of San Domingo from Gonzalez Byass, followed in 1975 by Spanish Sun from Domecq.

In 1976, despite its growth to 3.6% brand share and good distribution (eg 83% sterling distribution in multiple grocers), Croft Original was still a relatively small brand in the Spanish sherry market. So far, it had mainly attracted the more experimental (and less loyal) regular sherry drinker. The brand needed to strengthen its position in the market vis-à-vis competitor pale cream sherries, and widen brand usership to the targeted mainstream and ultimately more conservative sherry drinker. Growth of the brand was also essential for Croft Original to exploit the seasonal Christmas volume opportunity.

## THE EVOLUTION OF CROFT ADVERTISING

### Early Advertising

Initially, Croft's position in the marketplace was built on being pale, not a dark cream sherry, delivering 'a little Croft Originality'. When the other pale cream brands were launched in the mid 1970s this proposition was no longer competitive.

The key issues advertising had to address were:

— To give Croft (still a relatively new name in the conservative sherry market) real sherry credentials so that it would be a credible premium-priced mainstream contender, especially versus Harveys Bristol Cream.
— To continue to present paleness as a positive virtue in a market still dominated by the perception that cream sherries were dark, while also establishing Croft Original as *the* superior pale cream sherry.

'Dressage', developed in 1975 and the last execution before Jeeves and Wooster, sought to resolve these issues. However, in doing so it adopted an overtly upmarket stance. Although this execution implied (from the timelessness of the setting) Croft's permanence and heritage, nevertheless mainstream sherry consumers remained unconvinced that Croft had real sherry values and the credentials that were necessary to compete effectively against the established brands:

> 'I think either they are trying to seduce me into drinking a drink which has been drunk in directors' dining rooms for years, or on the other hand they are trying to rip me off by pretending they are'. (IDV Qualitative Research, 1977).

A new campaign was required that could tackle this problem.

### Jeeves and Wooster 1977 – 1989

*Advertising Strategy* – The role of advertising remained to promote Croft Original as *the* superior pale cream sherry, with real and accessible sherry credentials and heritage.

The communication objectives were defined as follows:

1. The product: paleness to be equated with quality.
2. The drinker: sophisticated and stylish, able to recognise the good things in life.
3. The brand: prestigious and long established.

The targeting remained unchanged, aiming at the mainstream sherry buyer. The primary target was described as the regular sherry drinker who kept a cream sherry in the home. It was thought that the secondary target, the occasional Christmas sherry buyer, would follow as the size and stature of the brand grew.

*Creative Development* – The creative idea developed used PG Wodehouse's characters, Jeeves and Wooster. The 1930s period scenario provided the brand with heritage and pedigree. But the problem of poshness and exclusivity evident in 'Dressage' was avoided. The use of wit and humour prevented the brand from being seen as either elitist or aloof.

The relationship between the likeable but basically inept Wooster and his butler Jeeves, the arbiter of good taste and discernment, provides a platform for projecting the quality of Croft Original and the stylish sophistication of its drinkers. The use of the end-line developed for 'Dressage', 'One instinctively knows when something is right', was continued as an appropriate summation of the brand's quality positioning.

The first execution in the series 'Suit' (1977), focused directly on the paleness of Croft Original. By drawing a comparison with Wooster's loud suit, the inimitable Jeeves leaves us with no doubt as to the discerning quality of Croft Original:

> Wooster: 'I say, top hole, but why is it that *colour*?'

> Jeeves: 'I imagine, sir, so that one may discern the quality of its taste merely by looking at it'.

The next three executions in the series, taking us up to 1981, all focus on the same theme of establishing the superiority of the visual appearance of the product. This is further illustrated by another comment from Jeeves:

> 'One can tell a great deal, sir, just by looking at things. Your Croft Original, for example, with its light delicate colour. One glance at the sherry tells one all one needs to know about the quality' (1981).

In total, 12 Jeeves and Wooster commercials have been developed. The campaign has proven to have real staying power and is flexible enough to carry a variety of more specific messages about the brand.

For example, later executions continued to reinforce the quality and sophistication of Croft's paleness, but in order to amplify the benefit over dark creams, increasingly linked paleness to modernity:

> 'now Croft Original with its light delicate hue has become ... the absolute thing' (1981).

A message of 'modernity' was entirely credible within the period scenario of Jeeves and Wooster, but it would have undermined the status of the brand to the sherry drinker if delivered in any other way.

Also, some executions were more directly aimed at Harveys Bristol Cream, referred to as 'the old brown stuff' in 'Aunt Agatha'. (1982)

The only departure from the dark-light contrast over this period was one execution developed to deliver a swipe at 'pale imitations', a response to the growth of own label.

*Media Strategy* – Television has been the only medium since Croft's launch, with buying concentrated around the crucial pre-Christmas sales peak. The same media

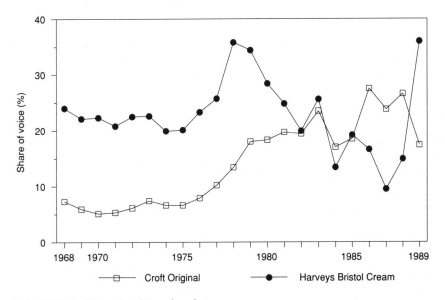

Figure 2. *Croft Original and Harveys Bristol Cream share of voice*
Source: MEAL

strategy was continued with Jeeves and Wooster, being the most effective way of reaching our target and building brand saliency and image.

Harveys Bristol Cream has traditionally been the biggest spender in the category, with an advertising share of 23% in 1976 compared with 8% for Croft Original. With the launch of Jeeves and Wooster, share of voice increased, so that by 1981 it was 20% for Croft Original versus 25% for Harveys Bristol Cream.

During the 1980s, Croft Original maintained share of voice at levels above 17%, narrowing the gap or even spending somewhat more than Harveys Bristol Cream when Harveys were supporting their new brands Finesse, Tico and John Harvey (see Figure 2).

## ADVERTISING EVALUATION

The evaluation of the Jeeves and Wooster campaign falls into two phases:

*1977 – 1981*: Jeeves and Wooster realised the brand's potential in an older, conservative market where there was not a natural dynamic towards lighter, more modern drinks (unlike wine and vermouth for example which have a more youthful orientation). This was crucial for the health of the brand during the 1980s.

*1981 – 1989*: Jeeves and Wooster continued to sustain the brand and grow share at a time when the market was in severe decline and brands were fighting the growth of own label. The less well-placed brands suffered disproportionately.

### *Phase 1 – Developing a Mainstream Brand: 1977 – 1981*

The Spanish sherry market was buoyant up to 1981, imports peaking at 6.4 million cases in that year (see Figures 3 and 4).

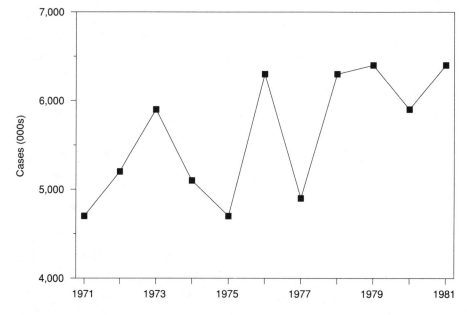

Figure 3. *Spanish sherry imports*
*Source:* HM Customs & Excise/IDV

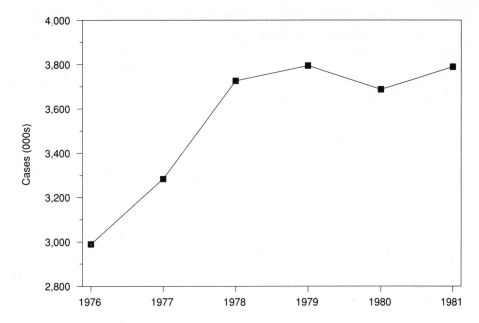

Figure 4. *Spanish sherry consumer sales*
*Source:* Nielsen

In this period, Gonzalez Byass and particularly Domecq lost share to Harveys and Croft. While Croft continued to grow share to 1981, 1978 was a notable turning point for Harveys, which for the first time saw its overall share decline (see Figure 5).

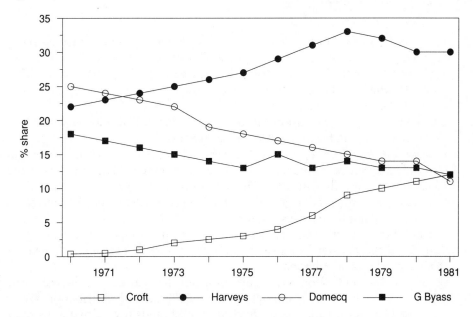

Figure 5. *Shipper shares*
*Source:* Nielsen/IDV

1. *Developing the Brand Franchise* – The most significant effect of the Jeeves and Wooster campaign was to build the size of Croft's consumer base. Up to 1976, growth had been slow, with virtually no growth at all between 1976 and 1977. However, after 1977 there was a substantial increase in Croft users from 2.4 million in 1977 to 7.5 million in 1981. Over the same period, Harveys Bristol Cream's consumer base remained relatively flat (see Figure 6).

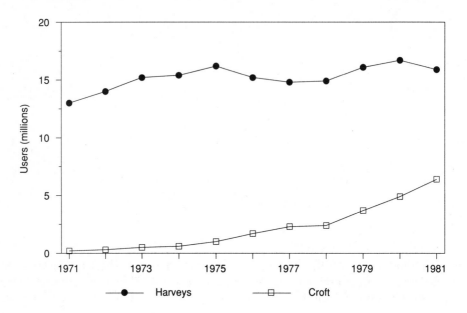

Figure 6. *Croft Original and Harveys Bristol Cream users*
Source: TGI

2. *Brand Sales and Market Share* – Croft's ex-factory sales grew strongly between 1977 and 1981, increasing by 88% to 631,000 cases. With a market share of 3.6% in 1976, Croft Original increased to 6.3% in 1977 and 10.7% in 1981, whereas Harveys Bristol Cream lost some share for the first time, from 19.6% to 18.5% (see Figure 7).

Other pale cream competition failed to make any real headway, with Croft Original accounting for over 80% of pale cream volume.

3. *Distribution and Rate of Sale* – The very substantial improvement in Croft Original's market performance in 1977 – 81 was largely due to the Jeeves and Wooster commercials with the increased advertising weight put behind them (of course, if strong sales growth had not been forthcoming, the increased support could not have been sustained).

The product, its packaging and pricing relative to the competition remained the same as in the first ten years of the brand's existence. The only other factor that changed was distribution.

Before Jeeves and Wooster, Croft Original had already achieved wide distribution – in 1976 in multiple grocers 83% sterling distribution versus 96% for Harveys Bristol Cream. By 1981 both brands had virtually the same distribution.

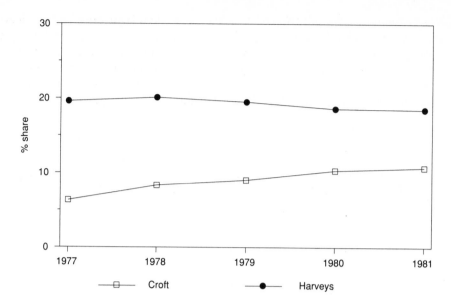

Figure 7. *Croft Original and Harveys Bristol Cream brand share*
*Source:* Nielsen

From the high distribution base of 1976, the effect of the additional distribution on Croft Original sales up to 1981, while positive, could not account for such a large sales increase. This is supported by the data we have on rate of sale (see Table 2).

TABLE 2: RATE OF SALE IN MULTIPLE GROCERS

|  | 1978 | 1979 | 1980 |
|---|---|---|---|
| Croft Original | 35.5 | 36.6 | 38.7 |
| Harveys Bristol Cream | 77.9 | 73.8 | 68.3 |

Source: IDV/Nielsen

Thus between 1977 and 1981 Croft Original developed from being a small niche brand to become the second largest brand in the sherry market with broad based consumer appeal. It did so by growing at a faster rate than the rest of the market, and taking share from dark cream sherries and notably from Harveys Bristol Cream. This allowed the brand to face the problems of the next decade from a position of strength.

### Phase 2 – Fighting for Share: 1981 – 1989

Two factors had a significant impact on the market in this period. First, the market went into decline from 1981 with a temporary recovery in 1984/85 (see Figures 8 and 9). The total number of sherry users declined by 22% between 1981 and 1989.

The second factor was the significant impact of own label. It increased from an estimated 3% of the market in 1979 to take 27% in 1985 and 29% in 1989. Own label was represented in all three sectors of the market, with both dark and pale cream variants.

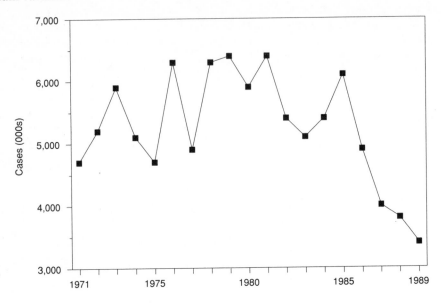

Figure 8.  *Spanish sherry imports*
*Source:* HM Customs & Excise/IDV

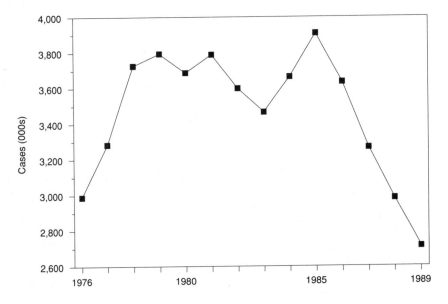

Figure 9.  *Spanish sherry consumer sales*
*Source:* Nielsen

As well as having to sustain its position vis-à-vis own label, Croft Original was directly challenged by Harveys who launched their pale cream, Finesse, in 1983.

Against this background Croft was the only shipper to continue to build share. Harveys share, which had peaked at 33% in 1978, declined to 28% in 1989.

Domecq, who had market leadership in 1970, declined consistently to hold only 4.0% of the market in 1989. Gonzalez Byass was rather more resilient, in part because they had developed stronger brand propositions than Domecq but also because they were more dependent for market share on the Amontillado and Fino sectors, which were unaffected by the activity in the cream sector (see Figure 10).

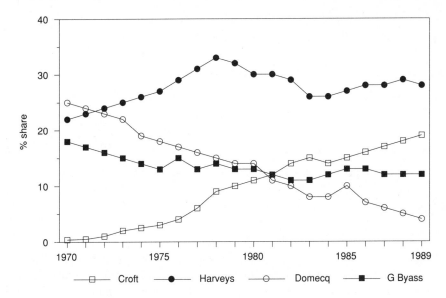

Figure 10. *Shipper shares*
*Source:* Nielsen/IDV

1. *Further Building the Brand Franchise* – Whereas both the market and Harveys Bristol Cream began to lose users in 1981, Croft Original continued to recruit to the brand up until 1987 (see Figure 11).

   Importantly, the nature of those users has changed over the last decade. As the brand grew, it attracted the more loyal mainstream sherry drinker (more 'most often' brand users) and also drew in the occasional buyer. Thus its profile is now less dependent on the regular, more experimental sherry drinker and is much like that of Harveys Bristol Cream (historically representing the mainstream sherry brand choice):

TABLE 3:  DEVELOPMENT OF CROFT ORIGINAL FRANCHISES

|  | Croft Original | | Harveys Bristol Cream | |
|---|---|---|---|---|
|  | 1980 | 1989 | 1980 | 1989 |
| User Base (000's) | 6,368 | 8,657 | 15,875 | 11,145 |
| % most often brand users | 68 | 78 | 81 | 78 |
| % lighter sherry drinkers | 60 | 75 | 71 | 79 |

Source:  TGI

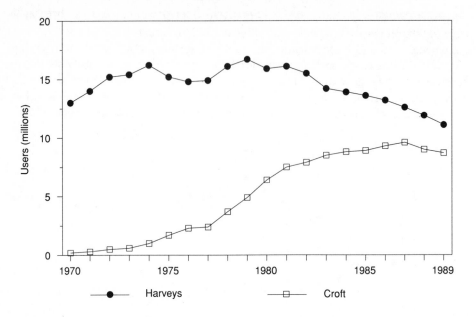

Figure 11. *Croft Original and Harveys Bristol Cream users*
*Source:* TGI

It is also worth noting that although the size of the Croft franchise increased substantially over the 1980s this was achieved without compromising the quality credentials of the brand. That Croft was able to maintain its upmarket profile also helps to explain why the brand has been in a better position to weather the market conditions of the last decade.

TABLE 4: SOCIAL CLASS PROFILE (ALL USERS)

| (Index v adults) | Croft Original | | Harveys Bristol Cream | |
|---|---|---|---|---|
| | 1980 | 1989 | 1980 | 1989 |
| AB | 153 | 154 | 101 | 109 |
| C1 | 122 | 122 | 112 | 107 |
| C2 | 88 | 81 | 100 | 95 |
| D | 64 | 66 | 90 | 95 |
| E | 69 | 73 | 92 | 93 |

Source: TGI

2. *Brand Sales and Market Share* – Croft's ex-factory sales peaked in 1983 at 692,000 cases, held reasonably steady to 1987, and have declined only in the last two years. However, Croft Original has been the *only* brand to consistently outperform the market and continue to build share, narrowing the gap with the brand leader Harveys Bristol Cream (see Figure 12).

   Despite the impact of own label, the launch of Finesse and the continuing presence of Gonzalez Byass, San Domingo, Croft Original has continued its domination of pale creams. The share growth of pale cream over the 1980s has predominantly been due to Croft Original's performance, and has been at the expense of the dark creams (see Table 5).

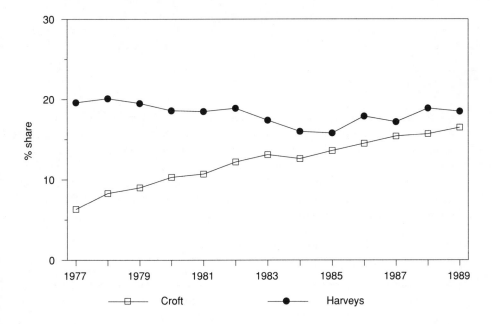

Figure 12. *Croft Original and Harveys Bristol Cream brand share*
*Source:* Nielsen

TABLE 5:  PALE CREAM BRAND SHARES

|  | 1983* | 1984* | 1985 | 1986 | 1987 | 1988 | 1989 |
|---|---|---|---|---|---|---|---|
| Croft Original | 13.0 | 12.6 | 13.6 | 14.5 | 15.4 | 15.7 | 16.5 |
| Finesse | — | 0.6 | 1.1 | 0.9 | 0.8 | 0.5 | 0.4 |
| San Domingo | 2.4 | 2.4 | 2.9 | 2.9 | 2.6 | 2.5 | 2.3 |
| Double Century Pale Cream | 0.3 | 0.7 | 1.1 | 0.8 | 0.7 | 0.5 | 0.5 |
| Own Label | 4.9 | 3.0 | 4.4 | 4.9 | 5.6 | 5.3 | 5.8 |
| All Other | | 2.4 | 0.4 | 1.1 | 1.4 | 1.7 | 1.4 |
| Total Pale Cream | 20.6 | 21.6 | 23.5 | 25.1 | 26.5 | 26.2 | 26.9 |
| Total Dark Cream | 36.3 | 35.0 | 33.3 | 34.5 | 32.2 | 31.9 | 31.0 |
| Total Cream | 56.9 | 56.6 | 56.8 | 59.6 | 58.7 | 58.1 | 57.9 |

Source:   Nielsen
Note:   *England and Wales only

Having made the transition to a 'safe' mainstream brand, Croft Original is fully able to capitalise on the Christmas market volume opportunity. Croft Original and Harveys Bristol Cream are now the two key brands to benefit from purchases by the infrequent once a year sherry consumer (see Table 6).

TABLE 6:   CROFT ORIGINAL AND HARVEYS BRISTOL CREAM CHRISTMAS BRAND SHARES 1986–89

|  | 1986 | | 1987 | | 1988 | | 1989 | |
| --- | --- | --- | --- | --- | --- | --- | --- | --- |
|  | Full Year | Dec/ Jan | Full Year | Dec/ Jan | Full Year | Dec/ Jan | Full Year | Dec/ Jan |
| Croft Original | 14.5 | 20.3 | 15.4 | 19.8 | 15.7 | 20.8 | 16.5 | 20.7 |
| Harveys Bristol Cream | 17.9 | 25.9 | 17.2 | 24.3 | 18.9 | 26.1 | 18.5 | 24.0 |

Source:   Nielsen

3. *Competitors' Distribution* – Croft Original's share growth in a declining market is a notable achievement. Of the other three shippers, Domecq has fared particularly badly. But until the last few years, Domecq's poor sales performance has not resulted in a loss of distribution (see Table 7). And the other two have fully maintained their distribution base. Thus, Croft's share gains have not been gained easily by taking over displaced purchases from competitors losing distribution: they have been won.

TABLE 7:   STERLING DISTRIBUTION IN MULTIPLE GROCERS

|  | 1983* | 1984* | 1985 | 1986 | 1987 | 1988 | 1989 |
| --- | --- | --- | --- | --- | --- | --- | --- |
| Croft Original | 100 | 99 | 100 | 100 | 100 | 100 | 100 |
| Harveys Bristol Cream | 100 | 100 | 100 | 100 | 100 | 100 | 100 |
| Gonzalez Byass | 98 | 98 | 95 | 94 | 96 | 97 | 97 |
| Domecq | 89 | 88 | 87 | 89 | 71 | 60 | 49 |
| Own Label† | 73 | 76 | NA | NA | NA | NA | NA |

Source:   Nielsen
Note:   * England and Wales only
    † Own Label with approximately one third volume share over this period.

4. *Pricing* – Croft Original has consistently pursued a premium pricing strategy maintaining only a 5 – 10p price discount to Harveys Bristol Cream (see Table 8). With other cheaper brands always available, and particularly own label in the 1980s, price in its own right has not contributed to Croft Original's share gains. Rather, price has been consistent with the brand's quality positioning and contributed mainly to its profitability.

TABLE 8:   PRICING (£ PER BOTTLE)

|  | All Spanish sherry | Dec/Jan period | | | |
| --- | --- | --- | --- | --- | --- |
|  |  | Croft Original | | Harveys Bristol Cream | |
|  |  | Multiple grocers | Off- licences | Multiple grocers | Off- licences |
| 1983 | 2.90 | 3.20 | 3.52 | 3.25 | 3.58 |
| 1985 | 3.24 | 3.56 | 3.85 | 3.58 | 3.86 |
| 1987 | 3.61 | 3.91 | 4.35 | 3.97 | 4.41 |
| 1989 | 3.90 | 4.30 | NA | 4.48 | NA |

Source:   Nielsen

Croft Original has reinforced its position as *the* superior pale cream sherry, continuing to build market share at the expense of dark cream sherries and narrowing the gap with Harveys Bristol Cream. The other shippers fared less well. Domecq in particular, being more dependent on cream volume than Gonzalez Byass, paid a heavy price for not having a strong quality brand.

## HOW HAS THE ADVERTISING WORKED?

Croft Original delivered the sweet tasting sherry most people's palate desired, yet it looked dry and therefore potentially a more sophisticated and contemporary drink. The contribution of Jeeves and Wooster was to present this seeming paradox to consumers in a credible and motivating way, and thus realise the potential of the brand in a conservative market where there was not a built-in dynamic towards lighter drinks (as evidenced by the static share taken by Amontillado and Fino sherries).

From the start of the campaign, Jeeves and Wooster equated paleness with quality. This quality message was reinforced by the 'posh' period setting of the campaign, which also gave the brand sherry credentials and heritage. The concept of paleness was later expanded, associating it with modernity (and dark with old-fashioned).

A message of modernity within the conservative sherry market was only credible within the traditional setting of Jeeves and Wooster.

The success of this communication is evidenced by the correspondence map shown in Figure 13, which uses data from a brand personality study conducted in 1986. The closer a brand to an attribute, the closer the perceived relationship between the two. The image of Croft Original is of a more stylish, sophisticated and fashionable drink (more like dry sherries in fact), whereas by comparison Harveys Bristol Cream seems more old fashioned.

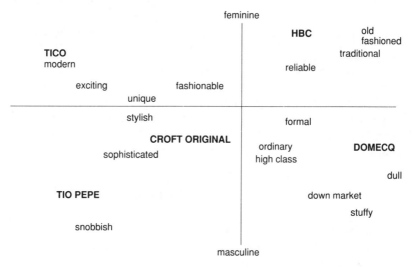

Figure 13. *Brand personality map*
*Source:* MAS 1986

Despite the similarity in sweetness of Croft Original and Harveys Bristol Cream, consumers believed they were drinking a drier product:

TABLE 9:  PERCEIVED SWEETNESS LEVELS

|  | Harveys Bristol Cream % | Croft Original % |
|---|---|---|
| Very sweet | 16 | — |
| Sweet | 57 | 16 |
| Medium sweet | 25 | 17 |
| Medium dry | 1 | 44 |
| Dry | — | 19 |
| Very dry | — | 4 |

Source:     NOP, 1981
Base:       Brand users

Jeeves and Wooster gave consumers licence to respond to the imagery associated with drier products, endorsing users as more sophisticated and discerning, without asking them to compromise on preferred taste. Thus, Croft Original developed into a good all-round brand to offer guests whatever their sweetness preference:

'Some people are embarrassed to ask for a sweet one as it's less sophisticated. So if you ask for Croft, you don't have to let on!'

'Croft is good because you can have it as the *only*  sherry. They ask for dry and you give them that and because it's pale, they don't realise it's sweet' (IDV Qualitative Research 1984).

With such a long-running campaign, the Jeeves and Wooster characters now represent the positive brand values of Croft Original. In 1989 executions still continue to be enjoyed and hold the attention of consumers:

'Croft Original advertising has high spontaneous recall and many consumers remember specific details of different executions with great clarity. Jeeves and Wooster embody the Croft brand values of discernment, enjoyment and good taste. At the same time individual executions are engaging and humorous' (IDV Qualitative Research 1989).

While both Croft Original and Harveys Bristol Cream have benefited from advertising investment, only Croft Original has maintained a consistent strategy and campaign in the late 1970s and 1980s. The effectiveness of Jeeves and Wooster has been enhanced by this lack of consistency from Harveys Bristol Cream.

## CONCLUSIONS

Between 1977 and 1981, Jeeves and Wooster transformed Croft Original from a small niche brand (which already had good distribution) to become the second largest, mainstream brand in the Spanish sherry market. The campaign realised the brand's potential in a conservative market where there was not a built-in dynamic towards lighter drinks. It achieved this by presenting Croft Original as a quality brand and paleness as a positive virtue in a market dominated by the perception that cream sherry was dark. The period scenarios of Jeeves and Wooster convinced consumers for the first time that Croft Original had real sherry credentials and heritage, and thus was a 'safe' choice, allowing the brand to capitalise on the Christmas volume opportunity.

As market conditions tightened, further growth was dependent on Croft Original maintaining its position as *the* pale cream sherry and taking share from other brands. Jeeves and Wooster continued to reinforce Croft Original's superior positioning and had the flexibility to deliver more focused messages, such as those targeted against 'the old brown stuff'. The communication of Croft Original as a more contemporary and sophisticated drink for discerning drinkers successfully sustained the brand, so that it continued to build its user base of more upmarket sherry drinkers up to 1987 (when sherry users had been declining since 1981). Croft Original is the *only* Spanish sherry brand to have consistently built market share during the 1980s, largely at the expense of dark creams and in spite of pale cream and Own Label competition.

Other less well-placed brands suffered disproportionately. The failure to build strong consumer-led brand propositions, through consistent advertising strategy and execution, meant decline for the brands of some shippers, notably Domecq. Croft Original's health as a brand is a direct consequence of the relevance and quality of communication from Jeeves and Wooster, and the flexibility and durability of the campaign. After 13 years, Jeeves and Wooster continue to communicate the qualities of the brand for those consumers who believe 'One instinctively knows when something is right', and the campaign continues to be the best remembered and best loved advertising in its category.

# 3

# The Ultimate Success Story

*How the Hippo & Duck Advertising Campaign Helped to Rebuild Silentnight's Business in the UK Bed Market*

## INTRODUCTION

This submission seeks to demonstrate the influential role of effective advertising in the transformation of the Silentnight Beds business in the second half of the 1980s.

The case history shows how manufacturers in underpromoted consumer durable markets can benefit from a genuine commitment to building a true brand franchise – built upon often-claimed, though seldom delivered 'advertising which works harder': in short, outstanding creativity.

The study is effectively the story of a manufacturer who broke the mould in a traditional, highly conservative industry (neither high tech nor low tech, but *no tech* according to the Chairman of the National Bedding Federation). This conservatism is nowhere more prevalent than in its reluctance to embrace fully the discipline of marketing and to recognise the benefits of investment in long-term advertising strategies.

Silentnight's story features the reversal of a five year decline in market share, the successful relaunch of a significant new product positioned at higher price points than previous Silentnight products, the rebuilding of retail trade credibility, the development of a strong consumer franchise for both the product and its advertising characters, a turnover and profit turnaround, and the creation of a resilient platform to both defend and support future growth.

The Institute of Marketing called it 'a highly innovative approach in product differentiation and the achievement of a competitive edge in an otherwise 'me-too' product market place' (1987 Marketing Awards).

At Silentnight, it is known as *The Tale of the Hippo and Duck*.

## BACKGROUND

In 1984 Silentnight was brand leader in the UK bed market.

However, its product range had no significant advantages over other beds, and leadership had been achieved largely through extremely competitive pricing and a superior delivery service.

Moreover, the market itself had been static for some five years; growth was not forecast; and Silentnight's share had been in decline since 1981.

Worse still, attempts to build a consumer franchise purely on name and image alone through the brand's first significant advertising commitment had proven a costly failure. Between 1982 and 1984 over £4 million at today's prices had been spent on TV and press.

Sales, market share and profit had fallen in each year.

A new added-value product, incorporating a mattress with significant consumer benefits, was launched in August 1984 in an attempt to reverse this trend. Though a partial success, sales targets in the following year were not met because of the effects of a serious industrial dispute which significantly reduced production efficiency, output and trade customer confidence.

As competitors took advantage of Silentnight's problems, market share fell by over a third.

And by the year end the business position was critical.

The beginning of 1986 saw both the end of the industrial dispute and product improvements in the shape of a new base unit designed to enhance the performance of the new mattress. Unfortunately, sales recovery remained slow and the company decided to review its advertising.

The relaunch of the new product range was vital to Silentnight. It represented a major marketing and advertising initiative following the company's supply interruptions. With the continuing concentration of buying power into fewer hands and the retailers' preoccupation with price, the programme represented the company's last opportunity to stop the downward spiral of reducing margins.

*If the launch did not succeed, it was unlikely that Silentnight would get another opportunity.*

## THE BRIEF

Not surprisingly, the sales and marketing objectives were simply defined:

1.  To regain market share lost in 1985.
2.  To firmly establish the new product range in its respective premium price sector.
3.  To strengthen Silentnight's position in the bed market.
4.  To provide a sound base for planned growth.

On the subject of advertising and promotion Silentnight concluded:

'Presented properly, we have a proposition in our (Ultimate) range that is desirable, credible and worthy of a price premium to the consumer. Getting the consumer to believe this will require a well co-ordinated and consistent strategy pursued over a period of years' (Silentnight Advertising Brief, 1986).

## THE CONSUMER PURCHASING PROCESS

At first sight, the available market research painted an unpromising picture for an advertiser. Furniture shopping, *particularly for beds*, was less popular than shopping for other consumer durables.

Beds were low in the public consciousness. People hardly ever thought of them except when engaged in the buying process. Often they could not even recall the make of their own bed.

Awareness of reputable makes of bed was poorly defined, and lacking the values and imagery associated with strong brands. In fact, most people could not determine where they had first encountered the brands remembered:

'I suppose it must be television. You don't go about discussing people's beds'.

'...but I can't remember any bed adverts off hand'.

Total category advertising spend in 1985 was *less than* £1 million, according to MEAL. There was a very low word of mouth exposure, and a total absence of casual window shopping.

In short, the market was asleep. Beds were boring – and sales fundamentally driven by consumers' changing domestic circumstances or, more likely, by distress purchases.

However, awareness of deterioration of the bed can take years to build up and fundamental signs of decay were generally necessary to establish the need to buy a new bed in the foreseeable future.

'When the springs start pushing up your behind, it's time to change' (Consumer respondents, Pegram Walters, 1984).

The research enabled a concise summary of the primary purchasing considerations and behavioural factors to be drawn up:

— Most people claimed to attempt to buy a *good bed*
— But perceptions of what made a good bed were extremely vague
— These centred on some unstructured combination of price, known brand name, appearance, sturdiness and to a lesser extent what it felt like
— There was an inability to grasp more than *superficial* judging criteria and a resigned acceptance that you could not really differentiate between beds
— The internal structure was regarded as a mystery and little inclination existed to improve this understanding
— Particularly as technical details and springing terminology were found to be little more than *confusing*
— Names were either known and trustworthy, or not
— Though brand loyalty did not exist, as consumers were happy to buy from any of their known repertoire
— First Time Buyers tried to be 'proper consumers' with their buying process often extended over several weeks in a genuine attempt to buy the right bed

— Replacers wanted to get it over with quickly. To them the purchase of a bed was a peculiar mixture: potentially very important, but too confusing to make any great expenditure of time and effort worthwhile.

This information enabled the Agency to construct a representation of the typical sequential purchasing process so that the role of advertising could be hypothesised.

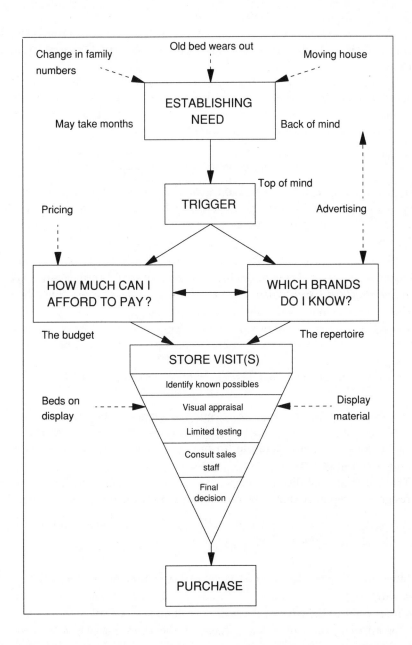

Figure 1: *Bed purchasing: the decision-making process*

In 1984, Pegram Walters summarised the outcome as being merely: 'the right bed in the right place at the right time'.

It can be fairly concluded that *the process was neither emotional nor truly rational*, reflecting the low historical level of marketing investment by the major manufacturers.


## ADVERTISING'S ROLE

After a four-way pitch, Bowden Dyble Hayes & Partners (BDH) were appointed in June 1986.

The Agency was optimistic about the research findings. The market clearly presented a genuine opportunity for a manufacturer to stand out from the crowd – by demonstrating a superior product to the consumer. A product whose features could be translated into meaningful consumer benefits.

### The Opportunity for Advertising

Having identified the characteristics of the market's typical purchasing process, the Agency derived a clear indication of the role which advertising could play in the communication of this product proposition to the consumer. Its contribution was modelled as:

1.  *Raising awareness*: to ensure the brand's position in the known category.
2.  *Competitively differentiating the brand* with a relevant consumer benefit to provide a rational basis for the purchasing decision.
3.  *Increasing pre-disposition* towards Silentnight.
4.  *With strong prompted recall* to create an opportunity in-store to relate the product's benefits to the purchasing process.
5.  And *cultivating an emotional discriminator* to resist switch-selling.


To achieve these objectives, the Agency recognised the need for a totally integrated campaign, above and below the line, fully supported by the trade.

It was obviously crucial, therefore, to motivate Silentnight's own salesforce and the retailers *as well as* the consumer.

### Towards a Communications Platform

The unique combination of mattress and base in Silentnight's new Ultimate Sleep System offered a desirable package:

1.  Individual support for two sleepers – no matter what the differential in weight.
2.  Support right to the edge of the bed – to eliminate roll off.
3.  A 'posturised' zone of extra springs in the central third to provide extra support where the bodyweight is greatest.

## The Consumer Proposition

Advertising's task was to translate these features into a credible consumer benefit. Research had identified the consumer's primary requirement as 'a good night's sleep'. The communications strategy had to convert this general desire into a tangible and rational proposition.

Pre-testing suggested the focus be turned onto individual support. Or, more accessibly, *the elimination of roll-together to prevent disturbance as two sleeping partners of unequal weights roll into the hollow in the middle of the bed.*

This had been experienced by most respondents, and was something all could relate to.

## The Creative Solution

*The Brief* – The requirements of the *creative concept* were complex:

— To brand the range in a memorable way.
— To differentiate Silentnight from its competitors by communicating the main benefits that the range can provide via credible and relevant claims – *in a non technical way.*
— To employ a logical approach enabling the consumer to make a rational decision with the right emotional 'feel'.
— To communicate enough to convince the consumer that this product should be considered before purchasing other beds.
— To confer quality imagery.
— To adopt a confident, friendly and engaging tone – appealing to a mass market audience of both sexes and all ages, but specifically relating to women (the initial movers in the purchasing process).
— To translate outstandingly at point of sale.

The *creative solution* was disarmingly simple: a unique product demonstration that was sufficiently novel to break through consumer apathy and to convincingly communicate the product's principal consumer benefit.

The stars of this demonstration were the Silentnight Hippo and Duck.

Consumers reacted enthusiastically to the concept exactly as intended:

— The major message communicated was *no roll-together.*
— The characters were noticeable, memorable, well-liked and their relevance understood.
— The response generated by the storyboard was that:

'These beds are well worth looking at'.

'Overall, the basic creative concept appeared to have tremendous potential to generate interest in and convey the benefits of Silentnight beds' (Pegram Walters, 1986).

### Implementation

The full extent of the broad implementation of the Hippo and Duck creative strategy may best be illustrated by means of the *Communications Pyramid*: whereby the most intrusive medium, television, spearheaded the campaign to gain the consumer's interest, and the requirement for further detail was satisfied as the consumer neared the point of purchase.

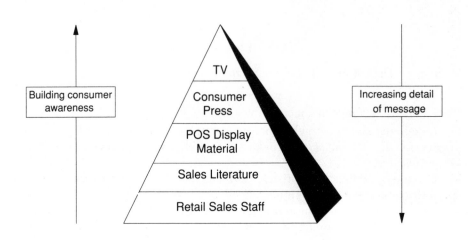

Figure 2:  *The integrated communications pryamid*

The pre-campaign research concluded that the animal characters set the tone for describing further product features and consumer benefits in a non-technical way.

The two reproductions on the next page are examples of this: a copy of the launch consumer press advertisement and the 1990 footmat. (The latter were formerly used purely to protect beds from dirty feet in-store during customer trial. At best they were simply logo branded. Since 1986 these have been used as an integral part of the sales story at point of purchase). Each is representative of the way the creative theme has been consistently employed throughout.

### Media Strategy

On a restricted launch budget the campaign began with a three area TV test supported by national colour press.

Results were so encouraging that the planned regional roll out was replaced by national television at the earliest opportunity: February 1987.

Since then the media strategy has been determined by the following key considerations:

## LAUNCH PRESS ADVERTISEMENT

**Why buy an ordinary bed, when you can have the Ultimate Sleep System from Silentnight?**

*A*LLOW us to introduce a remarkable new bed. The Ultimate Sleep System from Silentnight.

Its base and mattress are quite unique. Not least, because they have been designed to complement each other perfectly.

To give greater support and more comfort, and to successfully eliminate a failing all too common in ordinary beds. The problem of roll together.

**ABSOLUTELY NO ROLL TOGETHER**

Even the most perfectly matched sleeping partners tend to be of different weights, which in an ordinary bed can lead to the lighter partner rolling towards the heavier one. But, thanks to the unique construction of the Ultimate Sleep System, this is no longer a problem.

Silentnight's revolutionary continuous support spirals are connected from head to toe (not side to side like the springs in an ordinary mattress), ensuring that each sleeper has their own individual support.

**MORE SUPPORT RIGHT TO THE EDGE**

The continuous support spirals of the Ultimate Sleep System give a massive 50% more surface coverage than ordinary spring systems.

Right to the edge of the mattress, in fact.

So your whole body weight receives correctly distributed support. And none of the rolling off sensation often experienced in an ordinary bed.

**EXTRA SUPPORT WHERE YOUR BODY NEEDS IT MOST**

In an ordinary bed, you get uniform support across the whole surface area.

In the Ultimate Sleep System you get all this. And more.

A unique posture zone across the centre section of the mattress gives an area of extra support where your body weight is greatest.

Ensuring both a natural and restful position while you sleep.

**THE ULTIMATE BASE**

The base of the Ultimate Sleep System has been specially designed to enhance the unique features of the ultimate mattress.

It has its own anti roll zone and its own posture zone, plus extra support around the edge.

Mattress and base. Designed together to create the Ultimate Sleep System.

And with prices ranging from as little as £180 up to £480 you've even got the ultimate choice.

So why settle for an ordinary bed, when you can have the Ultimate Sleep System from Silentnight?

**Silentnight**
THE ULTIMATE SLEEP SYSTEM

## 1990 PROTECTIVE FOOTMAT

# This is no ordinary bed

### IT'S THE ULTIMATE SLEEP SYSTEM FROM SILENTNIGHT

**THE ULTIMATE SLEEP SYSTEM**
* EXCLUSIVE TO SILENTNIGHT
a mattress and base specially designed to work together to give you a perfect night's sleep

**THE ULTIMATE MATTRESS**
* NO ROLL TOGETHER
individual support for each sleeper
* NO ROLL OFF
more support right to the edge of the bed
* EXTRA SUPPORT
maximum support in the posture zone where the sleeper's weight is greatest

**THE ULTIMATE BASE**
A sprung base specially designed to work with the Ultimate Mattress, the Ultimate Base has special benefits of its own.
* EXTRA SUPPORT
* NO ROLL OFF
* NO ROLL TOGETHER

**THE ULTIMATE IN COMFORT**
* SUPERIOR COMFORT
in a range of comfort levels

* ULTIMATE COMFORT RATINGS
symbols from 3-9 appear on mattress label to represent comfort level – select a comfort rating that best suits your needs
* CFC-FREE FILLING

**FEEL THE DIFFERENCE**
There's only one way to experience the benefits of the Ultimate Sleep System. That's to try the Hippo Test at your local Silentnight stockist, and feel the difference for yourself.

**1** NO ROLL TOGETHER Lie on the bed and feel how the continuous support spirals connected from head to toe give you and your partner individual support, and eliminate roll together.

**2** EXTRA SUPPORT Sit in each zone and see how the posture zone gives you extra support where your weight is greatest.

**3** NO ROLL OFF Lie on the edge and see how extra edge support in mattress and base eliminates roll off, maximising the sleeping area.

Why buy an ordinary bed when you can have the Ultimate Sleep System from Silentnight?

**Silentnight**
THE ULTIMATE SLEEP SYSTEM

AS SEEN ON TV

1. *Budget* – Enough to dominate the category, though limited in national terms. The spend peaked in 1988 (£1.64 million, Media Register). Each year since it has declined in absolute and real (constant prices) terms, as well as in proportion to total Silentnight turnover.
2. *National support* – Dictated by the requirements of the retail multiples. Additionally it provides a key point of difference compared with the company's competitors.
3. *Targeting* – Silentnight is a true mass market brand, with a product range covering almost 90% of retail price points. For media buying the agreed target audience was defined as 25-55/ABC1C2/adults, with a high female conversion.
4. *Campaign frequency* – Dictated by the twin imperatives of building the brand and maximising the number of selling-in opportunities.

| MEDIUM | ACTIVITY | | | | | | | | | | |
|---|---|---|---|---|---|---|---|---|---|---|---|
| **TELEVISION (TVRs)** | 353 | 343 | 386 | 274 | 475 | 419 | 420 | 434 | 263 | 310 | |
| Regions | Granada YTV STV | Network | Network | Network | | Network | Network Exc. London | Network | Network | Network Exc London TVS Anglia | |
| Commercial Length (secs) | 30 | 30 | 30/10 | 10 | 20/10 | 20/10 | 20/10 | 40/20/10 | 10 | 20/10 | |
| Ratio (%) | 100 | 100 | 50:50 | 100 | 60:40 | 50:50 | 40:60 | 40:40:20 | 100 | 50:50 | |
| **COLOUR PRESS** | ▬▬ | | ▬ | ▬ | | | | | | | |
| **POSTERS** | | | | | | | ▬ | | | | |
| **IN-STORE POS** | ▬▬▬▬▬▬▬▬▬▬▬▬▬▬▬▬▬▬▬▬▬▬▬▬▬▬ | | | | | | | | | | |

Ju Se No Ja Ma Ma Ju Se No Ja Ma Ma Ju Se No Ja Ma Ma Ju Se No
**1986** **1987** **1988** **1989**

Figure 3. *Media plan (1986 – 1989)*

As Figure 3 shows, the campaign has evolved since 1986. Two key differences are evident:

1. The removal of press from the schedule – due to (a) the effectiveness of TV in building the brand, and (b) TV's rising cost, which has taken a proportionately greater share of the available budget.
2. The inclusion of posters – to upweight London when its relative cost threatened the balance of the TV campaign. This is being repeated in 1990 – and extended to other parts of the South East.

## THE ULTIMATE SUCCESS STORY

This paper sets out to demonstrate a copy-book example of advertising enhancing the effectiveness of other elements of the marketing mix – as well as exerting a primary influence in its own right.

*Results To Date*

The original sales and marketing objectives have certainly been met:

1. The declining market share trend has been reversed, with Silentnight recording highest ever levels in 1987, 1988 and 1989 consecutively.
2. The Ultimate Sleep System is now the biggest-selling premium product in the UK bed market.
3. It sells at higher price points than previous Silentnight products and now accounts for around 50% of company turnover.
4. The brand is now clearly seen as the market leader by the consumer, the retail trade and its competitors.
5. The characters in the advertising have proven to be a very effective PR vehicle, and so popular that Silentnight has introduced a range of associated products featuring them.
6. For the last three years, the brand's resilience and profitability have provided the basis for protected company growth.

During this turnaround the campaign has been evaluated on a number of measures. While sales, market share and profitability are the ultimate determinants of success, trends within the intermediary measures have been tracked to demonstrate advertising's initial effects in line with the Agency's understanding of consumer purchasing motivation.

It is this paper's intention, therefore, to show that we have not only moved minds, but that this has also helped to move beds.

*Campaign Evaluation[1]*

Advertising's first task was to ensure a position in the prospective purchaser's repertoire by building sufficient awareness to figure strongly in the 'known' category – especially amongst those actually in the market looking for a bed.

*Increasing Awareness of Silentnight Beds*

Recognising the importance of in-store assessment of the range displayed, prompted brand recognition is regarded as a key measure. Figure 4 demonstrates that prompted awareness amongst all adults has grown steadily since the campaign's launch.

Further, amongst the core target audience of *people who intend to purchase[2]*, an even greater increase has been recorded. In this category the gap behind Slumberland narrowed dramatically: from 16% in January 1988 to 9% in January 1989. In July of that year Silentnight became the top ranked brand by this audience.

---

[1] In 1986 and 1987 pre and post advertising checks were conducted. RSGB's national omnibus was used with a sample of 2,000 adults. From January 1988 onwards a monthly tracking study was set up with NOP in recognition of the need for improved understanding of the trends within long-term image changes. The sample size was maintained at 2,000 adults nationally.

[2] The sample consisted of respondents claiming to be 'currently thinking about buying a new bed' from the NOP national omnibus.

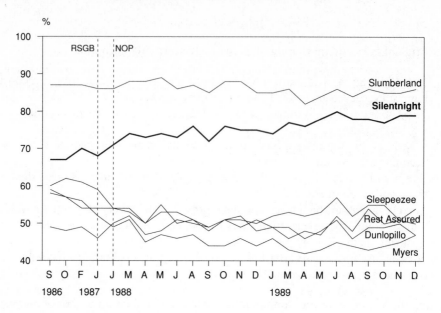

Figure 4.  *Prompted brand awareness*
*Source:* RSGB, NOP
*Sample:* 2,000 adults

Indexing advertising recall against brand awareness highlights the relative significance of advertising to each of the key manufacturer's profiles. Figure 5 demonstrates the trends within the market since the launch of the Hippo and Duck campaign on this particular measure.

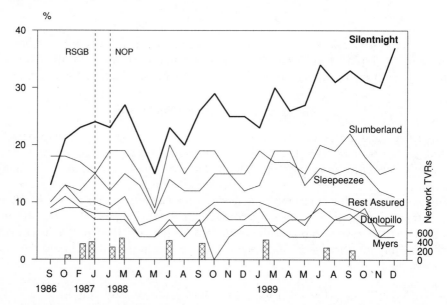

Figure 5.  *Advertising awareness indexed against brand awareness*
*Source:* RSGB, NOP
*Sample:* 2,000 adults

It can be seen that, in 1986, Slumberland had the highest index consistent with its *historical* position as the industry's biggest ad spender. By the end of 1989, however, the only brand to have moved significantly was Silentnight.

Its index had more than tripled, reflecting its three year commitment to advertising (between 1986 and 1989, MEAL shows that Silentnight's expenditure was greater than that for all its competitors combined).

This clear trend strongly supports the contention that advertising is increasingly playing a more important role as the source of awareness for the brand – thereby helping to ensure a place high in the 'known' repertoire.

### Redefining the Mental Shopping List

While the brand's profile has grown, it has also clearly differentiated itself from the 'me-too' morass of manufacturers that bed purchasers are *likely to consider*.

A snapshot Consumer Preference survey undertaken in December 1989 showed that Silentnight was the brand most consumers would look for when buying a bed. Figure 6 shows that almost one in two specified Silentnight; the next highest score was for Any Brand; and in total 80% *would consider* a Silentnight bed (ie a combination of 46% who would look specifically at Silentnight plus 34% who would consider any brand). The nearest competitor recorded less than two thirds of Silentnight's figure.

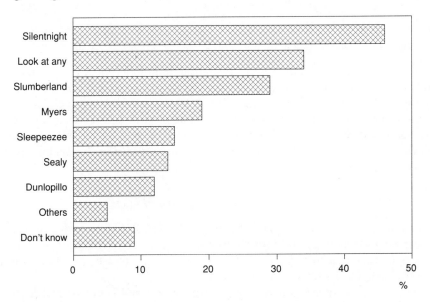

Figure 6. *Brands consumers would look for when buying a new bed*
Source: Scantest Research, December 1989
Sample: 235 adults

The findings of the tracking study confirm this benchmark; they also demonstrate the significant growth, since the beginning of 1988, in the level of interest in the brand amongst those intending to buy a bed in the future. Again, Silentnight has risen from an undistinguished position within the crowd to clear market leadership. Again we believe advertising to have played an important part.

Figure 7 plots future purchasers' brand consideration against advertising awareness. The significance lies in the fact that the sample base for each measure consists *not of people who have bought, but of people who intend to buy.*

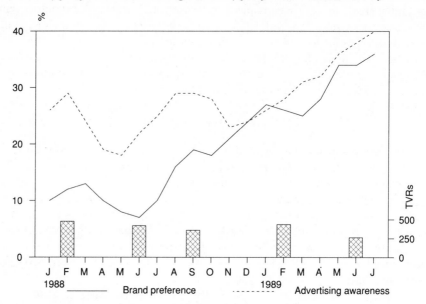

Figure 7. *Growing consumer preference for the Silentnight brand amongst those intending to buy a bed*
*Source:* NOP, AGB, BARB
*Base:* Those looking at present

At the same time as advertising awareness (amongst potential purchasers) has built up for Silentnight, so too has their *expressed preference* for the brand. The two sets of data in the figure above show a strong correlation which has increased as the campaign has progressed (between January and July 1989, r = 0.92)[3]. This would suggest that not only has the campaign been noticed by its target audience, but that it is also creating an increasingly positive impression, enhancing favourable pre-disposition towards Silentnight's products.

### The High Profile Hippo and Duck

After only one year of national advertising the two TV stars had generated 74% prompted awareness amongst all adults and 81% amongst the prime target market of people intending to buy a bed. The tracking study (see Figure 8) demonstrates that these high levels have been maintained.

The characters' appeal is particularly strong amongst 15 – 44 year olds and has a very broad socio-economic base. Yet, the strongest increases in 1989 were amongst ABC1s, the primary consumers of premium beds.

Figure 8 also reveals an instance of how this continuous monitoring contributed to the development of the campaign by helping to identify the area of underperformance.

---

[3] In both cases aggregated three month moving average totals were used to increase the statistical significance of the base sample.

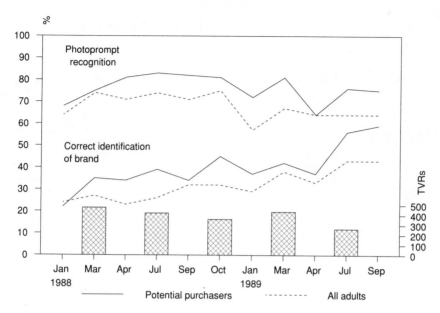

Figure 8.  *Hippo and Duck photoprompt recognition*
*Source:* AGB, BARB, NOP

## *Making more use of our strengths*

From the outset the intention was to capitalise on the high profile of the Hippo and Duck in an attempt to overcome the no-loyalty, weak consumer franchises typical of the market's brands.

This strategy relied upon the widespread distribution of character-branded display material prompting recall at point of purchase. In those outlets where POS material was not merchandised (as with many multiples), Silentnight had a potential problem. Were the Hippo and Duck linked sufficiently to the brand?

As a potential Achilles heel, this formed the point of departure for a new creative brief:

— To introduce a new means of intrusively grabbing the consumer's attention.
— To continue to capitalise on the no roll-together proposition.
— To lay greater emphasis on the ultimate end-benefit: a good night's sleep.
— To counter the danger of switch-selling by strengthening the bond between the characters and manufacturer, achieved by ending each commercial with a four second animated Silentnight logo.

The storyboard for the second television commercial, *The Ultimate Alarm*, is shown on the following page.

Figure 8, above, demonstrates how correct identification of the Silentnight brand from the Omnibus' photoprompt has improved significantly since the introduction of the new TV commercial in February 1989.

Silentnight believe this is further evidence of the contribution made by creativity to the building of their brand. In this case, creative development has been the key to sustaining and improving the advertising campaign's effectiveness.

# THE ULTIMATE ALARM SYSTEM (40 SECONDS) 1989

(Tom Baker): With Silentnight you get a revolutionary spring system not just the mattress but ...

... also in the base. So no matter how heavy your partner is there's no roll together.

The result – a perfect night's sleep.

We would recommend, however ...

... that when you've got the Ultimate Sleep System...

...you get the Ultimate Alarm System as well. The Ultimate Sleep System – from Silentnight

*A Successfully Differentiated Brand – With a Unique Identity*

Qualitative research conducted in June 1986 indicated that Silentnight was best known for its availability and wide range of prices (in fact a reasonable résumé at the time, though undoubtedly these are general claims which could be applied to most known manufacturers in the market). In short, no performance benefits were strongly associated with its products.

Two years later, prior to the development of the second TV commercial, a second qualitative exercise confirmed that the two characters 'appear to work exactly as hoped': communicating individual support – no matter how heavy your partner, substantiated by a clear product message, and giving viewers a very confident feeling about the brand (Pegram Walters, 1988).

Indeed, by 1989 Silentnight had clearly established itself, thanks to Hippo and Duck, as the bed that ensures 'no roll-together'. The tracking study shows how this benefit has increasingly become associated with the brand – on both the spontaneous and prompted level (see Table 1 and Figure 9).

TABLE 1: SPONTANEOUS RECALL OF ADVERTISEMENT CONTENT (%)

|  | 1986 | | 1987 | | 1988 | | | | | | 1989 | | | | | |
|  | Sep | Oct | Feb | Jul | Jan | Mar | Apr | Jul | Sep | Oct | Jan | Mar | Apr | Jul | Sep | Oct |
|---|---|---|---|---|---|---|---|---|---|---|---|---|---|---|---|---|
| Any mention of Hippo and Duck | — | 14 | 33 | 43 | 39 | 39 | 48 | 37 | 50 | 53 | 49 | 61 | 48 | 51 | 55 | 54 |
| Any mention of 'no roll together' | 1 | 5 | 9 | 19 | 25 | 25 | 22 | 18 | 22 | 29 | 27 | 31 | 32 | 29 | 33 | 28 |

Source: RSGB, NOP.
Sample: 2,000 adults.

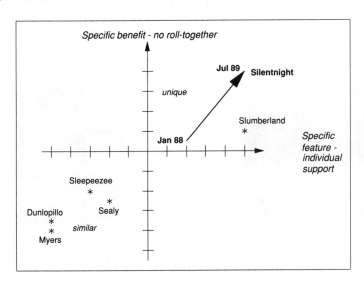

Figure 9. *The establishment of a positively differentiated positioning*
*Source:* NOP 1988/89

The image map shows how Silentnight is moving away from the brands perceived as 'me-too' to claim sovereignty over the principal claimed benefit. No competitor has made any statistically significant movement in this area over the past two years.

It seems reasonable to presume that the shift in these dimensions has been even greater since 1986 when the campaign began. Realistically, then Silentnight would most likely have been in the lower left-hand quartile of this diagram (see Table 1).

Consequently in the decision on which brand to buy, the consumer now has a rational 'reason to choose' Silentnight: it is *the brand* which eliminates roll-together. And remember, this explicit proposition did not exist before Silentnight established it on the consumer's agenda through the Hippo and Duck campaign. Importantly, its continued relevance was endorsed by the creative development research prior to the making of the second TV commercial.

### *The Market's Only Dynamic Image*

As we have seen, prior to the launch of the campaign the brand's perception was indeterminate. However, its positioning in commercial terms was at the lower end of the mass market.

Consequently, a move up-market in product terms had to be supported by shifting brand imagery qualitatively upwards.

Figure 10 plots the improvement in perception of the brand over 1988 and 1989. The brand map represents two key dimensions, Luxurious/Good Quality Beds and Price Perceptions from cheap to more expensive.

Silentnight has shown positive movement in the desired direction relative to its competitors (though a further question on the Omnibus shows perceived *value for money* has remained consistent). In fact it is the only brand in the market demonstrating any statistically significant positive image shift along these dimensions.

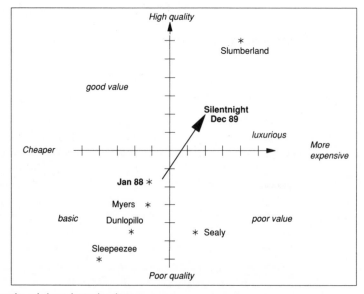

Figure 10. *Brand map: bed manufacturer brand images*
Source: NOP 1988/89

### The Importance Attached to Advertising by the Retail Trade

A research survey conducted on behalf of an independent third party by Marketlink provides a valuable insight into trade perceptions of the role of advertising in the furniture industry.

Fundamentally, 'the vast majority of respondents thought that bed manufacturers could and should create customer pull through by increased expenditure'. They also confirmed that 'if they were particularly impressed by a manufacturer's marketing strategy (in essence consumer advertising on a grand scale), then they would be *receptive to stocking* that manufacturer's products'.(Marketlink, 1988).

According to this research, Silentnight had obviously impressed:

> 'It would appear that Silentnight has 'set the standard' in terms of consumer advertising, a certain reverence for this company's strategy was detected' .

Retailer feedback clearly indicates a belief that the campaign has been 'tremendously successful' in terms of generating business:

> 'The Hippo and Duck are real crowd pullers'.

> 'People come in and ask for a Hippo and Duck bed' (Retailer Respondents, Marketlink, December 1988).

### Advertising Which Works Harder

The broader aspect of advertising practice involves realising the benefits of *advertising which works harder* – wherein its effects cross over to drive other elements of the marketing mix.

The Silentnight campaign has been successful beyond the originally envisaged parameters, reflecting the marketability of the two advertising characters – and their undoubted consumer franchise.

The following summary highlights some of the more extraordinary responses:

— Letters began to pour in from consumers as soon as the campaign began – over 500 in the first year alone.
— The Hippo featured in newspaper competitions, retailer and exhibition promotions, and charity bed races.
— He was seen in aeroplanes and was invited to, and attended, a wedding.
— Since the launch over 800 large scale cuddly Hippos have been sold to retailers at £200 each for in-store displays.
— Even 'Hippo Heists' became national news. Missing Hippos from at least four stores around the country were reported on the BBC TV programme *Crimewatch*, seen in two episodes by a combined audience of over 24 million. In West London, one heist was accomplished by hauling the beast through a shop's skylight with a crane.
— The campaign has also featured on *Reporting Scotland* (the national BBC News programme, four days consecutively), on *Beadle's About* (twice), as an extended promotion (to reproduce a model alarm) on *Ghost Train*, on *This*

*Morning* and on Channel 4's *Business Daily*, as the company's upturn in fortunes was appraised.
— Both the Hippo and Duck have proved so popular (and profitable) that Silentnight introduced a range of products featuring them. Not only do people *like* the advertising characters, they actually *pay* for them.

To date, for instance, over 140,000 toy 'baby hippos' have been sold.

Even ignoring the promotional opportunities and spin offs for the company's retailers, the returns have been enormous: profits on the licensed Hippo toys equate to those on several million pounds worth of additional beds turnover! Nevertheless, even this is part of the long-term strategy – developing the brand's franchise with the bed buyers of tomorrow, and providing bed retailers with an additional source of revenue.

## The Sales Response

Enhanced brand perceptions as well as increased consumer demand have helped Silentnight to achieve their business objectives (see Table 2). For ease of interpretation and business confidentiality, the data have been indexed from 1986, the year of the launch.

TABLE 2:   INDEXED UK BED MARKET SALES TRENDS

|      | Volume | | | Value (at constant 1986 prices) | | |
|      | Market | Total SNT | Ultimate | Market | Total SNT | Ultimate |
|------|--------|-----------|----------|--------|-----------|----------|
| 1980 | 98     | 107       | —        | 104    | 126       | —        |
| 1981 | 97     | 115       | —        | 93     | 122       | —        |
| 1982 | 98     | 115       | —        | 90     | 112       | —        |
| 1983 | 100    | 111       | —        | 91     | 105       | —        |
| 1984 | 102    | 110       | 5        | 93     | 106       | 8        |
| 1985 | 104    | 75        | 62       | 99     | 75        | 59       |
| 1986 | 100    | *100*     | *100*    | 100    | *100*     | *100*    |
| 1987 | 118    | *120*     | *149*    | 110    | *121*     | *161*    |
| 1988 | 134    | *136*     | *156*    | 120    | *133*     | *168*    |
| 1989 | 132e   | *144*     | *142*    | 115e   | *129*     | *148*    |

Source:   Business Monitor, Silentnight Sales History.

1.   The five year trend in declining sales volume and value has been reversed.
2.   Volume sales have increased significantly since the launch of Ultimate – with a rate of growth in excess of that of the market.
3.   More importantly, the richer model mix has enabled Silentnight to significantly increase sales value and share.
4.   Sales growth for the Ultimate Range has far exceeded the market in both volume and value.
5.   It is now the single most significant product on the market – accounting for 10.2% by value.

6. Silentnight's volume and value shares have grown substantially more than those of any major competitor (see Figure 11).

7. Even in the tougher market conditions of 1989, brought on by the interest rate squeeze on consumer expenditure, Silentnight has demonstrated the extra resilience of strong brands by gaining market share. In this year volume growth was maintained as consumers with less money to spend traded down.

8. Since the advertising launch of Ultimate, Silentnight products have resisted the downward pressure on prices significantly better than the market average. Again this is a reversal of the trend prior to 1986. Ultimate has actually kept pace with the RPI, so that 1989 sales were at an average unit selling price 20.3% higher than the market norm (see Table 3).

TABLE 3: INDEXED BED MARKET PRICE TRENDS

|      | RPI | Market | Total SNT | Ultimate |
|------|-----|--------|-----------|----------|
| 1980 | 68  | 73     | 80        | —        |
| 1981 | 77  | 73     | 81        | —        |
| 1982 | 83  | 76     | 81        | —        |
| 1983 | 87  | 79     | 83        | —        |
| 1984 | 91  | 83     | 88        | —        |
| 1985 | 97  | 92     | 96        | 97       |
| 1986 | 100 | 100    | 100       | 100      |
| 1987 | 104 | 100    | 105       | 108      |
| 1988 | 109 | 98     | 107       | 113      |
| 1989 | 119 | 103e   | 106       | 117      |

Source: CSO, Business Monitor, Silentnight Sales History

Silentnight interpret the industry figures as vindication of their long-term branding strategy. The company's reliance on trade discounting has been reduced as advertising has added value to their products in a price-led, price-sensitive, almost commodity market.

## REVIEW OF THE COUNTER-ARGUMENTS

Clearly Silentnight's fortunes have been reversed; equally clearly, we believe, the Hippo and Duck advertising campaign has played a significant role in facilitating this turnaround.

It has never been BDH's intention to credit advertising as the sole 'saviour' of a troubled company. Indeed this paper seeks to demonstrate, not isolate, advertising's contribution to enhancing the effectiveness of each element of the marketing mix.

Nevertheless, every fully reasoned case must appraise those other factors which might have brought about the successes.

### Countering the Counter-Arguments

The sales increases have obviously not been *bought* by price cuts.

However, the credit, if such is due, could perhaps have been conferred on the upturn in the bed market, the new product's superior capabilities, increased salesforce efficiencies or enhanced distribution. This section seeks to demonstrate that none of these could have been the *primary* factor in Silentnight's resurgence.

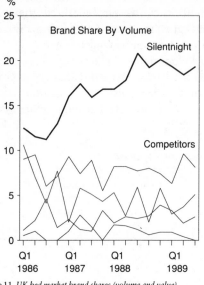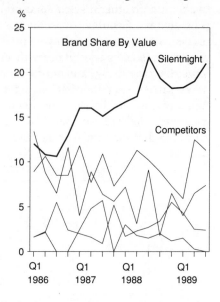

Figure 11. *UK bed market brand shares (volume and value)*
Sample:   *3,746 housewives*
*Source:* TMS[4]

1.  *Increased market buoyancy* was undoubtedly a feature of the years between 1986 and 1988. Unfortunately the current economic climate began to adversely affect the furniture market late in 1988. Yet neither of these trends is crucial to the case, for Silentnight has consistently *outperformed the market*, whatever its status. The company has increased both volume and value share in each year since the campaign launch.

2.  The *new product* itself was clearly crucial to repositioning Silentnight within the market. However, it is our contention that this could never have been effected without shifts in awareness, brand image and trade, as well as consumer motivation – driven by the Hippo and Duck advertising campaign. This argument is upheld by three principal factors:

—   Firstly, new product advantages were first made available in 1984 with the launch of the new mattress in the Perfect Sleeper range; and the full specification of interdependent mattress and base was introduced in January 1986.
    Sales take-off, however, did not occur until after the launch of the advertising campaign.

—   Secondly, within a year of the introduction of the Ultimate Sleep System, with its 'unique combination of consumer benefits', its claims had been widely copied by most of Silentnight's major competitors.

[4] TMS is the only source that monitors all the major bed brands. Prior to their methodology amendment in 1988 there was some discrepancy between their data and that from other sources (Business Monitor, Trade Estimates). For this reason the Silentnight data has been weighted in accordance with Business Monitor data.

Few credible manufacturers now promote their beds without some form of 'no roll-together' platform. Yet we have seen how advertising has helped to make this Silentnight's proposition.

— Thirdly, the Republic of Ireland forms a crucial *control* area. Ultimate was launched in Eire with the same product range, the same positioning, the same display material package and the same concentrated sell-in.

Only the advertising was omitted.

A comparison of indexed sales trends with those of the UK highlights the differences (see Table 4). After the initial impetus of the launch which generated a short-term sales blip, there was a complete collapse in Ultimate sales in Ireland.

TABLE 4:  SALES VALUE COMPARISON: UK/EIRE

|      | United Kingdom | | Republic of Ireland | |
|      | Total SNT | Ultimate | Total SNT | Ultimate |
|------|-----------|----------|-----------|----------|
| 1986 | *100*     | *100*    | 100       | 100      |
| 1987 | *121*     | *161*    | 125       | 119      |
| 1988 | *133*     | *168*    | 112       | 17       |
| 1989 | *129*     | *148*    | 70        | 31       |

Source:   Silentnight Sales History

3. *Enhanced Salesforce efficiency* is again one of the broader effects of having a stronger story to sell. Though paradoxically this particular case history demonstrates a further benefit of the long-term commitment to building the brand. For the consistency of the advertising campaign, where previously there had been none, has provided a key element of *stability* – playing down the impact of high sales staff turnover which would normally be expected to adversely influence performance.

4. *Distribution* was long regarded as the absolute key to success in the bed market driven by the maxim, 'You only sell what you display'.

Analysis of the realities of the past three years should prove sufficient to provoke a re-appraisal of this conventional wisdom; though the launch saw initial gains in retail outlets and floor models displayed, the picture by the end of 1989 showed a net decrease of 5% in absolute distribution (Silentnight's Floor Model Tracking Survey).

## CONCLUSIONS

'The cleverest campaign of the last two years – they caught the imagination and backed it up very strongly' (UK Bed Retailer, Marketlink).

In conclusion then, in what ways has Silentnight's advertising campaign affected its business performance?

1. A direct influence on sales has been demonstrated through appraising the ways in which the campaign has impacted upon consumer purchasing behaviour. Each of the original communications objectives has been met: the brand is now top of mind in its marketplace and strongly associated with a desirable benefit, providing a meaningful point of difference – so that Silentnight is now the purchaser's preferred brand. The Hippo and Duck characters seem to enhance this rational process with their own emotional franchise. They now feature on all Ultimate bed labels.

2. Advertising's *broader* effects have been demonstrated by the campaign's impact across the spectrum of the marketing mix. Its perceived success has contributed enormously to restored trade customer confidence. And the character-branded display material could not have functioned as successfully without the relevance conferred by the TV campaign.

3. The very nature of the beds' marketplace (with a repeat purchasing cycle typically somewhere between 10 and 25 years!) dictated a *longer* perspective from the outset.

Yet compared with the scenario in 1986, the company is now selling more beds, at higher margins and generating increased profits.

Is this entirely coincidental?

The Hippo and Duck don't think so.

Note: In December 1990 Silentnight overtook its nearest competitor for prompted brand awareness *amongst all adults* for the first time in the NOP tracking study

# 4

# Champagne Lanson: 'Why Not?'

## INTRODUCTION

This paper charts a five year period (1985 – 1989) in the successful development of Champagne Lanson in the UK market.

Lanson began this period with a new distributor, a commitment to brand marketing and, for the first time, an advertising agency. The 'raw material' was excellent: a high quality product, a Grande Marque heritage and reasonable sales. Despite this, Lanson had low awareness, little real consumer franchise and, in consequence, a weak price position.

Five years on, Lanson has greatly improved its price position, more than doubled sales and grown share in an increasingly competitive market. It is now a brand that genuinely means a lot to consumers (and the trade), and is in excellent shape for the future.

We will demonstrate the important and profitable role that the 'Why not?' campaign has played in this success, both in terms of its direct effects on consumers and its broader role in instilling confidence in the trade.

## BACKGROUND

Champagne is no ordinary product, Lanson is no ordinary Champagne, and the market is no ordinary fmcg market.

### Champagne

Champagne's special status is rooted in the unique qualities of the product itself. It can only be made from grapes grown in the designated Champagne region surrounding Reims and Epernay, whose chalk-based soil and unique micro-climate permit vines to flourish in an unusually northerly latitude.

Champagne grapes are among the most expensive in the world; the grape cost alone is now approaching £4 per bottle, which added to the labour intensive production process and stock-holding costs – Grandes Marques spend a minimum of three years maturing in the bottle – this explains Champagne's high price.

As an 'agricultural' product, annual production is heavily weather-dependent. New plantings and better viniculture have increased average yields but, with virtually all available land now under vine, the production ceiling is close. The long-term 'game' in Champagne is more about supporting higher prices than increasing volume.

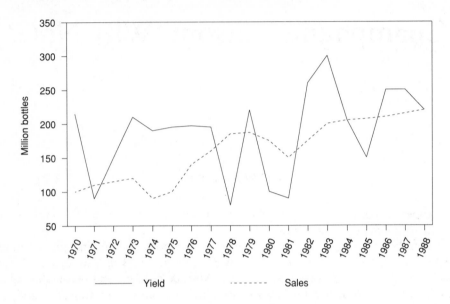

Figure 1. *Total champagne yields and sales since 1970*
*Source:* CIVC

### Champagne Lanson

Established in 1760, Champagne Lanson is one of the oldest of the Grandes Marques. Though now part of a bigger group – Lanson was acquired by BSN in the early 1980s – the Lanson family retain responsibility for the quality of Lanson Champagnes, and in particular the 'style' of their non-vintage cuvée, Lanson Black Label. The great Champagne Houses all guard with great care the 'style' of their non-vintage cuvées (which represent the bulk of their sales). Careful blending ensures a consistency, whenever or wherever you drink it.

Black Label accounts for c90% of Lanson sales. It has a distinctive 'style'; 'a full and fruity flavour that is quite, but not astringently, 'dry'. Though product connoisseurship is not high, Champagne drinkers can generally discern a difference.

The UK has been Lanson's most important export market for many years. However, until 1985 brand support was confined to trade marketing, plus PR directed at traditional areas of Champagne consumption such as horse-racing. There had been no real attempt to communicate with a broader Champagne audience.

### The UK Champagne Market

Champagne is a well-established drinks category in the UK and very much a universal symbol of status and celebration.

Several factors have fuelled growth in Champagne during the 1980s: greater affluence, good harvests, low real prices in historical terms, plus wider distribution (especially through supermarkets).

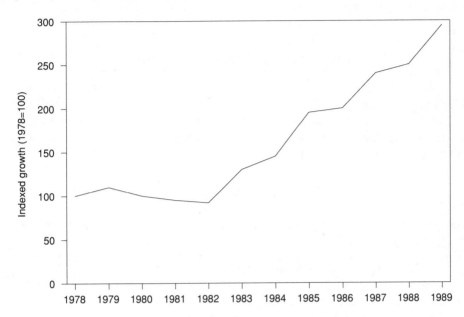

Figure 2.  *Growth of champagne exports to the UK*
*Source:* CIVC

Shipments to the UK almost doubled between 1984 and 1989; from 1 million cases to 1.9 million. Drinker and purchaser penetration also increased by over 50% during this period – with many new buyers – but the target market remains narrow; estimated annual purchase penetration in 1989 was just 3% (TGI and Lanson Brand Standing Monitor).

The trade structure is complicated and diverse, with volume breaking down as follows:

— Off-trade (specialists and grocers) c40%
— On-trade (hotels, restaurants, pubs) c30%
— Other (corporate entertaining, race-courses, etc) c30%

Sales split roughly 50:50 between 'bulk purchase' and 'personal purchase'.

'Bulk purchase' decisions relate to corporate entertaining, weddings and the like; the people who actually drink the Champagne typically do not make a brand choice. Such decisions tend to be based on price, personal contacts, the Chairman's preference, etc, and are unlikely to be advertising sensitive.

'Personal purchase' relates to occasions where individuals choose a brand for personal consumption. This sector is our main focus for advertising, and its subsequent evaluation. We will focus particularly on the off-trade – which accounts for c.80% of personal purchases – where we have good data via the Stats MR audit.

Neither the relative importance of these trade channels nor the market's 'brand structure' have changed greatly during the 1980s. Moët has maintained a 20%+ volume share, followed by Lanson with approaching 10%, and other Grandes Marques at 5% or less.

## CAMPAIGN DEVELOPMENT AND HISTORY

J R Phillips was appointed in early 1985 to bring distribution muscle and a greater marketing orientation to Lanson. A commitment to above-the-line activity was part of the change; J R Phillips appointed Saatchi to work with them on developing brand strategy and advertising.

### Early Strategy

The overall Lanson marketing objectives were straightforward, if somewhat daunting:

— Develop a real consumer (and trade) franchise for Lanson.
— Improve distribution.
— Increase sales at least in line with the fast growing market.
— And, crucially, greatly improve the brand's price position.

Champagne is a status product and it was clear that any advertising must be stylish, understated and high in 'production values'. To develop a strong identity on a limited budget any advertising would also need to be *relevant but different* from the established images associated with Champagne, especially given Moët's dominance in the public consciousness.

Established Champagne imagery was entirely generic, reflecting overt status, tradition and traditional celebration occasions. What little advertising there was tended to be of the 'bottle, glass and château' variety.

We sensed a new, 'flexible' dynamic emerging in the UK. Based largely on intuition – people in advertising agencies *do* drink more Champagne than most – this was confirmed by qualitative research, which also showed the failure of traditional Champagne images to capture the special relationship that many consumers have with it. Many view, and use Champagne in a more flexible way. They value the intrinsic *spirit* of Champagne – style, romance, spontaneity, the way it can add to any special moment – as much as its traditional celebration role and status.

The initial 1985 creative brief was loose, being essentially to:

— Appeal to these new, flexible users.
— Avoid expected, traditional Champagne values (whilst reflecting status qualities).

In retrospect it may have been too loose.

## The Creative False Start

Two executions, 'Topiary' and 'Model Railway', were produced and run in highly targeted 'lifestyle' press in autumn 1985 (magazines such as *Tatler* and *Vogue*; total spend c£100,000).

This first stage of advertising certainly helped in trade and consumer terms, but qualitative research showed both executions to be flawed. 'Model Railway' strayed too far into traditional party territory; it was 'expected', failed to capture the intrinsic emotional potential of Champagne, and implications of overt wealth and 'Hooray Henry's' could alienate. 'Topiary' was much more successful, being seen as imaginative, involving and intriguing, but perhaps lacked the executional magic to evoke the emotional potential of Champagne.

Nevertheless, the development of these executions, and the subsequent research, helped crystallise the creative brief which produced the 'Why not?' campaign.

## THE REFINED CREATIVE STRATEGY

### Advertising objectives

1. Develop a strong and distinctive identity for Lanson (by being relevant but different).
2. Appeal to the new, flexible user dynamic.
3. Appropriate the intrinsic emotional values of Champagne rather than obvious generic, status imagery.

### Target Audience

— Affluent, men and women aged 25 – 40, biased London/South.
— Like Champagne, and the emotions it triggers, too much to restrict its usage just to traditional Champagne occasions.
— Imaginative, flexible, confident of their own style and not bound by conventions (a group we term 'Flexibles').

### The Single-minded Proposition

Lanson, the Champagne for people with the imagination to create their own Champagne occasion.

### Tone

Unexpected but desirable, emotionally special and enjoyable. Sophisticated and stylish, but not elitist.

### Additional Guidelines

— Champagne must be integral to the occasion.
— Seek non-traditional situations with Champagne potential.
— Groups trigger traditional associations; two people is enough.

### The 'Why Not?' Campaign

This brief came to life as the 'Why not?' campaign:

— The 'Why not?' line encapsulating the 'flexible' attitude to Champagne.
— The situation, relationships and 'atmosphere' triggering the intrinsic emotional values of Champagne.
— The distinctive look appropriating these values to Lanson, and conferring style and status on the brand.

The creative inspiration was Cartier Bresson's 'reportage' style of photography, based upon observed moments rather than 'staged' poses. The press work is shot in black and white then 'post-tinted' to give a 'limited colour' look.

Four double page magazine executions have been run: 'Beach' and 'Ballroom' (from 1986), 'Pie & Eel' (from 1987) and 'Ferry' (from 1988). The last three have also been produced as single page executions for occasional use in national press.

A 40 second film, 'Lanson D'Amour' was made in 1987. Shot in black and white, using the Manhattan Transfer song 'Chanson D'Amour' (re-recorded as 'Lanson D'Amour'), it was inspired by 'Beach' and highly synergistic with the press campaign. It appeared on cinema in 1987 and 1988, and on London TV in 1989.

### Media

Lanson media strategy has been driven by budget (limited), efficiency of targeting in terms of demographics and psychographics (aided by TGI lifestyle data), and environment.

Lifestyle magazines such as *Tatler*, *Country Living* and *Homes and Garden* were a natural choice. These offer limited cover and we have aimed to reach a broader audience by selective use of national press, supplements, cinema and TV.

*Why not?*                                                                *Lanson*

The gradual extension to cinema and then TV was triggered by increasing budgets (based on brand success), and the sheer power of the 'Lanson D'Amour' film to motivate consumers and the trade. Nevertheless, effective use of TV was only made possible by careful targeting – buying selectively at a very low strike weight – and exceptional media buying by Zenith.

TABLE 1: MEDIA SUMMARY 1985 – 1989

| Medium | Period | Schedule delivery (vs AB adults aged 25–40) | Media cost* |
|---|---|---|---|
| Lifestyle magazines | Oct–Dec 1985 | 30% cover at 1.5 OTS | £100,000 |
| Lifestyle magazines | Jun–Dec 1986 | 35% cover at 4 OTS | £240,000 |
| Lifestyle magazines plus *The Times* (x5) and *Daily Mail* (x2) Cinema (London/TVS) | Mar–Dec 1987 May–Dec | 50% cover at 3 OTS 25% cover at 2 OTS (within areas covered) | £200,000 £60,000 *£260,000* |
| Lifestyle magazines plus *Independent* (x5) and *Daily Mail* (x3) Cinema (London/TVS) | Mar–Dec 1988 May–Jul/Oct–Dec | 60% cover at 3.5 OTS 25% cover at 2 OTS (within areas covered) | £220,000 £60,000 *£280,000* |
| Lifestyle magazines plus *Independent* (x1) TV (London) | Feb–Dec 1989 Jul–Dec | 45% cover at 3 OTS 275 TVRs (ABC1 adults aged 25–44) giving 70% cover at 4 OTS | £210,000 £240,000 *£450,000* |

Note: * Approximate actual cost (below MEAL/Media Register figures shown later); consumer press only.

## EVALUATION – OUR APPROACH

Though Lanson is a well-researched brand (see Appendix 1), it is difficult to isolate the contribution of advertising on a year to year basis. Advertising has been integral to the general plan of the brand, spend relatively low and, with a consistent overall approach, we have no real 'peaks and troughs' to help us see the effects of advertising.

The development of Lanson was always seen as a long-term exercise and it makes sense to evaluate it that way. We have undertaken a 'brand audit', looking at relevant measures of brand performance and status at the end of 1989, comparing them with equivalent measures when we began in 1985, and looked at some of the 'signposts' in between. The five year contribution of advertising can be isolated by eliminating, or otherwise taking into account, other influential factors on brand success.

The next section outlines brand achievements over the five year period. We then aim to isolate the contribution of advertising, and finally discuss how the advertising has worked.

## EVALUATION – BRAND ACHIEVEMENTS

### *The Overall Sales Picture*

Lanson volumes out-performed the market by 32% between 1984 and 1989. Figure 3 shows official CIVC figures for shipments to the UK: total Champagne shipments were 92% higher 1989 vs 1984, cf+124% for Lanson.

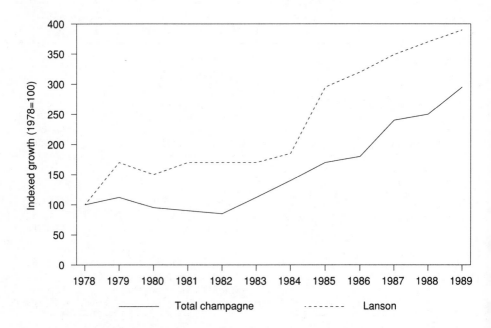

Figure 3. *Champagne shipments to the UK: total vs Lanson*
*Source:* CIVC

## *Off-Trade Sales*

As already stated our main focus will be the off-trade, where we have good data via the Stats MR off-licence audit (no market data is available for Champagne in the on-trade or 'bulk purchase' area). Lanson's off-trade sales performance is similar to the total picture shown above and it seems a reasonable basis for analysis.

We measure Lanson's performance in two ways:

— Against the total market.
— Against a 'Raft' of leading brands.

The 'Raft' comprises Lanson, plus its most direct Grande Marque competitors in price and volume terms: Moët & Chandon, Mumm, Mercier, Veuve Clicquot and Charles Heidsieck. In 1989 it accounted for 50% of total of trade sales. Remaining sales come mainly from 'cheapies' and own label, but also included 'exclusive' high price, low volume brands such as Roederer and Krug.

Table 2 shows Lanson out-performing the market by 32% and the 'Raft' by 60% over the five and a half year period that data is available to us.

TABLE 2: OFF-TRADE VOLUME SALES TRENDS

|  | A/M '85 | D/J '86 | D/J '87 | D/J '88 | D/J '89 | D/J '90 |
|---|---|---|---|---|---|---|
| Total Champagne (index) | 100 | 113 | 124 | 133 | 159 | 166 |
| The 'Raft' (index) | 100 | 108 | 111 | 117 | 135 | 138 |
| Lanson (index) | 100 | 115 | 149 | 154 | 175 | 198 |
| Lanson % market share | 8.8 | 8.9 | 10.6 | 10.2 | 9.7 | 10.5 |
| Lanson % share of the 'Raft' | 14.6 | 15.5 | 19.6 | 19.2 | 18.9 | 20.9 |

Source: Stats MR

## *Pricing*

This excellent volume sales performance has been achieved whilst improving Lanson's price position by over 10% vs the market average, and c5% vs the 'Raft'.

TABLE 3. OFF-TRADE PRICE TRENDS (RSP/VOLUME WEIGHTED)

|  | Indexed prices: | |
|---|---|---|
|  | Lanson vs market av. | Lanson vs 'Raft' av. |
| F/M 1985 | 98 | 93 |
| J/J 1985 | 103 | 95 |
| D/J 1986 | 102 | 93 |
| J/J 1986 | 103 | 93 |
| D/J 1987 | 105 | 95 |
| J/J 1987 | 106 | 97 |
| D/J 1988 | 110 | 98 |
| J/J 1988 | 110 | 98 |
| D/J 1989 | 109 | 97 |
| J/J 1989 | 110 | 97 |
| D/J 1990 | 107 | 96 |
| F/M 1990 | 110 | 98 |

Source: Stats MR

(There can be anomalies because of the phasing of price increases. In December/January 1990 Lanson's price increase lagged Moët; the latest February/March 1990 data shows Lanson price indices returning to previous levels.)

### Distribution

Increased distribution was a key Lanson objective. Since J R Phillips took over and started talking to the trade about its plans – it has almost tripled. In a growing market, other 'Raft' brands have also improved their distribution, though to a lesser extent; Lanson's share of total 'Raft' brand distribution points has increased from 16% to 26%, showing a strong performance in terms of opening and retaining accounts.

TABLE 4: OFF-TRADE DISTRIBUTION TRENDS (STERLING DISTRIBUTION)

| | F/M 1985 % | D/J 1986 % | D/J 1988 % | D/J1990 % |
|---|---|---|---|---|
| Lanson distribution | 27 | 45 | 62 | 75 |
| Total 'Raft' brand distribution points (ie sum of the 6 brands % distribution) | 170 | 193 | 244 | 284 |
| Lanson share of 'Raft' distribution points | 16 | 23 | 25 | 26 |

Source: Stats MR

Lanson's distribution increases have obviously helped support higher sales volumes, but have had no direct effect in supporting higher prices.

The presence, quality and quantity of consumer advertising support is frequently cited as an important determinant of trade stocking behaviour, and this has certainly been the case for Lanson. The London TV test in 1989 is an example of advertising giving the trade extra confidence in a brand. A trade panel had voted the 'Lanson D'Amour' film the Grand Prix (ie the best single drink's advertisement) in the inaugural Off-Licence News Drinks Advertising Awards in March 1989 (when it had run only on cinema). This was one of the reasons we finally chanced our arm on TV. The J R Phillips National Accounts team directly attribute major new listings to the decision to use TV:

— Nationally Lanson's sterling distribution rose from 64% in December/January 1989 to 75% in December/January 1990.
— Because of the way the trade works, the benefit was as great outside London (distribution rising from 57% to 67%) as in the London TV area (rising from 75% to 87%).

The trade's confidence was repaid in full.

## The London TV Test

The London TV test run July-December 1989 was in effect a 'test and control' experiment for Lanson. TV advertising was the only variable: Lanson press advertising was running nationally; as we have seen, distribution increases were similar in London and elsewhere; prices are set nationally; there was no difference in promotional activity. The overall market was weaker in London (because of the differential impact of interest rates), but we can take account of that.

Table 5 is based on the audit periods likely to be most affected by the advertising (cover did not build to 50% until October), and shows how Lanson sales in London out-performed the market by 26% (cf+11% elsewhere). With all other key influential variables in balance across areas, the additional 15% sales uplift during the advertised period in London must be primarily the result of the TV campaign.

TABLE 5: TV TEST: SALES IN LONDON VS ELSEWHERE

| | Oct–Jan 1989/90 vs Oct–Jan 1988/89 | | |
| | Total market % | Lanson % | Lanson vs market % |
| --- | --- | --- | --- |
| Total GB | −1 | +16 | +17 |
| London TV | −4 | +22 | +26 |
| Elsewhere | +1 | +12 | +11 |
| London vs elsewhere | −5 | +10 | +15 |

Source:   Stats MR

## Brand Standing

The development of a strong consumer franchise was another key marketing objective. We regard improved brand standing as a tangible achievement because it will provide the basis for stronger and more certain future profits.

Table 6 shows the standing of Lanson has increased steadily on all key measures across a five and a half year period. Lanson is a brand which now means a lot more to Champagne buyers than it did in 1984.

TABLE 6: LANSON BRAND STANDING TRENDS 1984 – 89

| | NOP | NOP | Lanson brand standing monitor (BMRB) | | |
| | Jul 84 % | Jan 86 % | Jul 87 % | Jul 88 % | Dec 89 % |
| --- | --- | --- | --- | --- | --- |
| Spontaneous brand awareness | 5(16) | 8(17) | 22 | 24 | 26 |
| Total brand awareness | n/a | 28(45) | 53 | 63 | 67 |
| Preferred brand: | | | | | |
|   1st choice | 1(2) | 2(3) | 5 | 8 | 9 |
|   1st or 2nd choice | 5(10) | n/a | 15 | 21 | 21 |
| Rated as 'particularly | | | | | |
|   good quality' | n/a | n/a | 45 | 51 | 53 |
| Claimed purchase in last year | n/a | n/a | 13 | 17 | 19 |

Base:   Buyers of Champagne in the past year.

The figures in brackets are our attempt to correct for technical differences between the two NOP surveys (omnibus) and the three Brand Standing Monitors (ad hoc). By assuming there was no real change over the 1984, 1986, and 1987 surveys for the average brand, we have derived a corrective weight for each measure to apply to Lanson (see Appendix 2 for further explanation).

None of the competitive brands covered in our research have made a consistent improvement in brand standing in the period monitored. Though its position has been eroded, Moët remains the highest rated on all measures. Lanson is steadily gaining on Moët and is well ahead of all other 'Raft' brands on all key measures.

## EVALUATION – ISOLATING THE CONTRIBUTION OF ADVERTISING

We have already seen strong evidence of Lanson TV advertising causing a sharp short-term uplift in sales in London in 1989; we will be monitoring longer term effects with interest, but have already extended use of TV in 1990. In this section we will concentrate on the longer term 'five year' effect, by looking at all the possible influences on Lanson sales.

### Lanson Marketing Activity

Lanson PR expenditure covers standard activity such as consumer and trade press releases, the supply of product for events and competitions, and presentations/tastings for the trade and winewriters. In addition Lanson has sponsored the Vintage Stakes at Goodwood for many years and the Ladies' International Challenge at York since 1987. Trade marketing expenditure (including promotions, point of sale, incentives, etc) remains a large part of the overall budget.

Marketing expenditure covering the above has grown at a lower rate than turnover 1984 – 89. The main change was consumer advertising – before 1985 there was none – and the gradual increase in advertising budget. In addition much below-the-line activity has reflected the 'Why not?' theme.

### Competitive Activity

The market has become considerably more competitive with overall a much more professional approach to marketing. As brands attempt to support higher prices, increasing expenditure has been made both above and below-the-line. Table 7 shows the sharp increase in consumer advertising over the period.

Given these increasing levels of competitive activity, Lanson would almost certainly have considerably under-performed the market without advertising investment.

TABLE 7: CHAMPAGNE ADVERTISING EXPENDITURE 1984 – 89

| £(000s) | 1984 | 1985 | 1986 | 1987 | 1988 | 1989 |
|---|---|---|---|---|---|---|
| Lanson | — | 104 | 291 | 318 | 396 | 572 |
| Mumm | 158 | 196 | 165 | 362 | 264 | 390 |
| CH Heidsieck | — | — | 2 | 177 | 370 | 288 |
| Veuve Clicquot | 73 | 58 | 64 | 106 | 187 | 344 |
| Total 'Raft' | 231 | 358 | 522 | 963 | 1,217 | 1,619 |
| *Total market* | *231* | *465* | *744* | *1,051* | *1,354* | *1,740* |
| Lanson share of voice(%) | 0 | 22 | 39 | 30 | 28 | 33 |

Source:  Media Register (except 1984/85 – MEAL)

## Competitive Strategies

Creatively all other brands which advertise have stuck with fairly traditional Champagne images. 'Raft' brands have increased their prices ahead of the market average, but under-performed the market in sales terms as a result. Lanson has increased its prices faster than the 'Raft' and increased volume well ahead of the market (Tables 2 and 3).

## Distribution

The retail trade needs a good reason to stock a given brand in a crowded market. Competitive pricing can be one such reason but, as we have seen, Lanson have not been playing that particular game. Trade and salesforce feedback indicates Lanson advertising has been crucial in driving up distribution. Advertising is a tangible sign of a brand's professionalism and commitment and gives the trade confidence. Moreover, the trade particularly likes Lanson advertising, and sees it as adding a new dimension to the Champagne market.

The promise of advertising helped drive up distribution in 1985, the increasing commitment to it – and good sales performance – has helped distribution increase further to its current high level. Without advertising the best we could have expected was for Lanson distribution to increase in line with the 'Raft'. This would have taken it from 27% in February/March 1985 to 45% (rather than the 75% level actually reached in December/January 1990). Given increased competitive activity, even growth to 45% would have been highly optimistic without advertising.

## The Financial Contribution of the Advertising

We have aimed to demonstrate, largely by process of elimination, that the various brand achievements outlined are primarily a result of the effectiveness of Lanson advertising.

To get an idea of the financial impact of the advertising, we can compare actual brand performance with projected performance on two 'baseline' assumptions:

Assumption 1: That Lanson would have performed in line with the total Champagne market in sales and price terms 1984/5 – 89.

Assumption 2: That Lanson would have performed in line with the 'Raft'.

Given increased competitive activity, neither of these assumptions seems pessimistic for 'zero advertising' scenario projections.

Projected figures for 1989 based on these two assumptions can be made from a single arithmetic calculation using the figures underpinning the indices in Tables 2 and 3; Table 8 shows the results.

TABLE 8: PROJECTED 1989 OUTCOMES FOR LANSON VS ACTUAL
(Based on Off-Trade data)

|  | Projected vs Actual | |
|  | Assumption 1 (vs total market) (%) | Assumption 2 (vs 'Raft') (%) |
| --- | --- | --- |
| Lanson volume sales | −16 | −30 |
| Lanson price | −9 | −4 |
| Lanson sterling value | −23 | −33 |

Computed at average retail (off-trade) selling price, Lanson UK sales were worth almost £30 million in 1989. Even on these 'baseline' assumptions – that Lanson would have maintained its competitive position without advertising – we can see that actual turnover in 1989 is as much as £10 million above its projected value.

Information on margins and profitability must remain confidential but with media costs still under £500,000 in 1989, advertising has clearly been a highly profitable activity for Lanson over the past five years.

No less importantly, Lanson is clearly a much stronger brand now than it was in 1985 before advertising began; *future* profit flows should be much greater and more secure than they otherwise would have been.

## EVALUATION – HOW THE ADVERTISING HAS WORKED

We have seen that the advertising has worked in business terms – but how has it produced these business effects?

A lot of the evidence has already been produced.

The effects of the quality and quantity of Lanson advertising on the trade have already been discussed. In many ways we regard the trade effects as of equal importance to the consumer effects, although the trade effects would not of course have persisted if consumers had not been prepared to buy Lanson in increasing quantities at increasingly higher prices.

'Trends in brand standing amongst consumers (Table 6) show that Lanson is now a brand which is more 'top of mind', better known, better thought of, and in more people's repertoires of preferred and 'usually bought' brands'.

These quantitative measures show a familiar pattern of 'familiarity and favourability', but are too crude to expose the 'emotional bond' built by the advertising between Lanson and many Champagne buyers. This can only really be seen in qualitative research.

> 'It is clear from this research that Lanson's advertising works very effectively in the post-opening, emotional world of Champagne. As such it is unique: all other Champagne advertising concentrates on the formal, pre-opening world, with little or no reference to what follows. The Lanson approach was found to have singular appeal and interest among consumers ... (it) never failed to convey a very potent message, that the world of Lanson was the world of a special, spontaneous, personal celebration' (Strategic Research Group 1990).

The bond is particularly strong with our core target audience of 'Flexibles' who use Champagne flexibly and value Champagne for its emotional, enhancing properties rather than (just) the social status it confers. 'Flexibles' account for c50% of Champagne purchases (and rather more of sales). Lanson is the only brand making a pitch for them in advertising and this we believe has been the bedrock of its success.

Not surprisingly, the remainder of the market – 'Inflexibles' – tend to get less involved with the Lanson advertising. The exception is the 'Lanson D'Amour' film which appears to refresh the parts the press does not reach. This indeed may be the reason for the 'sales kick' produced by the use of TV in 1989.

> '(The film) managed to win the approval of *everybody* interviewed ... even those respondents who were otherwise uninterested and found it difficult to become involved with the campaign were finally impressed with this film' (CWA 1987).

> 'Very few respondents were left unaffected by the execution... (which) operates in the realm of fantasy/ideal, not reality' (Strategic Research Group 1990).

Finally, it should be noted that the 'Why not?' campaign has won several high profile creative awards including five silvers in the Campaign Press Awards and the Grand Prix in the Off-Licence News Drinks Advertising Awards. This has generated considerable PR for the brand, especially within advertising and marketing (an important market for Champagne), and amongst the retail trade.

## IN CONCLUSION

We believe that this is a valuable case history for a number of reasons; it shows:

— The important long-term brand building role of advertising.
— How advertising can improve margins as well as sales.
— How relatively small budgets, applied consistently and creatively, can have large effects.
— How breaking some of the accepted 'rules', and using advertising imaginatively in a market where advertising was under-used, can give a brand competitive advantage.
— How advertising greatly admired for its creative qualities can also be highly effective in business terms.

Much of the analysis covered in this paper comes from a 'brand audit' conducted to ensure that Lanson strategies continue to drive the brand forward in the changing circumstances of the 1990s. We hope that the reader shares our conclusion that we can look ahead with confidence.

## APPENDIX 1

### Research Sources

1. CIVC UK Shipments data – the CIVC is the Champagne producers trade body; all production and shipments have to be notified by strict regulation.
2. Stats MR Off-Licence Audit – the 'market standard' retail audit for drinks; covers all sectors of the off-trade; J R Phillips have data from the beginning of 1985 with MAT sales data back to the 12 months ending April/May 1985.
3. BMRB Lanson Brand Standing Monitor – three waves to date; dedicated Lanson/Champagne survey; nationally representative; 300 interviews with buyers of Champagne in past year, male and female, ABC1, aged 20 – 64; using Champagne drinkers identified via the TGI in the previous year as a contact sample; interviewed by telephone after being carefully screened to ensure they had bought at least one bottle of real Champagne in the past 12 months.
4. NOP July 1984 – Omnibus research; face-to-face; based upon 154 claimed Champagne buyers (purchased in the past year); contact sample nationally representative of all GB adults.
5. NOP Jan 1986 – data based on 143 claimed Champagne buyers (purchased in the past year) identified as part of the 1986 NOP Alcoholic Drinks Survey; technically similar to the 1984 omnibus research.
6. Fusion – Strategy research conducted in April 1985; four groups conducted with AB Champagne buyers aged 25 – 50, male and female.
7. Fusion – Creative Assessment/Strategy Refinement; October 1985; seven groups, sample as above.
8. CWA – Creative Assessment/Brand Update; February 1987; four groups with Champagne buyers.
9. Strategic Research Group – part of overall brand audit and development of strategy for the 1990s; February 1990; eight groups (two extended), nine individual depths with Champagne buyers aged 28 – 50; sample stratified by attitude to Champagne, 'Flexibles' vs 'Inflexibles'.

## APPENDIX 2

### Corrective Weighting of Brand Standing Data

Although question wording and sample definition (all claimed purchasers of Champagne in the last year) are broadly consistent, there were technical differences between the two NOP surveys (omnibus) and the three Brand Standing Monitors (dedicated to Champagne/telephone). All brands registered much lower levels in the

NOP research: omnibus surveys generally produce lower levels than dedicated surveys, and there was less careful screening in the omnibus surveys to ensure that respondents were real Champagne buyers. The BMRB research also had a tighter sample (ABC1, 20 – 64).

The figures in brackets in Table 6 are our attempt to correct for these differences by applying corrective weights to the NOP data for Lanson. On each measure, separately for 1984 and 1986 surveys, corrective weights have been computed on the assumption that there was no *real* change between 1984, 1986 and the first BMRB survey in 1987 *for the average brand*. The figures preceding those in brackets are the actual figures produced by the research.

# Section Two

*Established Consumer Goods and Services*

# 5
# Marketing Sleep: The Relaunch of Karvol

## INTRODUCTION

It could be said that there are two distinct if not separate effects of advertising: a short-term effect which stimulates additional sales over a defined and limited period of time; and a longer term effect which contributes to the more enduring 'saleability' of a brand.

This paper sets out to demonstrate how a brand made vulnerable through restricted distribution, and a fragile consumer base, used highly creative advertising to achieve short-term sales growth and also contributed to the longer term brand development and 'saleability'.

### Background

Throughout the 1980s, there has been a steady trend by the British consumer towards self medication. This means dealing with everyday minor ailments with a non-prescription medicine.

This trend has been helped by the present Government. In an attempt to reduce escalating NHS costs, they have been committed to encouraging greater personal responsibility for healthcare.

In 1985 the 'Limited List' was introduced in order to prevent certain brands, considered to have a price premium, from being prescribed. Most of the brands had 'Over The Counter' (OTC) equivalents (ie similar products, which could be sold to the consumer without a prescription). Consequently manufacturers began to invest heavily in advertising in order to build consumer brands, and create consumer demand, rather than rely on doctor recommendation. At the same time, increasing numbers of drugs were made more freely available to the consumer. Brands originally with 'P' or 'Pharmacy Only' status (restricted to sale by a pharmacist, and therefore kept behind the pharmacist's counter) were able to switch to 'GSL' or 'General Sales List' status, so allowing them to be positioned out front in the pharmacist's store, and sold in other outlets.

The net effect of these changes has been the creation of a highly favourable environment for the growth in household medicines with 'GSL' status.

Whilst pharmacies have benefited, and have continued to dominate total sales, the real growth opportunities have moved to the other retailing outlets. The virtual sales monopoly once enjoyed by pharmacies has given way to increasing competition from the major grocery multiples and from drugstores.

The challenge for any healthcare manufacturer has been to ensure that its brands survived in this changing healthcare environment, and to take advantage of future retail opportunities thrown up by the changes.

## The Opportunity for Karvol

Karvol had originally benefited from the trend towards self-medication. As a nasal decongestant, it comes in the form of small gelatine capsules containing a mixture of natural oils, such as menthol and cinnamon. When sprinkled onto bedclothes warmed through body heat, the oils provide a steady release of aromatic vapours. These clear and soothe a blocked nose throughout the night, helping easier breathing and so aiding sleep.

Karvol operates in a market sector with the somewhat tortuous definition of 'Children's Non-Ingested Decongestants', known more familiarly, if not correctly, as 'Vapour Rubs', given the format of a number of products in the sector. The market definition originates more from the trade than the consumer, since historically brand choice has depended on the pharmacist. Apart from Karvol, the key brands include Vicks VapoRub, a well known family brand, and Snufflebabe, a vapour rub positioned as a decongestant for very young babies. It also includes Olbas Oil, the brand physically most similar to Karvol given its liquid format and its method of use (also sprinkled onto bedclothes). Olbas' difference lies in its natural herbal positioning, and its use of a dropper bottle, rather than capsules, which allows for a more liberal use of liquid. This market has recently been benefiting from the significant advance in the incidence of colds (Figure 1).

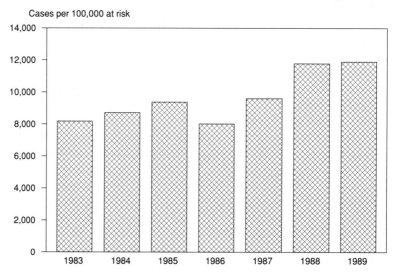

Figure 1. *Rate of incidence of common cold*
*Source:* CDSC

## ORIGINAL KARVOL PACKAGING

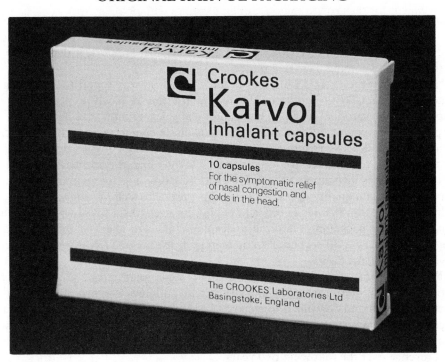

## RE-PACKAGING OF KARVOL

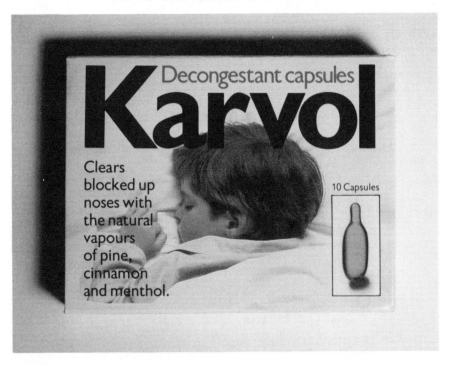

### History of the Brand

Karvol itself has not always been a child's brand. It was originally launched in 1951 as a decongestant for both adults and children. Packaged in an ethical, non-pictorial pack and receiving little, if any, consumer support, it depended on a fifth of its sales coming from doctor prescription.

However, by the early 1980s, the brand's franchise was found to be strongest amongst mothers with children. The reason for this is partly explained by the format of the product itself. The use of capsules ensures a safe method of application for young children, since it avoids direct contact with a child's delicate skin. The capsules also ensure correct application of a single night's dosage, and so provide extra reassurance for an anxious parent. And the intricate method of opening the capsule (snipping the top off with scissors), together with its small size, give the product a quality of preciousness appropriate to a child's brand.

In the winter of 1981/82, in order to exploit its strengths, Karvol was relaunched with consumer packaging featuring a sleeping child. For the first time the brand was supported by a 30 second TV commercial featuring a six year old child being given Karvol by his father.

The campaign originally ran nationally, and sales grew. Following the introduction of the 'Limited List', the brand suffered a sharp drop in sales. However, the brand continued to receive yearly advertising support, and pack sales regained their momentum. In the winter of 1986/87, the pack of 10 capsules was joined by an economy pack of 20. Sales responded accordingly with 24% growth in real revenue over the following two years.

## THE PROBLEM

By 1988 the brand was performing well. Karvol was experiencing year on year growth in a static market (see Figure 2).

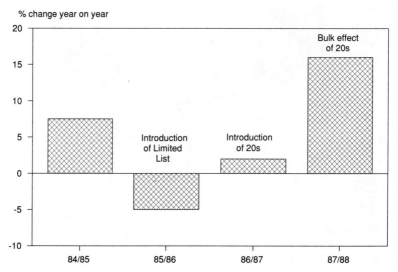

Figure 2. *Volume growth year on year*
*Source:* Nielsen

Karvol was also brand leader in pharmacies and enjoyed high levels of pharmacist recommendation (see Table 1).

TABLE 1:  BRANDS RECOMMENDED BY PHARMACISTS
FOR CHILD USAGE

|  | % |
| --- | --- |
| Karvol | 75 |
| Vicks VapoRub | 52 |
| Snufflebabe | 15 |
| Olbas Oil | 2 |

Source:  HIPPO Research 1987
Base:  Pharmacists
Note:  Numbers add up to over 100% since pharmacists
are able to recommend more than one brand

It was felt, however, that the brand was vulnerable. First of all, most of the recent growth had come through distribution gains for the 20s pack. This had now reached over 70% distribution and hence could not be relied on to provide further 'easy' growth.

Secondly, Karvol was the only inhalant to possess 'P' status. In contrast, its competitors have always been registered as 'GSL' brands, allowing them far greater access to consumers.

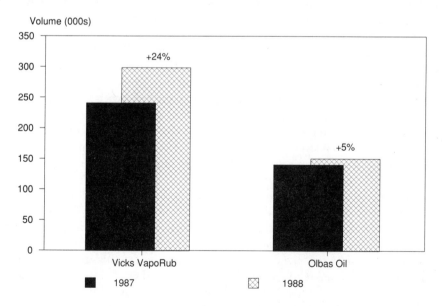

Figure 3. *Performance in grocery and drugstore of Karvol's competitors*
*Source:* AGB

While Karvol benefited from the medical credibility bestowed on the brand as a result of pharmacist control, it also meant that future growth for the brand would be restricted in sales. And despite pharmacies accounting for around 80% of the market, it was evident that drugstores and groceries share of sales had grown significantly over the last few years (+90%: AGB, Nielsen and Crookes' Estimates). Karvol's competitors were not only available in more outlets, but accessible to the mother shopping on a more relaxed, everyday basis. An omnibus survey had revealed that 60% of adults with children 0 – 9 bought decongestants 'just in case', in advance of any symptoms (RSGB 1987). There was a danger, therefore, that Karvol would increasingly miss out as a regular purchase, and instead become a distress purchase for extreme occasions.

While Crookes had little data available on the groceries/drugstores sectors, it did indeed appear that both Vicks VapoRub and Olbas Oil were benefiting from their presence in other outlets, and had increased sales considerably over the previous few years (Figure 3).

But perhaps one of the greatest concerns regarding the brand's future existence was the threat of Karvol's uniqueness being challenged by the launch of a 'me-too' capsule, already in possession of 'GSL' status, and thus able to be more widely distributed.

## Marketing Objectives

The long-term objective had to be the acquisition of 'GSL' status for the brand, in order to fight back at its competitors (both existing and potential), and to bring in new users. This meant passing stability tests, possible product reformulation, and a lengthy application for the licence. It was estimated that, at the earliest, 'GSL' status would be achieved by mid 1990.

The short-term objectives were therefore to maintain Karvol's growth as a 'P' status brand, whilst at the same time start laying the foundations for expansion into a new distribution network. It would be difficult for Crookes to extend the brand since, as a pharmaceutical marketing company, their links with groceries were not as strong as with pharmacies. If groceries and drugstores were to consider stocking Karvol in two years' time, it was necessary to ensure its position as a clear brand leader, and use this to justify its consideration by the trade. Both of these objectives meant a strengthening of Karvol's brand leadership within pharmacies, and the development of a distinct consumer benefit.

They also meant a high level of advertising support. In the 'P' status medicines market advertising plays a fundamental part in supporting sales. Without advertising, brands are dependent on pharmacist recommendation and existing users. The pharmacist, however, in his role as salesman, can be easily influenced in his choice of brand by perceived consumer appeal. And existing users, of children's brands like Karvol, quickly move on to new brands as their children grow older.

An advertising to sales ratio of c17% is therefore the norm for this market, with some brands spending up to 30%. In fact before the new campaign, Karvol's advertising to sales ratio was almost 21%.

It was decided that advertising investment had three roles to play:

1.  To support existing volume (because without it a 'P' registered brand such as Karvol would decline rapidly).
2.  To boost short-term sales.

3.  To support long-term investment, allowing Karvol to venture successfully into the 'GSL' market.

It was accepted that with such a high advertising to sales ratio it would be unlikely that any investment would pay for itself through short-term incremental sales growth. However, Crookes believed in the long-term potential of the brand, and took the decision to invest in it as necessary. It was agreed that specific short-term targets would be set which would establish a significant dominance for Karvol over its competitors. These were:

1.  To increase volume share from 31.8% to 33%.
2.  To increase brand awareness in line with the more famous VapoRub.
3.  To encourage a corresponding increase in trial and penetration.

### The Options

There were a number of options, however, as to how these objectives could best be met by advertising. The brand's strengths appeared to lie mostly amongst mothers of younger children. By contrast, Vicks VapoRub had for years successfully maintained a family positioning, and had as a result generated usage across a far wider age span. Olbas Oil also had a broader marketing proposition, and concentrated its advertising on adults (Table 2).

TABLE 2:  MAIN USAGE BY BRAND

|  | Karvol % | VapoRub % | Olbas % | Snufflebabe % |
|---|---|---|---|---|
| **Children** | | | | |
| Under 3 | 24 | 3 | 2 | 62 |
| 3–5 | 21 | 6 | 3 | 31 |
| 6–10 | 11 | 7 | 2 | 5 |
| 11–15 | 7 | 8 | 4 | — |
| Adults 15+ | 38 | 77 | 89 | — |

Source:  RSGB 1987
Base:  All adults

At the other end of the age spectrum, Snufflebabe had adopted its own tightly defined positioning as a rub for young babies (particularly up to the age of one). However, Snufflebabe was a tiny brand with only around 2% value share of the market, and so was not considered a serious competitor. The option for Karvol was whether to compete with Vicks directly on a family usage basis, or to define its target user more precisely.

### The Decision

Qualitative research confirmed that the brand's strengths of preciousness and cosseting made it most appropriate as a younger child's brand. Toddlers were naturally the focus for considerable parental concern. Whilst older children were considered more self reliant, once able to speak and to express their feelings fairly clearly, a younger child was felt to be particularly helpless and vulnerable. And this generated a greater level of anxiety amongst mothers.

'They can't tell you what's wrong'.

'The first time they get a cold, you think it's the end of the world, because you've never been through it before'.

'It's easier as they get older because they sit up more and they don't seem to congest as much by that time, and you've got used to them having colds, but their first..., to me it was as if she had something she could die of...' (Winstanley Douglas Research, 1988).

Already, amongst loyal users of the brand, Karvol was regarded somewhat as a guardian angel, looking after the child during the night in the mother's absence.

'You look after (the child) during the day, Karvol takes over during the night' (Winstanley Douglas Research, 1988).

Of all the brands, only Karvol possessed such a high level of cosseting values. The decision was taken therefore to build on its emotional potential as a 'carer' for younger children, and so reposition Karvol single-mindedly as a decongestant for toddlers aged under three.

Despite the danger of limiting usage further by losing older children, it was felt that the opportunity outweighed the risk. There still remained considerable untapped potential for the brand amongst younger children; the RSGB Omnibus survey had revealed that only 22% of adults with children under three years old had bought the brand in the previous 12 months. And it was also not forgotten that population trends were indicating a likely growth in the number of young babies of up to 11% during the 1990s.

## DEVELOPMENT OF ADVERTISING

### The Role For Advertising

Any change in positioning demanded a change in advertising. The research had indicated that the previous film had failed to portray either a genuine problem or a clear benefit from using Karvol. The execution featured a six year old child, clearly able to communicate his symptoms and therefore lacking the helplessness and vulnerability necessary to set up the problem. The need was to make the problem more dramatic, and demonstrate Karvol's ability to offer a distinct solution. At the same time, the advertising had to capture all the emotional and rational benefits of using Karvol.

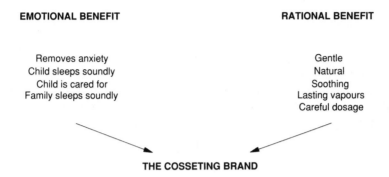

**EMOTIONAL BENEFIT**

Removes anxiety
Child sleeps soundly
Child is cared for
Family sleeps soundly

**RATIONAL BENEFIT**

Gentle
Natural
Soothing
Lasting vapours
Careful dosage

**THE COSSETING BRAND**

## Creative Development

Television was chosen as the best means of capturing the key emotional properties of the brand. A script was developed which grew directly out of an understanding of the mother's emotions, and her actions at various stages whilst caring for her child.

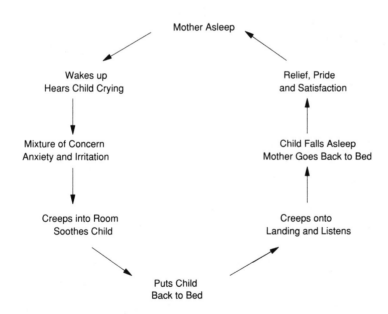

Mother Asleep

Wakes up
Hears Child Crying

Relief, Pride
and Satisfaction

Mixture of Concern
Anxiety and Irritation

Child Falls Asleep
Mother Goes Back to Bed

Creeps into Room
Soothes Child

Creeps onto
Landing and Listens

Puts Child
Back to Bed

The script focused on a helpless one year old throughout, playing on the natural instinct of mothers by highlighting the vulnerability of a disturbed child. Unlike the previous campaign the drama of the situation was clearly resolved by the child visibly falling asleep before the viewer's eyes. There was no voice over, only the sound of a child's tearfulness turning to gentle breathing. The respondents were able to understand both the rational benefits (child falls asleep) and emotional benefits (child cared for), of the brand. Moreover, the ad was found to be highly enthralling and captivating.

### Media Activity

A breakfast and coffee time media strategy was chosen as one that would provide an extremely rich opportunity to reach 'housebound' women. In the first year the finished film ran from November to March, to coincide with the winter sales peak. The weighting was staggered, with the bulk of the campaign running from December to February, and with a total spend of £448,000.

Because of the resulting uplift in sales, the ad was repeated in the winter of 1989/90, this time running from January through to March, and with a slightly increased spend of £548,500 to keep in line with media inflation.

For the second year there was some concern that the breakfast/coffee time strategy might exclude working mothers. As a result, a single page press ad, depicting a distressed child, ran in *Mother & Baby* for two months prior to the second winter burst with a spend of £50,000. It was hoped this use of a secondary medium might extend the Karvol message throughout the autumn/winter season and also provide further reassurance to the more anxious mothers.

To announce the new advertising to the trade a double page spread ran twice in *Chemist & Druggist* the autumn prior to the first year's activity. A further single page trade ad ran twice in the autumn of 1989.

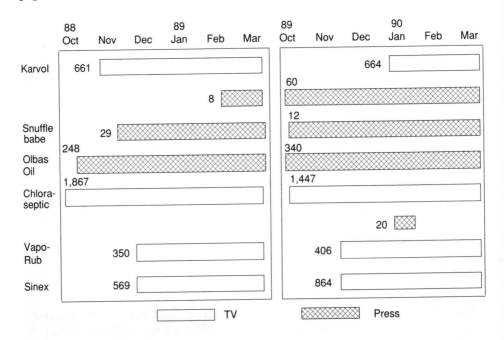

Figure 4. *Advertising expenditure – £000s*
*Source:* Media Register

## 'BABY'

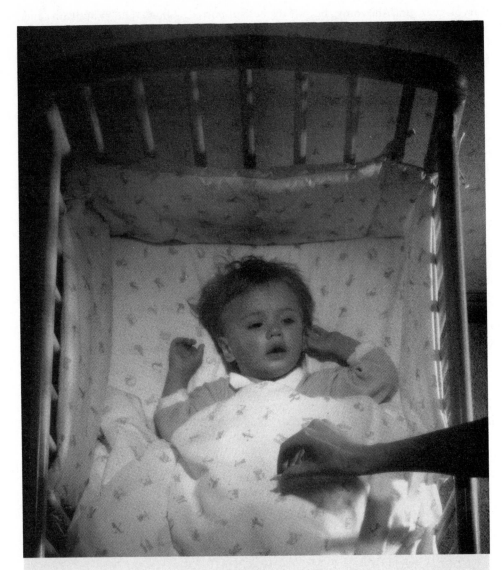

## Give your child Karvol and you'll both have a peaceful night.

A blocked nose means a sleepless night for your child and a worrying one for you.

Fortunately a child's nasal congestion can be cleared simply and effectively with Karvol.

The natural vapours of pine, cinnamon and menthol work through the night to help a child breathe easily.

*One capsule dabbed on to your child's bedclothes will help unblock a stuffy nose.

Just what you need for a good nights sleep.

Behind the best names.

**Karvol. Says goodnight to a child's blocked nose.**

• See pack for details. Available from your pharmacist in packs of 10 and 20.

*Competitive Activity*

Karvol was not the only brand to be supported. Olbas Oil, VapoRub and Snufflebabe advertised over the two year period. VapoRub would also have indirectly benefited from advertising for Vicks Sinex and Vicks Chloraseptic. The full media schedule is shown in Figure 4 (see p96).

*Further Support*

As further support to the repositioning, a new pack design was developed. The older child originally featured was replaced by a visibly younger child of 18 months. The new packs only began to be stocked during the summer sell-in of 1989. They were therefore only present for the second year's activity.

## MEASURING THE EFFECT OF THE CAMPAIGN

An analysis of sales over time had indicated that the brand was already performing well. The key question to be asked was: had the repositioning been effective not only in growing the brand in pharmacy, but also in preparing it for future expansion?

We analysed sales of Karvol and its competitors from November/December 1983 to January/February 1990, as measured by Nielsen (bimonthly data). Our findings were as follows:

*Sales*

The new campaign started running in November 1988. Karvol's sales immediately increased, and in the first month alone achieved an increase in capsule sales of 27%

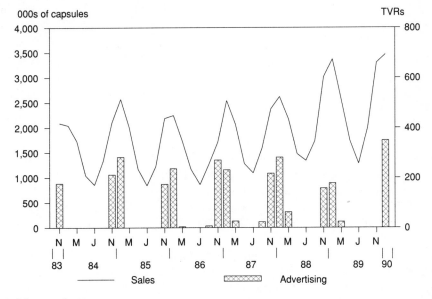

Figure 5. *Sales versus advertising*
Source: Nielsen, BARB

year on year. Altogether over the advertised period the brand experienced an increase in sales of 21.3% on the previous year.

For the following year, sales exceeded the winter 1988 peak, so that the 1989/90 sales were a further 7.1% up on the previous year (Figure 5).

### Rate of Sale

Rate of sale had been static over the preceding three years for both Vicks and Karvol. With the launch of the campaign, however, Karvol's rate of sale saw a 19.1% increase for January/February 1989 vs January/February 1988, whilst Vicks remained static.

The following year saw a slight fall of 2.9% possibly affected by the reduction in share of voice (Figure 6).

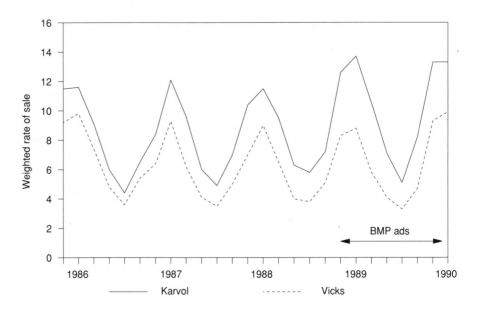

Figure 6. *Rate of sales in GB pharmacies*
*Source:* Nielsen

### Share

Although some of the sales growth was undoubtedly due to market growth, the advertising also appeared to have a significant effect on share. To arrive at a true picture we needed to make an adjustment for the two pack sizes; we have therefore treated 20s as equivalent to two 10s. From this it can be seen that market share rose when the ad went on air, and fell back slightly as share of voice declined (Figure 7).

In analysing market share we found that Olbas Oil, which had been included in Nielsen's data since July 1984, had a slightly different seasonal pattern to the other brands in the market, and in particular to Karvol. Its sales were more seasonal than Olbas, reflecting the different usages of the two brands (Figure 8).

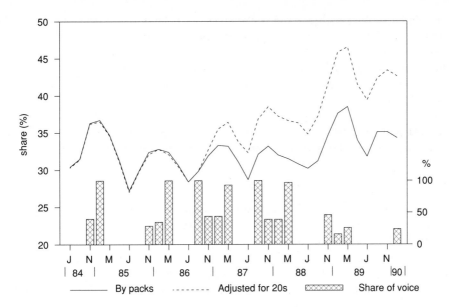

Figure 7. *Karvol market share, by volume share in GB chemists*
*Source:* Nielsen, BARB

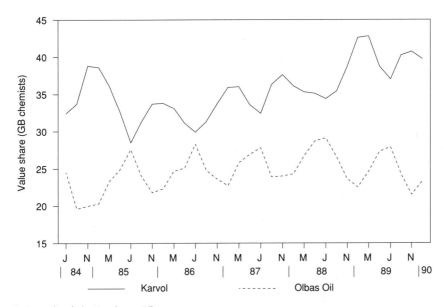

Figure 8. *Seasonality of sales, Karvol versus Olbas*
*Source:* Nielsen, BARB

Both qualitative and quantitative research show that Karvol is more exclusively used for colds than Olbas, and is more likely to be bought for young children. In contrast Olbas Oil appears to be used mainly by adults, and is also used for hay fever in summer months. Attempts to include Olbas' price, distribution or advertising in our subsequent analysis failed to show any significant effect on

Karvol's sales. We concluded that Olbas was not behaving as a true competitor. We therefore reverted to the original pre-1984 Nielsen definition, and excluded Olbas from our analysis.

In the first year of the campaign the objective of attaining 33% MAT share was more than achieved, with share rising to 39% whilst the advertising was on air. Despite losing share of voice in the second year, Karvol held on to an MAT share of over 36%.

Karvol remained brand leader, and, indeed, widened the gap between itself and competitive brands. It appeared to have taken share at the expense of Vicks.

### Regional Analysis

Although Karvol's weight of advertising was fairly even across the country, Vicks' was more variable, and as a result Karvol's share of voice showed some regional variations. This enables us to correlate share of voice with gain in market share. In so doing we can see broadly that during the first year of advertising, the higher the share of voice, the greater the gain in market share (Figure 9).

This is further evidence to suggest that the advertising was responsible for the growth in sales.

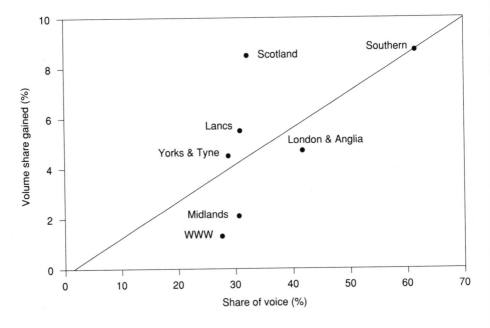

Figure 9. *Share gains versus share of voice, GB pharmacies 1988/89*
Source: Nielsen, BARB

## HOW THE ADVERTISING WORKED

Consumer reaction to the advertising supports the hypothesis that the advertising was a contributory factor to share growth.

## Reaction Amongst the Target Audience

There is no doubt that Karvol's advertising succeeded in generating high levels of awareness for the brand amongst the target audience. After the first winter's advertising, awareness rose to its highest level ever and, indeed, higher than any other brand in the market, despite the competitors having their own advertising support (see Tables 3 and 4).

TABLE 3:  SPONTANEOUS ADVERTISING AWARENESS

|  | Pre 1st Burst Nov 88 % | Post 1st Burst Mar 89 % | Pre 2nd Burst Dec 89 % | Post 2nd Burst Mar 90 % |
|---|---|---|---|---|
| Karvol | 9 | 18* | 6 | 23* |
| Vicks VapoRub | 6 | 7* | 3 | 10* |
| Snufflebabe | 1 | 1 | 1 | 1 |

Source:  ISL
Note:  * denotes a significant increase at the 95% confidence level.
Base:  Mothers of children under three

TABLE 4:  PROMPTED ADVERTISING AWARENESS

|  | Pre 1st Burst Nov 88 % | Post 1st Burst Mar 89 % | Pre 2nd Burst Dec 89 % | Post 2nd Burst Mar 90 % |
|---|---|---|---|---|
| Karvol | 23 | 49* | 24 | 52* |
| Vicks VapoRub | 9 | 12* | 8 | 18* |
| Snufflebabe | 2 | 3 | 4 | 4 |

Source:  ISL
Note:  * denotes a significant increase at the 95% confidence level.
Base:  Mothers of children under three

Advertising awareness recall rose further when prompted with a show card. 82% of our key target recognised stills taken from the commercial.

TABLE 5:  PROMPTED BRAND AWARENESS

|  | Pre 1st Stage Nov 88 % | Post 2nd Stage Mar 90 % |
|---|---|---|
| Karvol | 75 | 84* |
| Vicks VapoRub | 90 | 78 |
| Snufflebabe | 61 | 47 |

Source:  ISL
Note:  * denotes a significant increase at the 95% confidence level.
Base:  Mothers of children under three

The increase in advertising awareness coincided with a similar increase in brand awareness. Amongst mothers of children under three, prompted brand awareness grew by 12% to 84%, a gain which, for the first time, made Karvol the most well-known brand in the sector for our target audience, overtaking the historically more famous VapoRub. We had exceeded our second objective of raising awareness in line with Vicks (Table 5).

Not only did the advertising appear to affect brand awareness but it also seemed to have achieved the more difficult objective of gaining trial for the brand. Claimed usage in the last six months for Karvol doubled from 22% of mothers (with children under three), up to 40%, putting usage of the brand amongst our core target now well above that of Vicks (Figure 10).

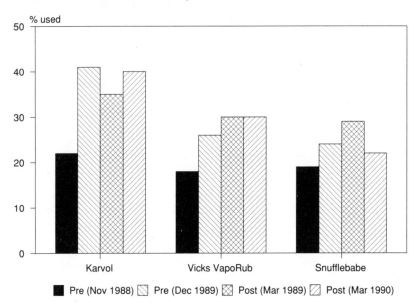

Figure 10. *Brands used in last six months*
*Source:* ISL
*Base:* Mothers of children under three years

Propensity to use also grew significantly; from 49% to 68% after the first year's advertising. It settled at over 60% of the target, indicating a level of goodwill towards the brand which is greater than that of Vicks (Figure 11).

That we can attribute the growth in usage to the success of the campaign is supported by the target's claimed reason for choice of brand. Karvol is the only brand to show significant advertising influence. After the first burst of advertising, 33% of the target asserted that advertising had influenced their choice (Figure 12). Whilst this declined after the second year of the campaign, there was a proportional rise in the percentage claiming to have 'always used the brand'. It would appear that as mothers became more familiar with the brand, so the conscious impact of the commercial on their actions declined accordingly (Figure 13).

Despite tightly defining our target as mothers of children under three, we were encouraged to discover that the advertising appeared highly effective amongst mothers of older children. Prompted advertising awareness reached 47% amongst mothers of children 3 – 5, and 44% amongst those of children 6 – 9.

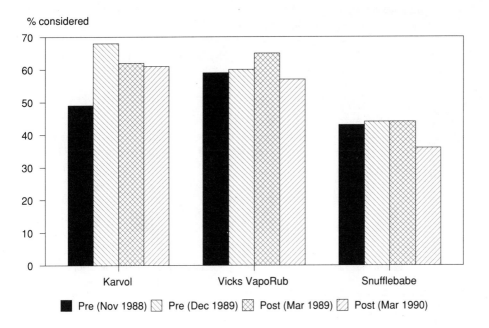

Figure 11 *Brands would ever consider using*
*Source:* ISL
*Base:* Mothers of children under three years

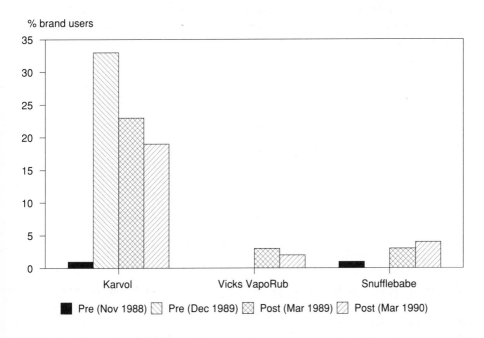

Figure 12. *Chose due to advertising*
*Source:* ISL
*Base:* Mothers of children under three years

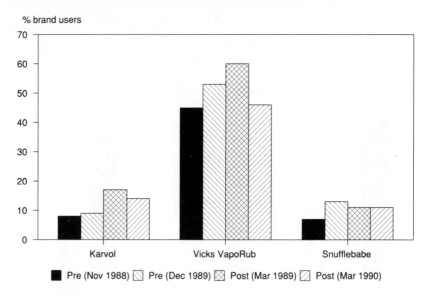

Figure 13. *Chose because always use*
*Source:* ISL
*Base:*    Mothers of children under three years

There was also a significant increase in the percentage who would consider using the brand: up to 58% of mothers with children 3 – 5, and 49% of mothers with children 6 – 9.

And as a further indication of the success of the brand's intended repositioning, we looked to an impact on image. Over the last two year period, Karvol's role as a decongestant for young children has become more firmly established amongst all mothers (Table 6).

TABLE 6:  PROMPTED IMAGE DIMENSIONS

|  | Pre 1st Burst Nov 88 % | Post 1st Burst Mar 89 % | Pre 2nd Burst Dec 89 % | Post 2nd Burst Mar 90 % |
|---|---|---|---|---|
| Is suitable for young children | 47 | 53* | 54 | 57 |
| Is particularly for adults | 7 | 4 | 3 | 5* |

Source:  ISL
Note:  * denotes a significant increase at the 95% confidence level.
Base:  Mothers of children 0 – 9

The strengthening in brand image as 'one for young children' by March 1989 could only have come from advertising, since the new packaging had not been introduced at this stage.

We concluded therefore that the advertising had not only helped generate high levels of brand awareness, but had also established the desired repositioning, and encouraged purchase.

## Influence on the Trade

The response of the Crookes Healthcare salesforce to the commercial was extremely positive. The advertising enjoyed a misty-eyed reception at the 1989 Annual Sales Conference. It was evident that the salesforce responded to the ad not just on a professional, but on a human, emotional level as well. As one rep said:

'This just finishes me off every time – it just makes me want to be back home with my kids'
Crookes Healthcare Sales Conference, Bournemouth 1989.

Feedback from the salesforce over both advertised periods suggests that retailers were also responding well to the ad. It was considered successful in highlighting Karvol's unique younger child positioning to the trade, and justifying pharmacists' recommendation of the brand.

## Further Indication of Impact

Some further peripheral evidence of the effectiveness of the campaign can be found in Appendix 1.

## ISOLATING THE ADVERTISING EFFECT

Although Karvol's sales growth, and the very positive movements in additional measures of consumer response implied the campaign's effectiveness, there were other factors which could have assisted the sales increase.

To isolate more completely the effect of advertising, we carried out an econometric analysis investigating relative contributions to Karvol's growth of pricing, the introduction of the 20 pack, favourable demographic trends, competitive activity, the pattern of colds in the population, and the advertising itself.

## The Growth in the Number of Children with Colds

Karvol's sales are slightly more sensitive to both the incidence of colds in the population and to changes in the numbers of children in its key target group.

Both of these increased over the last three winters, and thus contributed a relatively small proportion of Karvol's growth. Figure 14 shows the net effect of both these changes.

## Price Variations

Another potential contributor to Karvol's growth was the decline in real price over the last period. This price decrease resulted from both the real price per pack having fallen and the 20s (which are cheaper per capsule than the 10s) making up a larger proportion of sales (Figure 15).

However, the model indicates that Karvol is not exceptionally price sensitive. A 1% decrease in the real price per capsule leads to only a 0.6% increase in Karvol's share of the market (by value).

At the time when the decline in real price was having its maximum effect, it was only contributing 1.9 incremental share points (July/August 1989). No statistically significant effect of competitive pricing was found.

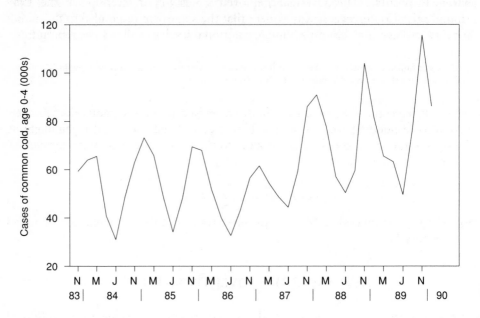

Figure 14. *Colds among young children*
*Source:* CDSC, CSO

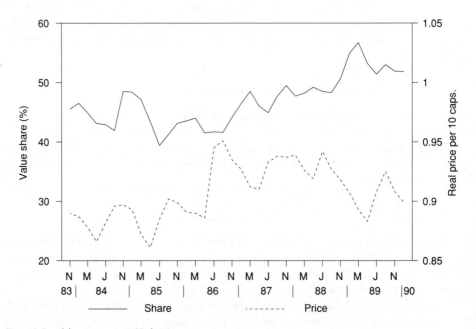

Figure 15. *Karvol share versus price in GB chemists*
*Source:* Nielsen

*Launch of the 20s*

The launch of the 20s contributed substantially to Karvol's growth between late 1986 and mid 1988 whilst their distribution was growing rapidly. Some of this was a result of their lower price/capsule (incorporated in the price effects discussed above), and some a result of the larger share of front stocks they helped to occupy (Figure 16).

However, since mid 1988, the distribution of 20s has grown more slowly, increasing from approximately 70% to 80% sterling. Model simulations show that this has added only 0.4% share points in the last two years.

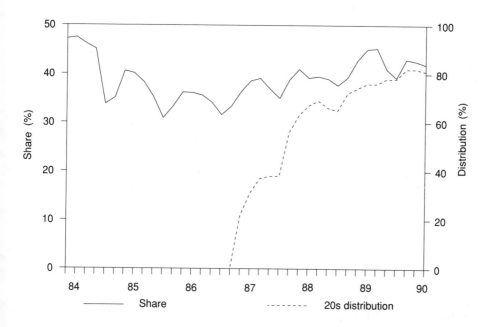

Figure 16. *Karvol share versus 20s distribution, GB pharmacies*
*Source:* Nielsen

## Impact of New Packaging

It was not possible to use the econometric analysis to disentangle any effect of Karvol's new packaging as its introduction coincided with Karvol's autumn press advertising.

But, intuitively, as even at the time of writing the new packs have yet to gain full distribution, they can only have had a limited impact on growth.

## Promotions

Because Karvol is a 'P' status medicine, it is unable to run promotions directly connected with the brand (such as price discounts, money-off coupons etc).

During the two years of advertising, a leaflet and book of Nursery Rhymes were used as prizes/mailouts in a number of competitions run in *Mother & Baby*. The uptake of the material, however, was minimal.

*Advertising*

The above sections indicate that some of the growth in Karvol's sales must be attributed to factors other than advertising.

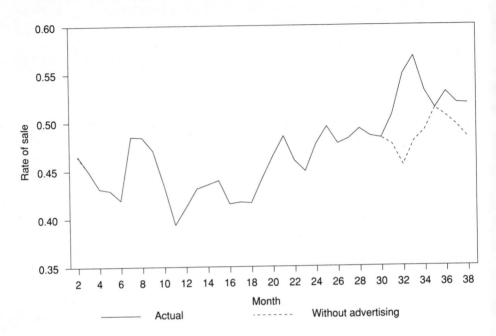

Figure 17. *Advertising effect*

Figure 17 shows Karvol's actual sales plotted against the model's projections for sales levels had there been no advertising. This demonstrates that the new campaign has been the largest contributory factor to Karvol's recent growth, and has led to Karvol achieving its highest ever brand share (over the period for which we have data). In fact the model suggests that 61% of the incremental volume over this period can be attributed to the advertising. Furthermore, whilst the old campaign generated an extra 1.9 share points/100 TVRs, overall the new campaign has been four times as effective per TVR.

Additionally, whilst any gain generated by the old campaign could be easily negated by an equivalent burst of Vicks advertising, this is not true of the new campaign. If both were to advertise simultaneously with 100 TVRs, the model shows us that Karvol would still make some share gain.

Finally, the BMP advertising proved roughly four times as effective as Karvol's previous advertising, with the sales up-lift being larger and lasting longer. Figure 17 shows the effect on Karvol's market share.

The econometric study confirms that Crookes' attempt to reposition Karvol as a young child's brand has been successful, since from the model, Karvol's sales appear now to be more sensitive to the increase of colds amongst young children (0 – 4) than other brands in the market.

## SUMMARY

The econometric analysis has demonstrated very clearly that despite a number of variables acting in Karvol's favour, the one which has had by far the greatest impact on sales in the last two years is the new BMP DDB Needham advertising campaign.

As regards short-term sales effects, the advertising was the overriding factor in growing the brand, and not only achieving but exceeding the short-term share target.

Crookes's stated objective for Karvol was to achieve and maintain 33% volume share (of all 'Vapour Rubs') in GB chemists. This target has already been substantially exceeded: in March/April 1989, Karvol attained a share of 38.5%. A year later, even with a substantially lower share of voice, volume share is still well above target at 35.8%.

As for broader and longer term effects, we have already seen a strengthening of the brand's franchise amongst its newly focused target audience. And finally we have seen evidence to suggest that this stronger franchise is already restricting competitive activity – particularly launches aimed at our target audience.

## THE FINANCIAL CONTRIBUTION OF ADVERTISING

Many of the effects of the advertising campaign are difficult to value in terms of financial contribution. For example, in January 1990 we saw the launch of a copy-cat version of the Karvol product, called Flurex. This product is also an oil in a gelatine capsule, but has 'GSL' status. And it retails at a lower price than Karvol. However, this new brand appears to be experiencing difficulties in gaining sales and indeed distribution. By May 1990 Flurex had achieved only 15% distribution against Karvol's 100% and a bimonthly volume share of c0.7% against 35.8% for Karvol. We believe that the success of the Karvol advertising must have played a part in restricting the growth of this rival. Unfortunately, it is impossible to put a financial value on this.

However, we can provide quantified proof of the new campaign's profitability in other ways.

For the two years previous to the BMP campaign, Karvol had an annual advertising to sales ratio of 21%. As previously mentioned such a high figure is not uncommon for a 'P' registered product. Even with an advertising to sales ratio of this magnitude the brand was profitable.

As we have seen, in the two years since the BMP campaign first started to run, sales went up, producing an increase in average annual revenue of c30%. In addition this occurred against a background of lower advertising expenditure – in fact 28% lower.

Hence the advertising to sales ratio for Karvol has fallen from 21% to 11.1% since the campaign began. Without disclosing actual profit data, it must be clear that since the brand was profitable on its previous advertising to sales ratio then it must be even more profitable when this falls to c11%, while volume and turnover are still increasing.

Finally we have already shown that 61% of the sales uplift was directly attributable to the advertising (as were substantial cost savings since ad spend went down). It is therefore fair to conclude that the profit increase was largely due to the new advertising.

## CONCLUSIONS

Karvol has now gained its 'GSL' licence, and by November 1990 will have started to negotiate its introduction into drugstore and grocery.

The short-term effect of Karvol's new advertising on sales and share has been significant. But it is in the long run that its broader effects will be fully appreciated. With its strengthened franchise, and strong consumer allegiance, it now has the opportunity to take advantage of wider distribution, and a wider consumer base.

## APPENDIX 1

### Further Indication of Impact

1. *Awards* – The new campaign won a Lion D'Or at the 1989 Cannes Advertising Film Festival. It was also a winner in the Pharmaceutical section at the 1989 Eurobest International Advertising Awards, and was shortlisted for a D&AD in March 1989.
2. *Additional Publicity* – The first trade ad received further publicity in a *Campaign* feature on trade press advertising. With the focus of the article being the general low quality of trade advertising, the ad received welcome praise:

> 'Another BMP ad I admire is for Karvol, a medication to help you sleep....'

> 'With all the other ads around shouting about how everyone will find their multimillion pound TV campaign so riveting, this one must have really taken people by surprise in a totally relevant way'. Mike Shafron, 12th May 1989.

## APPENDIX 2

### Econometrics

Karvol's sales have been modelled from November/December 1983 to January/February 1990 using bimonthly Nielsen data (GB chemists). Sales volume (in packs) is not an accurate measure of the brands true performance, since it does not reflect the increase in the number of capsules sold after the introduction of the 20 capsule packs in 1986. We therefore chose real revenue as the dependant variable for the model. This is in fact closely correlated (99.8%) with the number of capsules sold, and has the advantage that it enables us to construct meaningful measures of market share.

Since July 1984, Olbas Oil has been included in the vapour rubs market as defined by Nielsen. However, as previously shown, Olbas Oil has a different seasonal pattern of sales to Karvol, and its price, distribution and advertising were shown to have no statistically significant effect on Karvol's sales. We therefore concluded that Olbas Oil does not behave as a true competitor to Karvol and reverted to the pre-1984 definition of the market.

Using this definition, we regressed Karvol's real revenue on that of the market (together with the other marketing variables), and found that the model could be restricted to a model of the market share:

|  | Result | Critical value |
|---|---|---|
| F Test on linear regression | 0.52 | 4.35 |

The model of Karvol's market share was estimated by ordinary least squares regression, and performs well against a range of standard statistical tests for both fit and specification. The actual and fitted values are shown below.

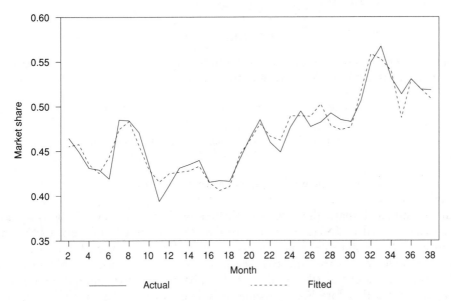

Figure 18. *Karvol revenue share model*

| Statistical tests | Result | Critical value |
|---|---|---|
| $R^2$ | 0.920 | — |
| $R^2$ (adjusted) | 0.900 | — |
| Standard error of the regression | 0.028 | — |
| Sum of squared residuals | 0.022 | — |
| Durbin Watson | 2.000 | — |
| LM(1) | 0.160 | 3.84 |
| LM(4) | 3.750 | 9.49 |
| Arch(1) | 0.280 | 3.84 |
| Arch(4) | 2.380 | 9.49 |
| Variance ratio test | 1.420 | 2.91 |
| CHOW (parameter stability) | 1.010 | 2.30 |
| CHOW (post sample predictive failure) | 1.520 | 2.55 |

## Interpretation of Price Coefficient

If a is the price coefficient in a value share model, it can be shown that, for a market of fixed value, the volume elasticity with respect to price is $1 - a$

This may be a slight under-estimate for a large brand, where an increase in price may actually depress the size of the overall market. On this basis, Karvol's price elasticity is about 1.6.

## Forecasts for March/April 1990

When the model was constructed, data was only available up to January/February 1990. However, by making some reasonable assumptions about the likely behaviour of the independent variables, it was possible to forecast that Karvol's revenue share would rise again in March/April 1990, as the remainder of the advertising effect filtered through. The forecast brand share was 53%. When data finally became available, the prediction was confirmed: share rose to 52.8%, well within the standard error.

## Advertising Effect

The table below shows Karvol's sales volume as measured by Nielsen, and how much of this is attributable to the new advertising.

| Year (to April) | Sales (Packs) | Sales due to new ads |
|---|---|---|
| 1987/1988 | 969,230 | — |
| 1988/1989 | 1,125,730 | 128,863 |
| 1989/1990 | 1,173,310 | 91,870 |

Hence the new campaign was responsible for 61.2% of the volume growth seen over the last two years.

It is estimated that, allowing for Nielsen pick-up, the advertising will have generated a total of £531,131 extra sales at RSP by the end of May 1990. This represents the combined effects of press and TV advertising. By and large it has not been possible to separate the two, because they tend to occur simultaneously. However, during October/November of 1989, BMP ran a press ad in the absence of TV, and it has therefore been possible to isolate its effect. This increased market share by an extra 2.4 share points during the autumn period.

## APPENDIX 3

*Analysis of 'P' Status Brands*

The table below shows the advertising expenditure and sales for thirteen 'P' status brands.

| Brand | Sales £000 | MEAL spend £000 | Advertising to sales ratio (%) |
|-------|-----------|-----------------|--------------------------------|
| Nurofen | 8,800 | 2,341 | 26.6 |
| Solpadeine | 4,400 | 922 | 21.0 |
| Benylin | 17,150 | 1,122 | 6.5 |
| Actifed/Sudafed | 7,350 | 1,222 | 16.6 |
| Nightnurse | 6,800 | 488 | 7.2 |
| Sinutab | 4,500 | 367 | 8.2 |
| Oxy 10 | 1,900 | 548 | 28.8 |
| Dulcolax | 880 | 262 | 29.8 |
| Senoket | 4,220 | 248 | 5.4 |
| Arret | 1,700 | 291 | 17.1 |
| Preparation H | 2,000 | 301 | 15.1 |
| Germoloids | 1,760 | 284 | 16.1 |
| HC45 | 1,320 | 345 | 26.1 |

The average advertising to sales ratio of these brands is 17.3%. The table below shows how much Karvol would have to spend to achieve a similar ratio.

| | Turnover | Implied ad spend |
|---------|-----------|------------------|
| 1988/89 | £2,600,000 | £449,667 |
| 1989/90 | £2,900,000 | £501,886 |

# 6

# Adding Volume to Vorsprung durch Technik

## INTRODUCTION

This paper concerns the launch of the 1990 Audi model range (with catalytic converter engines) and the success of the advertising campaign in generating increased sales (and thus greater profit for VAG United Kingdom and its dealer network) in the period October 1989 to March 1990.

The background sets out the position Audi had reached by the end of 1988, key information about the car market in the period under consideration, and the difficulties Audi had to overcome in order to succeed.

The sales increase that was achieved and the response to the advertising campaign are analysed in the Results section. Other possible influences on Audi sales, namely, model line up, price, specification, distribution and weight of advertising, are then discussed, and it is argued that these factors were not decisive in generating increased sales volume.

Finally, catalytic converters are discussed in some detail so as to establish that it was not the introduction of catalytic converters per se, but the way they were advertised, that contributed to the sales success, given that other manufacturers also introduced catalytic converters and advertised them.

A brief explanation of how the advertising worked is given before the conclusions, which also indicate the next steps for Audi.

## BACKGROUND

### Audi and the Market

In 1983 Audi had a weak image and was not known to be German. Knowing they were to introduce a new technically improved range at higher prices, Audi set out to reposition the marque (brand). So, from 1983 to 1988 the Vorsprung durch Technik advertising campaign repositioned Audi as a prestigious German marque. Image improved so that by 1988 consumers grouped Audi with Volvo and Saab alongside BMW, Jaguar and Mercedes rather than with Ford and Alfa Romeo as they had in 1982.

This enabled Audi to introduce more expensive cars into the more prestigious sectors of the market and to increase the retained profit per unit. While Audi volume remained approximately constant during this phase of repositioning, the market was buoyant and saw unparalleled growth from 1984 to 1989, with the effect that Audi market share declined from 1.13% to 0.82%.

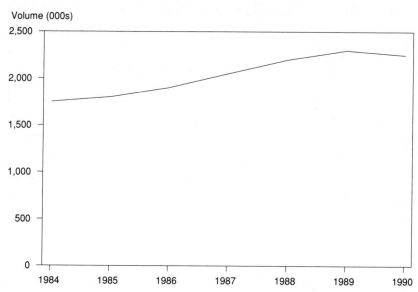

Figure 1. *The car market*
Source: SMMT

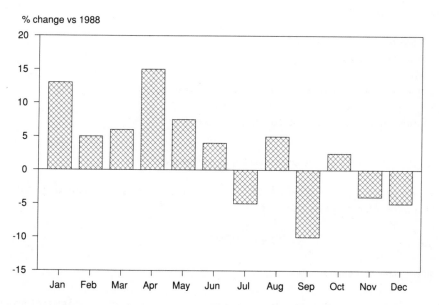

Figure 2. *The car market, 1989*
Source: SMMT

Having achieved the repositioning, the objective became to increase volume in the 1990 model year, which began in September 1989. Ironically, at exactly this time the market began to decline. This made the task of increasing Audi volume all the more onerous.

### The Growth of the Green Pump

One opportunity was to introduce cars equipped with catalytic converters. Audi in Germany had developed such a range of cars which reduce toxic exhaust pollutants. However, these cars *have* to run on unleaded petrol.

1988/89 had seen a dramatic increase in the availability of unleaded petrol. In March 1988 unleaded petrol sales accounted for less than half a percent of total petrol sales. By June 1989 unleaded had grown to 14% and green pumps were springing up all over the country, making the introduction of catalyst equipped cars a viable proposition.

In the summer of 1989 Audi UK took the decision to import *only* catalytic converter equipped models for the 1990 range. This range of cars was the first to be launched in the UK with catalytic converters as standard and was available from September 1989.

### Inhibiting Factors

To put into context the introduction of catalyst equipped cars it is important to clarify how the rise of green consumerism was affecting motorists and car buyers at that time.

It may *seem* that with the growth of environmentalism, the launch of a range of cars with catalytic converters was a guarantee of success. In fact the opposite is true, for six reasons:

1. Confusion over unleaded petrol.
2. Inaccurate press coverage.
3. Misleading advertising.
4. Scares about unleaded petrol and catalytic converters.
5. The prevarication of the Government.
6. Consumer fears about performance and economy.

### Confusion Over Unleaded Petrol

The introduction of unleaded petrol caused confusion. Unleaded petrol was continually referred to by the press as 'green'.

'Fast road to the green pump' (*The Times* 12/6/89).

'Green pump war hots up' (*Today* 22/3/89).

The implication was that once a car had been converted to unleaded petrol no more was needed to make it environmentally friendly.

Unleaded petrol was being hailed as an end in itself, not as a means to run catalyst equipped cars.

'Act now: end the petrol menace' (*Daily Mail* 2/1/88).

'Unleaded sales soar since Mail pioneered drive for clean fuel' (*Daily Mail* 11/3/89).

## Inaccurate Press Coverage

The press *themselves* were often confused, which made things more difficult for consumers. For example, *The Guardian* managed to cross breed the issues of unleaded fuel and catalytic converters, and come up with the phrase 'lead converters' which means nothing.

'PM rejects plea for lead converters' (*The Guardian* 21/11/88).

## Misleading Advertising

Motorists were being bombarded with advertisements about green issues which were often confusing or inaccurate. The ASA, in July 1989, criticised car manufacturers, dealers and oil companies for misleading advertisements.

'However a problem has arisen with some advertisers (and their agencies) who appear to be paying more attention to making sure that their wares are perceived as sitting on the green side of the fence than to checking the factual accuracy of their claims and thereby maintaining the truthfulness of their advertising' (ASA Case Report 171 12/7/89).

## Scares

This situation was exacerbated as scares about the damaging and unsafe effects of unleaded petrol began and alarming headlines appeared

'Fire fear over lead free fuel' (*Today* 12/12/88).

Nor are catalytic converters without their critics. Some scientists have claimed that catalytic converters cause *further* damage to the environment. As ever, this has been faithfully reported by the press in their own inimitable style:

'Green exhaust pollution peril' (*Today* 22/5/89).

'Catalytic converters, hailed as the answer to pollution, are under attack for adding to the greenhouse effect and destroying the ozone layer' (*Today* 22/5/89).

## Government Prevarication

The Government did nothing to clarify the situation. Having opposed catalytic converters as a solution to car pollution, in May they suddenly dropped their opposition to the EC directive requiring catalytic converters to be fitted to all new cars (regardless of size) by 1993.

'The Government dropped its opposition yesterday to a European directive that will impose American-style exhaust standards on new small cars by 1993' (*The Times* 25/5/89).

Even the Government was no authority on the subject.

### Consumer Fears

Furthermore, amongst those motorists who had some awareness of catalytic converters, we knew from our own qualitative research, there were further worries: namely that cat cars cost more to buy and run, and that they suffered in terms of performance. This fear was not made any easier by the fact that a catalytic converter has no *visible* benefit. The owner cannot point to the catalytic converter or show it off to his friends. This is important because it is the visual statement a car makes that gives it (and its driver) status and prestige.

It was in this highly complex situation that Audi decided to launch their cat only range. So, despite the growth of environmentalism, it was by no means a foregone conclusion that this would be a success.

## THE OBJECTIVES

### Marketing Objectives

The marketing objectives were simple. There were two:

— To increase sales volume whilst retaining a premium positioning.
— To introduce the catalytic converter equipped range of cars.

### Advertising Objectives

Advertising had a critical role to play in the launch. The advertising objectives were:

1. To generate awareness of the Audi offer.
2. To create interest immediately.
3. To seed sales for January 1990.

### Advertising Strategy

Use the introduction of catalytic converters as the latest example of Vorsprung durch Technik from Audi.

## THE CAMPAIGN

There were three elements to the campaign:
— Posters
— Press
— TV

The role of each of these is described below.

### The Role of Posters

Posters were used to give the start of the campaign impact, and generate awareness of the issue of reducing toxic pollution from car exhausts.

We used Adshel superlites specifically because their on street position was extremely relevant to the story we had to tell. We also used a VAG holding of poster sites on British Rail stations. There were two executions.

### The Role of Press

We used press to communicate detailed information about the complex subject of catalytic converters, to confront consumer fears that catalysts impair performance and economy, and to provide further information about the 1990 Audi model range. This was necessary in order to overcome the inhibiting factors explained previously.

We launched with five press advertisements which invited people to send for more information via a coupon, thus generating sales leads for dealers.

### The Role of TV

TV had been used in the repositioning of Audi and continued to be used to build the Audi marque image. TV aimed to raise the issue and benefits of catalytic converters in an *emotionally* appealing way. A freephone telephone number was included to facilitate response.

The TV commercial was a 60 second ad entitled 'In the Nick of Time' and featured an Audi 90 quattro. This is the flagship of the main volume model – the 80/90 series.

### The Timing of the Campaign

The campaign broke at the beginning of October. Press and TV ran in conjunction at a heavy weight during October and the early part of November. The advertising was sustained at lighter weight in press until March and with very short sharp bursts of TV in January and March.

The posters ran in a concentrated two week burst at the beginning of October. This timing was planned so as to seed sales for January, traditionally a peak month because people have the chance to buy 1990 registered cars rather than 1989 models.

*Client:* Audi

*Date:* 19 October 1989

*Title:* IN THE NICK OF TIME

*Length:* 60 seconds

| VISION | SOUND |
|---|---|
| Open on a receiver hurriedly being thrown down. | |
| A man quickly grabs a jacket. | MVO: Life is full of decisions. |
| His son, aged six, struggles to do up his own shoelaces in time. | Some of the head, some of the heart. |
| Cut to outside. It's late afternoon, early evening. | Take your next car. |
| The man and his son hurry to their parked and gleaming Audi 90 Quattro. | Will it have a catalytic converter that removes 95% of toxic pollutants? |
| They drive off through the German countryside. The sun gets lower and lower. | |
| They enter an elegant, yet deserted, German city. It begins to rain. | |
| The rain gets heavier and heavier. | |
| They come to a set of lights. They seem to be stuck on red for an eternity. | |
| The man drums his fingers on the steering wheel. | |
| Eventually the lights change and they set off. | Will it be clean, yet lose nothing in performance? |
| They continue down the lonely streets past a series of shops. One shop has its burglar alarm going. | |
| They eventually come to a large, imposing turn-of-the-century building. We have no idea what its function is. | Will it have all this at no extra cost? |
| The man parks the car outside the main entrance. He rushes up the stairs. | |
| He realises he's forgotten something. He rushes back down and lets his son out of the car. | |
| They rush inside. | |
| We see their POV of a long empty corridor. They get to a pair of swing doors. | In short, will it be one of the advanced new generation of Audis? |
| Cut to an arm holding up a baby. It's crying. | SFX: smack and baby cries. |
| Super: Vorsprung durch Technik. | |
| Cut to blank screen. | Vorsprung durch Technik. As both your head and heart would say. |
| Super: Audi (logo) | |
| Call 0800 800 800 for an information pack. | |

## 'IN THE NICK OF TIME'

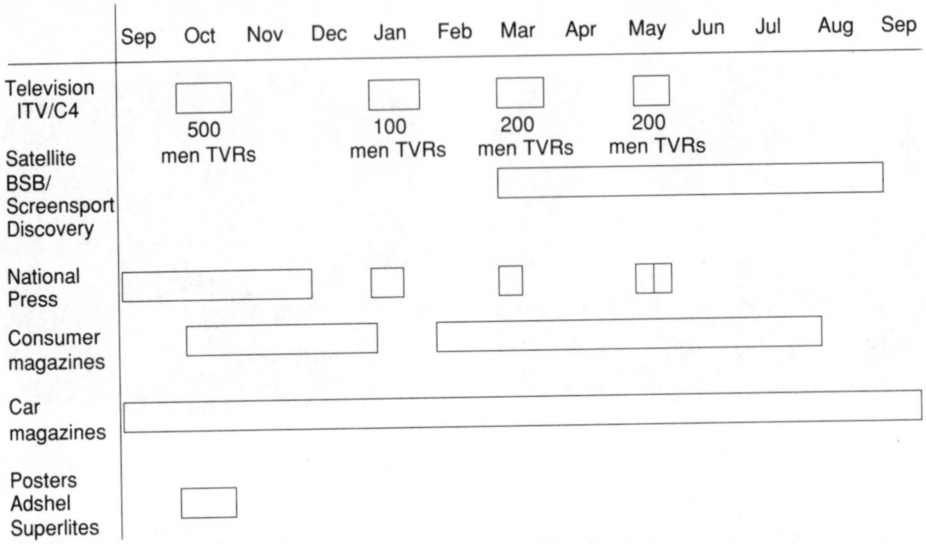

Figure 3.  *Media plan*

# THE RESULTS

The results of this campaign have been measured in terms of advertising sales and advertising responses. Having established what sales effect and response there was, other factors that may have contributed to the sales success are analysed later.

*Sales*

The car market is highly seasonal. In order to analyse Audi sales we have therefore used data for the six month period of the campaign and the six months prior to the campaign (compared to the year before) to make it easier to view the volume changes.

Since market share is not affected by seasonality this has been analysed by month over the same period, ie six months prior to the campaign and six months of the campaign.

Audi sales were up 13% for the advertised period (October – March 1990) versus the previous year. This 13% increase year on year represents a significant turnaround from the previous six month period (April – September 1989) during which Audi sales had declined by 11%.

This was not due to market movements. In fact, over the campaign period the market declined.

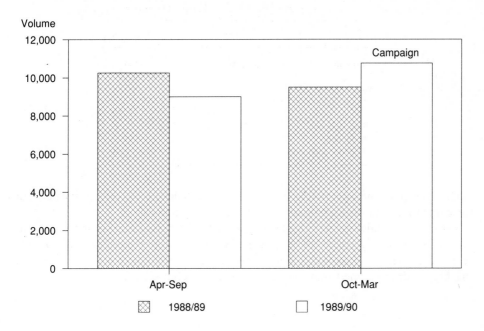

Figure 4. *Audi volume*
*Source:* SMMT

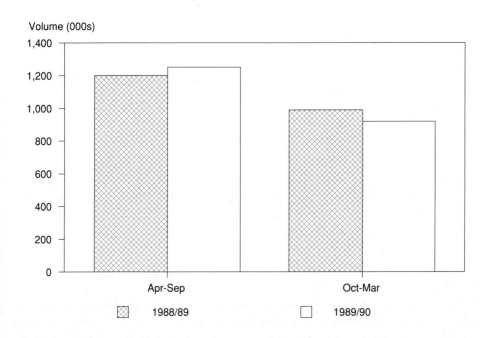

Figure 5. *Total market*
*Source:* SMMT

TABLE 1:  AUDI VOLUME VS TOTAL MARKET

|  | Apr – Sep | Oct – Mar |
|---|---|---|
| Audi volume 1988/89 | 10,433 | 9,553 |
|  |  | CAMPAIGN |
| Audi volume 1989/90 | 9,239 | 10,763 |
| % change |  |  |
| year on year | –11 | +13 |
| Total market |  |  |
| % change |  |  |
| year on year | +4 | –5 |

Thus, prior to the advertising Audi were losing sales in a growing market. Once the campaign began Audi gained sales in a declining market.

Naturally this sales growth has been reflected in increased market share for Audi.

More importantly, since all Audi cars fall in the upper medium and executive sectors, this volume increase has not been due to sector buoyancy within the total market. Audi has gained share of the sectors in which it sells.

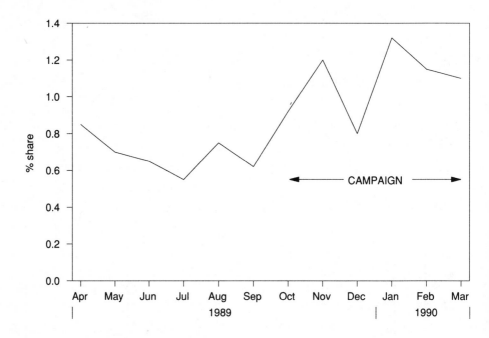

Figure 6. *Audi market share*
*Source:* SMMT

The increase in sales is even more marked for the cars featured in TV advertising. The car in the TV commercial was an Audi 90 quattro. This body shape is shared by all 80 and 90 variants, so effectively the commercial was for *all* Audi 80s and 90s.

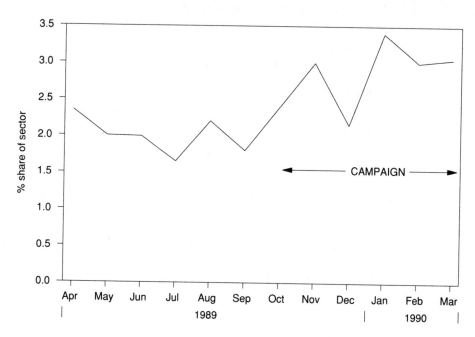

Figure 7. *Audi share of upper medium and executive sectors combined*
*Source:* SMMT/VAG Research

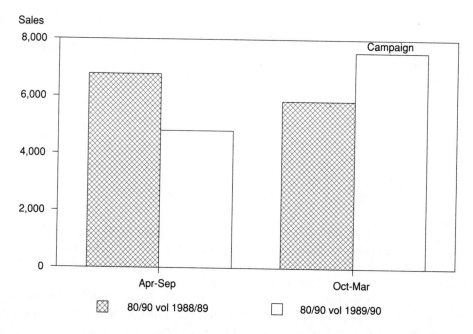

Figure 8. *Audi 80/90 volume*
*Source:* SMMT

TABLE 2:   AUDI 80/90 VOLUME

|  | Apr – Sep | Oct – Mar |
|---|---|---|
| Audi 80/90 vol 1988/89 | 6,772 | 5,844 |
|  |  | CAMPAIGN |
| Audi 80/90 vol 1989/90 | 4,796 | 7,551 |
| % change |  |  |
| year on year | –29 | +29 |
| Total market |  |  |
| % change |  |  |
| year on year | +4 | –5 |

Sales of 80/90 grew by 29% for the advertised period (October – March 1990) compared to the same period the year before; and reversed a decline of 29% for the previous six months (April – September 1989).

Audi 80/90 also increased its share of sector, achieving the highest ever (3.1%) in

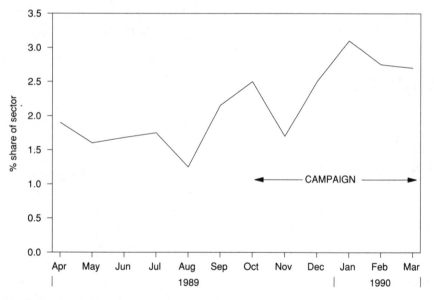

Figure 9.   *Audi 80/90 share of upper medium sector*
*Source:* SMMT/VAG Research data

January 1990.

Sales of the Audi 80/90 range also show that the increase began with the onset of advertising in October, not when the cars became available (in September).

It is also interesting to note that there were peaks in total Audi share, and 80/90 share of sector in *January 1990* as indicated in Figure 8.

The campaign was planned to seed sales for January as mentioned in 'advertising objectives'. This was based on data from Audi owners surveys which tell us that the average consideration period for an Audi buyer is 13 weeks (see Table 3).

Since people spend 13 weeks considering their purchase, the maximum effect of the advertising should be observed 13 weeks or so after the heaviest activity, by which time more of those who were considering during the advertised period will be buying. The heaviest weight of activity was in October. The market share peaked in January (13 weeks later), so the sales data bear this out.

Table 3: CONSIDERATION PERIOD

| | 4 weeks | 8 weeks | 18 weeks | 30 weeks | 38 weeks | 52 weeks | average |
|---|---|---|---|---|---|---|---|
| | | | | % considering for | | | |
| 100 Estate | | | | | | | |
| Oct 89 | 19 | 47 | 25 | 6 | 1 | 3 | 13 |
| 100 Saloon | | | | | | | |
| Oct 89 | 26 | 45 | 20 | 5 | 1 | 3 | 12 |
| 80 | | | | | | | |
| Aug 89 | 21 | 33 | 30 | 5 | 5 | 6 | 15 |
| Average total weeks | | | | | | | 13.3 |

### Sales Summary

— Total Audi volume increased by 13% for the advertised period compared with the same period the previous year.
— This was achieved in a declining market.
— Audi also gained share of its market sector so growth did not come from market dynamics.
— The sales decline of the six months prior to the advertising campaign was reversed.
— The model series which was featured in the TV commercial (Audi 80/90), saw an even larger increase of 29% for the advertised period compared with the same time a year ago.
— The maximum sales effects were observed in January 1990, so the advertising objective of seeding sales was achieved.

### Direct Response

TV and press advertising carried a response mechanism – Freephone on TV and a coupon (and Freephone) in press. This allows us to measure the interest generated by the campaign *directly*.

Audi normally receives customer enquiries at the rate of approximately 10,000 a year. Figure 10 shows the number of enquiries received in the October to March period of 1988/89.

In 1989/90 these customer enquiries continued at a slightly lower level than the previous year. These are people telephoning or writing to VAG directly not as a response to advertising.

However, in addition to this our campaign generated nearly 12,000 responses in only six months.

These were people filling in the coupon or phoning the Freephone number, so they are a *direct result of advertising*. The advertising effectively generated more than an extra *year* of leads for Audi!

The pattern of response closely followed the weight of activity. A breakdown by month is given in Table 4.

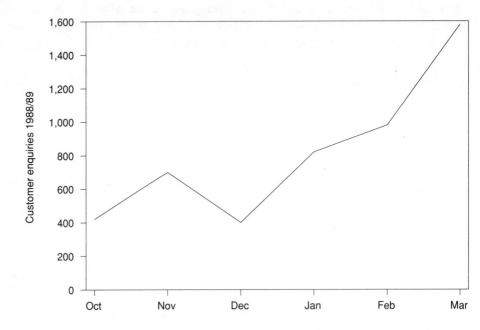

Figure 10. *Customer enquiries, 1988/89*
*Source:* VAG Research

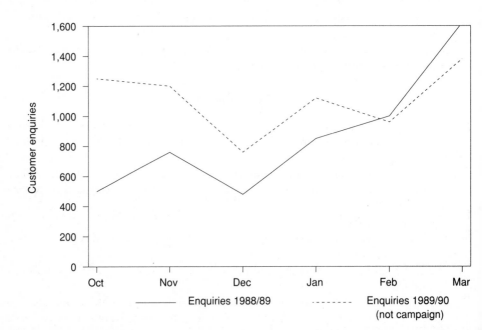

Figure 11. *Customer enquiries*
*Source:* VAG Research

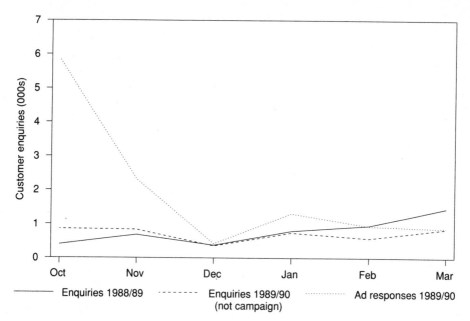

Figure 12. *Customer enquiries*
*Source:* VAG Research

TABLE 4: CAMPAIGN RESPONSES

| | Oct | Nov | Dec | Jan | Feb | Mar | Total |
|---|---|---|---|---|---|---|---|
| Customer enquiries 1988/89 | 399 | 683 | 378 | 797 | 954 | 1,457 | 5,668 |
| Customer enquiries 1989/90 (not on coupon/Freephone) | 859 | 833 | 359 | 745 | 580 | 859 | 4,235 |
| Campaign responses 1989/90 | 5,830 | 2,310 | 422 | 1,309 | 938 | 870 | 11,679 |
| Campaign responses as % of previous year's enquiries | +417 | +338 | +112 | +164 | +98 | +60 | +206 |

This total includes both telephone and coupon response. The split between Freephone and coupon was approximately 50:50 so both TV and press were generating responses.

Over 4,000 responses were handled by a specialist telephone unit. As well as having their enquiry answered callers were questioned, which allows us to establish the quality of the responses. These data tell us that 17% *immediately* arranged a test drive. 58% of callers were intending to replace their car within six months, 11% were Audi drivers and only 4% called to register another comment or complaint. The advertising was attracting the interest of people in the market, who were in the main, non-previous Audi owners, ie potential conquest customers. Thus it has enabled Audi to build a database of 12,000 leads which dealers can pursue.

## Advertising Awareness

In addition to the response data we conducted a national pre- and post-survey amongst car driving ABC1 men aged 30 – 55. It was timed to measure the initial impact of the campaign. The pre stage was conducted at the end of September and the post stage in mid October. We found *statistically significant* increases in advertising awareness both spontaneously and prompted.

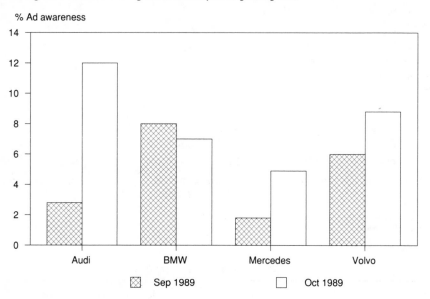

Figure 13. *Spontaneous advertising awareness*
Source: VAG Research

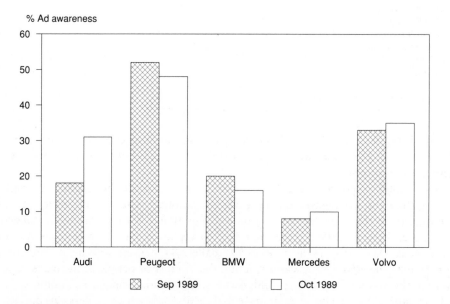

Figure 14. *Prompted advertising awareness*
Source: VAG Research

More interestingly, the advertising, as well as generating awareness was communicating that Audi make environmentally friendly cars.

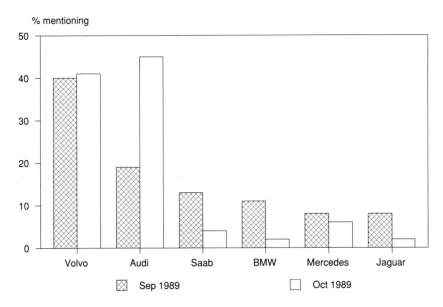

Figure 15. *Manufacturers ahead in building environmentally friendly cars*
*Source:* VAG Research

In this period Audi overtook Volvo (who are thought to be very strong in this respect). While the number of people thinking any manufacturer ahead is low, the change is still *statistically significant.*

TABLE 5: MANUFACTURERS AHEAD IN BUILDING
ENVIRONMENTALLY FRIENDLY CARS

|          | Pre (62) % | Post (49) % |
|----------|-----------|-------------|
| Volvo    | 40        | 41          |
| Audi     | 19        | 45*         |
| Saab     | 13        | 4           |
| BMW      | 11        | 2           |
| Mercedes | 8         | 6           |
| Jaguar   | 8         | 2           |

Source: VAG Research.
Note: * Statistically significant at 95%.
Base: Those thinking any manufacturer ahead

## OTHER FACTORS

In order to establish the effectiveness of the advertising campaign, this section analyses the other factors which may have had an effect on sales, namely:

— model line up
— price and competitive position
— specification
— distribution
— weight of advertising
— catalytic converters

It is argued that none of these factors were decisive in themselves in explaining the increase in volume sales.

### Model Line Up

The 1990 Audi model line up that was available from September 1989 was not substantially different from the 1989 line up that was available until August 1989.

For those not familiar with the car market this requires some explanation. It was previously mentioned that between 1983 and 1988 Audi introduced new cars in more expensive sectors of the market. These were introductions of entirely new cars, eg the old and new Audi 80.

With the 1990 model range there were no such changes. No new body shapes were introduced. The 1990 cars are virtually impossible to distinguish from the 1989 versions. The changes that occurred to the line up in September 1989 were changes of detail. Most of these changes concerned high performance low volume variants. The high volume models of Audi 80 and Audi 100 (which together make up 80% of total Audi volume) remained constant.

AUDI MODELS

| July 1989 (pre) 24 models £10,875 – £31,079 | Sept 1989 (post) 27 models £11,125 – £32,994 |
|---|---|
| 5 80s | 5 80s |
| 3 90s | 4 90s |
| 5 100s | 6 100s |
| 5 100 estates | 6 100 estates |
| 2 coupes | 5 coupes |
| 1 quattro | 1 quatrro |
| 3 200s | |

### Price

Was price responsible for the sales increase? Analysis of Audi pricing in the context of the whole market shows that the cars did not become relatively cheaper in September 1989. *What Car?* magazine ranks all the new cars available in the country by price. There are over 600 from the Fiat 126 at £2,995 to the Aston Martin Vantage for £135,000! Using this data it is possible to see where the Audi models fell in relation to all the other cars available before and after the new range was launched in September. We have plotted the Audi models by their *position* in this cost rank and since the cheapest Audi was approximately £11,000 we have analysed only cars costing £10,000 or more. The position on the vertical axis represents the position of the Audi models in that rank order. The higher the number, the more expensive the car.

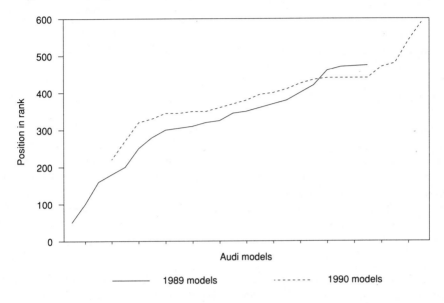

Figure 16. *Audi position in cost rank*
*Source:* What Car?

It can be seen that by far the majority of the new range is slightly more expensive. Only at the top of the range, where the volumes sold are very low indeed, does the 1990 range include cars that were relatively better value. We can also see that the top price position of the range was extended upwards.

If in the market overall Audi did not become cheaper, how did pricing change versus the immediate competition?

BMW is a key competitor for Audi, as the nearest alternative German prestigious marque.

We know from the New Car Buyers Survey (a syndicated study conducted by MIL Research) that Audi is most considered against BMW, within its sector. A comparison of prices for Audi and BMW before and after the introduction of the new Audi range in September shows that there was little change either in absolute terms, or versus BMW.

TABLE 6:  AUDI PRICING

| | Average price of cars available | | % change |
| | 1989 range (Aug 1989) | 1989 range (Sep 1990) | |
|---|---|---|---|
| 80 | 13,152 | 12,967 | −1 |
| 90 | 16,973 | 17,154 | +1 |
| 100 | 17,198 | 18,254 | +8 |
| Coupe | 19,728 | 18,880 | −4 |
| Quattro | 31,368 | 32,994 | +5 |

TABLE 7:  COMPETITIVE PRICING – BMW

|  | Average price of cars available | | |
|  | Aug 1989 | Sep 1989 | % change |
| --- | --- | --- | --- |
| 3 Series | 16,612 | 16,689 | 0 |
| 5 Series | 23,188 | 23,835 | +3 |
| 7 Series | 37,655 | 37,655 | 0 |
| 6 Series | 41,320 | 41,320 | 0 |

Thus, the price position of Audi cars available before and after the launch relative to the market and relative to the key competitor BMW does not alter. There are no sudden changes that explain an increase in sales of +13% in a declining market.

Consumers were not buying cheaper versions either. The price of the most frequently bought Audi (modal price) did not change significantly. It was £12,577 in the six months preceding the campaign and £12,475 during the campaign.

### Specification

The addition of a three way catalytic converter as standard equipment will be dealt with in a separate section. This section demonstrates that other standard equipment was not a significant influence on Audi sales.

The readiest source of comparative data for standard specification is *What Car?* magazine. This is where most consumers go to establish the specification of cars. By looking at the standard specification listed in *What Car?* we can objectively assess whether or not the new model range was significantly better equipped, and ascertain whether this could account for the volume increases. Changes in specification were very much a case of swings and roundabouts: some extra things being added and others taken off, but overall remaining at a comparable level.

The 1989 year models were equipped with stereo radio cassette (worth £230) as standard which none of the 1990 models had. Against this power steering was added to the Audi 80s (the other cars already had it). Other general changes were that the 1990 cars had only front electric windows instead of front and rear electric windows.

It is difficult to conclude that the increased value from specification was a major factor. While obviously some particular cars would be better equipped this was by no means general and many cars were, in terms of equipment, less attractive in their 1990 form.

### Distribution

No changes were made to the manner of ordering, stocking and selling Audi. Nor was distribution increased.

Indeed the number of dealers selling Audi has been reduced from 350 two years ago, to 275 by the beginning of 1990.

## Weight of Advertising

According to MEAL, Audi advertising achieved a share of voice of 4.7% in the car category. Thus Audi was still a small voice in a very crowded advertising market. Moreover, this weight was comparable with that of competitors. Volvo for example had a share of voice of 3.7% in the same period (and yet their volume declined by 9% in that period where Audi volume grew by 13%).

The level of spend is not such that a significant volume increase would be expected automatically.

## Catalytic Converters

It is important to consider catalytic converters themselves. It may be that at this stage the reader supposes that with the growth of environmentalism cars equipped with catalytic converters were bound to succeed and that it was this item of equipment alone and not the successful advertising of this item of equipment that resulted in increased sales. There are several pieces of evidence which establish that this is definitely not the case.

As set out in the introduction, Audi competes in a 'club' of prestige marques. The closest in image positioning is Volvo. Volvo also made changes to their cars for the 1990 model year, offering a catalytic converter on every model as a *free* option. What this meant was that every Volvo was *available* with a catalytic converter, and that Volvo customers were free to choose a catalytic converter equipped car *without* paying extra. The difference between this and what Audi offered was that every Audi had a catalytic converter as standard – you cannot buy an Audi without one. This is extremely important because it gives us a point of reference for Audi in trying to ascertain the significance of catalytic converters themselves.

The first significant fact is that Volvo admit the uptake of cats to have started off slowly. This refers to the period September 1989 to April 1990.

'It started off slowly but about half of new Volvo orders are now coming in for catalyst cars, said a Volvo spokesman' (*Autocar Motor* 18/4/90).

Volvo are currently predicting that only 50% of their 1990 volume will be sold with a cat even though cats *do not cost the consumer* anything to fit to a Volvo! How many other *free* offers would only be taken up by half those people eligible? One can only conclude that the latent demand for catalytic converters is low.

More importantly Volvo volume does not show the same growth over the period as Audi. In fact it declines.

TABLE 8: VOLVO VOLUME

|  | Apr–Sep | Oct–Mar |
|---|---|---|
| 1988/89 | 41,261 | 39,070 |
| 1989/90 | 45,241 | 35,534 |
| % change | +10 | −9 |

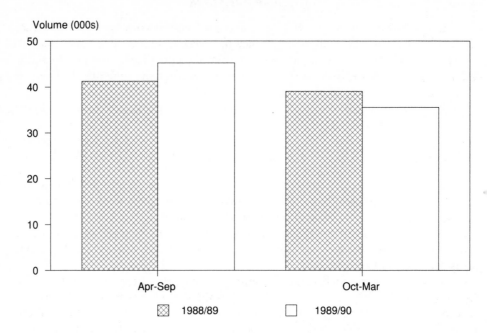

Figure 17. *Volvo volume*
*Source:* SMMT

If it were the case that catalytic converters alone were the cause of Audi's success, Volvo volume too should have benefited. If anything, Volvo should have benefited more than Audi because they were already thought to be a manufacturer concerned about the environment (see Table 5).

Nor did a catalytic converter add much value to the car. A survey by MORI on behalf of the Lex group, conducted in the autumn of 1989 (exactly when the Audi campaign ran), allows us to quantify this. Motorists were asked whether they would be prepared to pay for a catalytic converter.

The survey found that only 26% would be prepared to pay £200. Since the modal price of an Audi sold is approximately £12,500, for a quarter of motorists, a catalytic converter as standard on an Audi represented a marginal price decrease of just under 2%. For the remaining 75% of motorists it represented *even less than this*. On this basis the catalytic converter alone could not make the car sufficiently better value to account for an increase of 13% in Audi sales, in a declining market, during the advertised period.

This was reflected in the telephone responses to our campaign. Callers were asked 'what would you say most influences your choice of car?'. Very few of them cited environmental issues (eg catalytic converters) as an important influence. Instead the long-standing qualities of appearance, performance and reliability still came out as most important.

TABLE 9: FACTORS INFLUENCING VEHICLE PURCHASE

|  | (4385) % |
| --- | --- |
| Style/appearance | 26 |
| Performance | 20 |
| Reliability | 16 |
| Fuel economy | 7 |
| Acceleration/speed | 6 |
| Size | 5 |
| Initial cost | 5 |
| Environmental issues | 4 |

Source: VAG Research
Base: Telephone responses to advertising
(October 89 – January 90)

These data all suggest that a catalytic converter, as an additional item of standard equipment, would not have increased sales suddenly or significantly.

## HOW DID THE ADVERTISING WORK?

It may seem paradoxical that latent demand for catalysts was low and yet advertising based on the story about catalysts was successful in generating increased sales. Qualitative research in ·the summer of 1989 had warned us of growing dissatisfaction amongst consumers with car advertising in general, which was criticised as being hackneyed and hollow. Consumers were asking for more substance (of any kind) and less superficial imagery in car advertising.

In this context the catalytic converter provided the substance that was missing from so much car advertising. It was news. The advertising also made the catalyst offer feel contemporary and relevant without making implausible or self-righteous claims. While in itself it was not the reason to buy a particular car, it was sufficient reason to make motorists think again about *an Audi*. The catalytic converter was a hook, which interested people. If you like it was literally a catalyst, for consideration. Qualitative research is not the only evidence for this. The TV commercial has run many times in TV programmes from Dimbleby's 'Review of the Decade' to 'Washes Whiter'. As well as being evidence that the commercial was exactly right for the time it was made, this is an added benefit of the campaign – free PR on TV (and BBC no less).

The press campaign confronted more specific consumer fears about performance and economy. Again, from qualitative research we know that potential purchasers appreciated the direct explanation and information about the new car technology that the advertising offered. This contrasted with other manufacturers advertising about catalytic converters, which made reference to being green or saving trees. Consumers dismissed these as either boring or environmentalist bandwagoning.

## SUMMARY AND CONCLUDING REMARKS

This paper has set out to establish that increases in sales volume for Audi cars in the first half of the 1990 model year (September 1989 – March 1990) are due in no small part to an effective advertising campaign.

In a declining market, where confusion over the benefits of catalytic converters abounded, Audi adopted a strategy of launching a catalyst *only* range. The advertising had to overcome consumer ignorance and fear, and make Audi cars with catalytic converters desirable. During the period of the campaign Audi has achieved 13% growth in a declining market. This growth has not come from the market or from sector growth. The largest sales volume increases occurred in January – exactly when given the purchase lead times, the campaign would have maximum effect. The cars featured in TV advertising increased sales even more dramatically; +29% for the six month period of the campaign versus the same period a year previously.

The advertising created interest in Audi cars – with nearly 12,000 responses to the advertising (the equivalent of an *extra* year of leads). Other factors cannot explain the sales increase. Model line up and price positioning changed only slightly, and the timing of the change did not coincide with the increase in sales (which in fact coincided with the onset of advertising). Specification did not make the cars better value. Distribution was down and weight of advertising was comparable with competitive and previous Audi activity. Equipping cars with catalytic converters and advertising this did not yield a sales increase for Volvo. Finally, catalytic converters were not considered to be a major influence on purchase by consumers.

What this advertising *did* do, was use the catalytic converter story as the latest example of advanced Audi technology to maximum effect, creating interest in and consideration of the 1990 Audi models, which resulted in significant volume increases for Audi.

The next campaign for Audi, which is already in hand, will use a different example of advanced Audi engineering; or, as we call it, Vorsprung durch Technik.

# 7

# Knorr Stock Cubes

*How Thinking 'Local' Helped CPC Develop Advertising which Toppled the Brand Leader*

## INTRODUCTION

This paper sets out to demonstrate how, in a world of increasing focus on '1992', 'pan-European' strategies and 'global brands', thinking locally can still pay handsomely!

It shows how CPC exploited distinctive, local characteristics, ie home-made soup-making in Scotland, to develop a campaign that has become akin to popular Scottish folklore, and against all the odds, taken Knorr to brand leader in the Scottish cube market.

## BACKGROUND

Knorr Stock Cubes were launched in the UK in 1954, as the first real alternative to Oxo. In many ways Knorr could hardly have been more different.

1. Whilst Oxo had its *own* distinctive flavour, Knorr cubes (available in beef or chicken) had a more authentic meaty taste, enhanced with herbs.
2. Oxo tended to mask other flavours with its own particular taste: Knorr more subtly *enhanced* other flavours.
3. Oxo was a 'dry' cube which could be crumbled into cooking. Knorr had a 'moist' format and required dissolving in boiling water before addition.
4. Knorr was launched at a significant price premium (+200%) relative to Oxo.

In effect, Oxo was a flavour and colour additive. Knorr was more akin to real stock.

## Knorr's Position by Mid 1970s

Some 20 years after launch, Knorr had carved a small but profitable niche in the UK cube market.

TABLE 1: UK VOLUME SHARE 1975

|        | %    |
| ------ | ---- |
| Knorr  | 7.8  |
| Oxo    | 89.6 |
| Others | 2.6  |

Source: Nielsen

## Usage

Whilst Knorr's characteristics of subtlety and lightness made it particularly appropriate for chicken dishes (casseroles and soups), the more robust flavour of Oxo was particularly suited to red meat (casseroles, minces and gravies). As a result, Knorr volume was biased towards its chicken cube, with Oxo volume biased towards its beef cube.

TABLE 2: UK CUBE MARKET PROFILE, 1975
(VOLUME)

|         | Total Market % | Knorr % | Oxo % |
| ------- | -------------- | ------- | ----- |
| Beef    | 84             | 42      | 88    |
| Chicken | 16             | 58      | 12    |

Source: Nielsen

## Attempts to Grow Knorr 1970 – 1977

Knorr was regularly supported by national TV advertising during the 1970s, with the proposition:

'Only Knorr stock cubes have a subtle enough flavour to truly complement the flavour of poultry and meat'.

TABLE 3: KNORR PENETRATION AND VOLUME SHARE
1970 – 1975

|                 | 1970 % | 1974 % | 1975 % |
| --------------- | ------ | ------ | ------ |
| *UK Penetration* |        |        |        |
| *Total Knorr*   | 14.5   | 13.7   | 13.2   |
| Red Oxo         | 54.7   | 60.8   | 61.7   |
| Chicken Oxo     | 18.9   | 17.6   | 19.2   |
| *UK volume share* |      |        |        |
| *Total Knorr*   | 7.8    | 7.9    | 7.8    |
| Total Oxo       | 89.6   | 89.8   | 89.6   |

Source: Nielsen, TGI
Base: All UK housewifes

These attempts to grow the brand, however, met with little success.

*Factors Holding Back Knorr Growth*

In competing with Oxo, Knorr faced a challenging task!

1.  It is difficult to overestimate the strength of the emotional bond between the British public and Oxo. Oxo was, and still is, one of the truly great food brands, enjoying both huge loyalty and unquestioning, almost ritual purchasing behaviour.
    The following comment was typical:

    'I don't know really why I use Oxo – I just do. Mum always used it I suppose, so I do too'.

2.  People *liked* the strong, beefy taste of Oxo. Most people, therefore, saw no potential benefit from a more subtle tasting alternative.
3.  Knorr's 'non-crumble' format was unfamiliar.
4.  Knorr was much more expensive than Oxo.

In addition, even if Knorr *could* increase penetration, clearly its *nature* excluded it from the real volume of the market, which Oxo dominated – red meat casseroles and gravies.

Thus, whilst Knorr was left little choice but to play the same game as Oxo, the odds seemed heavily stacked in Oxo's favour.

## KNORR'S POSITION IN SCOTLAND IN 1975

Although the cube market in Scotland as a whole behaved similarly to the UK, Knorr's position in Scotland was very different. As a result, Scotland accounted for over 25% of Knorr's total volume.

TABLE 4:  CUBE VOLUME SHARE 1975

|        | UK % | Scotland % |
|--------|------|------------|
| Knorr  | 7.8  | 35.2       |
| Oxo    | 89.6 | 62.2       |
| Others | 2.6  | 2.6        |

Source:  Nielsen

Behind this difference lay an activity firmly entrenched in Scottish tradition, the making of home-made soup!

## HOME-MADE SOUP IN SCOTLAND

In a region characterised by long, cold winters, and where family budgets were traditionally stretched, it is not difficult to see how home-made soup became so firmly rooted in Scottish heritage. As one respondent described her grandmother's lifestyle:

'It was economy cooking then; big families, pots of broth and potato stovies'.

In many ways, home-made soup seemed to form the backbone of the family – always there as a warm welcome, and a powerful expression of the 'provider' role which Scottish women strongly adhered to.

'The pot was always boiling on the stove'.

'I remember coming home from dances and having a bowl of soup'.

Quantitative data strikingly confirmed the role home-made soup continued to play in Scottish family life.

TABLE 5:  HOME-MADE SOUP-MAKING, 1977

|  | Scotland | Rest of UK |
| --- | --- | --- |
| % housewives claiming made any home-made soup in past 4 weeks | 91 | 14 |

Source:  Marplan, April 1977

### How was Soup Made?

At the heart of a good soup, was good stock. Stock was made by simmering meaty bones in a large pot for a number of hours. After this, the liquid would be drained off to form the 'base' of the soup, to which vegetables or meat were then added.

Traditionally, women would obtain bones free from their local butcher for soup-making. Any left-overs, like chicken carcasses, would also find their way into the stock pot (the Scots were not ones for waste!).

### How did Soup-Making Influence Knorr's Position in Scotland?

1. Stock making was a time-consuming business. Bones needed to be boiled for several hours and this process needed on-going attention. With Scottish women living more busy lives, they were less willing than their mums to 'spend all day over the stove'.
2. It was becoming increasingly difficult to obtain bones for soup-making. Many women complained that their butchers simply didn't seem to keep bones like they used to and bones certainly weren't easy to find in supermarkets!

Despite no previous soup-related promotional activity for Knorr cubes, 'discoverers' of Knorr felt they had found a genuine alternative to bone-boiled stock, which both looked and tasted like home-made. Oxo, with its distinctive taste and dark colour, did not.

This explained Knorr's strength in Scotland.

## DEVELOPING A NEW STRATEGY FOR KNORR IN SCOTLAND

Research in 1977 in Scotland revealed both an untapped opportunity, and a cause for concern.

### A Growth Opportunity for Knorr?

Many Scottish women, it seemed, had not yet discovered Knorr. When we talked to them, we found they were very interested in Knorr's benefits over home-made stock. However, they clearly felt somewhat guilty at the prospect of using a convenient alternative. If we could assure them that Knorr gave results as good as the real thing, it seemed we could exploit this potential. Quantitative research confirmed this opportunity.

Despite home-made soup accounting for half Knorr cube volume in Scotland, *only 25% of all home-made soups contained any cube at all* (Marplan 1977).

### A Long-Term Threat to Knorr?

Younger women, in particular, seemed to be making home-made soup less often. It seemed very possible that these women were starting to adopt a more UK pattern of behaviour, only making soup when left-over carcasses were available, and otherwise using packet or canned soup.

Outside soup-making, Knorr's product characteristics clearly left it ill-equipped to challenge Oxo. If Knorr could not retain a soup-based 'foothold' in cupboards, there was a real danger of being squeezed out completely.

To sum up, we identified a real opportunity for Knorr to grow volume by actively exploiting Scottish soup-making. This potential growth, however, could only be realised if, in the long-term, Scottish women maintained their desire for home-made soup.

## 1977 – A NEW MARKETING STRATEGY FOR SCOTLAND

Knorr's most competitive positioning outside Scotland seemed to remain one of focusing on its more subtle flavour contribution in the context of casseroles. Soup-making was infrequent and a 'real stock' claim had little relevance – most women had never made real stock in their lives!

We decided to be bold, and to tailor a new strategy specifically to Scotland. Instead of playing the same game as Oxo – we were changing the rules.

## MARKETING OBJECTIVES

We set out to exploit Knorr's unique competitive benefit in Scotland, to grow sales, share, and via maintaining our price premium over Oxo, to increase profit. We hoped to achieve this by:

*Primarily*
1. Increasing frequency of usage of Knorr in soups among existing Knorr users.
2. Encouraging trial of Knorr in home-made soups by non-Knorr users.

*Secondly*
3. Maintaining levels of home-made soup-making.
4. Increasing Knorr usage in other meals.
   (Qualitative research suggested that once Knorr was in cupboards, usage tended to spread to other dishes).

## THE CREATIVE BRIEF

### Advertising Objectives

1. To reinforce existing users' perceptions of Knorr as a genuine alternative to home-made stock and so encourage more frequent usage in soups.
2. To make more women aware of the benefits of Knorr cubes in home-made soup-making and so encourage them to try Knorr cubes in soups.
3. To maintain the frequency and appeal of home-made soup-making.

### Proposition

*Because stock made with Knorr stock cubes is as tasty as home-made stock, but more convenient, they are particularly suitable for making soup.*
   NB: Convenience in this sense meant more than just time-saving. It embraced the broader issues of no mess, no need to have key ingredients (eg a chicken carcass) etc.

### Tone

This needed to reflect the cultural context of soup-making in Scotland, ie everyday, family cooking.

### Target Market

All home-made soup-makers (over 90% of housewives in Scotland).
   We knew that our target felt a degree of guilt at the idea of 'cheating' by using stock cubes – we therefore needed to assure them that Knorr produced stock that was as good and wholesome as the 'real thing'.

*Executional Guidelines*

We decided to feature Knorr Ham Cubes – a flavour introduced in 1974. Ham cubes were sold predominantly in Scotland, where they were particularly popular for making Pea and Ham soup.

## THE CREATIVE SOLUTION

BMP produced a creative idea called 'Monday Night' – centred on two Highland friends, Hughie and Jamie.

The men were so naïvely innocent of the cooking process that they could only assume that chicken the night before inevitably meant chicken soup the night after.

They were left totally bewildered when Hughie's wife somehow managed to create a wonderful Pea and Ham soup the next day. Her little secret – Knorr Ham Stock Cubes.

## PRE-TESTING THE CAMPAIGN

'Monday Night' was qualitatively tested – with extremely positive results. The campaign was felt to be perfectly in tune with Scottish values: the wry humour, the ignorance of the men about cooking, and the value attached to good home cooking. The message was felt to be relevant and appealing to both Knorr users and non-users. The campaign clearly showed the potential to meet our stated advertising objectives.

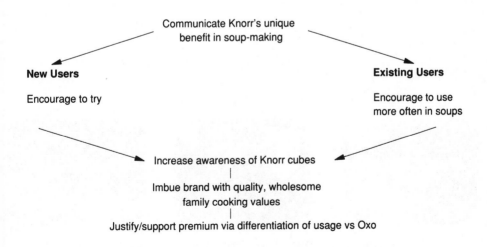

Figure 1. *How the campaign would work*

# 'MONDAY NIGHT'

'What d'you think the wife's cooking tonight Hughie?'
'Oh, I don't think at all – chicken soup. We had chicken soup yesterday.'

VO: Hughie doesn't know his wife uses Knorr Stock Cubes.

Boiling water over a Knorr Ham Stock Cube gives a delicious meaty tasting base for lentils and beans.

'This'll be the chicken soup then?'

'No Hughie, this'll be the pea and ham.'

'mmm. pea and ham...'

'How was your soup last night Hughie?'
'Oh delicious and the remarkable thing was it wasn't chicken, it was pea and ham.'

'Pea and ham from a chicken, now that's clever.'

VO: Knorr Stock Cubes – good soup and no bones about it.

*From Small Beginnings...*

Few people could have predicted, back in 1977, that we were embarking on a campaign which would still be running 13 years later! Few could have imagined the extent to which Hughie, Jamie and friends would touch Scottish hearts.

'Pea and Ham from a chicken' quickly became a national catchphrase. Phil McCol (the actor playing Jamie) became a 'celebrity' over-night. And even now, women in groups talk about 'Pea and Ham' cars (Morris Minors!) and 'Pea and Ham' roads (winding Highland roads!).

## CAMPAIGN DEVELOPMENT HISTORY

### *1977 – 82*

'Monday Night' ran annually from the winter of 1977/78 until 1980. The CPC account then moved agency, where it was recommended that given the strength of Knorr cubes in Scotland, all available monies be deployed behind more aggressively trying to grow Knorr cube volume in the rest of the UK – where sales remained static.

As a result, Scotland received no support after December 1980 until the winter of 1982, when BMP regained the account.

Analysis at this time revealed indications that Knorr's hold had begun to slip in Scotland.

TABLE 6

|  | 1980 % | 1981 % | 1982 % |
|---|---|---|---|
| Knorr volume share | 39.1 | 39.1 | 35.1 |
| Knorr penetration | 39.2 | 38.6 | 34.5 |

Source: 1980/81 Nielsen, 1982 NMRA, TGI

It was decided to re-air 'Monday Night' in December 1982, with a 'holding' objective.

In 1983, the strategy in Scotland was re-evaluated.

### *1983*

Research concluded that whilst the soup-making strategy was still the optimum route for Knorr in Scotland, and whilst 'Monday Night' was as popular as ever, some younger women were beginning to feel it portrayed Scottish life in a somewhat negative way. The *appearance* of Hughie's wife was the main cause of this criticism.

'She really annoys me – she looks very old fashioned – a 'wee wifey' in her pinney'.

The wife's role as a 'provider' was clearly not contentious – Scottish women respected this. It was agreed to develop a new execution within the same campaign which updated the *look* of the wife, rather than her *role*. The objectives of the advertising remained the same.

A new creative idea, 'Moira', was developed. Jamie and Hamish were seen lamenting the apparent sad demise of their hen 'Moira', as they approvingly ate a fine Cock-a-Leekie soup – only to be interrupted by 'Moira' miraculously appearing in the door-way!

Pre-testing confirmed 'Moira' as tremendously appealing and clearly having the potential to refresh the campaign as intended. 'Moira' ran for the first time in December 1984.

### *1984 – 1989*

One interesting finding from developing 'Moira' was that Hamish's more contemporary looking wife seemed to set 'Monday Night' back in context – to the extent that both executions ran in tandem until 1989.

'Monday Night' was then replaced by 'Hen Night', which brought the campaign raucously up to date. Hamish is seen proudly relating how his wife had gone all the way to Inverness for a hen night – such was her dedication to finding just the right hen for his soup. Instead we see her catching a stripper's sporran to the strains of 'What's New Pussycat?'!

This idea received a tremendous reception in research (with lots of cock-a-leekie jokes!). The idea of the wife using a stock cube for her *own* benefit (ie, so she could get out) while, importantly, the men still enjoyed a great tasting soup, was clearly a very modern expression of Knorr's 'real stock' benefit.

'Little do they know we're not at home slaving over their soup!'

'It's brilliant – even better than the Pea and Ham one'.

'Hen Night' ran with 'Moira' in November/December 1989.

### MEDIA

The media strategy has been broadly similar since the beginning of our campaign: a burst of activity focusing on the key Knorr cube sales periods in Scotland (ie November, December and January) at an average weight of 1,000 housewife TVRs.

Some years have differed slightly. If additional advertising monies have become available at the end of the CPC fiscal year, it has been agreed to deploy them in Scotland to give the campaign an additional 'kick' at the beginning of the soup-making season.

## 'MOIRA'

'This is a great drop of Cock-a-Leekie Hamish'
'Aye, she was a fine wee bird was Moira'
'Best soup I've ever tasted'
'Aye, she never let us down, even to this day. I miss the eggs though.'

VO: What Hamish doesn't know is that his wife uses Knorr Stock Cubes.

Simply pour boiling water over a Chicken Stock Cube and you've a delicious meaty tasting base

for Cock-a-Leekie soup without the bones.

'Och, it's how she would have wanted it.'
'Aye, I suppose...'

SHOT OF CHICKEN AT DOOR

'Moira?'

'Moira...'

VO: Knorr Stock Cubes – good soup and no bones about it.

## 'HEN NIGHT'

'On your own tonight Hamish?'
'Aye, Elspeth has gone to Inverness for a hen night.'

'All that way just to pick up a chicken?!'
'Aye, she doesn't make the best soup in the Highlands for nothing'

VO: Hamish doesn't know his wife uses a Knorr Stock Cube to make a delicious meaty base

for Cock-a-Leekie soup

'Probably spent hours deciding on just the right hen for your soup'
'Aye well, that's devotion for you'

MUSIC STARTS: Tom Jones, 'What's new Pussycat'

MUSIC CONTINUES

MUSIC CONTINUES

MUSIC FADES OUT...

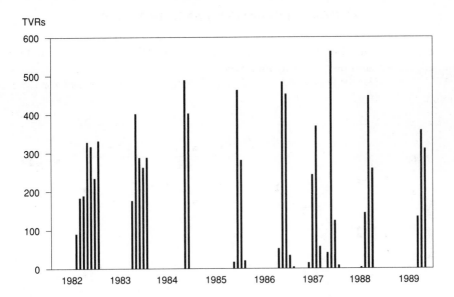

Figure 2. *Knorr housewife TVRs in Scotland*
*Source:* 1981–90 BARB

## EVALUATING THE CAMPAIGN

We have faced a number of difficulties in evaluating this campaign.

1.  Stock cubes sales are highly seasonal. Knorr sales in Scotland (due to the soup-making bias) are even more so. We have thus had to attempt to remove the effect of seasonality from our analysis.
2.  Knorr has been supported every year in Scotland (as has Oxo), with the exception of 1981. As such, there is little inbuilt variability in the advertising data to help in isolating advertising effects.
3.  In the year Knorr received no advertising, the retail audit company was changed – altering pick-up on both market and brand level. Our *sales* trend analysis has thus largely focused on the period since 1981.
4.  Bovril cubes were launched nationally in 1978, which introduced a considerable change in the structure of the cubes market, at the same time as the start of the Knorr campaign in Scotland.
5.  Research budgets only allowed ad hoc tracking of usage behaviour in Scotland.

In spite of these difficulties, we are able to demonstrate how:

—  Sales and share increased steadily over the 13 years from introduction of our campaign, to the extent that Knorr is now *brand leader* in Scotland.
—  Knorr's volume gains have resulted from long-term changes in soup-making behaviour which exactly match those set out in our advertising objectives.
—  Behavioural changes and hence Knorr's growth, were a direct *result* of our Scottish campaign and would not have occurred in its absence.

## KNORR SALES IN SCOTLAND, 1977 – 1990

While the cube market has remained static in Scotland over the 13 year period studied, Knorr sales have steadily increased.

At the end of 1989, Knorr became volume brand leader in Scotland for the first time.

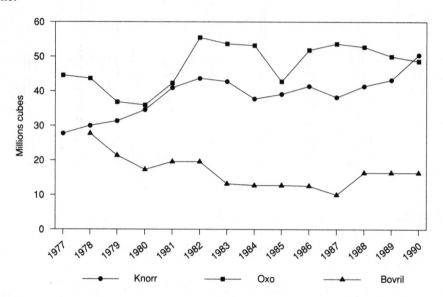

Figure 3. *Cubes volume Scotland*
*Source:* Nielsen 1977–81, NMRA 1982–90

TABLE 7:  VOLUME BRAND SHARES

|        | 1977 % | 1981 % | 1989 % |
|--------|--------|--------|--------|
| Oxo    | 60.6   | 40.5   | 43.7   |
| Knorr  | 37.4   | 39.1   | 45.8   |
| Bovril | —      | 18.8   | 5.5    |
| Others | 2.0    | 1.6    | 5.0    |

Source:   1977 & 1981 Nielsen, 1989 NMRA

Because of Knorr's continued price premium relative to the rest of the market, the volume share in 1989 equated to a value share of almost two thirds of total market value.

Knorr cubes are now a £4m brand in Scotland – more than twice the value of Oxo (NMRA, 1989).

### Effect of New Varieties

Two new varieties of Knorr cubes were successfully introduced in 1984 (lamb and vegetable).

However, these varieties still account for less than 14% of annual volume in Scotland. The best selling varieties (chicken and ham) have both steadily grown in volume by more than 40% since 1984.

Therefore, overall brand growth is due to core variety growth, not just new introductions.

## WHERE DID KNORR GROWTH COME FROM?

Bovril cube volume has been in long-term decline as its distribution has steadily been eroded. Bovril cubes are very similar to Oxo in both flavour (strong, beefy) and format ('dry', crumbly) – as such it seems highly probable that Bovril's volume is being picked up by Oxo. This has therefore 'buoyed up' Oxo sales and share.

What seems to be emerging in Scotland is not *one* cube market but two!

— A soup-making cube market (Knorr) which is increasing.
— A non soup-making cube market (Oxo/Bovril) which is declining.

Although we don't have quantitative data to validate this hypothesis, it seems the most probable scenario from both sales and qualitative data.

Thinking back to our objectives, this is exactly what we would expect to see if advertising was working as we planned.

We were not expecting Knorr volume to be gained primarily from other cubes at all – our 'competitors' were either bones or convenience soups. We would therefore expect additional Knorr cube volume to be largely incremental to the rest of the market.

This would also seem to explain why Scotland is increasing its share of all cubes sold in the UK, soup-making being the only major difference between the two markets.

## SOUP-MAKING BEHAVIOUR IN SCOTLAND, 1977 – 1990

Long-term trends illustrate that the behavioural objectives of our advertising have been met.

*Home-made soup has remained popular in Scotland*

Home-made soup-making has not collapsed in Scotland as we feared.

TABLE 8:  TOTAL HOME-MADE SOUP OCCASIONS IN SCOTLAND
(MILLIONS OF OCCASIONS)

| 1981 | 1985 | 1986 | 1988 | 1989 |
|------|------|------|------|------|
| 57   | 53   | 61   | 56   | 59   |

Source:  Family Food Panel, Winter/Spring

Neither has home-made soup lost out to more convenient versions.

TABLE 9:  HOME-MADE SOUP IN SCOTLAND
PERCENTAGE OF ALL SOUP OCCASIONS

| 1981 % | 1985 % | 1986 % | 1988 % | 1989 % |
|---|---|---|---|---|
| 47 | 47 | 45 | 45 | 48 |

Source:   Family Food Panel, Winter/Spring

We had a particular fear that a new generation of women would reject making soup. This has not occurred.

TABLE 10:  PERCENTAGE OF HOME-MADE SOUPS MADE BY YOUNGER WOMEN

| Age | 1981 % | 1988 % |
|---|---|---|
| 17–34 | 17 | 19 |

Source:   Family Food Panel, Winter/Spring
Base:   Home-made soup occasions

Therefore, the long-term platform on which Knorr depended, ie home-made soup-making, remained stable. We achieved our first objective.

*With the home-made soup-making platform stable, cube usage in soups has increased.*

There has been a dramatic increase in both the number of Scottish women who regularly use cubes in soups, and in the number of soups made with a stock cube.
    The possible scenario whereby women only make soups when they have a left-over carcass available does not seem to have materialised.

TABLE 11:  PENETRATION OF CUBES AMONG HOME-MADE SOUP-MAKERS IN SCOTLAND

|  | 1977 % | 1983 % | 1986 % |
|---|---|---|---|
| Ever use cubes in soups | 25 | 35 | 48 |
| Always use cubes in soups | 22 | 27 | 43 |

Source:   Marplan 1977, Schlackman 1983 & 1986
Base:   All housewives in Scotland

Our second objective of effecting a long-term increase in cube usage within home-made soups has been met.

TABLE 12:  PENETRATION OF CUBES IN HOME-MADE SOUPS IN SCOTLAND

|  | 1977<br>% | 1986<br>% |
|---|---|---|
| Soups containing<br>a cube | 25 | 47 |

Source:  Marplan 1977, Schlackman 1986
Base:    All home-made soups in Scotland

*Knorr usage within soups has increased*

A growing proportion of soups contain a Knorr cube. Knorr is the dominant brand of cube used in soups – by 1986 accounting for nearly 75% of all 'cube soup occasions'. This has led to a dramatic increase in the penetration of Knorr in soups.

TABLE 13:  PERCENTAGE OF ALL HOME-MADE SOUPS
CONTAINING A KNORR CUBE IN SCOTLAND

| 1977<br>% | 1986<br>% |
|---|---|
| 24 | 35 |

Source:  Marplan 1977,
         Schlackman 1986
Base:    All home-made soups in Scotland

We have achieved another of our objectives.

*Knorr usage in other dishes has increased*

Having gained a presence in cupboards via soup-making, Knorr cubes are increasingly being used in other dishes.

TABLE 14:  KNORR USAGE IN OTHER DISHES

| Using in casseroles | | | Using in gravies | | | Using in mince | | |
|---|---|---|---|---|---|---|---|---|
| 1981<br>% | 1983<br>% | 1986<br>% | 1981<br>% | 1983<br>% | 1986<br>% | 1981<br>% | 1983<br>% | 1986<br>% |
| 41 | 63 | 74 | 20 | 41 | 50 | N/A | 21 | 23 |

Source:  SRA 1981, Schlackman 1983 & 1986
Base:    Knorr buyers in Scotland

We have therefore met our final behavioural objective – that of increasing Knorr usage in meals other than soups.

*In Summary*

Long-term behaviour has changed exactly as we planned in our advertising objectives.

It appears that the home-made soup-making platform has been maintained, and Knorr has been able to capitalise on this, in a way which has increased both penetration among soup-makers (as shown earlier) and frequency of use (see Table 15).

TABLE 15:   AVERAGE NUMBER OF KNORR CUBES USED
PER YEAR PER USER IN SCOTLAND

| 1977 | 1981 | 1986 | 1989 |
|------|------|------|------|
| 41   | 58   | 63   | 78   |

Source:   Nielsen 1977, NMRA 1981/86 &
1989, TGI

We hope by now to have demonstrated that we have met our sales and share objectives for Knorr and that these were achieved via behavioural changes exactly as planned.

It could well be argued that all this is completely unrelated to the advertising. We will now show that this is not the case.

## EVALUATION OF 'INTERMEDIATE' DATA

### Appeal

This campaign is hugely popular. It is always discussed spontaneously in groups and despite the high exposure, women never seem to tire of seeing it.

Hughie, Hamish and friends are perceived as charmingly naïve, but totally believable – people have taken them to their hearts.

'That ad's been out for years and we're still laughing at it'.

'I come from the West Highlands and I know these people. I know lots of people like that and I just relate to them'.

'It's a nice humour as well – very sort of dry – a Highland humour'.

This is supported by tracking data. 60% of women recalling the Knorr cubes advertising in Scotland in 1989 stated that they liked it (50% higher than the Millward Brown average).

### Awareness

1. Knorr's 'Base Level' of advertising awareness, as measured by Millward Brown, has more than trebled over the monitored years. This is a rough

measure of awareness 'credit' – the higher the base level, the longer the campaign would be remembered after it stopped.

2. Spontaneous awareness of Knorr cubes has steadily increased over the period tracked, and in 1989 moved above that of Oxo.

   As media spend has remained relatively static, it seems that we are benefiting from an accumulating advertising effect; with each new burst building on the success of the former. (NB: As we will discuss later, econometric modelling supports this view).

3. Absolute levels of advertising awareness are also very high. Photoprompted awareness of Knorr advertising in Scotland stood last year at over 75%, with two thirds of those aware remembering the brand correctly.

### Communication

The campaign clearly communicates the proposition of good, natural stock, ideal for soup-making.

TABLE 16:  COMMUNICATION (SPONTANEOUS)

|                                      | %  |
| ------------------------------------ | -- |
| Tastes as good as the real thing     | 30 |
| Makes good soup without the bones    | 25 |
| Quick and convenient                 | 20 |

Source:   Millward Brown, November 1989 – January 1990
Base:   All recalling Knorr cubes advertised in Scotland

### Knorr Imagery

The imagery of Knorr stock cubes in Scotland is one of goodness and wholesomeness – not a convenient cop-out!

TABLE 17:  KNORR STOCK CUBE IMAGERY

|                             | Scotland % | UK % |
| --------------------------- | ---------- | ---- |
| Makes a good stock          | 89         | 76   |
| Suitable for home-made soup | 94         | 80   |

Source:  Millward Brown
Base:   All Knorr users

### In Summary

The advertising seems to have met all of its 'intermediary' objectives – generating awareness for Knorr cubes and communicating their benefit via a very popular, high profile campaign (and at much lower levels of TVRs than our largest competitor).

TABLE 18: SCOTLAND TVRs, 1982 – 1989

| Total Oxo | Knorr |
|-----------|-------|
| 16,136 | 8,876 |

Source: BARB

## PROVING THE CONTRIBUTION OF ADVERTISING

We have shown how Knorr sales and share have grown as a result of behavioural changes, in exactly the way we planned. We have also shown how we have met our advertising objectives, in terms of 'intermediate variables'. The question now is, did our advertising *cause* these changes?

There are two methods by which we will answer this question:

1. By eliminating other variables.
2. By validating our hypotheses through an econometric model.

## ELIMINATING OTHER VARIABLES

### Distribution

Sterling distribution has remained constant for both Knorr and Oxo at nearly 100% since our advertising began, thus it cannot have been a significant catalyst for change.

### Packaging

There have been only very minor modifications to packaging.

### Other Activity

There have been no significant PR or promotional campaigns over the period. CPC have intermittently developed press campaigns for Knorr to a 'rest of UK' strategy (ie, non soup-making). These have of course run in Scotland, but research has consistently suggested they have limited relevance to Scottish women.

Although Knorr markets other products in Scotland, any activity during the advertised period has been on a national level.

### Meat Consumption

Meat consumption has remained constant in Scotland since 1979. There seems no indication therefore that a decline in 'left-overs' has resulted in an increased need for cubes in soup.

*Pricing*

Knorr has, in real terms, become better value relative to Oxo by about 10%, over the period analysed. We would hypothesise however than the influence of this is probably relatively small, for two reasons:

1. The absolute premium of Knorr is still very significant. Qualitative evidence suggests that for people for whom price is important, the reduction of a few pence per packet for Knorr would make minimal difference to purchase intention.
2. Knorr is not primarily competing with Oxo or any other cube – certainly not in the key usage area of soups.

As we show later, econometric modelling confirms that Knorr price has minimal influence on sales.

*In Summary*

We find it difficult to see what factor, other than our advertising, could have produced the behavioural and sales effects which we planned and have achieved in Scotland.

## VALIDATING OUR HYPOTHESES THROUGH AN ECONOMETRIC MODEL

In order to validate our conclusions concerning other possible causal variables, and in turn *quantify* the sales contribution of advertising, we constructed an econometric model.

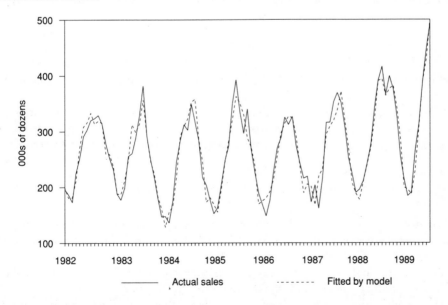

Figure 4. *Knorr Stock Cubes volume sales – actual vs fitted*
Source: NMRA

The technical details of the model are appended, together with appropriate tests to demonstrate its statistical validity.

Figure 4 shows Knorr's actual sales volume and the model's fit to it. The model explains 94% of the variation in Knorr sales from September 1982 to January 1990.

The model investigated the influences of the following factors on Knorr sales over the period 1982 to 1990:

1. Pricing and distribution for Knorr, Oxo, Bovril and own label.
2. New Knorr varieties.
3. Seasonality.
4. Knorr, Oxo and Bovril advertising.

## Pricing

Knorr sales were found to be remarkably price insensitive. The decline in real price since 1982 would seem to have contributed only 1.6% of Knorr volume over the period studied.

No impact of competitive pricing was found.

## Distribution

This had no significant effect on Knorr sales.

## New Knorr Varieties

Introduction of new Knorr varieties was found to have minimal influence on sales.

## Seasonality

Temperature was found to be the key seasonal variable. More cubes will be sold in a cold winter, the reverse in a hot summer.

However, the model found that although temperature accounts for slight variation in the seasonal peaks from year to year – it was not responsible for generating the long-term sales volume increases that we have seen for Knorr.

## Quantifying the Contribution of Advertising

After isolating the effect of all other variables, the model was able to quantify the direct contribution of advertising as *12.5% of total Knorr volume* in Scotland, over the period September 1982 – January 1990.

This means that advertising alone is responsible for *90% of Knorr's volume* increase over this same period (the remainder is due to price).

The model also confirmed our hypothesis that the sales volume directly attributable to advertising was growing from year to year.

# UNDERSTANDING HOW THE ADVERTISING WORKS

*Shorter and Longer Term Effects*

In our evaluation of this campaign, two 'levels' of effect have emerged.

1. *Short-term Effects:*
   These mirror the timing of the advertising bursts and produce discernible short-term uplifts in sales. This is a result of an immediate behavioural response, advertising increasing both immediate purchasing of Knorr cubes, and also usage of those cubes already in the cupboard at home (resulting in re-purchase a short time later).

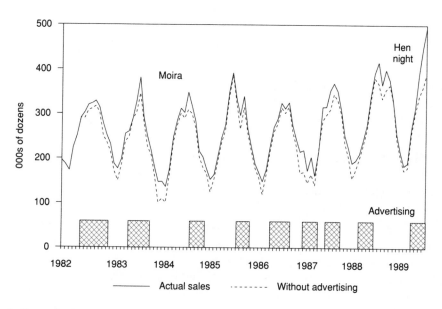

Figure 5. *Knorr stock cubes volume sales, actual versus without advertising*

The introduction of new executions seems to have effected a particularly marked short-term uplift in sales over the advertised period.

Awareness data mirrors this pattern of short-term response.

2. *Longer term Effects:*
   Even though the model was not specifically set up to measure a genuine, long-term accumulating effect of advertising on sales, the previous figure shows:

   — Each burst produces a sales effect with a very long 'tail' (to the extent that there is no point during any year when advertising is having no effect on sales).
   — Sales are always above the level preceding the last burst, when the subsequent burst of advertising takes place.

As we have seen, this pattern is reflected in both brand and advertising awareness data. Awareness is steadily building over time, despite an almost constant level of media weight.

It seems, therefore, that advertising effects are by no means restricted to the short-term. Instead, there seems to be a 'building' effect over a longer period of time.

This longer-term effect has undoubtedly played a key role in the success of the campaign – enabling us to achieve a significantly higher level of return over the 13 year advertised period than we would perhaps otherwise expect to achieve from a low absolute level of media spend.

It is interesting to speculate whether Knorr could have realistically achieved long-term volume growth, without the benefit of these carry-over effects.

## PROFITABILITY

We have shown that advertising directly contributed 12.5% of total Knorr cubes volume in Scotland, from 1982 to 1990.

On the basis of the following factors:

1.  The profit generated by this additional volume
2.  An average annual media spend of £110,000 (BARB)
3.  Low production costs, as a result of the stability of the campaign

the advertising paid for itself 1.8 times over.

NB: Although we couldn't apply the model to data prior to 1982, it is probable that advertising generated similar levels of incremental profit *before* this date.

However, even if, before 1982, advertising had no effect at all, subsequent incremental pay-back has been at a level which *alone* ensures profitability of the overall campaign (from 1977 to 1990).

### The Real Value of the Advertising

In estimating that advertising directly generated 12.5% of total Knorr volume (1982–1990) the model had to assume that had the campaign never run, there would have been no adverse market trends working to reduce Knorr's sales.

However, as we have seen, we believe this assumption to be highly optimistic.

Our research in 1977 clearly highlighted the likelihood that home-made soup-making and cube usage within it would gradually decline. A decline in Knorr volume would inevitably follow.

The *real* contribution of our advertising to CPC profit is therefore likely to be considerably higher.

## THE IMPLICATIONS OF ADOPTING A 'LOCAL' STRATEGY

We have proved that our advertising successfully generated incremental profit for CPC in Scotland.

Fundamental to this success was our decision to adopt a 'local' strategy.

Only by doing so could we effectively exploit a unique competitive benefit, ie Knorr's suitability for making home-made soup.

Only by thinking 'local' were we able to 'change the rules' and consequently topple Oxo to become brand leader.

A comparison with the performance of Knorr cubes in the rest of the UK confirms this view.

Continued support (on a 'more subtle flavour' platform) has encouraged some volume growth for Knorr, but this growth has largely been flavour and distribution-led.

Oxo still massively dominates the market.

TABLE 19:  VOLUME BRAND SHARES

|        | Scotland % | Rest of UK % |
|--------|------------|--------------|
| Knorr  | 45.8       | 10.3         |
| Oxo    | 43.7       | 74.6         |
| Bovril | 5.5        | 10.8         |
| Others | 5.0        | 4.3          |

Source:   NMRA, year to January 1990

## SUMMARY

CPC adopted a bold, new strategy when they agreed to develop advertising for Knorr cubes which specifically targeted Scotland, in order to exploit and defend a unique competitive advantage.

We have shown that these objectives have been very successfully achieved.

Since its inception in 1977, a famous, long-running campaign has developed – the effects of which have built year on year, with the result that Knorr now outsells all other cubes in Scotland.

The advertising worked exactly as we planned:

— By helping to maintain Scottish women's commitment to making soup.
— By encouraging more Scottish women to use Knorr cubes more often in their home-made soups.
— And by fuelling increased use of Knorr cubes in other meals in Scotland.

Most importantly, not only has the advertising *worked*, it has also demonstrably contributed to overall CPC profit.

## CONCLUSIONS

We acknowledge that we have set ourselves a difficult task – that of proving that *only* by developing advertising to meet the specific needs of Scotland, were CPC able to defend and grow a vital proportion of their total business.

We feel convinced however that this is so and it is only thanks to Hughie, Hamish and friends, that Knorr is now brand leader in Scotland.

Maybe sometimes *only* thinking and acting 'local' can pay.

## TECHNICAL APPENDIX

*An explanation and validation of the econometric model*

For reasons of space and confidentiality, this is an abbreviated version of the technical appendix submitted to the judges.

Stock cubes are essentially a store-cupboard item of which consumers tend to hold several weeks supply. Advertising may not therefore necessarily prompt any immediate purchase but simply encourage faster use of existing stores.

This led us to develop the hypothesis that any Knorr advertising potentially had two effects, one reducing the existing level of stores in consumers' cupboards, the other prompting actual purchase at, or close to, the time of advertising.

We developed the following theoretical model which relates the quantity purchased in any four-weekly period to a range of marketing factors, both Knorr and competitive, to consumers' *usage* and expected usage in that period and to the *change in household stores* between any one period and that prior to it.

### The Theoretical Model

(1)　$Q_t = a_0 + a_1 S_t + a_2 E(U)_t + a_3 T + a_4 P + a_5 A$

Q = quantity purchased, S = consumers' stores at the beginning of the period, E(U) = expected usage, T = temperature, P = price, A = advertising, for both Knorr and competitors.

(2)　$S_t = S_{t-1} + Q_t - U_t$
(3)　$U_t = b_0 + b_1 T + b_2 A$
(4)　$E(U) = f(T)$ proxied by $c + c_1 T_t + c_2 T_{t-1}$
　　ie expected usage in period t is a function of temperature.

By rearranging equation (2), substituting for household stores in equation (1) and taking first differences, we obtained a theoretical equation linking Knorr sales in any four-weekly period to usage, store levels and marketing activity. In order to estimate the model, the empirical specification necessarily differed from this theoretical one in two minor respects.

We used the model to test the following hypotheses:

1. That the model specification is appropriate.
2. That as stores increase, quantity purchased will decrease, all else remaining equal.
3. As temperature increases, stores will be depleted less quickly and less will be bought.
4. As advertising increases, stores will be depleted.
5. As temperature rises, purchases fall.
6. An increase in price leads to a drop in sales.
7. An increase in advertising leads to an uplift in sales.

The final empirical model was estimated by non-linear least squares using four weekly NMRA retail audit data over the period July 1982 to January 1990 – 99 data points. The advertising data was in TVRs, the source of which was BARB. The model includes an additional advertising term for the recently introduced 'Hen Night' film which appears to be working harder than previous films and a dummy variable for a most unusual data period in February/March 1984.

The coefficients of the model all had signs consistent with the above hypotheses, demonstrating the appropriateness of the model. Apart from the 'Hen Night' campaign which was significant at the 90% level, all of the variables were significant at the 95% level. The model passes a range of diagnostic tests indicating that the data supports the theory. The reported statistical tests were: $R^2$, $\overline{R}^2$ standard error of regression, sum of squared residuals, Durbin's h-test, Lagrange multiplier tests (portmanteau tests for higher order autocorrelation) with up to 1, 4 and 13 lags, ARCH tests for auto-regressive heteroscedasticity (up to 1, 4 and 13 lags), the variance ratio test for homoscedasticity, Chow (parameter stability), Chow (post sample pred. failure), Q test (Box-Cox) 13 lags.

# 8

# Making Warburton's a Breadwinner

## INTRODUCTION

This paper examines the influence of a new advertising campaign on the bread sales of Warburton's, a regional baker based in Lancashire.

The main thrust of the paper will centre around an attempt to demonstrate three things:

1. That new advertising investing Warburton's with emotionally based brand imagery instead of product-based imagery generated a significant increase in consumer demand and sales.
2. That the nature of new consumer advertising was marketed to the trade and significantly changed their image of Warburton's – assisting in increasing distribution.
3. That the new advertising served to successfully cushion Warburton's against the subsequent launch two years later of a competitive brand, Kingsmill, marketed on a product quality platform, to which it would otherwise have been vulnerable.

The paper covers the first two years following the campaign, from 1987 to 1989. Specific ad hoc research and a computer programme were employed to monitor the effect of advertising over that period, which were then discontinued. The sales increase continues in 1990, but it is less easy to isolate the advertising effect.

Warburton's sales area at the time was confined to all of Lancashire and half of Yorkshire. Sales in both areas increased following the advertising, but the data used to demonstrate and explain the advertising effect is largely taken from Lancashire. This is for two reasons: first, the status of the brand in each region was very different – with a 19% share and good distribution in Lancashire, Warburton's was number two brand; with low distribution and 6% share in Yorkshire, it was still not yet a major player. There are effectively two different stories, and time does not allow us to go in detail into both. Second, the sample sizes available in Yorkshire from AGB and Omnibus data are considerably less robust due to the limited geography of Warburton's sales area. The focus will therefore be on Lancashire although the results in Yorkshire will be briefly summarised where possible.

## BUSINESS BACKGROUND

### *The Story of Warburton's*

Warburton's have been a family of bakers for five generations. In 1876 Ellen Warburton started baking and selling her own loaves in her husband Tom's corner shop in Blackburn Road, Bolton. She sold out on the first day; the takings were about 2½d. On the second day she baked twice as many loaves; she sold out again. Within a year they invested in a new coke-fired two-deck oven and turned the corner shop into a bakery.

Today, the main Warburton's bakery stands opposite the original corner shop. It is still run by the family; the current Marketing Director, Jonathan Warburton, is Ellen's great, great nephew. They bake over 40 different types of bread, although they are best known for their large, wax-wrapped, white sliced loaf, which accounts for 23% of their total sales.

Warburton's business philosophy is based on the belief that they should produce the finest possible quality bread. Everything else is subservient to this. It costs them a great deal of money in better ingredients and a longer baking time, and this cost is passed on to the consumer – in 1987 they were charging a 20% premium for their large white sliced loaf over its nearest competitor.

They trade in just two areas. Lancashire remains their heartland, although in the 1970s they extended their trading area into Yorkshire as well. In 1987 they were still struggling to establish themselves as a player of significance in Yorkshire: their 6% share there lagged well behind a robust 19% of the market in Lancashire. In 1990 they launched into a third area, Tyne Tees.

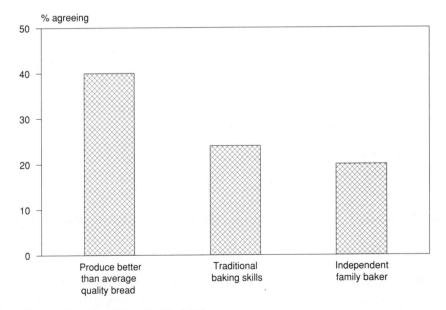

Figure 1. *Warburton's brand image in Lancashire, March 1987*
*Source:* RSGB
*Base:* All housewives

## Warburton's and the Bread Market

By 1987 the bread market in the North-West, like the rest of the UK was static.

Warburton's continued to enjoy some growth (about 2% a year), partly due to distribution, and partly due to a consumer recognition that it was an excellent quality product. This was, however, the only side of the Warburton's story that appeared to be known (see Figure 1, p169). It had little or no emotional brand imagery associated with it at all.

The trade, like the consumer, had a healthy respect for Warburton's as quality bakers, but research showed that they took a dimmer view of them as marketeers (see Figure 2).

They expressed a reluctance to give them much more business while they appeared to be production-led rather than marketing-led.

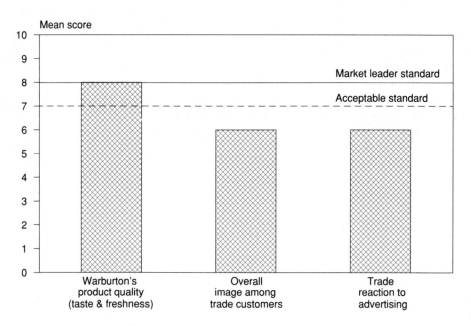

Figure 2. *Quantitative assessment of Warburton's performance amongst key trade personnel – performance vs acceptable standard*
*Source:* Research Associates, July 1986
*Base:* 37 senior trade buyers, 16 competitive sales managers

## DEVELOPING A NEW CONSUMER POSITIONING FOR WARBURTON'S

### The Brief

In 1986 Warburton's appointed a new Marketing Director, Jonathan Warburton, and a new agency, Still Price Court Twivy D'Souza. The task facing the agency in July 1986 was unusually not that of turning a 'problem child' around – Warburton's sales were doing fine – but rather to see if there was a way of boosting *still further* the performance of a brand that was already growing in a static market, but was felt by an ambitious Warburton's board to have the ability to perform still better. Their marketing objectives were threefold:

1.  To become Brand Leader in Lancashire.
2.  To become a Major Player in Yorkshire.
3.  To build a reputation in the trade as market leaders, not followers.

The agency was to go back to basics: to identify the most motivating consumer proposition Warburton's could appropriate and develop an impactful and appealing new advertising campaign around it.

### Strategic Development Findings

Warburton's were rightly very proud of their product. Our initial views were that the strongest strategy must surely centre around dramatising some aspect of the product story: the fact that Warburton's were the only baker to use the finest imported wheat, for instance, whose superior quality allowed the bread to rise 10% more than competitors' loaves. Or perhaps that the wheat's protein content kept Warburton's bread fresher longer. Or that they used less water and more wheat than the competition – all supportable claims directly talking about Warburton's product quality.

What we found in consumer research, however, is that the difference between two different loaves of bread is not seen to lie in what they are made of, but who they are made by. If you and Anton Mosimann both set out to cook the same meal, the fact that the latter's end-product turns out (the consumer thought) to taste rather better than yours is due not to the ingredients you both used, but to his skill, expertise and special 'touch'. So too with baking. We found that the fact that Warburton's had passed down the baking tradition within the family for five generations communicated product quality *far more strongly than any direct claim about the product.*

The 100 year heritage implied a knowledge of baking gained in the golden past, when bread was thought to be baked 'properly', and the family's involvement suggested a personal care in the bread's quality that was unique in a world of faceless mass-production.

In effect, the research suggested that the best way to communicate physical product quality was to talk about something else altogether: the emotional image of the people who made it. We believed this emotional imagery was so strong that people would 'self complete' all sorts of other attributes in their own minds about the physical qualities of the bread: that because the family cared, they would only use good quality, natural ingredients and so on.

All we needed to do was link the tradition of expertise and family involvement to the product on the shelf and we had our strategy: 'You can taste over 100 years of family baking in Warburton's bread'.

## THE CAMPAIGN

### *The Advertising Objectives*

Warburton's already enjoyed a high consumer loyalty and average weight of purchase amongst its existing user base; the only way to increase share would be to attract new users. The advertising objectives were therefore formally defined as:

1. To increase trial of Warburton's bread in both regions.
2. By increasing the saliency of Warburton's in the housewife's mind.
3. And by positioning Warburton's in her mind as a family baker with over 100 years of experience.

### *The Proposition to the Consumer*

'You can taste over 100 years of family baking in Warburton's bread.'

### *Target Market*

Housewives with children, 25 – 55

## DERRICK WARBURTON

# DERRICK AND JOYCE WARBURTON

### What We Wanted the Consumer to Think After Seeing the Advertising

Every Warburton's loaf looks like it has been hand baked by a member of the family, the way bread used to be.

### The Advertising Idea

The campaign idea was a very simple one: to use the family themselves in the commercials, talking about their tradition of baking and demonstrating through various comic scenarios that although they were not very talented actors, they were passionately committed to producing superb quality bread.

Three commercials ran in the first year introducing three different characters within the family. The two that launched the campaign were 'Derrick' and 'Joyce'.

*Client:*   Warburton's Limited
*Product:* Bakery range
*Date:*     4.6.90

*Title:*    JOYCE
*Medium:* TV 30 seconds

VISION

SOUND

HALF SECOND SILENCE.

Open on the real honest-to-goodness Mrs Warburton. She's wearing a pinny over her dress. In front of her, she has assembled the ingredients for making a loaf. She mixes everything together.

MVO: THIS IS MRS JOYCE WARBURTON, A MEMBER OF THE WARBURTON BAKING FAMILY.

FOR FIVE GENERATIONS, THE WARBURTONS HAVE TAKEN THE FINEST INGREDIENTS....

She kneads the dough...allows it to prove – and then tests it expertly. Before popping it confidently into the oven.

...ADDED THEIR OWN BAKING SKILLS...

Clock wipe to Joyce, looking at her watch to time the loaf to perfection. But surprisingly, it's a black leaden disaster. Mrs Warburton looks depressed.

...AND PRODUCED BREAD AS ONLY THEY KNOW HOW...

SFX: Thud!
MVO: OF COURSE, MRS WARBURTON – NÉE BOOTH – IS ONLY A MEMBER OF THE FAMILY BY MARRIAGE.

Behind her, Derrick, her husband, enters, bearing a deliciously, crusty, golden, Warburton's loaf. Mrs Warburton smiles wryly.

SO SHE HAS TO RELY ON HER HUSBAND DERRICK.

Cut to packshot. SUPER:
WARBURTON'S. BAKERS, BORN AND BRED.

WARBURTON'S. BAKERS, BORN AND BRED.

## The Media Strategy and Spend

The values embodied by the proposition were highly emotive, to do with tradition and care; television was felt to be the most effective and quickest way of putting these values across to the consumer. It was therefore the primary medium used. Posters and radio were secondary media used to maintain awareness.

TABLE 1: WARBURTON'S ADVERTISING 1987–89

|  | 1987 Lancs & Yorks | 1988 Lancs & Yorks | 1989 Lancs & Yorks |
|---|---|---|---|
| Television ratings | 1,769 | 1,600 | 1,700 |
| Poster sites | 24 | 29 | — |
| Radio bursts | 3 | 3 | 5 |

TABLE 2: WARBURTON'S MEDIA SPEND IN LANCASHIRE AND YORKSHIRE

|  | £000 |
|---|---|
| Year ending April 1988 | 415 |
| Year ending April 1989 | 664 |

## Trade Activity

Six months before the campaign broke, we produced a ten minute video, in which a media celebrity (Barry Took) presented to the trade the new advertising, and the consumer research and strategic thinking which had led to its development. This video was shown to trade buyers during the selling period and formed a key sales tool for the pre-production distribution drive.

## THE IMMEDIATE CONSUMER RESULTS

### Sales and Share

Over the next two years, the rate of growth of Warburton's bread sales increased dynamically in a slightly declining market (see Figure 3).

Brand share surged ahead in both trading areas. Warburton's gained brand leadership in Granada for the first time, ahead of Allied Bakeries, and rose to a 9% share in Yorkshire, establishing it as a major player (see Figure 4). In sales terms then, the marketing objectives had been achieved, but could we report back to the Warburton's board with confidence that advertising had been the primary influence in meeting these objectives?

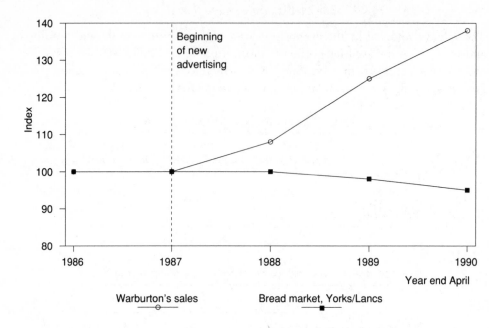

Figure 3. *Warburton's sales performance vs bread market in Granada/Yorkshire, indexed on 1986*
*Source:* Warburton's ex-bakery data, AGB
*Note:* Market index based on year ending September except 1990 – year ending March 1990

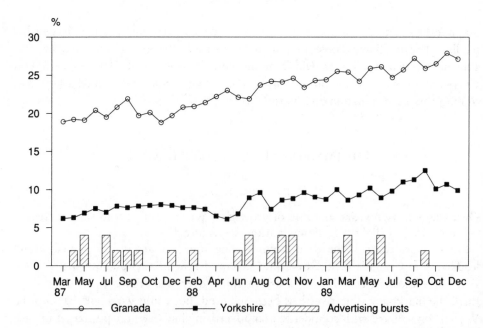

Figure 4. *Warburton's volume share in Lancashire and Yorkshire, March 1987 – December 1989*
*Source:* AGB

### Isolating the Advertising Effect

We knew only two other variables apart from advertising that might have influenced sales: packaging and distribution. The price premium of Warburton's had not changed significantly compared with its competitors.

### New Packaging

The packaging for the range had been completely redesigned, and launched in the trade in November 1986, five months before the new advertising broke. We looked at the total sales month by month over the year to see if we could identify when the growth started. We found that the upturn in sales growth only began in May. There had been no significant change for five months after the introduction of the new packaging: the sales results had only begun to accelerate once the advertising had broken. We therefore set aside packaging as the primary influence.

### Distribution

An unusual quirk of the bread market is that there is no independent distribution data; there is no available retail audit of a product that is only on a supermarket shelf for two or three days at a time. This posed a problem. Part of the marketing objectives of the relaunch had been to use the new advertising to stimulate a fresh distribution drive. They had been successful (see later) – but how could we take out the distribution effect without the availability of retail audit data?

Warburton's bread is delivered in vans, every morning, fresh to every shop that stocks it, including multiple grocers. Using the data kept by each van driver, we set up a panel of multiple grocers, who had been good customers before the new campaign broke, and who had taken no new lines of Warburton's, nor changed the number of facings over the two years following the new advertising. We then looked at the volume increase for all multiples over a six-month period (March–September) year on year, including distribution gains, compared with our panel of stores where the distribution effect had been taken out. The result – a primitive 'rate of sale', if you like – is shown below:

TABLE 3: VOLUME INCREASE DURING MARCH–SEPTEMBER AGAINST PREVIOUS YEAR

|  | 1987 vs 1986 % | 1988 vs 1987 % |
|---|---|---|
| All multiples (ie including distribution gains) | +32 | +9.3 |
| Control sample of multiples (ie excluding distribution gains) | +10 | +8.5 |

Although the increased distribution had clearly boosted sales considerably, something appeared to have increased rate of sale in the 'control' stores by 10% in the first year, and a further 8.5% the second. Advertising was the only variable left that could explain this; we therefore concluded that although distribution gains accounted for some of the sales increase, advertising had also been a primary influence.

## How Did the Advertising Work?

### Impact

Advertising awareness, brand awareness, and key image attributes were measured at four points between 1987 and 1989, using an omnibus. Of these four points, one was a 'Pre'-stage in March 1987 before the advertising broke, and the remaining three after each major burst of advertising during the following two years.

Levels of spontaneous advertising awareness doubled in the 18 months following the new campaign (see Figures 5 and 6).

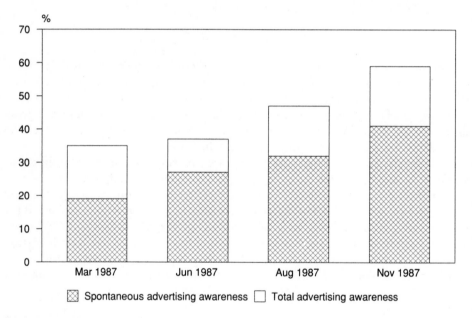

Figure 5. *Total/spontaneous advertising awareness in Granada of Warburton's*
*Source:* RSGB Omnibus
*Base:* All housewives

Prompted awareness had also risen to 59% in Granada and 58% in Yorkshire, so we were confident that people had seen and remembered the advertising. It also appeared to have increased the brand's saliency (see Figures 7 and 8). But had it affected their perceptions of Warburton's?

### Communication

We measured Warburton's and three main competitors on three key image attributes: 'An independent family baker', 'A baker using traditional baking skills' and 'A baker producing better than average quality bread'. The ratings of Warburton's over the two-year period are shown below (see Figures 9 and 10).

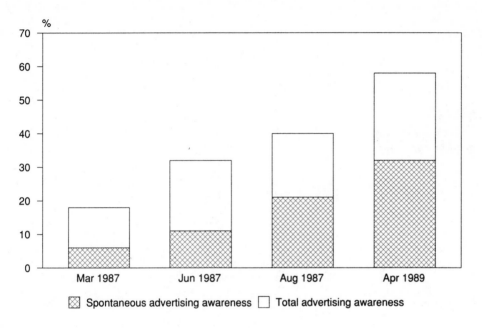

Figure 6. *Total/spontaneous advertising awareness in Yorkshire of Warburton's*
*Source:* RSGB Omnibus
*Base:* All housewives

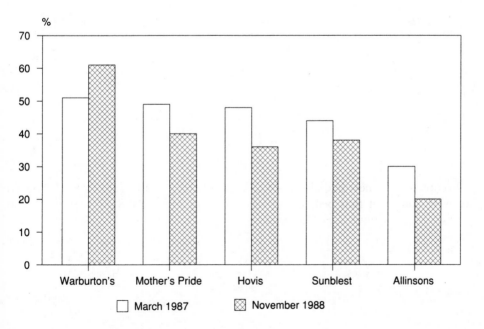

Figure 7. *Spontaneous brand awareness in Granada, March 1987 – November 1988*
*Source:* RSGB
*Base:* All housewives

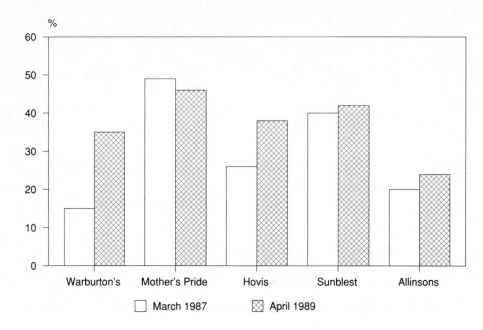

Figure 8. *Spontaneous brand awareness in Yorkshire, March 1987 – April 1989*
*Source:* RSGB Ominbus
*Base:* All housewives

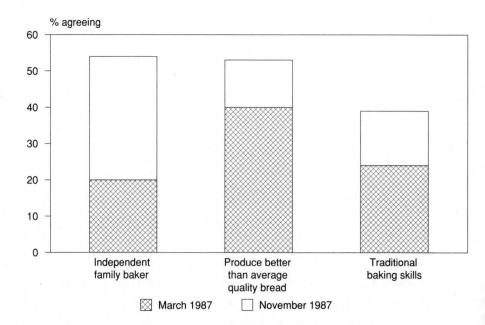

Figure 9. *Warburton's imagery for Granada, March 1987 – November 1988*
*Source:* RSGB
*Base:* All housewives

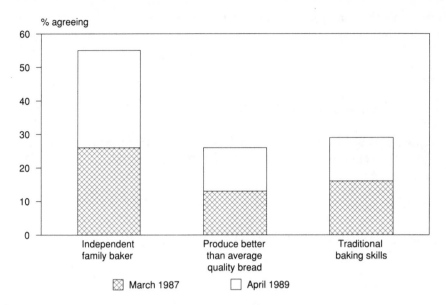

Figure 10. *Warburton's brand imagery for Yorkshire, March 1987 and April 1989*
*Source:* RSGB
*Base:* All housewives

The figures in isolation were extremely encouraging: Warburton's was beginning to develop a strong reputation as an independent baker, using traditional baking skills. This in turn seemed to have been accompanied by a significant rise in the product rating – confirming our initial strategic hypothesis. This disparity could not be explained unless advertising was influencing the image perceptions.

It was when we looked at the change in image attributes of Warburton's compared with the competition that the picture of how this image-shift was helping influence sales became clearer (see Table 4).

TABLE 4: IMAGE SHIFTS VS STRONGEST COMPETITOR

|  | Warburton's | | Competitor with strongest image | |
|  | 1987 % | 1988 % | 1987 % | 1988 % |
| --- | --- | --- | --- | --- |
| Better than average quality | 40 | 53 | 37 | 32 |
| Independent family baker | 20 | 54 | 26 | 26 |
| Traditional baking skills | 24 | 39 | 47 | 38 |

Over the 18 months following the new campaign, the brand had stopped jostling for position with other brands on a quality image and become *the* pre-eminent quality brand. Its image as a traditional family baker had also become substantially more clearly defined.

Qualitative research confirmed that the advertising was persuading consumers to think of Warburton's as being different, and of higher quality, because as bakers

Warburton's were unique in putting their hearts into baking their bread – unlike the factory lines of the competition.

'Having the family in them (the advertisements) is as if they care about the bread. It's not like a conveyor belt or factory'.

'It's as if they care about the bread; it's not like as if they're just flogging it'.

This proved, as we had hoped, an appealing idea in itself to the housewife, living in an age of faceless mass production; they saw Warburton's as not just another manufacturer, but as a small baker to whom the quality of the bread really mattered. It was then only a small step for them to imagine what the bread would taste like:

'I would like to think the bread would be substantial, wholesome, you know, really nice tasting. Not like dry bread'.

The result was an influx of new users.

### New Users

Between March 1987 and March 1989, over 200,000 more housewives in Lancashire began buying Warburton's bread.

TABLE 5:   HOUSEWIFE PENETRATION INCREASE BY REGION

|  | March 1987 penetration | March 1989 penetration |
| --- | --- | --- |
| Lancashire | 29 | 38 |
| Yorkshire | 8 | 13 |

The Yorkshire figure though, less substantial in absolute terms, was still a strong increase on 1987. The average weight of purchase over the same period dipped slightly in 1988, and then returned to the high 1987 loyalty by 1989.

Our conclusions were therefore that the advertising had been seen, and communicated the message of the family baking tradition. This had in turn not simply increased the saliency of the brand but succeeded in convincing a broader number of consumers that Warburton's was the best quality bread on the market. They had tried, and grown loyal, to the brand.

## IMPACT ON THE TRADE

Trade response to our 'marketing' of the development of the advertising was enormously positive. We were careful to repeat the exercise when we produced three new commercials to the same theme the next year. In order to gain an independent view of whether trade perceptions of Warburton's had really changed,

Warburton's bought into an independent syndicated survey of trade attitudes to the major bakers in the North.

This suggested that Warburton's had changed their standing in the trade to the point where it was now being rated *ahead* of the competition in its marketing ability and overall reputation (see Table 6).

TABLE 6:  TRADE RANKING OF WARBURTON'S FOLLOWING THE NEW CAMPAIGN

|  | % agreeing with respect to each baker | | |
|  | Warburton's | British Bakeries | Allied Bakeries |
| --- | --- | --- | --- |
| Have a good name in the trade | 60 | 50 | 29 |
| Have an efficient marketing approach | 45 | 40 | 29 |
| Are successful in controlling their market position | 50 | 36 | 32 |

Source:   Gordon Simmons 1989

What we cannot quantify, of course, is the extent of the distribution increase coming as a direct result. Qualitatively we know that the distribution gains have been considerable, and that trade buyers have gone on record as specifying the new campaign as a key reason.

## THE CONTRIBUTION TO BUSINESS

We cannot identify precisely the contribution made by advertising to business. All we know for certain is that advertising was the only variable that could explain the rise in consumer demand in the control sample of multiples, and that Warburton's profits from bread sales tripled between 1986 and 1989:

TABLE 7:  WARBURTON'S BREAD DIVISION: PROFITS 1986 – 89
1986 = (100)

| 1986 | 1987 | 1988 | 1989 |
| --- | --- | --- | --- |
| 100 | 115 | 169 | 292 |

Note:  Adjusted for inflation

(It should be noted that these figures are those of Warburton's Financial Year (ending September). The 1987 figure therefore only includes five months of sales following the new campaign).

We are unable to reveal precise figures, but we can note two further facts that may give a qualitative feel as to whether the advertising has paid for itself. The first is that the *incremental* share gains in Granada and Yorkshire according to AGB are worth over £8 million a year to Warburton's, which being a premium quality product, enjoys a higher profit margin than most.

The second is that the advertising would have to account for significantly less than half of the incremental sales in order to have paid for itself simply in terms of extra profit in the first two years alone.

Suffice to say that the Warburton's board are sufficiently confident in the power of advertising to have increased advertising budgets in both areas ahead of media inflation and have put a heavyweight advertising spend behind the launch into their second rollout area, Tyne Tees.

## THE LONGER TERM INFLUENCE OF THE ADVERTISING

In February 1989 Allied Bakeries launched a new premium brand of white bread: Kingsmill Top Grade. Their aim, trade sources suggested, was to produce a rival to Warburton's – except that Kingsmill would be launched nationally.

The launch package was a strong one. In quality, the product offered parity to the Warburton's product – consumers were equally divided on preference in blind monadic taste tests. They discounted heavily on margins to buy trade distribution, and priced their product slightly below Warburton's.

High quality, impactful white packaging reflected clearly a premium positioning, supported by heavy television advertising putting forward a 'finest quality ingredients' claim to the consumer – ie a straightforward product quality claim.

There are a number of interesting points to note about the subsequent performance of Kingsmill vis à vis Warburton's in its trading areas:

1. The share of Kingsmill is significantly lower in the Warburton's trading areas than in the rest of the country (see Table 8).

TABLE 8: KINGSMILL SHARE

| Region | Share (%) |
| --- | --- |
| National (excluding Lancs & Yorks) | 4.2 |
| Lancashire | 3.2 |
| Yorkshire | 2.8 |

Source: AGB.

2. Kingsmill's growth in Lancashire and Yorkshire does not appear to have grown at the expense of Warburton's, its most obvious competitor, whose share has also risen steadily (see previous charts). While we do not have a gains/loss analysis, brands that have lost share over this period are mainly Sunblest and Mother's Pride. This suggests that Kingsmill is only succeeding by growing the premium sector at the expense of the 'commodity' brands, rather than by taking share from the existing premium brand.

What this suggests is that Warburton's has been unaffected by the Kingsmill launch. In areas where Warburton's trade, Kingsmill have been unable to grow by taking share from the existing premium sector (and had to *grow* the sector – a harder task, hence a lower share). We would suggest that two years ago Warburton's would have been vulnerable to such a launch operating as it did, solely on a product quality platform. By switching to a unique, emotionally based consumer communication platform, Warburton's established a robust brand image. Through this, they were able to imply product values that circumvented the potentially damaging launch of a physically identical competitor (employing a quality ingredients advertising strategy alone). Two further pieces of data reinforce this belief.

3.  We quantitatively tested the Warburton's proposition (Brand X is a 'Bread from a Family Baker with Five Generations of Experience) against the Kingsmill proposition (Brand Y is a 'Finest Quality Loaf using the very best ingredients') in two regions in February 1990. The results are shown below:

TABLE 9:  COMPARATIVE PROPOSITION TESTS
Which of the two would you prefer to buy?

|                          | Tyne Tees | Lancashire |
|--------------------------|-----------|------------|
| Prefer Family Tradition  | 53        | 63         |
| Prefer Best Ingredients  | 31        | 25         |
| No preference/neither    | 16        | 11         |

Source:  SGA

Tyne Tees, exposed to only one month of Warburton's advertising and a year of Kingsmill, preferred the 'Family Tradition' story even if baldly stated in words alone. In Lancashire, 'educated' by two years of Warburton's advertising, this preference was even more pronounced.

4.  The same study included a more detailed competitive image battery. Interestingly, Warburton's outperformed Kingsmill on product attributes as well as the 'Tradition' and 'Care' attributes in Granada.

TABLE 10:  IMAGE OF WARBURTON'S VS KINGSMILL
% AGREEING

|                                | Granada |    | Tyne Tees |    |
|--------------------------------|---------|----|-----------|----|
|                                | Wrb     | Km | Wrb       | Km |
| Uses highest quality ingredients | 30    | 11 | 6         | 10 |
| Long history of bread baking   | 53      | 3  | 27        | 1  |
| Uses natural ingredients       | 34      | 10 | 15        | 11 |

Source:  SGA
Base:   All aware of each brand

The advertising (and the packaging) does not directly make any claims for Warburton's about ingredient quality, yet consumers have inferred such qualities from somewhere.

There are two conclusions we would draw from this. The first relates to Warburton's. Although the data is not conclusive, it suggests that the new advertising campaign repositioning Warburton's in terms of emotional 'Family Tradition' imagery allowed the brand to remain unaffected by the launch of a brand designed to mimic it in terms of product quality. Although Kingsmill's launch was not anticipated when we developed the new campaign, the latter seems to have done more for Warburton's than simply increase sales.

The second is a broader implication for the marketing and advertising of brands. It is this: brands marketed on product quality alone, at the expense of emotional imagery, leave themselves vulnerable to competitive attack. An emotionally-centred brand positioning may not only be more motivating and appealing in itself than a product story alone, but may also indirectly communicate key product attributes more effectively than a direct product sell.

## CONCLUSIONS

We conclude that:

1.  The advertising had a measurable effect on increasing consumer demand, and was directly responsible for the shifts in brand imagery which led to an increase in consumer trial in both Lancashire and Yorkshire.
2.  As such, it had been instrumental in meeting Warburton's marketing objectives of becoming brand leader in Lancashire and a significant player in Yorkshire.
3.  The advertising had served as the focal point for a trade re-evaluation of Warburton's and as such played an important role in securing the distribution increases that followed.
4.  The move from a reputation for product quality to a more emotionally led story had secured a stronger position for the brand to resist an unanticipated new launch of a direct competitor, marketed on a product quality platform, a launch to which in 1986 it might have been considerably more vulnerable.
5.  The image-based 'Family Tradition' story, although not centring around product attributes (eg 'made from natural ingredients'), seemed to have been communicating them more successfully *implicitly* than an attempt to do so overtly.
6.  Although an estimate of the increased profit resulting directly from the advertising is impossible (the lack of independent distribution data precluding econometric analysis), the evidence suggests that even if one ignores the help of advertising in gaining new accounts, it has played a major part in tripling Warburton's profits in the years following the relaunch.
7.  We may not have increased sales as rapidly as Ellen Warburton did over her first two days trading. But it has still been an impressive growth for a brand that has already been on the Lancashire market for 110 years.

## APPENDIX: THE WARBURTON'S (BRAND X) AND KINGSMILL (BRAND Y) PROPOSITIONS USED IN THE COMPARATIVE TEST

'Brand X are a family baker who made their first loaf in 1876. Their unique baking skills have been carefully passed down from father to son for five generations. Now, five generations on, they're still baking their traditional family loaf the way it used to be, with traditional quality you can really taste.'

'Brand Y spare nothing when it comes to choosing the ingredients for their bread. They believe that making the finest quality family loaf requires the very best ingredients in the baking process – only then can you taste the quality.'

# Section Three

*New Consumer Goods and Services*

# 9
# Crown Solo – The Paint That Rewrites The Rules

## INTRODUCTION

This is a case history about breaking from the straitjacket of the past. It concerns Crown – the number two brand in the UK domestic paint market. A brand which, like many others in a 'number two' slot, is constantly under attack from the market leader above it and cut-price own label competition below it.

Over the last decade Crown has stoically withstood this pressure. Within the gloss paint sector it retained a 19% volume share from 1980 to 1987 – never deviating more than one percentage point from this average. The company was successful but if it was ever going to grow it needed to do something dramatically different.

## THE TEAM BEHIND CROWN SOLO

The vehicle to lift Crown's fortunes came to be called Crown Solo. Its development involved a broad team of specialists: paint technicians at Crown, a new product development house, pack design specialists and layer upon layer of researchers at all stages. To tell the whole tale would be inappropriate in a paper about *advertising* effectiveness. However, the success of the launch does not 'belong' to JWT, but must be shared by the whole team: not least a client that was prepared to rewrite the rules in all areas, *including* advertising.

## MARKET BACKGROUND

In 1988 UK householders bought an estimated 165m litres of paint at a retail value of £450m. Gloss paint is an important sub-section of this market: on a narrow definition of 'top-coat' gloss (which we will use in this study), it comprises some 24m litres at £90m retail, while on a wider definition to include specialist exterior gloss, satin finish, primer and undercoat it reaches 41m litres at £170m retail.

Gloss has retained a stable share of paint purchases in recent years. However, since 1988 all paint sales have declined by some 10% pa due to the slump in house moving. It waits in line with most durable and DIY sectors for interest rates to fall and sales volume to recover again. These market conditions added further pressure for Crown to find a way to take competitive share without cutting prices.

## THE NEED TO INNOVATE

More sales *and* higher prices for a number two brand? Advertising alone was unlikely to be enough: Dulux could counter too quickly and in 1987 spent more than six times the Crown media budget of £1.4m (MEAL).

The chosen Crown strategy was to build share through the introduction of additional sub-brands at premium prices. These brands to stand alongside the existing Crown range. Success required the new brands to have added values which are both relevant and accepted by consumers and, vitally, the retail trade.

Two tasks were paramount:

1. Innovation in paint technology with a focus on the *process* of painting. Benefits were sought which would apply to the mass market of paint sales: gloss and emulsion, white as well as other colours.
2. Advertising to bring the benefits to life and thereby challenge the existing preconception that Dulux made the best paints. Their market dominance in sales terms inevitably led to an attitude leadership on all aspects of paint quality. Our advertising would need to cut through this preconception without the over-claiming that would subsequently lead to disappointment and, later, rejection.

## WHY GLOSS PAINT?

Crown tackled gloss paint first – emulsion following two years later in the form of Crown Advance. Gloss paint was given priority for several reasons:

— It has been relatively neglected by the leading manufacturers. The last major innovation was the development of non-drip gloss by Crown in 1967.
— Dulux has the more 'feminine' image of the two brands. An image which it reinforces with heavy advertising expenditure showing new paint styles and decorative effects in glossy magazines (£1.8m in 1987 and £3.5m in 1988: MEAL). We believe it to be more vulnerable to competitive attack when Crown adopts a more 'masculine' stance, ie talking about functional benefits. Functional benefits are particularly relevant to gloss paint because:

  1. Most people find gloss painting rather unpleasant, difficult and time consuming.
  2. A need for gloss paint tends to be triggered by a requirement to renew the surface on wood or metal, to give a durable coating and to provide protection, ie more performance-based criteria.

3.   Fashion is of little relevance to gloss paint since over two thirds of sales are in brilliant white, and much of the rest are shades of cream and off-white with just a splash of primary colour, typically for the front door.

—   The kind of gloss paint that people buy reflects the attitudes of the person in the family who does the painting (over 90% of men and two thirds of women). Those with higher levels of painting skill tend to choose liquid gloss (the preference of the 'professional painter'). Those who recognise themselves as 'bodgers' tend to always choose non-drip gloss. The vast majority of people lie between these extremes – changing between forms in response to the expected difficulty of the specific task ahead or as a reaction to the success or failure of the last job tackled. Neither form is entirely satisfactory.

—   With so little innovation white gloss was tending towards a commodity market with a growth of low-cost retailer brands and the regular price promotion of bigger brands as 'traffic builders' in the DIY multiples.

—   Crown itself had been making steady progress in its share of the coloured gloss market but was declining in the much larger white gloss sector (Figure 1). Something dramatic was needed to restore Crown white gloss sales share and improve profitability.

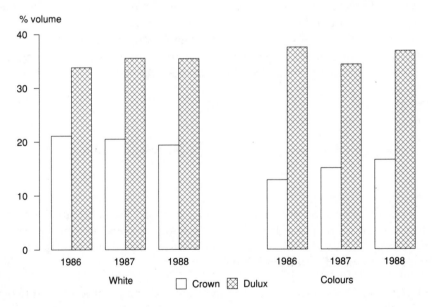

Figure 1.  *Market shares gloss paint, years to March*
*Source:* HPR 1986 – 1988

## WHAT IS CROWN SOLO?

The technical innovation behind the origination of Solo was the development of a new kind of thixotropic (thickening) system. This enabled a gloss paint to be made that has a creamy consistency rather than being thin, like liquid gloss, or jellified, like non-drip gloss.

Some of the advantages of Crown Solo to the user are:

— It is easier to apply than either liquid or non-drip. It is thick enough not to drip but unlike existing 'non-drip' does not break down and become runny when stirred or during application. The retention of a thicker consistency makes it both easier to apply on narrow difficult jobs (like small window frames) and also less likely to run on big surface areas (like doors).
— This ease of use means the 'non-expert' painter gets excellent results quicker.
— A thicker layer of paint is applied: thus obliterating the previous surface better.
— It is better than other paints in giving a smooth finish on poorer surfaces by filling small cracks and crazing.
— On most surfaces it needs no undercoat (also true of non-drip but never well communicated or accepted by consumers).
— It has a lower odour than most other gloss paints.

## THE ADVERTISING STRATEGY

We have already said that the key *motivator* for buying gloss paint is to renew surfaces, produce a durable coating and provide protection. Crown Solo is as good as other paints in these characteristics but not significantly better.

While giving reassurance on performance on these motivators for buying gloss paint, the advertising had to establish *discriminators* that would initially:

1. Promote trial.
2. Justify a premium price.

Later, a continuation of the same advertising theme would need to build the brand values to:

3. Ensure repeat purchase.
4. Safeguard the position of Solo against imitators who would eventually copy its thicker paint formulation. It was vital for Solo to become a 'brand' in its own right and not just a kind of paint from Crown that could be copied by all competition including retailer brands.

Product testing, pack testing and communication testing all proceeded in parallel through 1987 and into early 1988. A key requirement for communications was to keep the target group as wide as possible by not letting the application benefits so overwhelm the message that the response came back that this was a paint just for 'bodgers'.

From this work came a key descriptor of the Solo brand as the only 'self-undercoating' paint. From a product with many benefits (low odour, drip free, creamy texture, etc) came a brand which certainly had the advantage of not needing an undercoat but this is *not the sole basis of its appeal*.

## THE ROLE FOR ADVERTISING AND CREATIVE BRIEF

Although Crown is well known and has a good reputation, it inevitably stands in the shadow of Dulux. Dulux, being brand leader, is assumed to have the best paints overall, even though both brands sit side by side in terms of actual physical performance.

The role of advertising was to use the real product superiority of Crown Solo to attack Dulux with its *specific* benefits in the gloss market sector. Again there were problems posed by existing consumer attitudes. We found that most DIY painters feared that application benefits could only be achieved at the expense of ultimate quality and durability of finish.

The task was looking daunting:

1. Overcome an in-built belief that Dulux made the best paint.
2. Stress application benefits: but people will expect these to compromise the quality of the finish.

It was clear that the advertising was going to have to overturn existing beliefs about gloss paint on both fronts. The advantages of Solo lay in the quality of the product itself and in consumers' responses to it in the extensive home trials. Once it was tried even the most cynical or traditional paint user was utterly convinced.

The creative brief became quite straightforward. Talk to the large majority of gloss paint users who are neither bodgers at one extreme, nor semi-professional experts at the other. Tell them in the most dramatic way that everything that they believed about gloss paint is changed by the arrival of Crown Solo.

In response terms they should feel challenged and stimulated to find out for themselves if it is true (this being made easier by widespread availability of free or low unit price 250 ml trial packs).

The lead benefit was confirmed through research to be the self-undercoating claim: a tangible benefit that would help people to justify paying a premium price and which underpinned the whole proposition of being quicker and easier to use.

## THE CREATIVE SOLUTION

The creative solution featured a larger-than-life product demonstration, actually filmed in an airship hangar. The traditional rules about gloss painting are not just 'dismissed' but physically painted over with one coat of Crown Solo. You *see* the truth of the claim of not needing an undercoat.

The style is hard and challenging with an almost surreal quality, quite unlike any other advertising for paint. It is deliberately masculine in tone to provide reassurance that this is a serious, high quality, durable paint.

The contrast with the more feminine approach of Dulux and the Dulux dog is extreme. Against a backcloth of soft, enjoyable paint advertising Crown Solo stands out like a white pea in a pea-pod. It is, of course, deliberate. The style of advertising reinforcing the claim that Crown Solo is the Gloss Paint that 'Rewrites the Book' (subsequently amended in newer campaigns to Crown: Paint that Rewrites the Rules).

## CROWN SOLO PAINT

sound: music and location effects in background to end

male: YOU WILL NOT PAINT ON BARE PRIMED

YOU WILL APPLY A SECOND UNDERCOAT

YOU WILL RUB DOWN THE FIRST TOP COAT

YOU WILL ALWAYS USE...

2nd male: CROWN HAVE MADE A REMARKABLE NEW PAINT

3rd male: YOU WILL ALWAYS USE AN UNDERCOAT

NOT ANY MORE YOU WON'T

female: A CREAMY HARD WEARING GLOSS THAT NEEDS NO UNDERCOAT

WHATEVER PRECONCEIVED IDEAS YOU HAVE ABOUT GLOSS PAINT

BRUSH THEM AWAY

CROWN SOLO THE GLOSS PAINT THAT REWRITES THE BOOK

## THE MIDLANDS TEST MARKET

Crown Solo was launched into the Central ITV area in July 1988. It was initially available in brilliant white only. Colours followed from the time of the national roll-out in 1989.

Without doubt a most significant aspect of the launch was the brave stand taken on pricing. As Figure 2 shows, the branded white gloss market had become so deal oriented that both leading brands were regularly supporting their 'premium' over own label by offering 1.25 litres for the price of 1 litre. In effect this means that for much of the time the Dulux price per litre was no higher than that for own label.

Figure 2. *White gloss paint prices at Solo launch, one litre can*
Source: Nielsen Aug/Sep 1988

## MEASURING SUCCESS: WHY NO MARKET MODEL?

We are taking the unusual step of making an IPA Advertising Effectiveness submission without a market model. Let us be up-front with the reasons for this:

1.  Our data for the Midlands test is limited to 10 bi-monthly periods with the first period coinciding with the launch. This is not enough for reliable modelling.
2.  The success of the advertising is easily seen by eye and is confirmed by the national launch a year later. A model adds nothing in terms of *genuine* reinforcement of the case.
3.  Seasonality is not an issue because we consider only Crown *shares* of the total market.
4.  Price is not an issue because Solo was so much more expensive than anything else on the market. We will also show that other Crown lines were increased in price relative to both the market and Dulux.
5.  Distribution will be dealt with separately.

## THE DATA SOURCE

The primary data source is the Nielsen Home Improvement Index. Measurements have been available on a totally consistent basis from June/July 1988. Also from this date, and up until December/January 1990, a special panel boost was operating on behalf of Crown in the Central TV area.

The Nielsen audit covers all main trade sectors selling retail paint, ie DIY major multiples (eg Texas, Homebase, Payless, Woolworth), paint and wallpaper specialists (eg FADS), grocery multiples, superstores (eg Asda, Tesco etc), DIY and hardware independents.

## CAMPAIGN WEIGHT

For both the Central test and the national extension Crown Solo was advertised with one 40-second film plus a 10-second 'cut-down'. The MEAL estimated value of the campaign and adult ratings by spot length are shown in Table 1.

TABLE 1:  TELEVISION CAMPAIGNS MEAL EXPENDITURE AND ADULT TVRs

|                     | £000  | 40 sec | 10 sec | Total |
|---------------------|-------|--------|--------|-------|
| 1988 Central launch | 445   | 741    | 410    | 1,151 |
| 1989 GB launch      | 2,165 | 514    | 765    | 1,279 |

Press and posters were used as supplementary media.

TABLE 2:  PRESS AND POSTER MEAL EXPENDITURE

|                     | £000 | £000 |
|---------------------|------|------|
| 1988 Central launch | 28   | 15   |
| 1989 GB launch      | 65   | 350  |

At the time of the 1988 launch the bulk of the other Crown advertising (£3.6m MEAL) was supporting the full range of coloured paint (ie gloss and emulsion). This activity ceased in 1989.

## ADVERTISING SUCCESS IN CENTRAL

Figure 3 plots advertising in terms of 30-second equivalent adult ratings against volume shares of the white gloss market achieved for Solo and Total Crown (ie Solo plus liquid and non-drip brilliant white gloss). With a concentrated launch burst of advertising, Solo climbs rapidly to a share of just under 18%. Through the winter it falls while unsupported to 10%. The spend pattern in 1989 is more evenly spread and the shape of the Solo sales share responds accordingly, with a plateau of just under 20% during advertising, falling at turn of year to 13.5% when support is withdrawn.

The trend for Total Crown white gloss is similar. The original liquid and non-drip versions suffered a share fall from the launch of Solo of just two percentage points on average. *The net result was a growth of sales share* for total Crown from below 20% of the market to over 30% in October/November 1988 and for the whole of the peak April/September sales period of 1989.

We can be confident that this rise was caused by the advertised launch of Solo by comparing the 1988 results with the relatively flat performance of Crown white gloss paints in the rest of GB (see Figure 8).

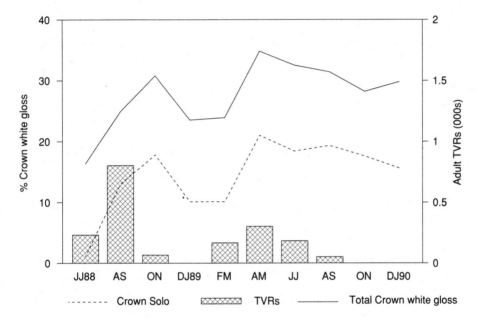

Figure 3. *Crown white gloss market share, Central TV area*
*Source:* Nielsen

On top of this volume share growth Figure 4 shows the effect of Solo on the average selling price of Crown white gloss paint. *From spring 1989 onwards Crown has moved from price parity to charge between 74p and 94p more than Dulux for each litre of white gloss paint sold.*

Combining share volume growth with higher retail prices has truly allowed Crown to rewrite the rules of the market as it has *gained sterling share leadership in white gloss paint in Central* (Figure 5).

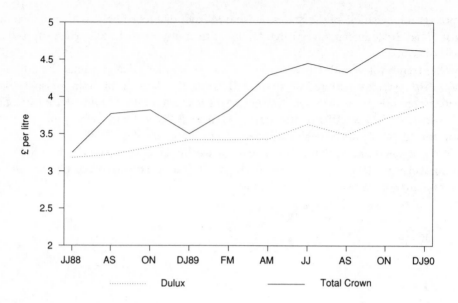

Figure 4. *Average selling price, Central TV area, white gloss paint*
*Source:* Nielsen

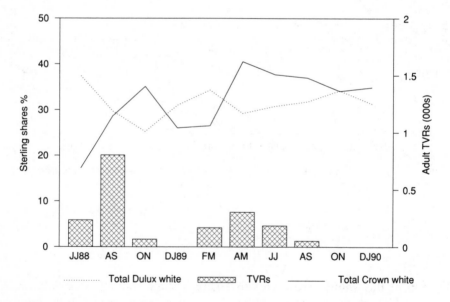

Figure 5. *Crown and Dulux white gloss shares, Central TV area*
*Source:* Nielsen

## DISTRIBUTION EFFECTS

Solo achieved approximately two thirds sterling distribution for its Midland test, rising to 85% at the time of the national launch in 1989.

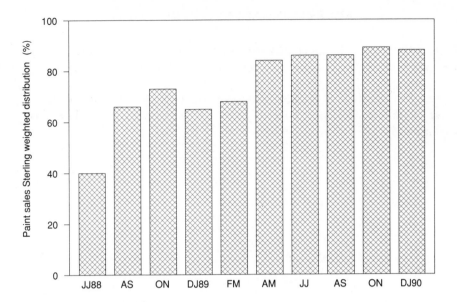

Figure 6.  *Crown Solo distribution, Midlands TV area*
*Source:* Nielsen

The effect of distribution on sales has been removed in Figure 7. This presents an estimate of the monthly sales of Solo per shop stocking. It is still clear that the sales trend closely matches advertising patterns (with a lag of one period). During the campaign, average turnover is around £200 per month against £100 without advertising.

Although they have a positive effect on sales, distribution gains in no way negate the case for the effectiveness of the Crown Solo advertising.

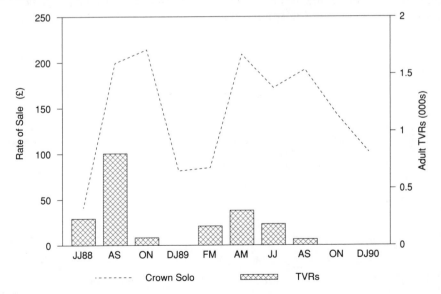

Figure 7.  *Central TV area, sterling rate of sale (average solo turnover per average shop per month)*
*Source:* Nielsen

## ADVERTISING SUCCESS IN REST OF GB

In its 1989 national launch, Crown Solo showed the same success that was recorded in Central. For brevity, the following figures are left largely as self explanatory.

From TV launch Solo rapidly achieves 18% volume share of the white gloss market – falling back after advertising to 13.5%. Total Crown white gloss rises from around a 20% to a 30% volume share.

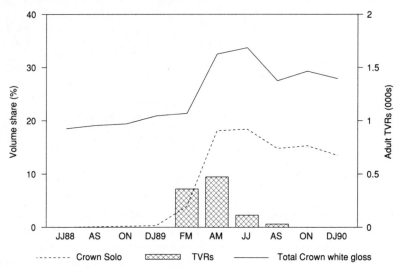

Figure 8. *Crown white gloss market share, rest of GB*
Source: Nielsen

Crown moves from selling at a discount to Dulux to charging on average an extra 68p for every litre of white gloss paint sold.

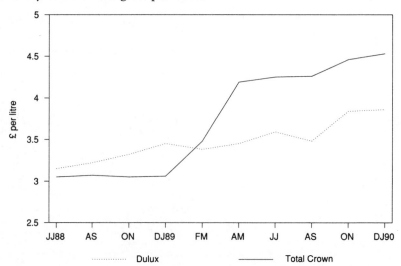

Figure 9. *Average selling price, rest of GB, white gloss paint*
Source: Nielsen

Crown has now overtaken Dulux in terms of its sterling share of the white gloss market.

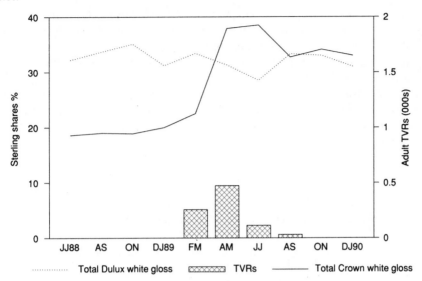

Figure 10. *Crown and Dulux white gloss shares, rest of GB*
*Source:* Nielsen

## TOTAL GB SALES PERFORMANCE

The long-term trend of decline in Crown's share of the white gloss market has been reversed in spectacular fashion. If we update Figure 1 – allowing for caution over an unavoidable switch of data source – it is clear that this is a number two brand which has really broken from the past!

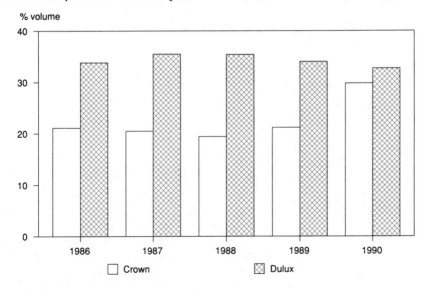

Figure 11. *White gloss market shares, years to March*
*Source:* Nielsen 1989 – 1990, HPR 1986 – 1988

## HOW DID THE ADVERTISING WORK?

We had developed creative work which we hoped would stand out and make people rethink their attitudes to gloss paint. We wanted to challenge people – particularly in the area of not needing an undercoat when using Crown Solo. Once challenged, the only way people could resolve any remaining doubts about our claim was to try the product.

Sales results for Solo at an unmatched price premium suggested the advertising could have worked in this way. Direct advertising research – qualitative, quantitative and on-air responses – is all coherent and consistent in confirming this interpretation.

### Pre-testing

Qualitative pre-testing by The Research Marketing Consultancy confirmed the strong appeal of the commercial. To quote from their report:

> 'The *curiosity* of all was raised by the bold simplicity of the claim in the commercial. The directness of the message helped it to sink in'.

> 'The *authority* of the Crown brand is sufficient to give credibility to the claim'.

> 'There is some scepticism and indeed cynicism about the 'no undercoat' claim, but the main motivating force of the ad is curiosity, which can only be satisfied by *trial* of the product'.

### Quantitative Communication Check

A Millward Brown impact and communication check on the finished film reinforced the strength of this commercial in conveying the core benefits of a new paint that does not need an undercoat.

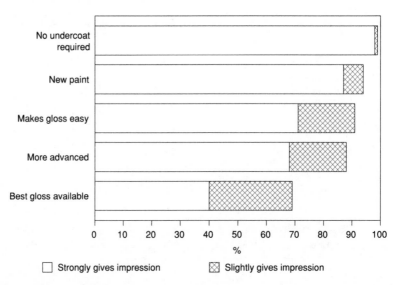

Figure 12. *Quantitative communication checks*
*Source:* Millward Brown

Given the market dominance of Dulux, the levels of motivation to try Crown Solo were also exceptional.

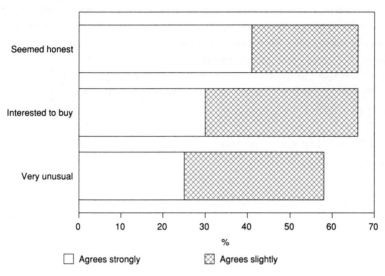

Figure 13. *Quantitative communication checks*
*Source:* Millward Brown

### Response to the Advertising on Air

A Mass Observation survey in May 1989 confirmed all of the pre-testing about the strong call-to-action generated by the advertising. Over half of respondents (56%) remembered the advertising and, although it was by no means as 'amusing' as the main competitor's current campaign, it scored exceptionally highly on being informative and leading to a desire to try the paint.

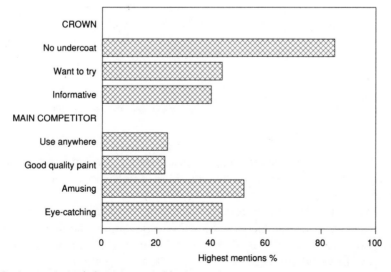

Figure 14. *On-air communication check, main messages and descriptors*
*Source:* Mass Observation, May 1989
*Samples:* Crown 248, Main Competitor 399

## THE TOTAL CROWN PORTFOLIO

The decision by Crown to concentrate its promotional activity behind Solo raised a fear of its vulnerability in other markets: notably emulsion paint. In fact these fears were totally unfounded and our promotion of Crown Solo appears to have helped the Crown brand to grow across the board.

Figure 15 traces the trend in six monthly volume sales shares for the major paint sectors before, during and after the launch of Solo. Total volume sales share for emulsion and, perhaps surprisingly, liquid gloss are both more than 10% up on the previous year. Where Solo has cannibalised previous Crown sales it has been confined to non-drip gloss but with the two combined, the total sales share is some 50% above a year ago.

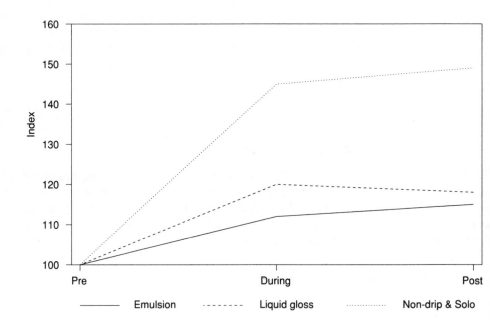

Figure 15. *Crown shares of paint markets, total GB index of volume share*
Source: Nielsen pre-August 1988 – January 1989, during February – July 1989, post August 1989 – January 1990

None of this growth can be attributed to price dealing. Crown has not responded to the temporary market decline by 'buying share' and has increased prices relative to the market as a whole in all sectors.

By accumulating all paint sectors (ie including those like exterior gloss and masonry paint where Crown has no national representation) the period of the Solo launch is associated with a 20% gain in volume share and a year on year 35% gain in value share for Crown in total.

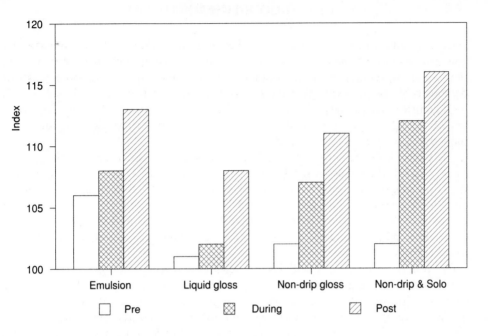

Figure 16. *Crown prices relative to the market*
*Source:* Nielsen pre-August 1988 – January 1989, during February – July 1989, post August 1989 – January 1990

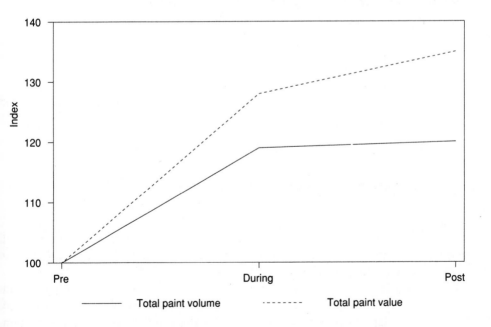

Figure 17. *Crown shares of total paint, total GB index of market share*
*Source:* Nielsen pre-August 1988 – January 1989, during February – July 1989, post August 1989 – January 1990

## CONCLUSION

This case history has been about a number two brand that used a combination of new product development and mould-breaking advertising to improve both its sales share and its retail prices. It would not have worked if Crown Solo was not demonstrably better than other gloss paints. Equally, a product with such a high market price would never have achieved rapid trial against the better regarded market leader if advertising had not stopped people in their tracks and convinced them that Crown Solo really was different.

The payback of the activity is difficult to assess. The Crown advertising spend in 1989 was *less* than that in 1988 (£2.5m vs £4.2m: MEAL). Instead of supporting the range of Crown paints, advertising was concentrated behind a single new brand designed to exploit what was perceived to be an aspect of vulnerability with a competitor. A key marketing lesson is that this focusing of marketing resources not only achieved brand leadership in the chosen sector but has actually been of benefit to the entire Crown range.

The full financial return will become clearer when people again start moving home and decorating more often. Share gains in a depression can be more fully cashed in during a recovery. Likewise a new respect from trade and customer alike has stood Crown in good stead to expand Solo into coloured gloss (where it has also now produced total Crown sterling brand leadership) and more recently Advance one-coat emulsion (launched in 1990).

Crown has adopted the mantle of a number two brand that tries harder. Advertising is the successful and visible manifestation of this: advertising which, like Crown Solo, has been determined to rewrite the rules.

# 10

# The Case for Radion Automatic: A New Brand in the Lever Portfolio

## INTRODUCTION

In October 1989 Lever Brothers launched their first dual variant (liquid and powder) detergent brand for over a decade. They did so in one of the most competitive and well established of all consumer markets; that for low-suds washing products.

In this, the largest of all grocery markets, dominated by heavyweight brands like Persil and Ariel, Radion established a significant 7% (value) market share within the first six months of its life supported by a distinctive product promise and an aggressive advertising campaign.

That the launch campaign for Radion Automatic has enjoyed a certain notoriety is perhaps an understatement. The campaign has been criticised, not least from within the advertising fraternity. The advertising has been described as harsh, brash, vulgar and offensive and is accused of setting the industry back 30 years. It has been parodied by 'alternative comedians' and widely reported in the national press.

This paper argues that while the Radion commercials were not the best-liked creative executions, they were strategically sound and highly effective in ensuring the successful launch of the brand.

Establishing Radion as a success in its own right, however, would not have satisfied Lever Brothers. Although it is a necessary condition of success, the performance of Radion must also be seen in its context as one of several Lever brands. Radion must be judged by its contribution to Lever's portfolio.

The risk of launching a detergent which cannibalised its stable mates was all too apparent.

Advertising, therefore, played a crucial role; not only by helping to establish a new brand in such a cramped market-place, but by positioning Radion as a complement to Lever's existing brands and as an alternative to those manufactured by the main competitor, Procter & Gamble.

## THE LOW-SUDS DETERGENT MARKET

The low-suds sector represents over 90% of the detergent market. Regarded by many as the epitome of a fmcg market, it is both well established and fiercely competitive.

In 1989 the GB grocers detergent market as measured by Nielsen was worth over £638 million (at RSP). The market has grown steadily from the early 1980s averaging an increase of 8.6% per annum since 1984 (by volume). Lever Brothers and Procter & Gamble dominate the market, between them accounting for over 85% of volume.

Prior to Radion's launch the market was divided as shown in Figure 1.

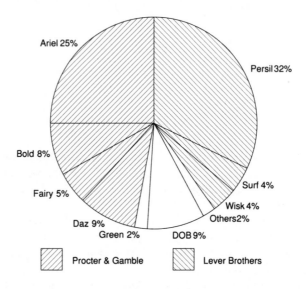

Figure 1. *Low-suds market segmentation, value share, September 1989.*
*Source:* Nielsen

While Lever held the market leader in Persil, its overall share was approximately 5% less than Procter & Gamble.

Throughout the 1980s some significant changes had taken place, the most important being the introduction of liquid detergents. The first liquid to be launched was Wisk, but this format was quickly adopted by all major brands. More recently powder concentrates have been introduced, notably Ariel Ultra.

Thus, while the market-place remained dominated by a few established brands, the introduction of new product variants and package sizes in recent years had increased choice for the consumer and competition for shelf space among manufacturers.

The level of advertising expenditure for low-suds brands bears testament to the competition between them. Media Register figures for 1989 show Persil spending £15.6m on advertising, Ariel £17.0m and Bold £8.1m. Total Ariel spend (powder, liquid and concentrate) made it the fourth best supported brand in all markets in 1989. Only the Water Flotation, Woolworths and Sky TV campaigns accounted for more media expenditure.

Persil and Ariel are brands with heritage. As market leaders they are universally known and widely trusted. However, Persil and Ariel have very distinct characteristics, appealing to housewives in different ways. Ariel is considered to be a modern and effective product particularly good at removing stains. Whilst Persil is also an effective cleaner, it is perceived as being used by more caring people and as being softer on clothes. This is demonstrated in the 1989 Millward Brown image statements below:

| | **Persil** % | **Ariel** % | |
|---|---|---|---|
| Bought by people who care about their family | 38 | 30 | |
| Leaves clothes feeling soft | 21 | 14 | |
| | 27 | 33 | Are modern and up to date |
| | 27 | 43 | Are particularly good at getting out stains |

It would be fair to say that Persil and Ariel tend to characterise the imagery for Lever Brothers and Procter & Gamble respectively. Procter & Gamble advertising has historically tended to depend upon a definitive functional platform whilst that for Lever products has offered a more emotional appeal.

## THE MARKETING TASK

In 1980 Lever Brothers held 61% of the market by value. Their share fell to 43% in 1984 when they were overtaken by Procter & Gamble as Persil lost 5%, largely to Ariel. By 1988 Lever's value share had slipped to below 40%.

How could Lever stem this decline?
Could Lever regain market leadership from Procter & Gamble?

International experience from the mid 1980s provided Lever with a possible key to the solution of this dilemma: 'Dirt and Odours'.

In 1984 a low-suds detergent with a dirt and odour removal proposition was launched in the USA. It was based on a Unilever patented technology, a unique deo-perfume system which deodorises clothes rather than merely masking odour. Exceeding all expectations it became the second best selling brand in the USA and has since been successfully launched into eight European countries.

Odour removal, it seemed, could be a motivating proposition and Lever Brothers believed that their international success could be repeated in the UK. The task for Lever's was to establish Radion Automatic as a major brand in this fiercely contested market-place.

The first year objective for penetration was set at 35% and that for repeat purchase at 24%.

These were bullish objectives and while the international record was encouraging, the enormity of Lever's task cannot be underestimated. Meeting these objectives depended upon two related issues of overwhelming strategic importance.

1. How was Radion to attract consumers away from long established brands?
2. Furthermore, how could Lever ensure that sales of Radion were not gained at the expense of their other brands?

## THE MARKETING SOLUTION

The strategy developed to overcome these issues was to position Radion as a *superior* alternative to competitive brands and a complement to Lever's. This strategy entailed two distinct but interrelated components.

First, Radion was to be promoted in a very different style from Lever's existing brands such as Persil and Surf. From packaging to advertising, support would be executed in a non-Lever manner.

In direct contrast to the gently toned lifestyle advertising which Persil employed, advertising for Radion would be required to promote modernity, vigour and uncompromising cleaning power.

Similarly the packaging was designed in bright 'day-glo' colours instead of the traditional soap powder bias towards white. Research showed that Radion packs communicated 'excitement', 'powerful cleaning' and 'modernity'.

This positioning was designed to ensure that Radion did not cannibalise its Lever stable mates. Introducing a brand which competed on the platform of uncompromising cleaning power, Radion would complement Persil, 'the caring brand'. It was intended that this would reinforce Persil's position in the battle for corporate market leadership.

Secondly, Radion was to redefine the parameters for judging a detergent's effectiveness. The issue of odour removal needed to be defined as an important additional part of the cleaning power of the product. Radion needed to be positioned as 'owning' this power, thereby offering a tangible benefit to the consumer and a proof of its greater cleaning effectiveness.

The bulk of this task fell to advertising and TV was chosen to execute this dual communication.

The strapline 'Removes Dirt *and* Odours' was reinforced by its appearance on other promotional material and on the pack itself.

Promotions were planned to support the launch: six million sample packs were to be distributed in stores between September and November 1989 and a further ten million door-to-door samples were to be dropped in February and March 1990. An on-pack cash-back promotion was also to be offered for the first two months of launch.

Lever's pricing policy for Radion reflected its positioning. Launch prices for Radion were set at parity with other premium brands for both liquid and powder.

## THE ROLE FOR ADVERTISING

Advertising had a critical role to play in defining Radion's positioning and credentials. Three objectives for advertising were laid down:

1. To *create awareness* of the launch of Radion.
2. To *communicate the brand's USP* – unbeatable cleaning across the wash with unique odour removal benefit.
3. To *help prompt consumer* trial.

The primary target audience was defined as front-loading automatic (FLA) owning housewives, especially those currently buying strictly effective detergents. Radion was designed to appeal to those housewives who were attracted to a functional cleaning promise and responded to a didactic and authoritarian tone in advertising. Radion advertising had, therefore, to confront the traditional cleaning promise head on and to surpass it with the unique odour removal benefit. The proposition used was:

> New Radion is as good as any other brand at cleaning and removes lingering odours that they sometimes leave behind.

## THE ADVERTISING SOLUTION

### Creative Executions

Advertising for the UK was not developed from this proposition in isolation. Given Radion's international heritage, executions for the UK drew heavily upon experience from the USA and Belgium. Both confirmed the potential of using a very direct creative execution.

The USA launch used a traditional 'slice of life' advertising format in which the product was presented in a 'real life' family situation.

Several executions were developed for the UK in this mould. Using scenes such as ('New Fence') a father and son erecting a fence or a father and children building a shed ('Reflections'), they emphasised the family's reaction to the father's offensively smelling shirt while working, followed by approval of the clean shirt once it had been washed by Mum using Radion. The odour removal message was reinforced in these executions by the use of a computer graphic representation of the shirt and a demonstration of Radion's deodorising action.

The style of the commercial was up-beat, lively and bright; the message was presented clearly, using perhaps larger-than-life characters. A male voice-over stressed the odour removal message in an authoritative tone while the computer graphics stressed the scientific validity of the product claims.

In contrast to the softer tone of, for example, Persil's lifestyle ads, Radion's advertising was hard sell.

In Belgium however, an even 'harder' format was introduced: the news-reader.

Experience there, later confirmed in the Ulster test market, showed the more direct approach to be particularly successful in creating heightened impact over the crucial first two months of launch. The commercial developed for the UK ('Presenter') used a news-reader to present Radion as a news story. On a screen behind him a woman was ironing and her family reacted to the odour from the clothes. The presenter solved her problem by handing her a packet of Radion.

The commercial was introduced by loud 'news style' music which, followed by the commanding tone of the presenter, made the advertising difficult to ignore. Again the presenter conveyed authority and validity. The message was delivered by the simple line 'Radion Removes Dirt *and* Odours'. The news style presentation added an urgency to the message and finished with the line 'New Radion. Try It'.

The consistency of this communication was maintained across all media for the UK launch.

Executions developed for radio followed the same news format. They capitalised upon the pervasive Radion news music to support the TV commercials and to add urgency to the message.

Posters supporting the launch were designed in a bold, impactful style. These featured simply a pack shot and the line, 'Radion Removes Dirt *and* Odours' printed large in Radion's bright 'day-glo' orange. The colour was eye-catching and an important branding tool for Radion, which the posters were designed to reinforce.


*Media Strategy*


The media strategy for Radion was designed to complement the creative executions. Radion was to achieve media dominance and ubiquity. Television was to run continuously over the first six months averaging nearly 1,200 TVRs per month. Throughout this time it was to be supported by radio and posters.

TV was targeted at all housewives but particularly heavy detergent users with a C2D bias. Flexibility was built into the media plans allowing spend to be switched, to combat competitive bursts. The importance of matching competitor media activity had been demonstrated by the test market experience. There Radion had suffered a temporary share decline six months into the launch. This coincided with a decrease in Lever advertising of 36% and a 50% increase in competitor advertising of another brand.

Posters and radio were used to outflank the competition. They both reiterated the core dirt and odour message and added to the presence of the campaign.

## 'PRESENTER' STILLS

## THE UK LAUNCH PROGRAMME

The launch of Radion in the UK took two discrete stages. A test market launch in Ulster in January 1989 which preceded by eight months its introduction to Great Britain.

### The Test Market

In a market where Procter & Gamble has traditionally held a higher share than in Great Britain (68% compared with 45%), Radion's functional and authoritative positioning worked well. The launch was successful in securing for Radion a 16% value share (14% volume).

Consequently Lever's corporate share rose from 31% to 46%, Procter & Gamble's fell to 51%.

These results encouraged Lever to continue their launch programme without delay.

### The Launch of Radion in Great Britain

Radion was launched on 2nd October 1989 supported by advertising, on-pack promotions and product sampling. The TV campaign broke with a 40 second commercial 'Presenter', which ran until late November when it was shown in rotation with 'New Fence'. 'Presenter' ran in 40 and 20 second formats throughout the first six months. 'New Fence' ran until January 1990, when it was replaced by 'Reflections'.

Radion accounted for over one third of total detergent market TV activity between October 1989 and March 1990 and consistently out-rated all other brands. Radion's rating pattern is shown in Figure 2.

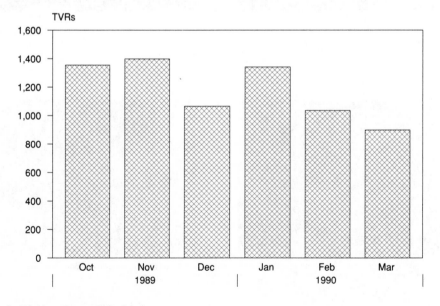

Figure 2. *Television ratings over Radion launch*
Source: AGB

From October 1989 Radion's market share had grown to 7% (value) by March 1990 (Figure 3). By that stage it had overtaken the smaller brands in the market such as Fairy, Wisk and Surf and was only 0.7% (value) behind both Bold and Daz after just six months.

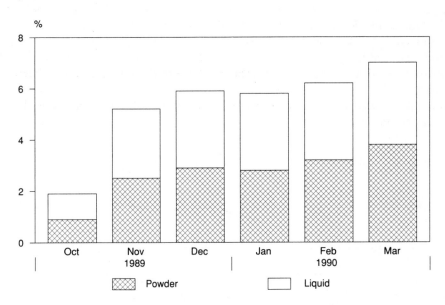

Figure 3.  *Radion market share (value)*
*Source:* Nielsen

By April 1990 cumulative penetration had reached 25% of the market, which was also on target for its first year objective.

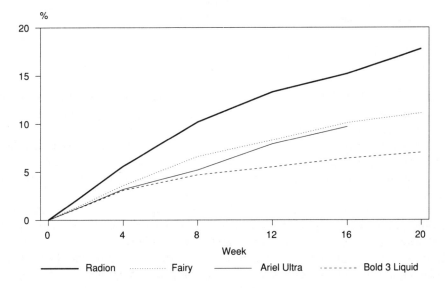

Figure 4.  *Cumulative household penetration for 1989 detergent launches*
*Source:* AGB

Radion has performed well by comparison with the other new detergent launches of 1989. Fairy Automatic, also a new brand to the low-suds market, was launched (in both liquid and powder variants) earlier in 1989. Bold 3 liquid was launched just two weeks before Radion and Ariel Ultra four weeks afterwards.

Figure 4 shows the cumulative household penetration built by Fairy, Ariel Ultra, Bold Liquid and Radion at equal intervals following their respective launches. It demonstrates that Radion has reached more households faster than any other new brand in 1989. Again this happened despite a considerable distribution disadvantage to its competitors and before door-to-door sampling had begun in January 1990.

Radion has also out-performed these brands in building market share. This is clearly demonstrated in Figure 5.

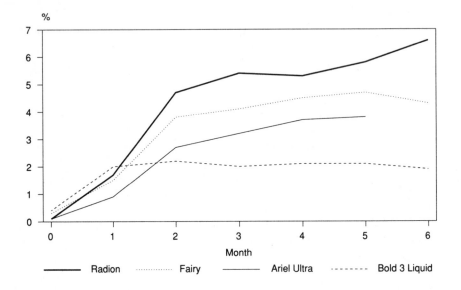

Figure 5. *Monthly market share (volume), for 1989 detergent launches*
*Source:* Nielsen

The success of Radion was achieved despite some significant adverse factors. First, distribution levels were limited by the fact that Radion was not stocked by Tesco until the end of March 1990.

Secondly, the number of new product launches in 1989 was atypically high. Although out-performed by Radion, they exerted competitive pressure through restricted supermarket shelf space and further exacerbated the distribution situation.

Finally, Radion successfully weathered competitor spoiling advertising. Procter & Gamble attempted to pre-empt Radion's odour removal claims by screening an Ariel odour removal commercial before and during Radion's launch.

Radion's success has not been as a brand in isolation, it has also met Lever's more fundamental objective of contributing to the company's portfolio. Over the period of Radion's launch, Lever's volume share of market rose from 41.7% to 44.8% and has overtaken Procter & Gamble in the process (see Figure 6).

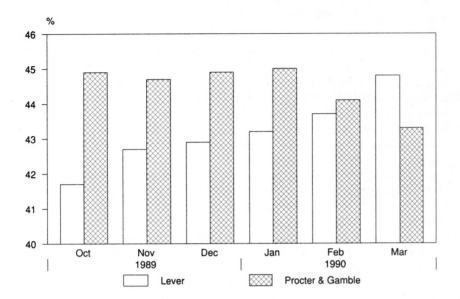

Figure 6. *Lever Brothers vs Procter & Gamble market share (volume)*
*Source:* Nielsen

## ADVERTISING PERFORMANCE

Having established both Radion's brand success and its contribution to Lever's portfolio, *advertising's unique contribution remains to be more fully demonstrated.*

Radion's advertising was certainly noticed, demonstrated by the high level of awareness it generated. The combination of high spend and branded memorability has led to Radion very rapidly obtaining 82% awareness (Millward Brown) within two months of launch.

The campaign also topped *Marketing*'s Adwatch list, a measure of consumers' spontaneous recall of advertising, for 21 weeks. Only recently has it slipped to fifth in the chart.

In could be argued, however, that Radion's advertising success was entirely a function of media weight. Indeed, Radion has enjoyed a considerable media spend in generating this level of awareness. High spend was required to endow Radion with the status and credibility otherwise reserved for established brands. However, in such a high spending market Radion's spend of £8.9m (October to January) would not be considered unusual for a launch. It represented approximately only half the annual spend of Ariel or Persil.

The requirement for such a spend and the evidence that it was employed efficiently is provided by the Millward Brown awareness index. This is a measure of the extra (ie that above base awareness) advertising awareness generated per 100 TVRs. Derived using a modelling process it enables the effectiveness of a campaign to be compared having allowed for, inter-alia, the difference in sheer media weight between campaigns.

Against these criteria Radion's launch advertising performed well, achieving an awareness index of 8, by far the highest in this market as shown in Table 1.

TABLE 1: MILLWARD BROWN AWARENESS INDICES (October – November 1989)

|  | Advertisement | Index |
|---|---|---|
| Radion | Presenter | 8 |
| Persil | Oil Change | 3 |
| Ariel Auto | Odour Campaign | 1 |
| Bold 3 | Michael Elphick | 1 |
| Ariel Ultra | Greener | 2 |
| Daz | Spiderman | 3 |
| Fairy | Sumo | 2 |

Advertising, however, has not worked simply to achieve success for Radion, but has positioned Radion to complement other Lever brands; achieved by a communication which stressed the modern and effective cleaning power of the brand. Furthermore, the advertising has introduced the concept of odour removal as an ultimate test of the product's cleaning power and has conferred ownership of this property on Radion.

Advertising's contribution to this positioning is demonstrated by a Millward Brown finding that of all those recalling 'Presenter', 70% stated spontaneously that 'Radion gets rid of smells'. The comparable figure for those recalling Ariel's odour removal ad was just 19%, despite the fact that this spoiling ad had run from prior to Radion's launch.

The impact of Radion's launch upon brand images in the low-suds sector is shown by the image map (see Figure 7). Based upon the images attributed to brands by consumers, the map shows how Radion is perceived relative to its competitors.

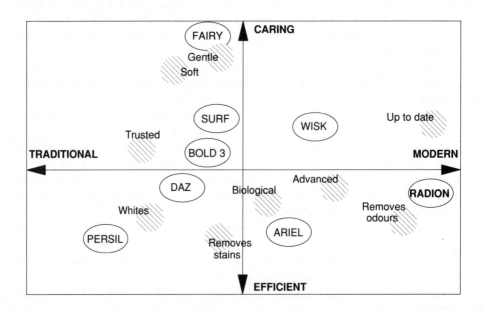

Figure 7. *Detergent brand image map*
*Source:* Millward Brown

The communication of odour removal as a vital part of the cleaning process has placed Radion in the modern/efficient quadrant of the map. It is clearly differentiated from the Lever portfolio, Persil in particular, and is placed high on the modern axis.

Analysis of AGB TCA panel data suggests that Radion's advertising has not only impacted in terms of brand imagery, but that it has also been successful in determining the source of Radion's share.

AGB gains/loss analysis estimates the expected share for a new brand. It is based upon the assumption that the expected source of volume for a new brand is taken from existing brands in approximate proportion to their market shares, with an adjustment made for differences in brand loyalty.

Thirty weeks of consumer panel data from pre and post launch clearly shows that Radion has not cannibalised the Lever portfolio. Naturally, Radion did take some share from all detergent brands; however, it did not do so simply in proportion to the market share of those brands.

Radion took a greater than expected amount of volume from the Procter & Gamble brands, Ariel, Daz and Bold, but less than expected from Persil. Specifically it took 15% more volume from Ariel than was predicted by AGB according to Ariel's market share and user loyalty. Conversely, the volume Radion took from Persil was 7% less than expected from the AGB prediction.

## HOW THE ADVERTISING WORKED

Radion advertising has not enjoyed popular support. It has achieved notoriety by flying in the face of the accepted advertising trend reflecting the caring 90s, the new man/woman, the lifestyle ad and the soft sell. It is rare to find anyone who would admit to liking the Radion advertising and yet the product has already been used by over 21% of households.

Qualitative research has revealed that this unusual result has been achieved *because* of the bold and even authoritarian style of the advertising. The news style presentation of Radion was extremely striking, impactful and authoritative. The message was clear and forceful: Radion is new, different and much more effective – it removes odours.

The research concluded that this communication worked by challenging the housewife. By challenging her confidence in her wash it dares her to try Radion. The loudness of the approach prompts some dislike and recoil but this only serves to strengthen Radion's position as a challenge to be met. The authoritative tone makes Radion more credible to the housewife who seeks perfection. This challenge is neatly summarised by the woman who said:

'That dreadful advert made me buy it'.

The research also discovered that the advertising polarised housewives' attitudes. The woman who seeks effectiveness and has her belief in Daz/Bold/Ariel shaken by Radion advertising rises to the challenge. The woman who seeks gentle caring values in a detergent brand, however, ignores the challenge.

In this way the advertising has tended to attract the competitor franchise to Radion but has repelled those who would constitute the core buyers of a 'caring' brand such as Persil.

This effect demonstrates the appropriateness of Radion's advertising. Radion advertising can be seen, therefore, as an accurate translation of the core marketing strategy into a creative execution.

## CONCLUSIONS

Radion's advertising campaign has contributed to the success of the brand both through its high level of impact and strong communication.

The bold manner with which a traditional advertising format was presented ensured a powerful impact. Awareness of the advertising has been high. Moreover, high awareness has been combined with strong endorsement of Radion's message.

Advertising has been highly successful in positioning Radion as a complement to Lever's portfolio. This has deflected competition from Lever's core brand Persil and has enabled Radion to steal share from competitor brands, rather than cannibalise its stable mates.

What has added interest to this case is that in achieving these results the campaign has attracted criticism. Importantly, as our tracking studies and qualitative research have shown, the campaign has not even been liked by its target audience.

The case also shows, however, that far from this being a barrier to success, the uncomfortable and assertive stance which provoked this dislike has been a key factor in the advertising's effectiveness.

# 11

# Advertised Without Compromise, Evaluated Without Mercy

## *How Advertising Helped Renault Successfully Launch the Renault 19*

### INTRODUCTION

The Renault 19 was launched in February 1989. This launch was key to Renault: the first model of a totally new range replacement programme, symbolising, according to Renault's annual report, 'a new era for the Renault Group'. The aim of this paper is to show that advertising made an important contribution to that objective.

The car market is an example of a market in which measuring advertising effectiveness is particularly difficult[1]. It has several important characteristics:

— It is a concentrated market. In 1989, the top ten manufacturers held 86% of the market[2].
— Consumers differentiate between domestics and imported marques. The 'big three' domestics (Ford, GM and Rover Group) share 55% of the market[3].
— Perceptions of marque images change extremely slowly and consumer prejudices are strong (bad experiences and expensive mistakes).
— It is an important, unusual purchase, and most people take the safe option. Loyalty is the norm: out of 100 people who replace their car with a new car, 35 buy the same model and 20 another model of the same make[4].

All these factors generate tremendous market share inertia: nine out of the top ten manufacturers in 1989 were the same as in 1984. It is therefore unrealistic to

---

[1] Paul Feldwick has himself made this point, 'Motor cars provide a particularly difficult field for evaluation where the long-term effects of advertising may pay off only after years for a particular individual. At the same time it is difficult to isolate the sales effect of advertising from the more obvious effect of model changes or competitive launches'. *The Longer and Broader Effects of Advertising*, IPA, ed. Chris Baker.
[2] Source: SMMT. Methodologies, sample sizes etc for sources quoted throughout this paper are indicated in Appendix 1.
[3] Source: SMMT.
[4] Source: NCBS, model year 1989.

expect that advertising, or any other short-term marketing action, can improve overall sales volumes significantly and permanently (except, of course, for very small marques).

Isolating the contribution of advertising in the car market is also difficult. Although some car buyers do fall in love at first sight, the decision-making process for most people is probably very long, compared to other markets. Clearly, innumerable influences are exerted on potential buyers, eg current driving experience, product ubiquity, advertising, press reviews, knowledgeable friends and salespeople in the showrooms. Empirically, we believe the real decision-making process takes up to three months, although advertising also has to influence the millions of drivers who are not, at a particular time, actively considering buying a car (see Figure 1).

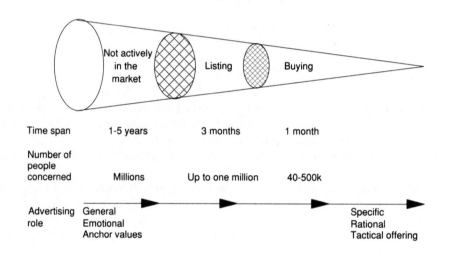

Figure 1. *An empirical car purchase model*
*Source:* Qualitative research

However, the task of assessing the advertising's contribution is made easier by the exceptional amount of existing information on the car market. Daily sales figures, syndicated studies looking at model and marque consideration and advertising tracking studies are available to all major manufacturers. Furthermore, Renault make it a priority to build a relationship with their buyers and to solicit information from them. The result of this effort is an important marketing tool for Renault UK: the Renault CustomerLink database which surveys customer profiles and attitudes.

In this paper we will be looking at the progress of the Renault 19 from its launch in late February through the key August selling period and beyond – the 'introductory' phase of this product's life cycle – and trying to assess the contribution of advertising. It is important to remember that during this period other variables were influential which we cannot quantify, eg accumulated prejudice, dealer bonusing, regional availability of Renault 19 and competitive models. We shall, therefore, be using traditional measures of success, eg recall, communication, attitudes, sales and buyer profile matched against the pre-launch situation and the strategic objectives of Renault UK.

What we will ultimately prove is that, while sector credibility was a key weakness impeding Renault's progress, *advertising helped build a perception of the Renault 19 as a good quality car.* Advertising therefore allowed Renault to attract a new type of driver who would previously not have considered the marque. Moreover, advertising made a positive contribution to Renault marque imagery, commensurate with corporate requirements to communicate the start of a new era for Renault.

## THE PROBLEM AND THE SOLUTION

Before demonstrating how the advertising worked, we need to explain briefly the context within which it was expected to perform, the brief upon which it was based and the creative thinking behind the campaign.

### *The Context*

1. *The Lower Medium Sector*
   No mass manufacturer can afford to ignore the lower medium sector of the car market: it is consistently the biggest sector. However, it has a reputation for being somewhat unsexy. The key volume models are the Ford Escort and Vauxhall Astra; the Volkswagen Golf is the image leader and there is a serious challenge from the Peugeot 309, theoretically a fellow French car, but increasingly perceived as European, or even, since the launch of the Ryton-manufactured Peugeot 405, as British. Hatchbacks like the Renault 19 dominate with 75% of sales. Lower medium sector buyers are less affluent than other buyers. Both qualitative and quantitative studies show that they are often reliability and price obsessed, more often concerned with the cost of ownership than the purchase price.

2. *Renault History in the Sector*
   The Renault 19 was designed to replace the Renault 9 saloon and Renault 11 hatchback, which had in recent years never exceeded 1% of the market. In their day (ie in the early 1980s), these models had been successful for Renault. They were perceived as typically Renault: comfortable, a bit stylish and different; and thus they attracted a loyal but small band of aficionados. These drivers were on average 8 – 10 years older than other sector drivers. So although it was important to retain them, it was essential to attract younger buyers, and in order to do this we would need to gain conquest sales from mainstream marques.

3. *The Product*
   Corporate literature extols the ingenuity of the Renault 19's design and the efficiency of its production process. Although the development of Project X53 (as it was known) had only taken 43 months, the testing of the product had been more rigorous than for any previous Renault model. The result was a car

that represented an exceptional improvement in build quality and aerodynamics for Renault. Significant consumer-oriented technological advances had been made, eg to keep running costs to a minimum, service intervals had been extended (first service now at 12,000 miles). The company was understandably proud. However, third parties such as journalists and car clinic (ie blind test) respondents considered the product evolutionary rather than revolutionary.

### The Brief

Renault UK briefed Publicis to produce advertising to the following brief:

1.  *Establish the Renault 19's credibility*. As a non-Germanic import, this meant building a strong perception of quality, solidity and modernity.
2.  *Widen Renault's appeal* in the sector by attracting a younger, more mainstream audience. Although the mere fact of being a French import keeps Renault off many buyers' shortlists (see Figure 2), the car had to be a clear departure from the 'specialist' or even 'eccentric' cars Renault had been selling in that sector.
3.  *Force a marque reappraisal* by sector buyers, ie 'Renault is now better than I previously thought'.

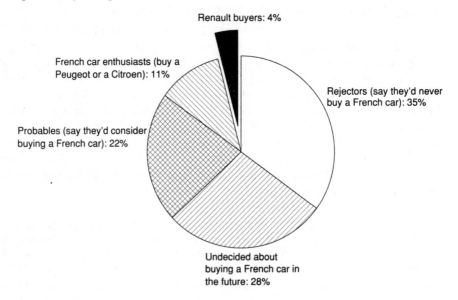

Figure 2. *Attitudes to buying a car of a French marque*
Source: MIL, QED, SMMT

Sales of the new model were expected to reflect the achievement of these objectives and an ambitious target figure of 27,000 units was set.

From this brief, Publicis developed an advertising strategy aimed at communicating design superiority, build quality and modernity based on the proposition 'It is the solidity and aerodynamic styling of the Renault 19 which make it desirable'. The brand personality was expressed as tough, modern, dynamic and strong. It was also intended that a strong feeling of progress and improvement for the marque should be communicated.

### The Campaign

Publicis developed an integrated multi media campaign, written by Chris Waite and John Aldred under the creative directorship of Tim Mellors. The campaign line was 'Renault 19 – Designed without compromise, tested without mercy'.

The campaign began with a poster teaser which featured the car's hallmark – a Picassoesque logo in yellow and white symbolizing modernity and dynamism. The idea of the TV commercial (directed by Steve Barron) was to show the car coming to life during design and testing phases and finally driving freely on a country road before merging into its yellow and white signature. The serious nature of the designing/testing message was complemented by an exciting 'technical' sounding version of the *Blue Danube* written specially by Malcolm McLaren. In creative development research, respondents were shown how the visual technique would work by using a well-known pop video (a-ha's *Take on me*) in which the mix of real life and drawings are cleverly mingled.

The press campaign reflected exactly the spirit and message of the TV commercial. On the first weekend, a specially developed spread appeared in the *Mail on Sunday*'s *You* magazine. This ad recreated the TV commercial even more realistically by combining the car's design on tracing paper over the car's full glory photographed below. Copy was written which specifically answered respondents, desires for 'all the information and homework but in an exciting way'.

Creatively the campaign bent one of the golden rules of car advertising: it eschewed always showing the new car in all its glory in favour of a better communication of the car's development process.

The media investment for the first year was £7.5 million. The launch TV burst in February/March consisted of 600 60-second men TVRs. The subsequent two bursts were 400 30-second men TVRs in June and November. 70% of the media spend was in TV, 23% in press and 7% in posters.

## HOW IT WORKED

To show how advertising contributed to the Renault 19's success, we will follow a simple five-step approach, summarized in Figure 3.

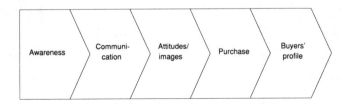

Figure 3. *A five-step demonstration*

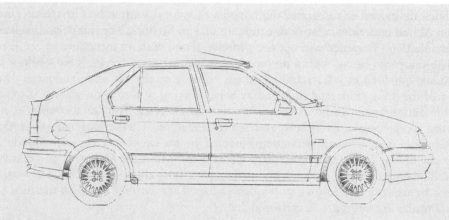

*Designed without compromise.*

*Tested without mercy.*

The beauty of the new Renault 19's profile is clear. But stylish new clothes, even ones with 0.30 Cd aero-dynamics, can deceive.

Too often they're just a cover-up for the same old model as last year's.

This car is an exception. It started life as a clean sheet of paper. The designers gave the Renault 19 an extra-long wheelbase for more space, secure roadholding and a smooth ride.

And inside, a thoughtfully planned driving environment where everything comes to hand and many 'extras' come as standard.

For example, the driver's seat has adjust-able lumbar support; and the front seat belts are height-adjustable. Consider too the new 1.4 litre 'Energy' engine. 80 bhp is more than many 1.6s can manage – and so is 108 mph.

Yet cruising at a test speed of 75 it squeezes 42.8 miles from each gallon. The

choice of leaded or unleaded is yours. Three other engines are available. They include an even quicker 92 bhp 1.7 litre, and a 65 bhp 1.9 litre diesel version.

All torture-tested in temperatures ranging from 50°C above zero to 30°C below.

And then tested again.

(The Renault 19's total test mileage before launch was equivalent to driving to the moon and back. Not once, but 10 times.)

You'll also welcome the back-up of the 300-strong Renault dealer network, plus a year's free membership of the RAC.

Yet one test is still to come. Your first drive in the new leader of the hatch pack.

The new Renault 19 from £6,520 – £9,520. Visit your local dealer or phone 0800 400 415 (24 hrs/free) for a brochure. All Renault cars have a 12 month unlimited mileage and 6 year anti-perforation warranty.

THE NEW RENAULT 19

FROM £6,520

CAR FEATURES RENAULT 19 TXE PRICES (CORRECT AT TIME OF GOING TO PRESS) INCLUDE VAT, CAR TAX, ELECTRIC GLASS SUNROOF AND SOUND SYSTEM, ALLOY WHEELS, DELIVERY AND NUMBER PLATES EXTRA. RENAULT FINANCIAL SERVICES PROVIDE A COMPLETE RANGE OF VEHICLE PURCHASE PROGRAMMES. RENAULT recommend elf lubricants.

## Awareness

The absolute advertising awareness figures achieved by the campaign (see Figure 4) are not unprecedented for Renault advertising in other sectors, but in this sector Renault was starting from a low base, ie zero residual advertising awareness. As a small brand, Renault demand that their advertising work hard for them. Their launches do not attract the sort of PR, rapid familiarity and general razzamatazz that domestic marques can expect and which appear to favourably affect their advertising awareness. Moreover, the idiosyncratic use of numbers by Renault to name their models tends to confuse people.

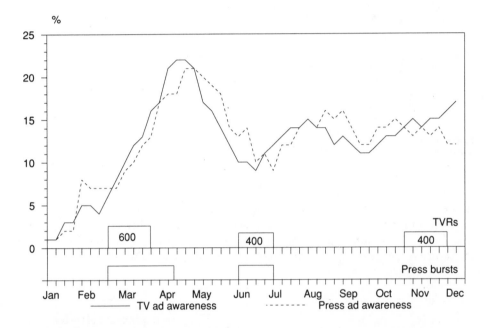

Figure 4. *Renault 19 advertising awareness, 1989 – 8 week rolling periods*
Source: Millward Brown

As Millward Brown noted in a report on the launch in July 1989, 'noticeability of the Renault 19 ad compares favourably with previous launch ads for other imports', thanks mainly to the graphics, which are 'a powerful creative device that gets the ad noticed'.

After the first TV burst, the Renault 19's awareness was number two in its sector, second only to the Peugeot 309, which continued to bask in misattributed awareness from the Peugeot 405 launch. And if we compare the Renault 19 with the launch of the Fiat Tipo, another import in the same sector suffering from a comparable lack of awareness and image problem, the model branding is five times higher and the marque branding six times higher (see Figure 5). To launch the Tipo, Fiat spent £7.2m, ie only marginally less than Renault.

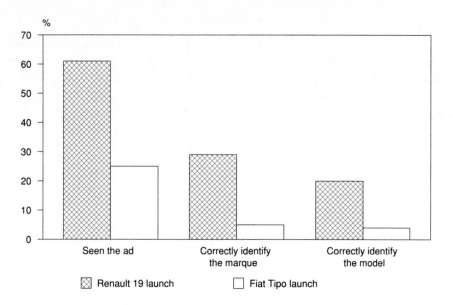

Figure 5. *Prompted recall of TV adverts from descriptions: Renault 19 and Fiat Tipo*
Source: Millward Brown

## Communication

Impressions given by the ad are precisely in line with the strategy. Figure 6 shows how the ad scored on all dimensions tracked by Millward Brown, at the end of the first burst. It is quite clear that quality, range improvement, specification and consumer-oriented design are effectively communicated by the ad.

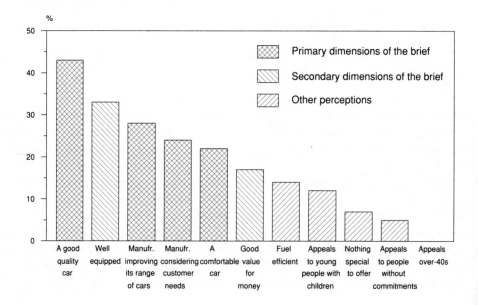

Figure 6. *Impressions given by the advertising*
Source: Millward Brown, 8 weeks to 19/5/90

## *Image/Attitudes*

The model's image, as shown by the ranking of all the descriptors prompted by Millward Brown, gave the Renault 19 perceptions of comfort, attractive styling, roominess, reliability and build quality (see Figure 7). These latter were all the more important as they are unusual for Renault.

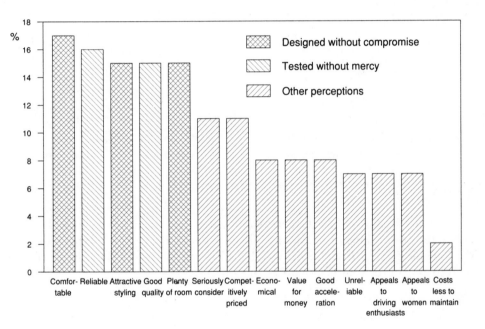

Figure 7.  *Renault 19 model image, July 1989*
*Source:* Millward Brown Model Images, 14/7/89

There is another way of showing how significantly Renault's marque image in the lower medium sector has been improved by the Renault 19 launch. The QED/RAP Monitor provides a useful indicator, called 'Perceived Net Improvement': it is the percentage of people planning to buy a car in the segment in the next six months who think the marque is changing for the better, less the percentage of respondents thinking the opposite. This indicator is slow-moving. Empirically, marques that top the Perceived Net Improvement chart prove to be image and market share winners in the medium to long run. In a nutshell, it is the best available indicator of a marque's *perceived dynamism* in a particular segment of the car market.

If we look at this dynamism indicator in the Renault 19 sector, Renault was a clear loser in July/October 1988, but a year later, the marque had overtaken Ford, VW, Nissan and Rover and ranked fourth in the 'dynamism' league (see Figure 8).

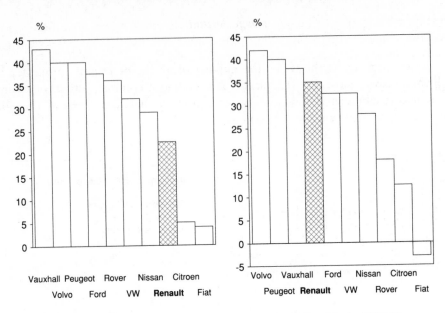

Figure 8. *Perceived net improvement of top 10 marques in the L.M. sector, October 1988 (left) and October 1989 (right)*
*Source:* QED

This was a totally unprecedented result for Renault (see Figure 9). Indeed, it was even a record-breaking result: despite previous marketing success, particularly with the Renault 5 and Renault 25, Renault had never achieved a 35% improvement score, in any of the sectors monitored by QED.

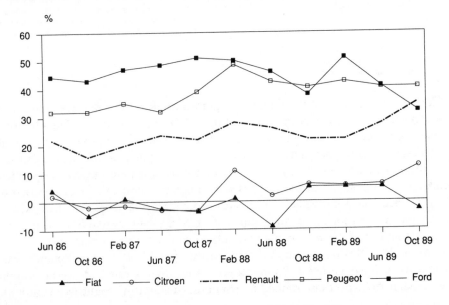

Figure 9. *Perceived net improvement of selected marques in the L.M. sector, June 1986 to October 1989*
*Source:* QED

Finally, the Renault 19 launch had a perceptible effect on the marque's image: perceptions of style and quality (which are, almost literally, the two key dimensions of the execution) for the marque at large, shot up when the car was launched, and have remained at the higher level since then. The improvement on these dimensions is all the more remarkable as marque images are usually extremely slow-moving (see Figure 10, and note how stable other image items are).

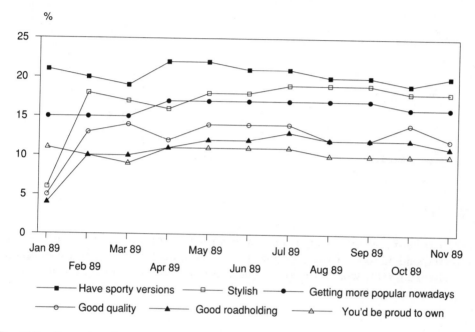

Figure 10. *Renault marque image, January-November 1989*
*Source:* Millward Brown

## *Purchase*

At the end of the year, the Renault 19 had achieved over 100% of its ambitious target, with 27,227 cars sold. (Until the end of September, the car was achieving results well above target, but in the autumn of 1989, the economic climate hardened and car sales started to slow faster than forecasters had predicted). But how do we know it was advertising that was contributing to this success?

Two indicators prove that it was:

1. *Buyers actually acknowledge the role of advertising.* Advertising is quoted as a reason for purchase in NCBS, more than for any model of its category. This is, of course, expected for a new model, but the comparison with the Fiat Tipo, which was launched at the same time, still shows a clear difference (see Figure 11).

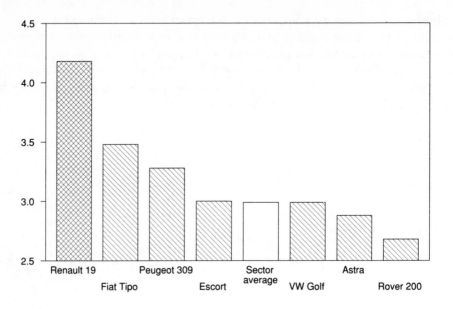

Figure 11. *Average rating by buyers (0-10) of importance of ads in purchase decision*
*Source:* NCBS

Furthermore, advertising is quoted as an important motive by Renault buyers
responding to the CustomerLink Survey, more than it used to be for buyers of
Renault 9/11, which is normal; but also more than for other Renault models
(see Figure 12).

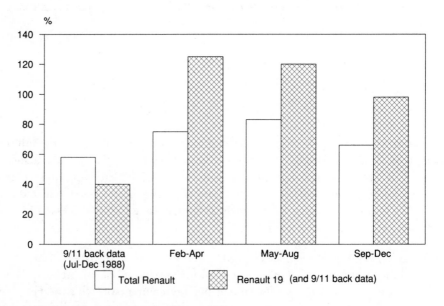

Figure 12. *Percentage heard or found out about the car thanks to advertising*
*Source:* Renault CustomerLink Survey

2.  *There is a correlation between ad awareness* and sales. For the purpose of
    correlation analysis, sales have to be entered as market share, to avoid the
    results being skewed by strong seasonality. As for advertising awareness, we
    took the higher of TV and press awareness (TV during the TV bursts, press
    between them) and simply averaged the figures for the four weeks ending
    during each sales month[5]. With these figures, a strong 'eyeball' link between
    awareness and share appears (see Figure 13).

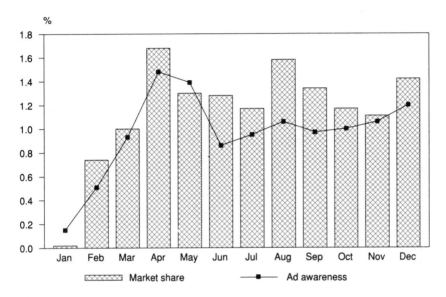

Figure 13. *Renault 19 ad awareness and market share, January – December 1989*
*Source:* Millward Brown, SMMT

If we now apply a simple regression to these figures, we find the R-squared
(correlation coefficient) to be 81.7%. A scatter diagram, plotting the ad
awareness and the sales for each of the 12 months of the year, is a visual
illustration of that correlation (see Figure 14).

Of course, a simple statistical correlation is not a proof of causality. But it is
reassuring and satisfying to find such a correlation between ad awareness and
sales in a market where so many other factors are playing a part.

## Profile

Finally and possibly most importantly for the marque's future, new buyers have
been drawn to Renault, who have a more attractive profile than Renault's usual
lower medium sector franchise: more women, younger drivers, and people who
come from the mainstream of the car market (ie not just French car aficionados).

The objective was not to alienate Renault's traditional customers in the sector.
Fortunately, Renault's CustomerLink Survey allows us to look at conquest buyers

[5]As Millward Brown publish rolling 8-weekly figures, this apparently simplistic method does take into
account the effects of advertising over a three month period ending at the end of the sales month. This is
consistent with our empirical model of the decision-making process.

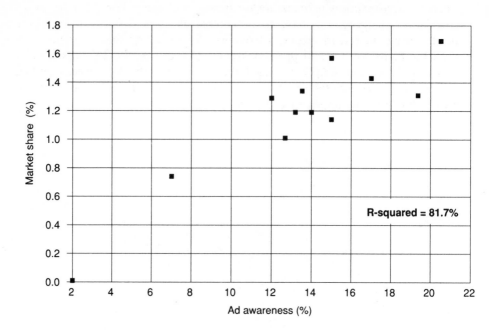

Figure 14. *Renault 19 ad awareness and market share, January – December 1989*
*Source:* Millward Brown, SMMT

and loyal buyers separately without having to resort to statistically insignificant samples. It also allows us to look at the buyer profile over time. This is useful because dealers logically serve their loyal customers first and franchise renewal only becomes clear after a few months.

1. *Conquest buyers.* The 'priority to loyalists' accounts for the low percentage of drivers with no previous experience of Renault in the first months (especially if compared to Renault 9 and 11 back data). However, the proportion of conquest buyers shot up as soon as the demand could be satisfied (see Figure 15).

   It is all the more remarkable then, that in figures given by the NCBS, which only relate to the February – July period, the Renault 19 had already achieved a level of conquest matched in this sector only by the Peugeot 309 (see Figure 16). It is clear from what we have just seen that this conquest rating would be even higher if figures were already available for the following months.

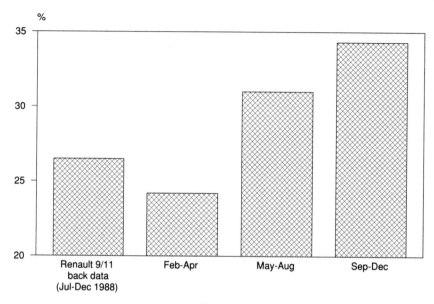

Figure 15. *Percentage of Renault 19 buyers with no previous experience of Renault*
*Source:* Renault CustomerLink Survey

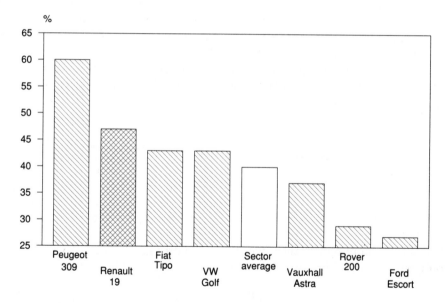

Figure 16. *Percentage of buyers replacing a car of another marque*
*Source:* NCBS

2. *Female drivers.* The percentage of female drivers increased steadily (see Figure 17). It was not a stated marketing priority to attract female buyers. However, it was recognised that the female market is an important and dynamic one and that it is vital that women regard Renault as having a relevant offer.

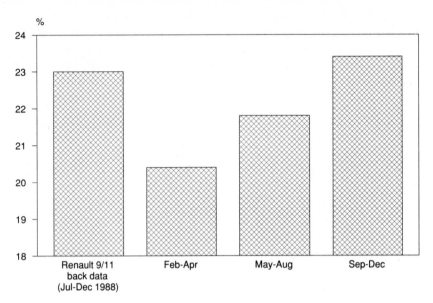

Figure 17. *Percentage of female buyers*
*Source:* Renault CustomerLink Survey

3.  *Younger customers.* Renault 19 buyers were on average appreciably younger than Renault 9 and Renault 11 buyers used to be; and their average age kept on decreasing over time. Furthermore, buyers with no previous experience of Renault were considerably younger than loyalists, which is a clear sign of franchise renewal. Last but not least, the percentage of young drivers among these conquest drivers goes up with time too: not only is the car attracting a new, younger clientele, but this clientele is itself getting younger. Figure 18 shows all these results.

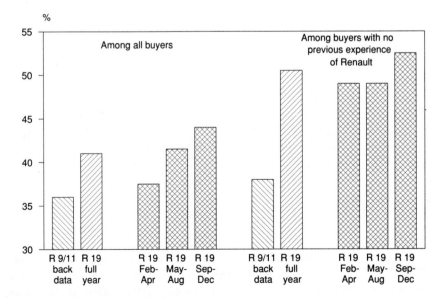

Figure 18. *Percentage of Renault 19 buyers aged under 44*
*Source:* Renault CustomerLink Survey

4.  *Not just French car aficionados.* Finally, it is worth noting that the cars conquest buyers were replacing were more 'mainstream' than Renault's usual competitors - showing that Renault is gradually escaping from its niche of eccentric loyalists and becoming a mainstream marque itself. The percentage of buyers replacing a Ford, a Vauxhall or a Rover was markedly higher for the Renault 19 than it used to be for the Renault 9 and 11 (see Figure 19).

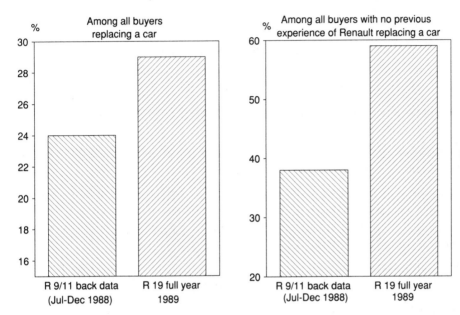

Figure 19. *Percentage of buyers replacing a domestic*
*Source:* Renault CustomerLink Survey

## SUMMARY

With the Renault 19, Renault gained access in its first ten months of commercialisation to over 27,000 customers, over half of whom had not previously bought a Renault. Despite a severe downturn in the market, it achieved its sales target, accounting for over a third of Renault's total car sales. Six months after launch 12% of sector buyers were considering the car and 6% were actually saying they would buy it (QED/RAP Monitor). Renault had gained *momentum* and advertising had played an important part in this success.

Moreover the Renault marque began to win the *respect* of a difficult group of buyers: they were now attributing values to the marque which had formerly not been associated with it.

This was only the first stage of a long process of building the Renault 19's *brand equity* – a process designed to ensure that the car enjoys better residual values than previous Renaults. This was a key objective: if new cars hold their price and are less subject to market fluctuations, long term profitability ensues. It was achieved beyond expectations, as at the end of 1990, the Renault 19 could boast the lowest depreciation in its class.

Ultimately, however, the most important communication objective would be to give the Renault 19 the long-lasting desirability among sector buyers which would guarantee future profitability. It would thus be vital during the 'growth' phase of the Renault 19's life to continue to preach the gospel of corporate and product renaissance, retaining the strong rational values now established, but adding gradually the more exciting emotional dimensions which would give the car 'badge' value.

## APPENDIX – SOURCES

The sources referred to in this document are:

SMMT (Society of Motor Manufacturers and Traders) – sales figures, market and sector share figures.

NCBS (New Car Buyers Survey) – a pan-European study conducted in the UK by MIL. 30,000 questionnaires processed annually.

Renault CustomerLink Survey – a postal questionnaire to all buyers of new Renaults. This study delivers a sample size of 20,000+. For Renault 19, the sample size in 1989 was 7,671. It is therefore possible to analyse finely the customer profile over time; or to look separately at conquest buyers.

Millward Brown Car Tracking Study – a tracking study reporting for 8-week periods, rolling weekly. About 100-200 respondents a month for each sector.

QED/RAP Monitor – a survey of people intending to buy a car reporting three times a year. About 3,000 respondents a year.

# Section Four

*Small Budgets*

SMALL BUDGETS

# 12

# Uvistat Case History
# Against All Odds

## INTRODUCTION

This paper describes the sales success of Windsor Pharmaceuticals' suncare brand Uvistat from 1988 to the present day, and demonstrates the genuine and lasting contribution the brand's advertising strategy and execution has made to this success. An examination of the effect of other brand and market variables leads us to conclude that the placing of a distinctive advertising message in selected media was the major contributor to the sales success of the Uvistat relaunch in 1988, and played a key role in the brand's continued growth to date. The sales effect of the advertising is made all the more interesting since the media spend was at a low level throughout the two year campaign (£231,000 in 1988, £311,000 in 1989) and in that time there were a number of brand and market factors which militated against the success of Uvistat, hence the title of this paper: Against All Odds.

## BACKGROUND

### The Company

In 1984, Boehringer Ingelheim, an international ethical pharmaceutical manufacturer, founded Windsor Pharmaceuticals in the UK. Windsor Pharmaceuticals was set up as a commercial pharmaceutical company in recognition of the fast-expanding self-medication market in this country.

Windsor Pharmaceuticals began its life with a portfolio of four brands, two laxative products, an anti-diarrhoeal, and a suncare preparation, Uvistat, which had been available on prescription and on request over-the-counter, and was now to be made self-select in pharmacies. Uvistat was the single largest Windsor brand accounting for 44% of Windsor value sales in 1985, the first year of trading under the Windsor name. This meant that the success of Uvistat, as Windsor's key brand, was crucial to the success of Windsor Pharmaceuticals itself.

## The Brand

Uvistat sun cream had been available on prescription for 20 years before it became a self-select product in 1984. It was prescribed by doctors and recommended in pharmacies for people with particularly sun-sensitive skins, even in the days before foreign holiday-taking was the norm, and before Sun Protection Factors were introduced. Consequently, Uvistat's heritage lay in the medical area with the emphasis on protection.

## The First Three Years

When Uvistat was introduced as a self-select brand in 1984/85 the range comprised Factor 10 and Factor 4 sun creams, a lip salve and an aftersun. The products were distributed in the top 200 Boots stores and in other pharmacies. It was launched into a marketplace where fashion, glamour and deep tanning messages were valuable currency with the consumer:

'A deep, dark tan is the most powerful product claim in suncare advertising. The deep, dark tan is the goal women work towards' (Susie Fisher Research Associates, August 1985).

At this time the fashion/tanning brands Ambre Solaire, Bergasol, Hawaiian Tropic and Coppertone accounted for half of all suncare sales. Their advertising talked 'tanning', featuring beautiful brown-skinned women and headlines which promised tanning results:

Ambre Solaire   'Deep tanning technology'.

Hawaiian Tropic   'Turns a North Sea islander into a South Sea islander'.

Bergasol's dark and light girls visual had become a familiar comparative theme in their advertising, and even the general purpose Nivea product was claiming:

'The loveliest tan under the sun'.

When Windsor launched Uvistat, the brand's advertising and promotional material assumed the established cosmetic market images and vocabulary. This is exemplified by Uvistat's 'Find Yourself a Sunspot' campaign which ran during 1985 and 1986. This used glamorous sunbathing shots and expressions such as 'enjoy a really deep, glorious tan'. In addition Uvistat sponsored a female professional windsurfer, who was used as the model for a glamorous Uvistat promotional calendar shot in exotic locations. At the same time as promoting Uvistat in this generic cosmetic manner, the decision was taken to produce a Factor 3 product, pushing Uvistat into the low-protection bracket and further away from its origins. At the end of 1986,, after two years of adopting an 'assumed' imagery communications strategy for Uvistat, a face-to-face survey carried out by Campbell Daniels revealed that the brand had not made any real inroads in terms of consumer awareness and usage (see Table 1).

TABLE 1: CONSUMER AWARENESS AND USAGE OF UVISTAT

|  | 1984 (598) % | 1986 (607) % |
|---|---|---|
| Brand last bought | 2 | 2 |
| Brand bought this year | 5 | 6 |
| Spontaneous brand awareness | 9 | 6 |
| Prompted brand awareness | 35 | 32 |

Source: Campbell Daniels, September 1984 and 1986

1987 heralded a different advertising approach for Uvistat and an increase in distribution in Boots from 200 to 600 stores. A new 'A–B' execution perpetuated the cosmetic Uvistat message, using familiar colour-change visual imagery, yet 'Nightmare' was in stark contrast to this tanning promise approach, focusing on the unpleasant effects of underprotected sunbathing by showing a badly sunburnt child. Whilst 'Nightmare' moved more towards a protection message, and therefore closer to Uvistat's origin, it concentrated on the *negative* aspect of being in the sun, showing Uvistat as the solution to a *problem* rather than promoting it as a beneficial preparation to use whilst enjoying the sun. At the end of 1987 Uvistat's sales volume was down 1.1% year on year in a market whose volume sales were up 6.4% and its unit brand share (January – October) dropped from its 1986 level of 2.1% to 2.0%, despite the presence of two new products, Factor 3 and Factor 8 creams, and the increase in distribution in Boots.

## Summary of the Brand's Position Before 1988

After three years of self-select status with increasing levels of distribution and reasonable media spend Uvistat had failed to increase its brand share within the total suncare market. A telephone survey conducted in 1987 revealed that amongst female sun preparation buyers levels of spontaneous brand awareness had fallen from the Campbell Daniels measure in 1986 (see Table 2).

TABLE 2: SPONTANEOUS BRAND AWARENESS

| Sep 1986 (607) % | Jun 1987 (104) % |
|---|---|
| 6 | 4 |

Source: Campbell Daniels, MRE

The brand had adopted a schizophrenic communication strategy with a cosmetic tanning advertising message and a wholehearted 'burning' message running simultaneously. Unsurprisingly, Uvistat did not seem to have developed any sort of distinct imagery for itself. The product range had been expanded with the addition of Factors 3 and 8 and the distribution base had increased without any demonstrable benefit to the brand's overall performance.

## THE RELAUNCH OF UVISTAT

Towards the end of 1987 Butterfield Day Devito Hockney were appointed by Windsor Pharmaceuticals to develop an advertising campaign for Uvistat for 1988 onwards. In developing an advertising strategy for Uvistat there were a number of factors which the agency had to consider.

### *The Market*

The suncare market was buoyant with year on year value increases around the 15% mark, but within that:

—   Only certain brands were growing.
—   These tended to be fashion or style orientated brands.
—   Others were static or in decline.
—   Many small brands were 'borrowing' imagery.
—.  Own label were making significant incursions.
—   A multitude of brands meant increasing pressure on shelf space.

This much was evident from historical syndicated suncare data and an examination of advertising in the category.

### *Awareness and Imagery in the Marketplace*

Analysis of previous qualitative and quantitative studies carried out by the Susie Fisher Group in 1985, Campbell Daniels in 1986, and considerable exploratory research conducted by BDDH in 1987 revealed that amongst consumers there was a high level of awareness of major brands, but low awareness of product differences between brands. In terms of advertising itself in 1987 there were 26 advertised brands, many of which advertised at low weights. There was a great deal of inconsistency both of message and of levels of spend by brand over time, Uvistat itself had been inconsistent in terms of message and level of media spend. Examining advertising in qualitative groups revealed that consumers:

—   Could not distinguish between the propositions of smaller brands.
—   Saw most advertising as 'showing perfectly tanned bodies', but did not read the copy.
—   Had a low level of awareness and involvement in suncare advertising.
—   Saw suncare advertisements as employing a narrow spectrum of communication which was *either* tanning *or* protection focused.

### *The Purchase Mechanism*

Consumers' basic requirements from a suncare preparation were that it would stop them burning and help them tan. Most people admitted that a known name and positive brand image values were desirable. In terms of the choice available to consumers there were 26 advertised brands, a massive own label and cosmetic brand 'offer', many variants within any one range, a mix of pack formats and product formulations and very few brands with real distinction in image terms. The net result of this for the consumer was mental simplification, and an assumption that brands were:

'all much of a muchness'.

It also meant that purchase choices were based on similarities (ie factors) *not* differences (ie brands), and resulted in highly promiscuous purchasing.

### Towards an Advertising Strategy

Given that it was the fashion/tanning brands that were experiencing growth, the obvious question was should Uvistat take the market on using the market's terms?

The answer to this question came from detailed qualitative exploratory research amongst the small number of consumers who used the brand, and through examining perceptions of the brand amongst non-users. A fashion orientated, overtly tanning message would not have worked for Uvistat because the brand was seen to lack relevant fashion heritage, also the product form (cream not oil), and name (technical not sexy or exotic sounding) were inconsistent with a fashion communication.

As we can see from looking at a consumer-generated map of perceived brand positionings, most other brands were already there and doing the fashion 'thing' better (BDDH Qualitative Research 1987).

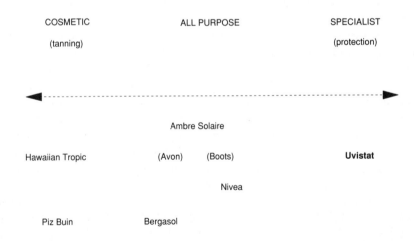

There seemed to be a level of interest being expressed in qualitative research, notably amongst the small core of Uvistat buyers, in information about the sun and its effects. In particular, women with children were conscious that there was little information about sunbathing and tanning communicated in suncare advertising which tended to focus on the promised end result. It seemed that from consumers' perceptions of the brand, Uvistat was ideally placed to build on its inherent strengths as a protection brand, and become an *authority* on suncare (because of the medical heritage).

Having uncovered what the distinguishing property of Uvistat was, it then had to be considered in the context of how suncare products are viewed and used generally.

Qualitative research amongst all sectors of sun tan product users revealed that holiday makers want to *enjoy* being in the sun, and also want to feel *in control* of their own tanning and protection levels. Historically, brands advertising in the category had veered *either* towards protection *or* towards tanning, eg:

| TANNING | PROTECTION |
|---|---|
| *Ambre Solaire*<br>'Deep Tanning Technology' | *Almay*<br>'The Golden Rule for Sun<br>Sensitive Skins' |
| *Hawaiian Tropic*<br>'Turn a North Sea Islander<br>into a South Sea Islander' | *Uvistat*<br>'Nightmare' |
| *Uvistat*<br>'Find Yourself a Sunspot' | |

In a market where advertising and consequently brands were seen as 'much of a muchness', where there was low user awareness and involvement in advertising and where there had always been a polarity of approach and language used in advertising (tanning *or* protection), there was a real opportunity to adopt a different and distinctive approach for Uvistat. Uvistat was a credible 'protection' brand that could, through advertising, identify itself with the unique understanding of consumers' desire to *enjoy* being in the sun whilst being *in control* of their tanning and protection levels. This combination of brand protection credentials and understanding of the emotional context in which suncare is used, afforded Uvistat the opportunity to sidestep the polarity of language/approach that had hitherto characterised suncare advertising. In reconciling these previously opposite ends of the communication spectrum it was also possible to expand Uvistat's franchise by being less categorical about targeting 'tanners' or 'protection seekers', and allowing consumers to self-define their requirements.

So Uvistat would talk about 'being in the sun', which is where all suncare product users are, rather than 'tanning'. Uvistat would talk about 'being in control' rather than specifying 'tanning' or 'protecting'. And the brand would be positioned as being for 'sun sensitive skins' rather than marginalising the brand's appeal by using 'problem' expressions like 'delicate', 'sensitive' and 'concerned'.

*Advertising Objectives*

To gain awareness and generate trial of Uvistat by positioning the brand as the definitive product range for sun sensitive skins.

## Advertising Strategy

By providing close identification between brand and user, and positioning the brand as specialist not generalist. By communicating that Uvistat puts you in control, allowing you to make the most of being in the sun.

## Advertising Proposition

Uvistat is the only range of products specially designed for people with sun sensitive skins.

## Tone of Voice

—  Positive, understands why you've gone on holiday.
—  Informative.
—  Relaxing, trustworthy.

## Target Audience

Knowing that the Uvistat communication would necessarily be an intelligent one, that women with children showed particular interest in expanding their knowledge about protection and the effects of being in the sun, and that Uvistat would be carrying a substantial price increase in 1988, ABC1 women 25 – 44 were selected as the target audience for the Uvistat campaign.

## Implications of the Strategy

The advertising strategy obviously had implications for the Uvistat range and it was the agency's recommendation that Windsor should look at discontinuing their lower factors (3 and 4), concentrate on developing higher factor range extensions, and in particular, look at producing a product specifically for babies and small children. The agency were also keen for the range to be repackaged giving the brand total synergy across all products.

## The First Concepts

The first two executions produced by the agency on this strategy sought to communicate the concept of 'putting you in control' using visual devices of a venetian blind and inconsistently spaced copy lines superimposed on a disproportionately large sun, over a beach. The line 'Same Sun Different Strengths' was used to express the idea of putting the individual in control of the amount of sunlight they exposed themselves to according to their choice of factor from Uvistat. The copy also explained the effects of the sun on different skin types, and Uvistat's ability to cater for all skin-types. These executions were subsequently exposed in research. Whilst they were considered by respondents to be 'different' and 'intelligent', the balance between enjoyment/relaxation in the sun, and 'hard facts' had not been struck. The executions were seen as 'too serious' because of the disproportionate focus given to the sun versus enjoyment and beach. This imbalance of visual elements led consumers to conclude that the executions were different and interesting but not appetising in the way of conventional suncare advertising.

## THE SECOND CAMPAIGN

What we learnt from researching the first advertising concepts was that a balance had to be struck between achieving the strategic objective of positioning Uvistat as the definitive brand for sun-sensitive skins, and including appealing 'holiday spirit' clues. It was the case that people found an 'informative' approach interesting, and 'different', but there was little association made with holiday taking and enjoyment. This new knowledge allowed the agency to move forward and develop the 'Gentle Art of Sun Control' campaign of *Girl Under Tree* and *Boy Under Water* (see pages 252 – 253).

The fact that the learning from exploratory research and the initial stage of creative development research had been injected into these new executions was evident in the responses to this campaign in subsequent research. The executions were viewed as both different and involving. The question format of the headlines, and the juxtaposition of the colour photograph and black and white diagram were seen as unconventional. They created impact and a high level of curiosity to resolve. The headlines were considered all the more powerful for being real consumer questions, frequently eliciting the responses:

'I've often wondered that'.

'I've asked myself that very question'.

The 'beautiful' pictures fulfilled the requirement for holiday spirit and appeal, but in conjunction with the diagrams went much further in telling 'the story behind the picture' in which there was a great deal of interest. The executions were seen as 'intelligent' and 'interesting' because of the content of the copy, and the authoritative stance it took, yet the colloquial copy style meant the advertisements did not cross the border into 'too serious for suncare' territory.

These two executions ran in the following women's magazines from May to July 1988.

> Best
> Family Circle
> Good Housekeeping
> Woman's Journal
> Options
> Cosmopolitan
> Prima
> Mother & Baby
> Under Five
> Essentials
> Woman & Home

The coverage and frequency of our target ABC1 women 25 – 44 that this represented was 60% at 3.5 OTS.

In addition to the advertising executions appearing in women's magazines the *Girl Under Tree* visual and the 'Gentle Art of Sun Control' line appeared in all point-of-sale material produced by Windsor for use with both consumers and trade.

### Data Source

The source of sales data quoted is Syndicated Data Consultants suncare retail audit. SDC are a division of Nielsen Marketing Services. Throughout this paper, sales comparisons made year against year are on a ten month January – October basis. 97% of all suncare is sold during this period.

### Did the Advertising Work?

With SDC volume sales of Uvistat up 31%, 1988 versus 1987 in a market whose volume had risen by only 8.5%, and with Windsor's own ex-factory sterling sales of the brand up 46%, 1988 versus 1987, it would seem that the advertising did work, extremely well. In order to demonstrate that advertising was indeed the major contributor to this sales success we can examine other factors which might have had an effect on sales.

## WHAT ELSE COULD HAVE CONTRIBUTED?

### Product Range

The only effect that could have been expected as a result of changes to the product range would have been a sales *decline* for Uvistat since the brand offering was reduced by one product, Factor 3, and there were no new Uvistat product introductions in 1988.

### Competitive Environment

There were no major new entrants to or exits from the suncare market in 1988.

### Media Expenditure

Far from being capable of expanding sales through increased media expenditure, the media budget for Uvistat was cut for the second consecutive year when 'The Gentle Art of Sun Control' campaign was launched. In the three years 1986 – 1988 total expenditure for the category had fallen, but this was due mainly to fewer brands advertising in 1987 and 1988. Of the brands which advertised consistently over the three year period, Uvistat was the only one to have its media budget cut for the second year running (see Table 3).

# "MY 12 YEAR OLD SAYS YOU CAN'T GET SUNBURNT

UVISTAT SUN CARE

This is a case of mother knows best.

You can indeed get sunburnt underwater. The sun's UV rays penetrate the sea down to a depth of about 10 feet.

UV rays, just to remind you, are the ones that have the power to both tan and burn.

An added complication is that being in the water keeps you cool, so you tend to stay exposed

to the sun for longer periods than you would on the beach.

All of which underlines the need for the right kind of protection throughout your holiday, especially if you have sun-sensitive skin.

Here, Uvistat can help. We make a range of high quality suncare preparations for the whole family.

For the budding Jacques Cousteau in the picture we'd recommend our water-resistant

# UNDERWATER. I THINK YOU CAN. WHO'S RIGHT?

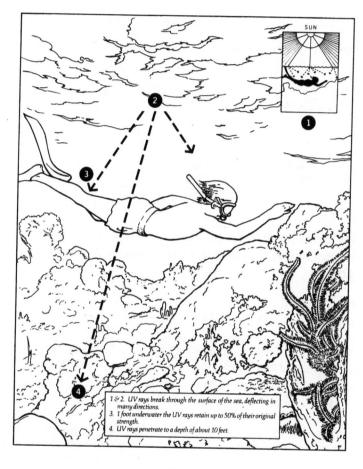

SUN

1 & 2. UV rays break through the surface of the sea, deflecting in many directions.
3. 1 foot underwater the UV rays retain up to 50% of their original strength.
4. UV rays penetrate to a depth of about 10 feet.

UVISTAT SUN CARE

formula, applied every two to three hours.

Like the rest of our range it is made to a unique specification, which is why you'll find it only in chemists.

But please don't think that good protection equals poor tanning.

With Uvistat you and your family will tan naturally, each in your own good time.

And you'll be delighted to know that natural tans last longer, because you're less likely to blister and peel.

On holiday everyone wants to make the most of being in the sun. All that takes is a little under-standing and a little control.

At Uvistat we're happy to hel you with both.

## UVISTAT
THE GENTLE ART OF SUN CONTRO

TABLE 3: MEDIA BUDGET

|      | Uvistat | Ambre Solaire | Bergasol | Coppertone | Market |
|------|---------|---------------|----------|------------|--------|
| 1986 | 100     | 100           | 100      | 100        | 100    |
| 1987 | 82      | 197           | 56       | 100        | 97     |
| 1988 | 75      | 196           | 86       | 57         | 86     |

Source: MEAL

## Pricing

In 1988 Uvistat's average price per item increased ahead of the market (see Table 4).

TABLE 4: AVERAGE PRICE PAID PER ITEM £

|               | Jan – Oct 1987 | Jan – Oct 1988 | % change |
|---------------|----------------|----------------|----------|
| Total suncare | 3.13           | 3.15           | +1.0     |
| Uvistat       | 3.15           | 3.40           | +7.9     |

Source: SDC

This increase meant that Uvistat products were more expensive than the market average price per product, making it unlikely that price played a part in volume sales increase.

## Distribution

Uvistat is only stocked in Boots and other chemists. Looking at the different retail outlets share of trade, 1988 versus 1987, we see that Uvistat had the disadvantage of not being stocked in outlets which were making share gains, ie discount drugstores and the grocery trade (see Table 5).

TABLE 5: RETAIL OUTLET UNIT SHARE OF RETAIL TRADE

|                                        | Jan – Oct 1987 % | Jan – Oct 1988 % |
|----------------------------------------|------------------|------------------|
| Boots                                  | 47.9             | 43.2             |
| Other chemists                         | 23.0             | 20.5             |
| Superdrug & other<br>discount drugstores | 9.5            | 15.5             |
| Grocery                                | 7.8              | 9.8              |
| Department stores                      | 2.9              | 4.1              |
| Other                                  | 8.7              | 6.6              |

Source: SDC
Note: Uvistat distribution base (Boots and other chemists) declined in importance to suncare whilst outlets where Uvistat had no distribution increased in importance to the category

Uvistat's distribution base did change in 1988 when the brand achieved total distribution in Boots with the addition of c400 small stores to its existing franchise in the other c600 medium and large stores. In order to understand the quality of distribution this gain actually represented, we need to look at the structure of Boots outlets (see Table 6).

TABLE 6:  BOOTS OUTLETS

|  | No. of stores | % Boots £ turnover |
|---|---|---|
| Type 1 (large) | c200 ⎫ | c80 |
| Type 2 (medium) | c400 ⎭ | |
| Type 3 (small) | c400 | c20 |

Source:  Windsor Estimates

We should recognise that Uvistat's gain of c400 smaller stores, whilst representing 20% of Boots total turnover would be of lower value than this figure suggests for sectors like suncare given the pressure on shelf space in outlets of this size.

### What Effect Might This Additional Distribution Have Had?

Clearly Boots is important to the market in total, and particularly to Windsor given that Uvistat is *only* distributed in pharmacies. Yet, if we look at Boots total unit share of the suncare market January – October 1988 versus 1987 we see that it actually went down (Table 7).

TABLE 7:  BOOTS UNIT SHARE OF SUNCARE IN RETAIL TRADE

| Jan – Oct 1987 % | Jan – Oct 1988 % |
|---|---|
| 47.9 | 43.2 |

Source:  SDC

If we look at what the key sales periods are in the suncare sector we can see that the period May – August accounts for 73.5% of total suncare sales (Figure 1).

Looking at Boots unit share of the market by period (Figure 2) we see that in the key suncare sales periods, Boots unit share was at its lowest.

Furthermore, for Windsor themselves, Boots relative importance (measured in sterling ex-factory sales) actually *declined* in 1988 over 1987 (Figure 3).

Finally, had the Boots distribution increase had a significant impact on brand sales we would have expected to see this from the beginning of the year when the distribution gain was made. In fact, this was not the case. If we look at Uvistat's unit sales performance against the market 1988 versus 1987 (Figure 4), what we see is that in the period March – April Uvistat sales were not only down on the previous year, but also considerably behind the market.

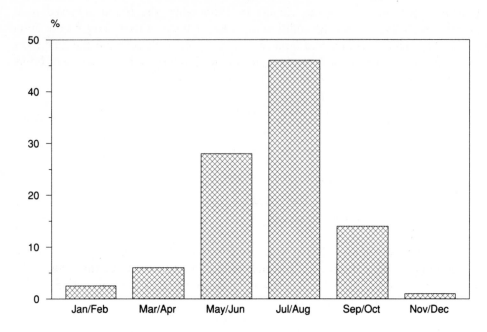

Figure 1. *Unit share of total suncare sales by bi-month, 1988*
*Source:* SDC

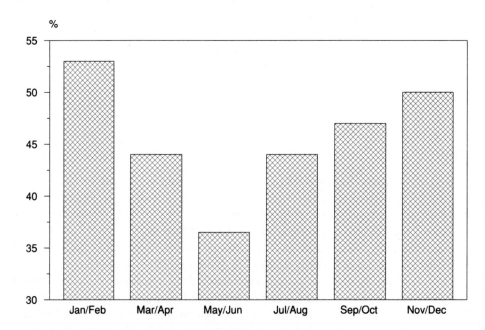

Figure 2. *Boots unit share of retail trade by bi-month, 1988*
*Source:* SDC

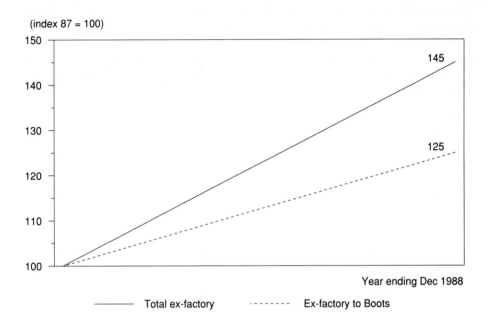

Figure 3.  *Uvistat sterling ex-factory sales*
*Source:* Windsor

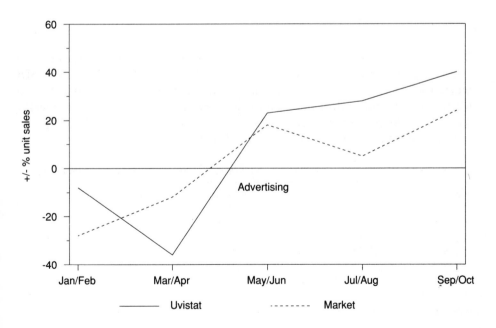

Figure 4.  *Uvistat and market unit sales by bi-month, 1988 versus 1987*
*Source:* SDC

It is not until the period beginning May when the advertising began, that Uvistat's sales forge ahead of 1987 sales levels and the market.

If we look at Uvistat's volume share performance by bi-month January – October 1988 over 1987 (Figure 5) we can see the same pattern emerging, with the brand's unit share down in the period March – April, and moving ahead considerably in the *peak sales* period May – August (73.5% total volume sales).

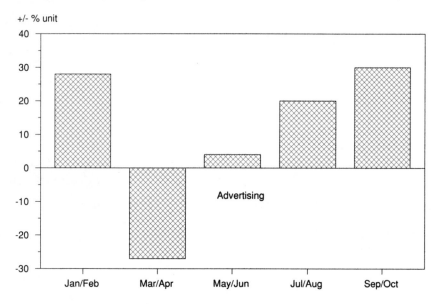

Figure 5.  *Uvistat's volume share performance by bi-month, 1988 versus 1987*
Source: SDC

But the 'bottom line' as far as Windsor, the manufacturer, was concerned, was the sterling ex-factory sales growth of 46% 1988 over 1987. Whilst the SDC volume growth of 31% is substantial in its own right, when we consider that this growth was at a time when the brand was carrying a price increase considerably greater than the market average (7.9% versus 1.0%), we see that Uvistat's value increase showed even greater improvement (Table 8).

TABLE 8:  UVISTAT'S VOLUME AND VALUE INCREASE, JANUARY – OCTOBER, 1988 VERSUS 1987

|         | Volume<br>% | Value<br>% |
|---------|-------------|------------|
| Uvistat | +31         | +41        |
| Market  | +8.5        | +9.4       |

Source:   SDC

So against the odds of:

—  reduced product range
—  reduced media budget

— price increase ahead of the market
— lack of distribution in outlets gaining importance to total suncare

distinctive and highly relevant advertising helped Uvistat to increase sales substantially and raise the brand's volume and value share of the total market (see Table 9).

TABLE 9:  UVISTAT'S MARKET SHARE

|          | Jan – Oct 1986 % | Jan – Oct 1987 % | Jan – Oct 1988 % |
|----------|------------------|------------------|------------------|
| Volume   | 2.1              | 2.0              | 2.5              |
| Value    | 2.0              | 2.1              | 2.7              |

Source:  SDC

In recognition of the advertising's success in 1988, Windsor decided that the same campaign should run in 1989, with an increase in media expenditure from £231,000 to £311,000. This meant that the publication list could be expanded to include:

Woman
New Woman
Essentials
Living
She
Parents
Ulster Tatler

This schedule represented a coverage and frequency against ABC1 women 25 – 44 of 61.3% at 3.7 OTS.

The campaign's impact was also recognised by the advertising industry with *Boy Under Water* receiving a commendation at the Campaign Press Awards in 1989.

This additional media investment paid dividends as Uvistat's volume sales increased by 9%, Jan – Oct 1989 versus 1988, in a market whose volume had increased by only 6%, and Windsor's sterling ex-factory sales were up 30% year on year. Again, an examination of factors other than advertising which may have contributed to this continued sales growth leads us to conclude that advertising played a major role.

*Product Range*

In 1989 the Uvistat product range changed. Factor 4 (50 ml and 100 ml variants) and the 50 ml variant of Factor 10 were discontinued, and Factors 20 and 15 creams, and Factors 8 and 6 lotions were introduced. But if we look at unit share of ex-factory sales by product type, 1989 versus 1988 (Figure 6), what we see is that the products which were present in the range across the two year period accounted for the same proportion of total sales in both years, indicating that the new products alone could not have accounted for the sales increase.

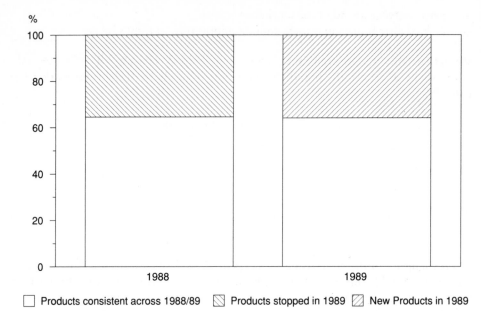

Figure 6. *Unit share of Uvistat ex-factory sales 1988 versus 1989*
*Source:* Windsor

## Competitive Environment

There were no major brand launches or departures in the suncare market in 1989.

## Media Expenditure

Although media expenditure was increased from £231,000 in 1988 to £311,000 in 1989, this was still below the £315,000 level of expenditure behind the brand in 1986. If we take into account media inflation in women's magazines in the period 1986 – 1989, it is obvious that media expenditure behind the brand was considerably below its historical level.

## Price

As with 1988, Uvistat carried a price increase ahead of the market increase in 1989, which makes price a factor unlikely to have affected the brand's volume sales increase (see Table 10).

TABLE 10: AVERAGE PRICE PAID PER ITEM (£)

|  | Jan – Oct 1988 | Jan – Oct 1989 | % change |
|---|---|---|---|
| Market | 3.13 | 3.39 | +7.6 |
| Uvistat | 3.15 | 3.84 | +12.9 |

Source: SDC

*Distribution*

There was no change in the Uvistat distribution base, 1989 versus 1988. However, Uvistat outlets (Boots and other chemists) continued to decline in importance to the total suncare market, to the benefit of outlets in which Uvistat has no distribution (see Table 11).

TABLE 11:   UNIT SHARE OF RETAIL TRADE JAN – OCT

|  | 1987 % | 1988 % | 1989 % |
|---|---|---|---|
| Boots | 47.9 | 43.2 | 42.7 |
| Other chemists | 23.0 | 20.5 | 20.0 |
| Superdrug & discount drugstores | 9.5 | 15.5 | 16.0 |
| Grocery | 7.8 | 9.8 | 11.0 |
| Department stores | 2.9 | 4.1 | 2.8 |
| Other | 8.7 | 6.6 | 7.4 |

Source:   SDC

*Packaging*

In 1989, a new packaging design for Uvistat, developed by Michael Peters and Partners, was introduced. The change in design gave the range a feeling of synergy, but represented only a minor change to the original design. The only retailer who had totally new pack stock in 1989 was Boots. All other retailers received new pack stock on a phased basis, meaning that some chemists had all or mainly old pack stock throughout the season, and many had a combination of old and new pack on display. Consequently, the only valid measure of the new design's contribution to sales is an analysis of Boots within the market, and more specifically, within the total Uvistat sales framework.

Looking at Boots unit share of total suncare sales by bi-month, 1989 versus 1988, (Figure 7) we see Boots share during key sales periods in decline.

Looking at Windsor's sterling ex-factory sales of Uvistat (Figure 8) we see that the brand had almost doubled in value in two years. What we also see is that Boots is declining in relative importance to Windsor for the second year running.

In order to confirm fully the advertising's contribution to the brand's success in 1988, and in 1989, BDDH commissioned a face-to-face quantitative survey, through Survey Research Associates, amongst female suncare buyers (ABC1 25 – 54), in April 1990. This survey matched the sample and structure of the 1984 and 1986 Campbell Daniels Surveys. Despite the fact that both of the previous surveys had been carried out in September, when suncare is top of mind, and the BDDH survey was carried out in May, what we see is a marked improvement in brand usage, awareness, and particularly in advertising awareness (Table 12).

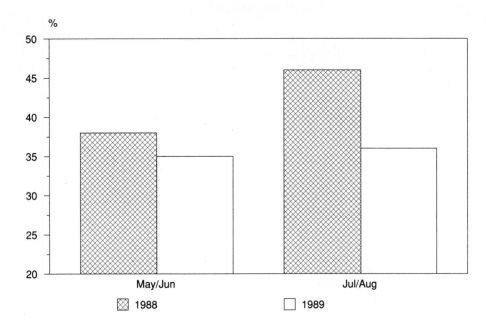

Figure 7. *Boots unit share of total suncare in key sales periods, 1989 versus 1988*

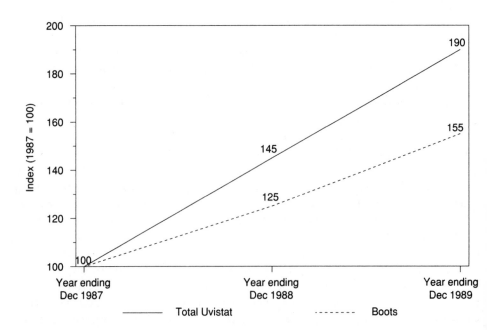

Figure 8. *Uvistat sterling ex-factory sales, 1989 versus 1988*

TABLE 12:  BRAND USAGE AND AWARENESS

|  | Sep 1986 (607) % | May 1990 (326) % |
|---|---|---|
| Brand last bought | 2 | 6 |
| Brand bought in last 12 months | 2 | 8 |
| Spontaneous brand awareness | 6 | 8 |
| Prompted brand awareness | 32 | 39 |
| Photo-prompt advertising awareness | 19 | 42 |

Source: Campbell Daniels, SRA

Unfortunately, Uvistat was not a listed brand on TGI until 1988, but on a 1988 – 1989 comparison we can see that the brand's penetration levels are on the increase (Table 13).

TABLE 13:  BRAND PENETRATION LEVELS

| Uvistat used | 1988 % | 1989 % |
|---|---|---|
| Most often | 3.3 | 3.4 |
| Other | 1.9 | 2.1 |
| Total | 5.2 | 5.5 |

Source:  TGI
Base:  All women

## THE FUTURE

Windsor have launched Uvistat 'Babysun', a range of suncare products specifically for babies and young children this year. This range started life as the agency's initiative, and indeed the agency helped Babysun gain listings in Boots with the use of convincing qualitative evidence that such a product from a protection brand was sought after by mothers of young children.

Windsor's Uvistat sterling ex-factory sales for the first five months of 1990, including Babysun, are up 72% versus 1989, showing that success in the consumer arena, helped by distinctive and highly relevant advertising, has meant the trade now recognise Uvistat as a force to be reckoned with in the suncare market. Latest SDC figures (see Table 14) indicate that Uvistat's substantial share gains 1986 – 89 will continue to increase into 1990.

TABLE 14: UVISTAT'S MARKET SHARE

|  | Jan – Oct 1986 % | Jan – Oct 1987 % | Jan – Oct 1988 % | Jan – Oct 1989 % | Jan – Apr 1990 % |
|---|---|---|---|---|---|
| Volume | 2.1 | 2.0 | 2.5 | 2.6 | 3.7 |
| Value | 2.0 | 2.1 | 2.7 | 2.9 | 4.6 |

Source:  SDC

# 13

# Value For Money in Charity Advertising

## *Advertising for Amnesty International 1988 – 1990*

### INTRODUCTION

This paper is an account of the effectiveness of a small press campaign for Amnesty International, over the last two years. This effectiveness was achieved in a charity sector which has become fiercely competitive.

Our short- and long-term profitability derived from capitalising on an unusual feature in the charity world – membership. In the short-term, it gave us a competitive edge. Research tells us that it was tantamount to offering better 'value for money' than just asking for donations, because it offered something back. As well as outperforming other charities, we also drastically improved on the results of previous Amnesty advertising. How we executed this strategy in advertising was therefore an important factor. The full benefit of recruiting members rather than raising money accrues in the long-term, as members pay annual subscriptions and generally stay in the organisation for a number of years. Overall, we can attribute the following achievements directly to members recruited by our advertising:

— An immediate return on media spend of 106%, compared with a 29% average for all charity advertising.
— A return, in members recruited, 12 times higher per insertion than previous Amnesty advertising, in the same newspapers and on a similar strategy.
— A projected long-term return on investment, which far outstrips the return from the best commercially available interest rates.

In addition, we have a list of names from which Amnesty can generate further profit through direct mail appeals and trading, and we have raised awareness of Amnesty. These are the two ways in which most other charities nowadays justify advertising as a cost.

## BACKGROUND

*Amnesty International*

Amnesty International was founded in 1961 by British lawyer Peter Benenson. It is a worldwide campaigning organisation which focuses on prisoners.

— It seeks the release of prisoners of conscience. These are people detained solely for their beliefs or origins.
— It works for prompt and fair trials for all political prisoners.
— It opposes torture and execution in all cases.

Amnesty has a very high success rate, for example, in 1988, 1,566 of the 4,640 prisoners whom Amnesty was campaigning for, were released.

In recognition of its work for human rights, in 1978 Amnesty International won the UN Peace Prize.

*Membership*

Amnesty neither seeks nor receives any government funding and relies totally on voluntary donations.

Amnesty is unusual in the UK charity sector in having a membership structure. Members pay annual subscriptions of £12.00 (individual), £15.00 (family) of £5.00 (student, under 18, claimant, OAP). Once enrolled, members receive a magazine every two months and campaigning literature. They are encouraged to write letters or telegrams on behalf of individual prisoners, take part in campaigns and join local group activities. They are also sent regular appeals for donations or for schemes such as 'Enrol a Friend'.

*The Competitive Environment*

In asking the public to give money to join, Amnesty is competing with all other charities. In the last four years the total voluntary income received by charities has barely increased, whereas the total spend on and total numbers of charities advertising has increased dramatically. Telethons, disaster appeals and major fund-raising events have all raised the stakes in the fight for a share of the public's mind and pocket. Figure 1 shows this fall off in income relative to advertising, using the latest information available from the Charities Aid Foundation.

Recent research has given us a clear picture of Amnesty's closest competitors. These are the other campaigning organisations such as Greenpeace and Anti-Apartheid and Third World charities such as Oxfam and Christian Aid (see Table 1). This clutch of concerns appeals to an educated liberal minority of perhaps a million individuals (calculated roughly using newspaper readership). The competition is fierce, with Amnesty having a 2.5% share of voice in 1989 according to MEAL.

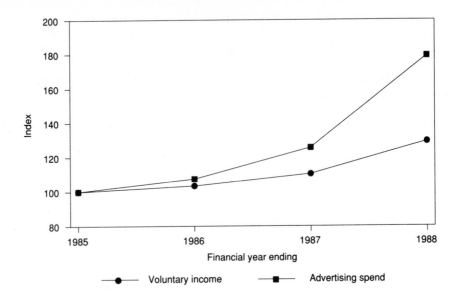

Figure 1. *Income and advertising; top 200 charities*
*Source:* Charities Aid Foundation, MEAL

TABLE 1:  AMNESTY SHARE OF VOICE, 1989

| Amnesty competitors | Spend (£000) | Share of voice (%) |
|---|---|---|
| ANC | 64 | 2.0 |
| Action Aid | 547 | 18.0 |
| Christian Aid | 231 | 7.5 |
| Disasters Emergency Committee | 77 | 2.5 |
| Friends Of The Earth | 433 | 14.0 |
| Greenpeace | 674 | 20.5 |
| Oxfam | 214 | 7.0 |
| Red Cross | 258 | 8.0 |
| National Anti-Vivisection | 159 | 5.0 |
| Save The Children | 112 | 3.5 |
| Shelter | 93 | 3.0 |
| Unicef | 200 | 6.5 |
| Amnesty International | 77 | 2.5 |
| *Total* | *3,139* | *100.0* |

Source:    MEAL

## Raising Money Off the Page

Experience on charity accounts and anecdotal information indicates that many charities have given up trying to raise money off the newspaper page. Instead they use it to recruit for direct mailing or to raise awareness for other activities such as door-to-door collections. Table 2 uses Charities Aid Foundation figures to estimate that charity advertising has an average return of 29% on expenditure.

TABLE 2:  AVERAGE RETURN ON CHARITY ADVERTISING

1.  Advertising accounts for 3.4% of total Voluntary Fundraising (1)
    Top 400 charities raised £127.8 million in Voluntary Fundraising (2)

    Advertising income    = £4.3 million

2.  Top 400 charities spent £15.1 million in advertising (3)

    Average return    = £4.3 million

    £15.1 million

    = 29%

Notes:

(1) Charities Aid Foundation, Household Survey 1988.
993 households were asked how much they gave and by what means. Donations in response to advertising accounted for 3.4% of total Voluntary Fundraising. ('Voluntary Fundraising' is the amount of money given by individuals, excluding legacies and covenants).

(2) Charities Aid Foundation Statistics, 1988.

(3) MEAL 1988. This does not include cinema, posters, inserts and local press advertising, which are likely to account for a substantial proportion of the 3.4% figure. On the other hand it measures ratecard costs and charities generally pay less. We have assumed these effects balance out to give a reasonable estimate of actual spend.

## MARKETING AND ADVERTISING OBJECTIVES

### Marketing Objectives

The fundraising department at the British Section of Amnesty has three objectives, in order of priority:

1.  To develop a large and active membership.
2.  To increase the groundswell of public support.
3.  To generate funding for campaigning, organisation and international activities.

The tools which it uses to achieve these objectives include:

— Advertising
— Direct marketing
— Trading
— Direct campaigning
— Local activities
— Events
— Media relations

Up until 1988 advertising had been used almost exclusively in a subsidiary role, in publicising and selling tickets for events such as The Secret Policeman's Ball. In June 1988 we were appointed to advertise to help to meet all three marketing objectives.

### Advertising Objectives

From the outset, we saw membership's potential as a fundraising tool. Firstly a new member provides a handsome £12 on joining (the average household only gave £24 in total to charities in 1987: CAF Household Survey) followed by further repeat subscriptions over a number of years. Additional profit could be made from these members through appeals and trading. Secondly membership offers 'value for money' – something back for the money you give – so it might attract more responses than just appealing for funds. We therefore made recruiting for members the primary objective.

Telephone research told us that, although awareness of Amnesty was high (82%) awareness of what Amnesty actually does was low (under 20%) (Audience Selection Telephone Research, April 1988). This convinced us that advertising would need to put across the problems Amnesty deals with, in order to recruit members most effectively. In doing this we would also be generating wider public support which was our secondary objective.

The third fundraising objective of raising money was principally to be achieved through membership subscriptions. However, we also included in the coupon a request for donations suggesting amounts from £15 to £50 so that those responding could donate more than (or if they wished instead of) the subscription.

---

I wish to join Amnesty International:

£12 (Individual) ☐          £15 (Family) ☐          £5 (Student, Under 18, Claimant, OAP) ☐

I wish to give a donation of:    £50    £25    £20    £15    Other £ _____

Name _____

Address _____

_____

Amnesty International British Section, 5 Roberts Place, Off Bowling Green Lane, London EC1R 0EJ

---

Figure 2. *Coupon design*

The advertising objectives were then, in order of priority:

1. To recruit new members off the page.
2. To raise awareness of Amnesty's activities.
3. To raise additional funds in the form of donations.

The primary objective was monitored by use of key codes on coupons which were entered onto the Amnesty membership computer files. We could not justify the cost of monitoring our performance against the other objectives, as our budget was so tiny.

## Target Market

At the outset we had no consumer research and used a common sense definition of the target market:

— Younger men and women.
— Liberal minded people.
— Having a basic awareness of Amnesty and of current affairs.
— Readers of *The Guardian*, *The Independent*, *The Observer*.

Subsequent research among Amnesty members yields a very similar picture – the 'Lifestyle' measures yield a particularly graphic picture.

TABLE 3: MEMBERSHIP SURVEY (SEPTEMBER 1989)

|  | Amnesty Members % of Total | UK Population % | Index |
|---|---|---|---|
| *Age* |  |  |  |
| Under 22 | 24 | 31 | 77 |
| 22–34 | 30 | 19 | 158 |
| 35–44 | 19 | 14 | 136 |
| 45–54 | 9 | 11 | 82 |
| 55+ | 18 | 25 | 72 |
| *Sex* |  |  |  |
| Male | 51 | 49 | 104 |
| Female | 49 | 51 | 96 |
| *Lifestyle* |  |  |  |
| Environmental concerns | 66 | 27.5* | 240 |
| Had further education | 63 | 12 | 525 |
| Earn more than £20,000 | 30 | 15 | 200 |
| Read *The* Guardian | 45 | 3 | 1,500 |
| Read *The Independent* | 36 | 2.5 | 1,440 |

Sources: HMSO/TGI.
Note: *Definitely disapprove of aerosols.

Members therefore tend to be educated, young, liberal, professional (and middle class).

Our advertising has aimed to recruit new members from the section of the population similar to this existing member profile. This assumes a greater tendency to join among this group and is borne out by experience which shows, for example that *The Guardian* elicits a very much higher response than *The Sunday Mirror*. It will remain profitable to recruit 'close to home' while an overwhelming proportion of this group have not joined Amnesty, and this is the case at present.

TABLE 4:   READERS WITH EDUCATION PAST THE AGE OF 19

| | |
|---|---|
| Guardian | 587,000 |
| Independent | 382,000 |
| Observer | 795,000 |
| Total | 1,764,000 |

Clearly not all of these are typical of their papers' editorial stances but we might expect at least a million of them to be potential Amnesty members – compared with the current membership of 67,000.

There will come a time when it is no longer profitable to recruit within this niche. Our long-term objective is to recruit a much broader-based membership but in the short-term we are constrained, by the need to maximise profit, to advertise further afield only when free space becomes available.

## DESCRIPTION OF CAMPAIGN

### Advertising Background

Amnesty advertising has necessarily been a process of learning by doing: every pound has been needed in the front line. Where possible the direct response data has been supplemented by small qualitative programmes of research, to help us understand how the advertising was working. This research was often conducted voluntarily – without cost to Amnesty.

Because few people knew what Amnesty did (although many were aware of the organisation) and because once Amnesty's mandate was explained the majority supported it (Table 5), we decided the advertising should focus on the problems Amnesty deals with.

TABLE 5:

QUESTION:   *'This is a summary of Amnesty International's aims – can you tell me how much you support them (READ CARD)?'*

| Support | Total (%) |
|---|---|
| A lot | 43 |
| Quite a lot | 32 |
| Not very much | 14 |
| Not at all | 5 |
| Don't know | 6 |

Source:   Audience Selection
            Telephone Survey,
            April 1988

Anybody reading the papers, particularly our core titles, is confronted by a barrage of similar charity advertising. Common sense, backed up by our qualitative research, tells us that in this environment impact is the first criteria for success. Impact rests on having a visual or verbal hook:

'It says the same thing, but stops you and gets through to your emotions somehow' (BMP Qualitative, April 1990).

This is particularly difficult in Amnesty advertising as the naked representation of what Amnesty deals with is too horrible – torture, hanging, sexual abuse – and positively deters readers' involvement. We have always therefore adopted a symbolic approach, but we do find that it has most impact when the full horror is lurking just below the surface.

In this competitive environment, research has also confirmed our initial hunch that asking for more than just money – ie membership – might be an advantage. Respondents spontaneously suggested that:

'Amnesty's not like any other charities, which just want your money' (BMP Qualitative, December 1989).

Advertising has mostly recruited members aged 22 – 24. (see Table 8). Nearly all the members we spoke to in this lifestage had joined because of a general feeling that they didn't do enough 'worthwhile' things. What made them choose Amnesty was the chance to feel involved rather than 'just throwing money at a problem'. Some went as far as to describe it as 'better value for money' (BMP Qualitative, December 1989).

In recruiting members to Amnesty, we not only have to overcome ignorance of the issues, but also the general feeling among non-members that Amnesty is:

'An organisation'
'Far from home and real life' (BMP Qualitative December 1989).

We therefore needed advertising which affected people personally and made people identify with the victims – rather than just setting out Amnesty's activities. Making people identify in this way with the victims of horrible abuses has been a tough creative challenge.

## Advertising Development

'Letters'
This advertising lets realistic translations of real letters from prisoners speak for themselves. In this way we hoped to achieve a very personal communication with readers. It also builds on any existing awareness of the letter-writing activities of Amnesty members.

## DEATH PENALTY

# IN AMERICA, HE CAN'T VOTE FOR ANOTHER 18 YEARS BUT HE CAN BE SENTENCED TO DEATH IN 10.

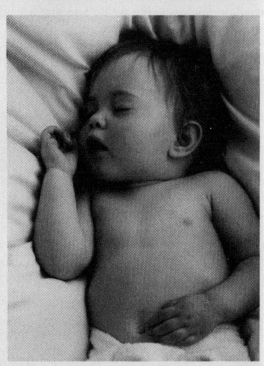

The International Covenant on Civil Rights states: 'Sentence of death shall not be imposed for crimes committed by persons below 18 years of age.'

This treaty was signed by the United States Government in 1977. Despite this, 17 states still set a minimum age below 18.

In both Indiana and Vermont, that age is just 10.

America is only one of 125 countries whose laws provide for the death penalty for ordinary crimes.

Amnesty International opposes the death penalty which is the ultimate cruel, inhuman and degrading punishment.

It seeks the release of men, women and children detained anywhere for their beliefs, ethnic origin, language or religion who have not used or advocated violence.

It is self financing and independent of any government, political faction, ideology, economic interest or religious creed.

It seeks your help to win these freedoms.

---

I wish to join Amnesty International:   £12 (Individual) ☐
£15 (Family) ☐   £5 (OAP) ☐   £5 (Student, Under 18, Claimant) ☐

I wish to give a donation of:   £100   £50   £25   £15   Other £____

Name _____

Address _____

_____

_____ Postcode

Amnesty International British Section, Freepost, London EC1B 1HE.

# AMNESTY INTERNATIONAL

## BAZOFT

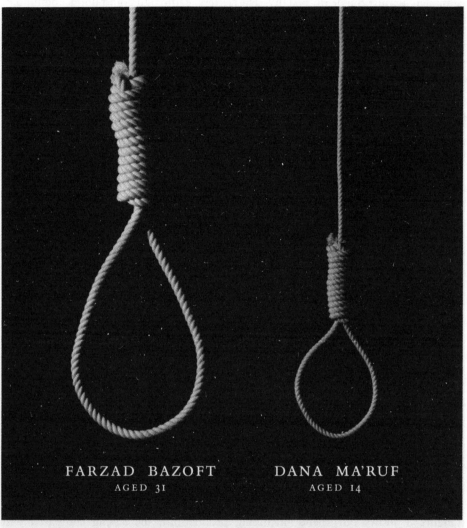

FARZAD BAZOFT
AGED 31

DANA MA'RUF
AGED 14

The Farzad Bazoft case has shocked public opinion all over the World.
Equally shocking, though, has been the execution of children as young as fourteen. The imprisonment
and torture of infants of five and six has also been reported. We're investigating allegations
that methods used by the Iraqi government range from pulling out fingernails to gouging out the eyes of their victims,
cutting off noses, ears and penises. And even hanging female prisoners upside down during menstruation.
Join Amnesty International and you can help fight the methods of all oppressive governments like Iraq.
This is an appeal on behalf of Farzad Bazoft. Something the Iraqis didn't allow him.

306

To: Amnesty International British Section, Freepost, London EC1B 1HE.
I WISH TO JOIN AMNESTY INTERNATIONAL: £12 *Individual* ☐ £15 *Family* ☐ £5 *OAP* ☐ £5 *Student, Under 18, Claimant.* ☐
I WISH TO GIVE A DONATION OF: £100 £50 £25 £15 OTHER £_____

NAME_____ ADDRESS_____
_____POSTCODE_____

**AMNESTY INTERNATIONAL**

### 'Death Penalty'

New advertising was developed to coincide with a major Amnesty publicity campaign against the death penalty. The 'letters' campaign could not accommodate this focus on an issue. The photographs were chosen to be visually compelling – the headlines to bring out the barbaric nature of execution.

### 'China'

An advertisement was prepared using an existing visual (*Times* cartoon) following the Tiannenman Square massacre.

### 'Bazoft'

Two advertisements were used at the time of the execution of Farzad Bazoft in Iraq. The first was all type (for speed), the second using photography of nooses as shocking symbols of hanging, followed on two days later.

### Media

The space sizes have generally been 25 x 4 column – one size larger than the plethora of 20 x 2 column size charity advertisements. We wanted to stand out from all the other charity advertising. We also then had more space to create the impact and communication which was needed given the low level of knowledge about Amnesty.

The total advertising budgets available to us have been:

|      |          |
|------|----------|
| 1988 | £30,000  |
| 1989 | £50,000  |
| 1990 | £150,000 |

The successive increases are obviously a vote of confidence. By being innovative and persistent we have managed to buy at a considerable discount. In many cases it has been sight of the advertisement and our topical approach which has got us free space. This is especially true of smaller publications like the *Spectator* who have actually contacted us offering free space.

The bulk of our money has been spent on our core publications – *The Guardian*, *Independent* and *Observer*.

Figure 3 shows our spend (including production), the saving compared with ratecard and the surrounding Amnesty publicity. We learnt early on that publicity has an effect on the response – the first evidence we had of this is shown in Table 6.

TABLE 6:   EFFECT OF HEAVY PUBLICITY IN DECEMBER 1988 (Running the Same Advertising)

| June–Oct 88 | Average Response: | Observer    | 119        |
|-------------|-------------------|-------------|------------|
|             | (Members)         | Independent | 122        |
|             |                   | Guardian    | 98         |
| Dec 88      | Average Response: | Observer    | 207 (+74%) |
|             |                   | Guardian    | 148 (+51%) |
|             |                   | Independent | 182 (+49%) |

Note:  PR in Dec 1988: Secret Policeman's Third Ball, TV screening of Amnesty World Tour and TV series on human rights.

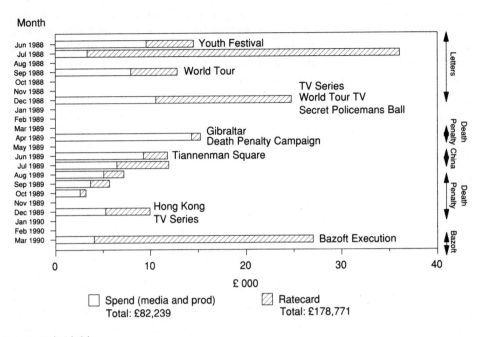

Figure 3. *Media Schedule*

While some of this effect might be cumulative – the campaign wearing in – other examples have convinced us that there is a genuine effect of publicity. This effect cuts both ways. The response in December 1989, when many people were upset about Amnesty's 'unpatriotic' publicity about Hong Kong, gives an example of a negative effect – responses fell by an average of 60% in our core publications, compared with the previous exposure of the same advertisement.

### Results

A summary of costs and responses is shown in Table 7. From this we can see that advertising directly recruited 4,718 new members. A full analysis of overall effectiveness is conducted in the next section. In this section we concentrate on lessons we have learned from these results.

TABLE 7

| | Inserts | Ratecard (£) | Actual cost (£) | Production (£) | Total spend (£) | Recruits |
|---|---|---|---|---|---|---|
| Letters (Jun – Dec 88) | 22 | 88,222 | 18,050 | 13,446 | 31,496 | 1,852 |
| Death Penalty (April 89) | 5 | 15,250 | 10,400 | 3,930 | 14,330 | 780 |
| Tiannenman (Jun – Jul 89) | 4 | 23,742 | 13,200 | 2,532 | 15,732 | 510 |
| Death Penalty (Aug – Dec 89) | 8 | 26,047 | 14,300 | 2,323 | 16,623 | 903 |
| Iraq (Mar 90) | 8 | 25,510 | 1,000 | 3,058 | 4,058 | 673 |
| Total | 47 | 178,771 | 56,950 | 25,289 | 82,239 | 4,718 |

The previous agency advertised on a similar strategy to ours early in 1988. Their responses were recorded, as ours were, in the membership computer files, so we can compare how our advertising did in the same publications (Figure 4). This gives the cleanest measure of the relative strengths of the advertisements themselves (rather than media efficiency, which is considered later).

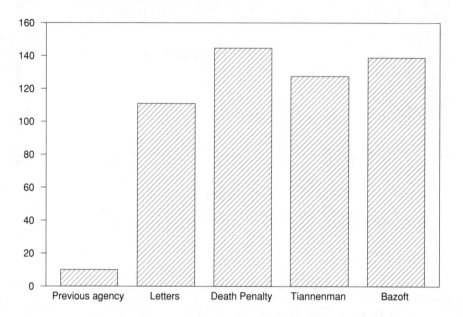

Figure 4. *Recruits per insertion, Guardian, Independent, Observer*

The 'Stones' death penalty advertisement achieved the highest return per insertion of all our advertising. It is gratifying therefore to note that 'Stones' was also rated highest by respondents in our research (December 1989) when they were asked which of our previous advertising they were most likely to respond to. And it is also interesting to note that this advertisement won an advertising creative award (Campaign Press & Poster, Silver).

The effectiveness of our advertising rests on media buying as well as creative strength. A better overall comparison of effectiveness is therefore gleaned from a graph of return in members on total cost of advertising (Figure 5). We do not have costs for the previous advertising, but a number of other interesting points arise from this graph.

1.  The results for the Tiannenman advertisement fell well below the standards set by our previous advertising. Part of the blame falls to us for getting to press over a week after the event. At this late stage we had little leverage for cheap space with the press on the basis of topicality, and public interest had fallen away.

2.  In March 1990 we learned the lessons from this affair and bent over backwards to get an advertisement in the papers the day after the execution of Farzad Bazoft. This approach paid off in pure responses per exposure, doubly

so as we managed to get nearly 90% of the media cost for free, and triply so as accompanying donations reached nearly £2,000.

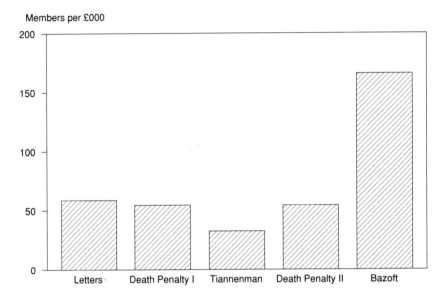

Figure 5. *Return from advertising*

As often happened with 'Letters' and 'Stones' it was sight of the advertising which contributed to our getting free space – a direct advertising effect. Smaller publications have often requested advertising which they ran for free, after seeing it in the national press.

## EVALUATION AND ISOLATION OF THE ADVERTISING EFFECT

### *Isolation of Advertising Effect*

The 4,718 new members were definitely recruited by advertising. The figure comes from return of coupons, which were only available in the advertisements – it is a clear, direct response and there is no need to isolate an effect in the normal sense.

The question could perhaps arise as to whether some of these people might have joined by other means if we had not advertised. Figure 6 shows that the annual rate of growth of membership increased once advertising began.

This graph in itself strongly suggests that advertising alone was responsible for its recruits and indeed that the advertising may have increased the effectiveness of other methods of recruitment like direct mail.

Further evidence is provided by the type of people advertising recruited. Amnesty is highly visible amongst young people, particularly students, due to events like concerts and activities at school and on campus. On the other hand the 1989 membership survey indicates that our advertising recruits are on average substantially older.

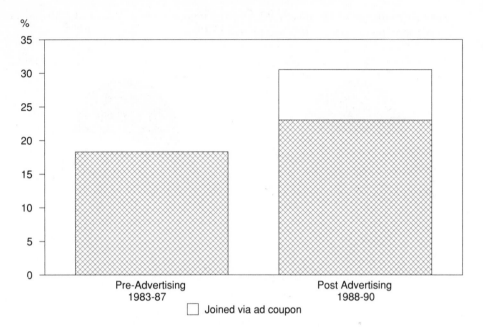

Figure 6. *Annual rate of growth of membership*

TABLE 8:   AGE PROFILE BY SOURCE OF MEMBERSHIP

| Base | Advertising (%) (440) | Other (%) (1850) |
|---|---|---|
| Under 22 | 11 | 27 |
| 22 – 34 | 32 | 30 |
| 35 – 44 | 26 | 16 |
| 45 – 54 | 12 | 8 |
| 55+ | 18 | 18 |

This is confirmed by the profile of membership types for advertising versus other recruits (Figure 7). Qualitative research with 25 – 44 year olds indicated a very low public profile. Given that advertising and press mentions are the principal contact for these people, and given that joining unsolicited is hard work, we would argue our advertising alone is responsible for their recruitment.

We have always recognised the beneficial effect of advertising when other favourable publicity exists. This generally pays back in increased responses and in our ability to get cheap media space by being topical (and therefore interesting to have in a newspaper). Obviously in these cases we have worked in synergy with PR. There is absolutely no evidence that our recruits would (or could) have joined in other ways. In many cases it was *only* our advertising which linked world events (such as the execution of Farzad Bazoft) with the idea of joining Amnesty.

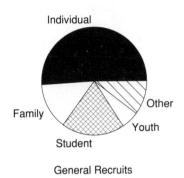

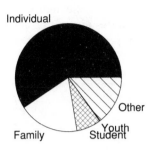

Figure 7. *Recruits by type, 1988–89*

## Short-Term Pay-Back

The first issue in assessing advertising effectiveness is what return advertising has provided in the short-term. Members provide Amnesty with income in the form of fees and donations, but also cost Amnesty money in magazine and campaign mailings. Ideally we would look at the net income from members recruited by advertising. This is however not available as a separate sample so we use the total membership base, and go on to show that the advertising recruits are above average in terms of net income.

The 1989 financial report gives us the overall net income.

TABLE 9

|  | Membership mid-year | Income from members (£) | Net cost of mailing & magazine (£) | Net income per member (£) |
|---|---|---|---|---|
| 1989 | 55,781 | 983,900 | 322,100 | 11.86 |

These figures exclude additional income from trading and donations made in response to appeals, but include any donations made with the membership application.

As mentioned above, advertising tends to recruit different sorts of people to other methods of recruitment. This has financial implications. A statistical analysis shows that the distribution of membership types is significantly different (see Appendix).

On average the recruits from advertising pay £11.00 per head in subscriptions, as opposed to the average of £9.99. And since they tend to be older (and hence wealthier), it is reasonable to assume that they will make larger donations (the Charities Aid Foundation Household Survey research confirms this view). We can scale up the £11.86, to take account of the higher subscriptions paid by advertising recruits. This gives a figure of £12.87 (11.86 + 11.00 − 9.99), which is the direct return from the advertising coupon.

It is then possible to assess the profitability of the advertising so far (Table 10).

TABLE 10

|  | Immediate income | | 2nd year income | Total |
|  | Ads 1988/89 | Ads 1989/90 | Ads 1988/89 | to date |
|---|---|---|---|---|
| Spend | £45,826 | £36,413 | — | £82,239 |
| Recruits | 2,632 | 2,086 | — | 4,718 |
| Renewals | — | — | 2,050 | 2,050 |
| Income | £33,885 | £26,856 | £26,391 | £87,133 |
| Profit | −£11,941 | −£9,557 | £26,391 | £4,894 |

The important point which we wanted to make from this snapshot of cashflow is that by April 1990, income from advertising had already outstripped expenditure by £4,894. All further income from these members is pure profit (allowing for administration).

It is interesting to note that a calculation of return on media spend using the accurate £12.87 figure gives a pay-back of 106% − compared with the charity average of 29%. In immediate responses, we have been nearly four times more effective than the average charity.

### Long-Term Profitability

We have stated all along that the greatest benefit of recruiting members accrues in the long term. By looking at people who have joined Amnesty over the last six years and calculating the percentage now lapsed, it is possible to get a picture of the typical lifecycle of a member. Figure 8 shows that it is possible to model this life cycle accurately (see Appendix for details).

The model is an equation in which the chance of members renewing their subscription increases with every year they have already stayed.

This means that people who stay with Amnesty for more that three or four years are likely to stay for a very long time − perhaps for life. This accords with Amnesty's own experience of having a hard-core of more committed members. It is also a well-known tenet of fundraising that people give in proportion to how often they have given before to that cause.

We showed earlier that advertising recruits give more income than other recruits. It is also the case that they stay longer. Looking at the period June − September 1988 (lapsing is not recorded on the computer files until attempts over six months to retain a member have failed), we find that recruits from advertising are significantly more likely to renew their subscriptions for a second year (see Appendix for significance test).

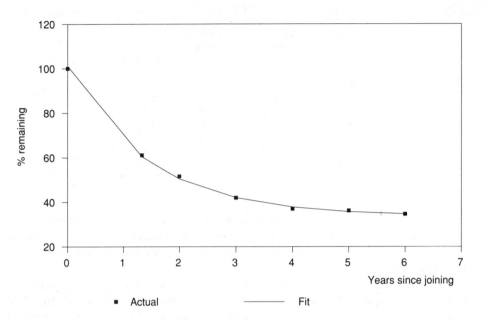

Figure 8.  *Model of decay rate*

TABLE 11

|         | Recruits | Renewals | % Renewing |
|---------|----------|----------|------------|
| Ads     | 832      | 648      | 78         |
| Non-ads | 5,346    | 3,128    | 59         |

Once again, this is understandable. Research (BMP Qualitative, December 1989) suggests that younger members often join because of peer pressure – it's a trendy thing to do. Older members are more likely to be going against the flow of opinion (prejudices about Amnesty being left-wing etc) and so if they do take the trouble to join, it is probably because of a deeper commitment. We actively encourage recruitment of more committed members by advertising on the issues rather than appealing to Amnesty's 'badge appeal'.

With only one year's data it is not possible to produce a separate model of the life cycle of new advertising recruits, so in what follows we will assume that they follow the pattern of ordinary members. This will tend to *under-estimate* the longevity of membership, and hence future income.

We can calculate the stream of future income by looking at the member life cycle graph and using our estimate of net income per member (£12.87).

TABLE 12

| Year | Ad Recruits left from year 1 | Ad Recruits left from year 2 | Income from recruits (£) |
|------|------|------|------|
| 1989 | 2,632 | — | 33,885 |
| 1990 | 1,354 | 2,086 | 44,287 |
| 1991 | 1,133 | 1,073 | 28,396 |
| 1992 | 1,022 | 898 | 24,715 |
| 1993 | 967 | 810 | 22,877 |
| 1994 | 939 | 766 | 21,959 |
| 1995 | 926 | 744 | 21,501 |

Total: £197,621

Thus, after six years, we can expect a profit of £115,382 for an investment of £82,239, a return of 140%. This is a *conservative* estimate for reasons outlined above – in fact, Table 12 shows that actual performance has already outstripped these predictions.

As a comparison, consider the sort of return we might expect from an alternative investment. Suppose Amnesty were able to invest the money at the best commercially available interest rate. Table 13 shows the expected stream of income.

TABLE 13

| Year | Interest rate** | Income* from year 1 | Income* from year 2 |
|------|------|------|------|
| 1989 | 13.9 | 6,370 | — |
| 1990 | 15.0 | 6,874 | 5,462 |
| 1991 | 13.0 | 6,957 | 4,734 |
| 1992 | 11.5 | 6,270 | 4,187 |
| 1993 | 12.0 | 7,499 | 4,370 |
| 1994 | 12.3 | 8,637 | 4,479 |
| 1995 | 12.1 | 9,545 | 4,406 |

Total: £41,152     £27,637

Notes: * Annual return on spend in year
      ** Henley Centre Forecast, 1990.

This gives a total profit of £91,436 after six years, a return of only 119%.

Thus, even on a conservative estimate, advertising can be shown to represent a very profitable investment in the longer term.

The actual profitability will be higher than the estimate shown because:

1.  Recruits from advertising stay longer than average.
2.  They make larger donations.
3.  Increased membership also increases the profitability of trading and direct mail appeals. On average Amnesty makes £2.80 from appeals and 92p from trading, per member, per year (Amnesty costings) – adding 30% to our profit.

4.  Members also recruit other members.
    13% of current membership joined in this way: there is a substantial 'snowball' effect which is encouraged through 'enrol a friend' schemes.

## CONCLUSIONS

The key to the success of our advertising was the recognition that membership offered a competitive edge and a long-term income. The whole paper has concentrated on how effective and creative advertising used these facts to secure a large profit for Amnesty International, and indeed a larger profit than their previous advertising had generated. This gives a very one-dimensional picture of what we have really achieved. Earlier this year the agency had a visit from a man who had been arrested, imprisoned and tortured continuously for four years in Argentina. Letters from ordinary Amnesty members and visits from Amnesty delegates kept him going through his ordeal, and he believes are the only reason he is alive and free today. If one member recruited by advertising wrote one letter that saved another human being's life – how could we possibly account for that on a balance sheet?

## TECHNICAL APPENDIX

### Membership Profile

As outlined above, the 1989 membership survey indicates that recruits from advertising show a different age profile from other recruits (see Table 8). A chi-squared test on the age distribution confirms that this difference is statistically significant at the 95% confidence level:

$\chi^2 = 65.5$     Critical value $= 14.1$ (7 degrees of freedom)

An analysis of new members recruited in the period June 1988 – May 1989 shows the following breakdown by category:

| Category | General recruits | Ad recruits |
| --- | --- | --- |
| Individual | 11,611 | 1,004 |
| Family | 3,156 | 312 |
| Student | 4,423 | 127 |
| OAP | 86 | 6 |
| Youth | 1,230 | 4 |
| Reduced | 2,200 | 240 |
| Twin | 47 | 1 |

The differences in the two distributions are highly significant at the 95% level:

$\chi^2 = 281.7$     Critical value $= 19.7$ (11 degrees of freedom)

## Longevity of Membership

By looking at people who have joined Amnesty over the last six years, and calculating the percentage now lapsed, it is possible to get a picture of the life cycle of a member:

| Date of joining | Average time elapsed* | % remaining |
|---|---|---|
| June 1983–May 1984 | 6 years | 35 |
| June 1984–May 1985 | 5 years | 36 |
| June 1985–May 1986 | 4 years | 37 |
| June 1986–May 1987 | 3 years | 42 |
| June 1987–May 1988 | 2 years | 52 |
| June–October 1988** | 16 months | 61 |
| May 1990 | 0 years | 100 |

* since subscriptions came up for renewal
** latest data available

It is possible to model this by the equation: $Ae^{-xt} + B$
Where:

$$Y = \% \text{ remaining}$$
$$A = 0.674$$
$$B = 0.336$$
$$x = 0.694$$
$$t = \text{time elapsed}$$

Figure 8 shows the actual and fitted values for the model, which has a remarkably accurate fit ($R^2 = 99.2\%$).

An analysis of recruits in the period June – October 1988 (the latest period for which such data is available) shows that recruits from advertising are significantly more likely to renew membership after the first year.

| | Recruits | Renewals | % renewing |
|---|---|---|---|
| From ads | 832 | 648 | 78 |
| Other | 5,346 | 3,128 | 59 |
| Test statistic | 8.35 | Critical value | 1.65 |

It is therefore likely that recruits from advertising will on average stay with Amnesty longer than other recruits. However, in the absence of longer-term data, it is impossible to produce a separate model for the life cycle of a recruit from advertising. We have therefore assumed for the purposes of profitability that recruits from advertising behave like all others. This will tend to *underestimate* their length of stay, and hence profitability.

# 14

## Lil-lets:

## *How a Small Investment Safeguarded the Future of a Brand*

### INTRODUCTION

The subject of this paper is the advertising for Lil-lets tampons since January 1988. At the end of 1987 the brand was in slow but long-term share decline. This prompted a change in agency and in advertising strategy, and it is the effect of the new strategy which is outlined in this case study.

This paper shows the campaign was successful in gaining unprecedented levels of trial for the brand in a market where trial is key. It justifies the focus of the advertising on one small variant which is particularly useful for trial gain – Lil-lets Mini. It demonstrates why this trial gain is essential to the long-term maintenance of the brand's business.

It will further show that this was achieved with great efficiency through creative and media targeting on an audience which is small in absolute terms but very fruitful. We will argue that this decision to concentrate relatively modest funds to the best effect will be repaid in the long-term.

### BACKGROUND

The tampon market is almost entirely a branded market. There are two broad categories of tampon: applicator – which is represented by Tampax – and digital – which is represented by Lil-lets.

The tampon market splits roughly 65:35 in favour of the applicator sector and, as Lil-lets and Tampax each command about 95% of these respective markets, any competition between the sectors is, per se, competition between these two brands (there is only a very small own label presence).

By the end of 1987 the Lil-lets brand (and therefore the digital sector) had shown persistent loss of share over five years. This loss of share was, given the nature of the market, to the direct gain of applicator tampons and, hence, Tampax (see Table 1).

TABLE 1:  MARKET SHARE: DIGITAL VS APPLICATOR TAMPONS

|  | 1982 | 1983 | 1984 | 1985 | 1986 | 1987 |
|---|---|---|---|---|---|---|
| *Volume* | | | | | | |
| Digital | 39.4 | 39.7 | 38.2 | 36.7 | 35.9 | 35.8 |
| Applicator | 59.7 | 60.0 | 61.8 | 63.3 | 64.2 | 64.2 |
| *Value* | | | | | | |
| Digital | 39.5 | 38.7 | 37.4 | 36.7 | 36.0 | 35.6 |
| Applicator | 59.8 | 61.1 | 62.6 | 63.3 | 64.0 | 64.4 |

Source:  Nielsen

### Why was Lil-lets Losing Share?

Lil-lets was losing share primarily because it was not recruiting new users. It was not recruiting new users because it was not gaining trial amongst girls entering the market. The importance of recruitment and of trial is explained below, as are the two main barriers to that trial which we had to overcome, specifically:

1.  The perceived 'difficulty' of using Lil-lets.
2.  A lack of salience in the market.

### A Failure to Recruit

The pool of menstruating women is constantly changing. Women enter the market when they reach the menarch (first period) at around thirteen and leave it when they reach the menopause at around fifty. To maintain brand volume it is necessary to replace the older women with new entrants to the market.

This Lil-lets had failed to do. It had once enjoyed a good share amongst the youngest users in the market but now fell behind its overall market share amongst the recruitment market (see Table 2).

TABLE 2:  LIL-LETS VS TAMPAX: VOLUME BRAND SHARES BY AGE

|  | Lil-lets | | | | Tampax | | | |
|---|---|---|---|---|---|---|---|---|
|  | 1984 | 1985 | 1986 | 1987 | 1984 | 1985 | 1986 | 1987 |
| 13 – 15 | 39.0 | n/a | 20.9 | 22.0 | 61.0 | n/a | 70.1 | 78.0 |
| 16 – 18 | 16.6 | 18.2 | 11.2 | 17.3 | 72.6 | 72.5 | 78.2 | 62.0 |
| 19 – 24 | 47.0 | 54.0 | 42.5 | 32.7 | 45.0 | 41.6 | 48.6 | 54.2 |

Source:  AGB/TCPI (1987 data)

As a result the brand's profile was getting older (see Table 3). Lil-lets was clearly losing its currency amongst young girls.

TABLE 3:  LIL-LETS – AGE PROFILE OF USERS

|  | 1981 | 1982 | 1983 | 1984 | 1985 | 1986 | 1987 |
|---|---|---|---|---|---|---|---|
| 15 – 24 | 47 | 42 | 42 | 38 | 38 | 36 | 35 |
| 25 – 34 | 29 | 34 | 33 | 36 | 34 | 36 | 34 |
| 35 – 44 | 18 | 15 | 18 | 19 | 20 | 21 | 22 |
| 45 – 54 | 5 | 7 | 6 | 7 | 7 | 6 | 8 |

Source:  TGI

This lack of share amongst the young augured very badly for the brand. Loyalty in the tampon market is established very early and is fiercely held to. The loyalty is to a system (ie a method of insertion) more than to a brand but, because brand *is* system in this market it appears as brand loyalty. It is very difficult indeed to unhinge a user's loyalty from her system and therefore her brand.

This presents any brand seeking growth with a large problem. It is not feasible in this market to encourage heavier consumption of the product by any one user. Women use only as many tampons as they need. Therefore growth can only come from new users. The high loyalty in the market makes it unlikely that new users will be found amongst an adult audience.

This high loyalty also makes irrelevant some of the factors which, in other markets, might offer an opportunity for conversion of established users. For example, price does not offer a competitive opportunity because consumers do not compare prices across systems. Therefore, as long as there is only one viable brand in each system, there is no point of comparison.

All this makes the lack of young recruits still more important. There is no other significant digital brand from which share can be stolen and it is unlikely to be got from the applicator sector. Furthermore, once the users have adopted a system they are virtually lost for ever (there are few occasions after this initial stage when a woman might contemplate or use something else – a change in contraceptive method or the birth of a baby might prompt a reassessment but in practice there is little opportunity). Therefore it is vital to recruit users as they enter the market (as young as ten to fourteen), when they are still considering their options and before they have decided on a brand/system.

## *Why Is Gaining Trial So Important?*

Trial is important in any exercise to recruit new users to a market or a brand. In Lil-lets case we had to be particularly aggressive in seeking trial for two reasons.

First, because the lack of salience and perceived difficulty of the brand made trial of digital tampons relatively unlikely (Tables 4 and 5).

TABLE 4: BRAND SALIENCE

| | Lil-lets | | Tampax | |
|---|---|---|---|---|
| | A % | B % | A % | B % |
| Spontaneous awareness | 84 | 64 | 91 | 79 |
| Prompted awareness | 99 | 96 | 100 | 100 |
| Tampons used nowadays | 40 | 23 | 66 | 69 |
| Tampons likely to use in the future | 44 | 32 | 68 | 72 |

Source: Usage and Attitude Study 1987.
Base: (A) 635 women 16–34
      (B) 103 tampon users 13–15

TABLE 5: TAMPON TRIAL

| Type of tampon first tried | |
|---|---|
| Applicator | 73% |
| Digital | 27% |

Source: Usage and Attitude Study 1987.

Second, because the first brand tried has an advantage in conversion (Table 6).

TABLE 6. TAMPON BRAND USED NOW BY SYSTEM TRIED FIRST

| Tried first | Applicator (1,124) | Digital (407) |
|---|---|---|
| Applicator used now | 62 | 42 |
| Digital used now | 26 | 49 |

Source: Usage and Attitude Study 1987

### Barriers to Trial

*The perceived difficulty of Lil-lets* – Digital tampons have a reputation for being more 'difficult' to use than applicator tampons. This is directly due to the method of insertion, which is with the finger (hence the description 'digital') rather than by a cardboard applicator which positions the tampon without the finger being required to intimately touch or enter the body.

Almost all tampon users can use an applicator tampon; not all can manage or countenance a digital one (thus it is rare to see a machine dispensing digital tampons in a school or public cloakroom; it is far more common to see a machine vending both towels and applicator tampons).

The perceived difficulty of the digital products is felt to be more acute for young users who are just coming to the market. The use of tampons touches on a number of taboos still prevalent in our thinking – the loss of virginity, the coming of age – which bear on the minds of mothers as well as of daughters. So it was not surprising in our qualitative work to come across tampon-using mothers who provided towels for their daughters, and Lil-lets-using mothers who bought Tampax for their daughters.

This situation calls for more education and explanation of the usage and benefits (notably discretion and reliability) of Lil-lets. In particular attention needed to be drawn to the existence of the 'Mini' variant of the Lil-lets brand which, due to its smaller size, was the ideal vehicle for young girls wishing to try the brand. There was a clear need to address these problems directly, in order to motivate and reassure both adult and child users.

*A Lack of Salience*

1. *Advertising* – Unfortunately Lil-lets was not addressing this need for education. Throughout the 1980s Lil-lets was consistently outspent by the larger brand Tampax in advertising terms (see Table 7).

TABLE 7:   ADVERTISING SPEND 1980–1987 (£000s)

|          | 1980 | 1981 | 1982 | 1983 | 1984  | 1985  | 1986  | 1987  |
|----------|------|------|------|------|-------|-------|-------|-------|
| Lil-lets | 457  | 502  | 637  | 783  | 967   | 980   | 747   | 0     |
| Tampax   | 649  | 782  | 857  | 989  | 1,161 | 1,287 | 1,516 | 1,329 |

Source:   MEAL

Furthermore its advertising was uncompetitive. The 'Ball and Chain' campaign which ran from 1979 until 1986, presented Lil-lets to a (mostly adult) audience of towel users. Lil-lets was positioned as 'the small key to freedom', a claim which, despite the reference to size, was essentially generic and offered no persuasive reason to try Lil-lets in preference to Tampax.

2. *Point of Sale* – Lil-lets has approximately one third of the market. This level is reflected in its share of facings on shelf – the only place where the small size of the pack works to its disadvantage, giving Tampax a great deal more space overall.

3. *Distribution* – Distribution of both brands was good. The highest volume lines, Regular and Super, not surprisingly enjoyed the best distribution and all variants were well represented in the pharmacy sector. However, in the grocery sector which was rapidly growing in importance Lil-lets fell behind Tampax (Table 8).

TABLE 8:   STERLING DISTRIBUTION

|                 | Slender/Mini | Regular | Super | Super Plus |
|-----------------|--------------|---------|-------|------------|
| *Total Pharmacy* |              |         |       |            |
| Lil-lets        | 62           | 97      | 98    | 96         |
| Tampax          | 89           | 100     | 100   | 99         |
| *Total Grocery* |              |         |       |            |
| Lil-lets        | 9            | 81      | 79    | 49         |
| Tampax          | 17           | 94      | 96    | 77         |

Source:   Nielsen N/D 1987

Neither brand's junior variant (Tampax Slender, Lil-lets Mini) was well distributed in grocery but comparison of the absolute levels was clearly in favour of Tampax. These smallest variants were particularly important for the youngest users (being easier to insert) and represented a vital stepping stone to the brand. Such low distribution, therefore, clearly worked against recruitment of the youngest users. So did the low awareness of Mini and its benefits.

In these three ways Lil-lets was failing to facilitate entry to the brand by menstruating girls.

## HOW COULD WE REVERSE THIS SITUATION?

Throughout the 1980s we had neglected the recruitment of our youngest market and we were now reaping the rewards of our inactivity. Only 20% of the brand's modest advertising budget had been directed at this crucial audience and our gateway to the brand – Lil-lets Mini – was effectively closed through lack of availability. It was agreed that for the long-term health of the brand we had to pursue the recruitment market and strengthen our profile amongst the young users who were just embarking on forty or so years of sanpro usage.

Even so, we were not likely to have more financial resources in the future than we had had in the past and we still needed to overcome the barriers posed by the brand's demanding image.

For the maximum benefit we decided to direct all the advertising funds at the recruitment audience leaving below-the-line activity to deal with existing loyal users. This meant we could mount a very aggressive attack on the young market which would make us highly visible and would provide an argument for better distribution of the Mini variant.

It was not ideal to abandon the older market completely. However, given what we knew about the strengths of our competitor and loyalty in the market, we knew we did not have the resources to offer a real challenge to it. What we could do was make the best use of our available funds, mounting the advertising campaign which was most likely to bring results and which would be an investment in our future. It is one of our objectives in this paper to show the benefits of this pragmatic concentration of funds to the long-term status of the brand.

## DEFINING A ROLE FOR ADVERTISING – TRIAL AND PERSEVERANCE

Advertising could be used as a means of gaining trial, by getting samples into the hands of our audience and by increasing distribution. But this was not enough. From the usage and attitude studies, from the low intention to try Lil-lets in future and from many years of girls' letters we knew that insertion of the first tampons was sometimes a very difficult experience (this could be for mental or physical reasons). While some failed trialists would postpone their entry to the market for some years, others, who persevered, would successfully learn how to use the tampon and would become loyal users.

Therefore the objectives for advertising were:

1.  To encourage trial amongst first-time users (benefits and sympathy).
2.  To try to limit rejection amongst those trialists (usage education and an acknowledgement of the difficulties).
3.  To inform.

The target audience was trialists and failed trialists ten to eighteen with a core target of girls aged ten to fourteen (the years immediately surrounding the menarch).

To meet these objectives with a target audience who were actively disinclined to try our product we needed to offer a persuasive competitive advantage over the competition. There was such an advantage inherent to the Lil-lets brand. This became the strategic focus of the advertising.

## CAMPAIGN EXECUTION

### Creative

The competitive proposition of the creative work was superior discretion. Many women are sensitive to the fact that other people might know when they are having a period. Amongst young girls this feeling is acute. The worst thing they can imagine is that anyone should know. The discretion offered by Lil-lets was what they most wanted from a sanpro product.

Furthermore the proposition was true to virtually every aspect of the product: its unbranded packaging, the size of pack and product (because there is no applicator), the fact that it is worn internally (generic) and the widthways expansion (a brand specific benefit protecting against leakage – the ultimate indiscretion).

Four executions were developed, 'Mental Block', 'Packet', 'Please Sir', and 'T-Shirt'. All had long reassuring copy which directly addressed itself to the process and problems of tampon use, particularly insertion. Each carried a freepost sample request coupon (which asked for name, address and age), and readers were invited to address queries to the in-house enquiry nurse, 'Marion Cooper'. A sample of ten tampons and an educational booklet was despatched to every girl who sent in a coupon.

Initially a Freephone line was also included in the coupon as a means of requesting a sample. It was intended to facilitate trial but it was subject to abuse and, as it was expensive and not particularly successful, it was closed down after a few months.

For 1989 three more executions were developed along similar lines. These were 'Silhouettes', 'Needle and Thread' and 'Paper Bag'.

### Media

The campaign ran exclusively in the teenage press with a bias towards readers aged ten to fourteen (first-time trialists). Because of the low cost of this kind of media the campaign was able to appear every week of the year (a fact which the sales force found particularly useful) on a budget which would have given us only two to three months of advertising against an adult audience (see Table 9).

## 'PLEASE SIR'

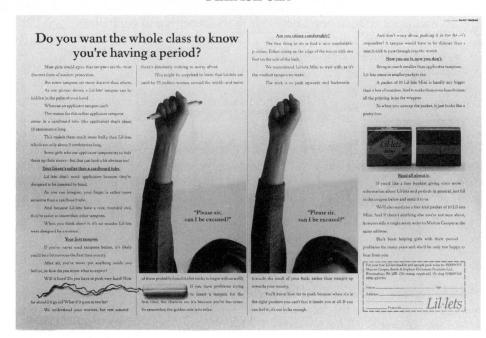

## 'T SHIRT'

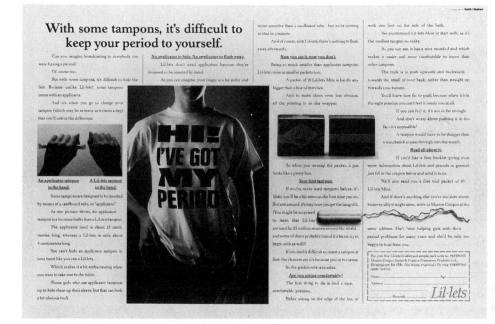

TABLE 9:  MEDIA PLACEMENT OF CAMPAIGN

| Title | 1988 No. of insertions | 1989 No. of insertions |
|---|---|---|
| Jackie (w) | 20 | 20 |
| Blue Jeans (w) | 16 | 15 |
| Patches (w) | 16 | — |
| My Guy (w) | 16 | 17 |
| Girl (w) | 16 | 17 |
| Just Seventeen (w) | 26 | 26 |
| Mizz (f) | 15 | 17 |
| Looks (m) | 10 | 10 |
| 19 (m) | 10 | 10 |
| Look Now (m) | 1 | — |
| Company (m) | 2 | — |
| More! (f) | — | 2 |
| Total | 148 | 134 |

Note:  (w) denotes weekly, (m) denotes monthly, (f) denotes fortnightly

By the end of the first year of advertising, the following coverage and frequency levels had been achieved (Table 10).

TABLE 10:  MEDIA COVERAGE AND FREQUENCY

| | |
|---|---|
| Coverage of girls 10–14 | 80% |
| Average OTS | 20.7 |

Source:   Carrick James/AMV Estimates

## CAMPAIGN EVALUATION

The evidence we will offer for the campaign's success is as follows:

1. Direct response coupon data.
2. Usage and awareness study data (quantitative and qualitative).
3  Qualitative evidence from AMV.
4. Distribution data: Nielsen and Company sales force.
5. Ex-factory sales.
6. AGB/TCPI share data 1989.

## THE EVIDENCE

### Direct Response Coupon Data

Sample requests showed a vast increase in 1988 and 1989 over any previous year. Coupons had been used before (1971 – 1978) and were known to generate more sample requests than offers hidden in the copy. However, 1988 requests were quadruple the previous high (1973).

TABLE 11: COUPON RESPONSE DATA

|      | Total sample requests | SOV |
|------|-----------------------|-----|
| 1971 | 32,138 | 34 |
| 1972 | 26,816 | 34 |
| 1973 | 32,841 | 33 |
| 1974 | 11,110 | 40 |
| 1975 | 29,915 | 29 |
| 1976 | 24,322 | 42 |
| 1977 | 20,293 | 44 |
| 1978 | 20,044 | 44 |
| 1979 | 7,340 | 44 |
| 1980 | 16,263 | 30 |
| 1981 | 13,613 | 26 |
| 1982 | 9,241 | 32 |
| 1983 | 7,989 | 27 |
| 1984 | 11,136 | 32 |
| 1985 | 27,520 | 35 |
| 1986 | 19,823 | 31 |
| 1987 | 3,863 | 0 |
| 1988 | 132,997 | 32 |
| 1989 | 102,324 | 31 |

This was particularly impressive as media share of voice within tampons was similar to previous years and the number of girls entering menarch (aged twelve to fourteen) was actually in decline (Table 12).

TABLE 12: NUMBER OF 12 – 14 YEAR OLDS IN POPULATION

|            | 1985 | 1986 | 1987 | 1988 | 1989 | 1990 |
|------------|------|------|------|------|------|------|
| Population in 000s | 1,202 | 1,128 | 1,063 | 1,019 | 980 | 958 |
| Index | 100 | 93 | 88 | 84 | 81 | 79 |

Source: OPCS/GAD

## Effective Targeting

The vast majority of responses, 68.5% in 1988 and 73.6% in 1989, were concentrated in the twelve to fifteen year old age range. This demonstrates the effectiveness of the creative and media targeting. As the campaign progressed, the demographic data gained from the coupon responses enabled us to refine our media targeting still further in a market notoriously short of readership audits.

## Usage and Awareness Study Data (Quantitative and Qualitative)

This annual or biannual study was last run in July 1988, only seven months after the inception of the campaign. Bearing this in mind, it is astonishing how quickly the campaign gained awareness and shifted attitudes to the brand. Many of the shifts outlined below are directional (ie not strictly statistically significant) but they are consistently positive for Lil-lets. Unfortunately, the survey was not re-run in 1989.

## Spontaneous brand awareness

There was a spontaneous brand awareness gain for Lil-lets and Tampax, 1988 on 1987 (Table 13).

TABLE 13:  SPONTANEOUS AWARENESS OF TAMPON BRANDS

|          | July 1987 % | July 1988 % |
|----------|-------------|-------------|
| Tampax   | 79          | 84          |
| Lil-lets | 64          | 71          |

Base:  All current tampon users, aged 13 – 15

Clearly, this is directionally positive for Tampax too. However, there are further data in the research which are in Lil-lets favour.

## Usership and intention to use

Claimed usership of Lil-lets in our target group had risen during the year. So had intention to use, which is probably more meaningful in the light of our competitive strategy (Table 14).

TABLE 14:  CLAIMED USERSHIP OF TAMPON BRANDS

|                            | July 1987 Stage IV % | July 1988 Stage V % |
|----------------------------|----------------------|---------------------|
| *Use these days*           |                      |                     |
| Tampax                     | 69                   | 67                  |
| Lil-lets                   | 23                   | 29                  |
| *Likely to use in the future* |                   |                     |
| Tampax                     | 72                   | 74                  |
| Lil-lets                   | 32                   | 39                  |

Base:  Girls 13 – 15

Interestingly, during the same period, current usership and intention to use Lil-lets among the sixteen to twenty four age group continued to fall. This is in line with the lack of trial-gaining advertising activity during their decision-making period (ie when they were aged ten to fourteen).

## Image Ratings

Image ratings among thirteen to fifteen year olds also improved for Lil-lets across this period.

TABLE 15:  PERCENTAGE CHANGE IN IMAGE DIMENSIONS 88 ON 87

|  | Lil-lets % | Tampax % |
|---|---|---|
| Is suitable for young girls | +2 | −3 |
| Is easy to carry without embarrassment | +8 | −12 |
| Its packs are more appealing than others | +16 | +7 |
| Understands women's/girls' needs | +1 | −2 |
| Makes products you can trust | +3 | −3 |

Base:   Girls 13 – 15.

It is possible that the rise in some of these scores, eg, 'Is easy to carry without embarrassment' which rises at the expense of Tampax, and 'Has more appealing packs', are attributable to the advertising, since they are closely related to the discretion benefit, and, indeed, to specific executions.

### Qualitative Evidence

Due to the sensitivity of the subject matter, research amongst the youngest members of our audience (girls aged ten to twelve) was conducted through a qualitative programme of fifteen depth interviews.

Most of the twelve year olds were already reading magazines and evaluating sanpro options. The interviews showed that despite endemic confusion about towels and tampon differences, brands and their benefits young girls were taking out the message that some tampons were more discreet than others because they did not have applicators.

'Lil-lets advertisements say they're smaller than Tampax – in the magazines they say that's their special thing, they make them smaller so if you go out you can just put it in your hand. You don't have to bulge it up your sleeve or something...I'll probably try these' (Twelve year old, W.Wickham)

Q. If you ever did use Tampons, do you know what kind you'd use?

'Probably Lil-lets or the ones without an applicator...they're better smaller' (Twelve year old, W. Wickam, Thornton Drummond & Brett).

These findings validated the competitive strategy and confirmed our belief that at this age girls will read long body copy with attention if it contains information that is of interest to them.

### Qualitative Evidence From AMV

AMV conducted qualitative groups on both the rough and finished advertising. The girls and mothers interviewed found the tone of voice sympathetic, understanding and encouraging. In fact the copy was so sensitively handled that most presumed it had been written by a woman (something of a tribute to Richard Foster and John

Horton, the creative team). The tone of ads such as 'T-shirt' was found straightforward, modern (ie free of shame), and attractively cheeky.

## Distribution Data

Significant distribution gains were made on Mini during 1988 and 1989.

The Smith & Nephew sales force believe that advertising was absolutely instrumental in building distribution and describe the campaign as an 'unqualified success'. The advertisements were placed in the sales force's presenter and were integral to the sales pitch.

## Trade Response

Resultant understanding of the strategy among retailers was 'very high'. The trade accepted the 'gateway to the brand' argument. Most were willing to stock Mini to ensure the future of a high value brand and help grow the tampon market. The trade also accepted the argument that rate of sale would remain low comparative to other variants owing to the small target audience. Stocking Mini was regarded as a 'service'. The creative approach was much liked.

## Specific Distribution Effects: Grocery

From the beginning of 1988 distribution grew rapidly in the hitherto problem area of multiple grocers.

TABLE 16:   LIL-LETS MINI TOTAL GROCERY: STERLING DISTRIBUTION

|            | Total grocery | Total multiples |
|------------|---------------|-----------------|
| May/Jun 87 | 7             | 8               |
| Nov/Dec 87 | 9             | 11              |
| May/Jun 88 | 16            | 23              |
| Nov/Dec 88 | 26            | 34              |
| May/Jun 89 | 49            | 66              |
| Nov/Dec 89 | 44            | 58              |

Source: Nielsen

In May/June 1988 Tampax began an aggressive distribution drive on their own trial variant, Slender. This was in direct reaction to Lil-lets' activity. In fact, the Smith & Nephew sales force undoubtedly paved their way into the trade but this did not happen at the expense of Lil-lets Mini which ultimately gained better distribution than Slender.

TABLE 17:   TOTAL GROCERY MULTIPLES: STERLING DISTRIBUTION

|            | Lil-lets Mini | Tampax Slender |
|------------|---------------|----------------|
| May/Jun 87 | 8             | 16             |
| Nov/Dec 87 | 11            | 13             |
| May/Jun 88 | 23            | 23             |
| Nov/Dec 88 | 34            | 30             |
| May/Jun 89 | 66            | 42             |
| Nov/Dec 89 | 58            | 55             |

Source:  Nielsen

## Specific Distribution Effects: Pharmacy

Pharmacies also saw a distribution surge in the first six months of 1988. Although distribution dropped slightly subsequently there was an overall sustained gain.

TABLE 18:   LIL-LETS MINI TOTAL PHARMACIES: STERLING DISTRIBUTION

|            | Total | Independent |
|------------|-------|-------------|
| May/Jun 87 | 64    | 62          |
| Nov/Dec 87 | 62    | 60          |
| May/Jun 88 | 76    | 75          |
| Nov/Dec 88 | 70    | 68          |
| May/Jun 89 | 68    | 66          |
| Nov/Dec 89 | 68    | 65          |

Source:  Nielsen

Boots and Superdrug, not monitored by Nielsen, were also receptive to the supported brand. Superdrug listed Mini in 1988 and Boots were 'particularly supportive' to the strategy, responding with extra promotional space. There was, overall, a growth in facings for this hitherto under-represented variant (Smith & Nephew sales force).

## Ex-factory Sales

The brand grew overall in 1988 and 1989 but the growth on Mini was far ahead of the brand.

TABLE 19:   INDICES OF EX-FACTORY VOLUME GROWTH FOR LIL-LETS

|             | 1987 | 1988 | 1989 |
|-------------|------|------|------|
| Total Brand | 100  | 107  | 108  |
| Total Mini  | 100  | 155  | 166  |

Source:   Smith & Nephew Ex-factory data (indexed on 1987)

## Did the Advertising affect the total growth of the brand?

The growth in sales force enthusiasm for the brand as a result of the campaign cannot be discounted as an advertising effect.

However, the sales force discount any direct knock-on effect on other variants from the Mini campaign. The advertising was part of a larger marketing push. The brand was repackaged in 1986 and this, along with merchandising promotions, led to increased distribution on other variants.

However, it is undoubtedly the case that the advertising played the largest part in Mini's disproportionate distribution gain and consequent volume growth. The variant's distribution had been struggling since launch in 1977 and only the catalyst of the advertising could really have pushed it out of its rut.

If one subtracts the brand's overall rate of growth from Mini's volume growth in 1988 and 1989 one can say that advertising was responsible for a growth of Mini volume of +48% in 1988 and +58% in 1989.

### AGB/TCPI Data 1989

A limited amount of AGB/TCPI data was re-supplied in early 1990. This data had been reworked and therefore showed slightly different share sizes than the previous tables. However, at the end of 1989 the data indicated a volume share gain of 5% for Lil-lets in the thirteen to fifteen year old age group, seemingly to the detriment of Tampax (Table 20).

TABLE 20: VOLUME BRAND SHARE (UNITS)

| | | % gain or loss | | |
| Year to Dec: | 1986 | 1987 | 1988 | 1989 |
| --- | --- | --- | --- | --- |
| Tampax | 100 | −1 | +2 | −1 |
| Lil-lets | 100 | +3 | +3 | +8 |

Base: Girls up to 15

Meanwhile brand share amongst All Women was static (see Figure 1), suggesting that the advertising was responsible for the gain amongst under fifteens. Share amongst young women aged nineteen to twenty four, who were not subject to recruitment efforts as young girls, continued to decline.

*If one attributes the 3% share gain 87 on 86 to the packaging changes in October 1986, this leaves a gain of +5% 89 on 86, to be claimed for advertising via increased trial and distribution.*

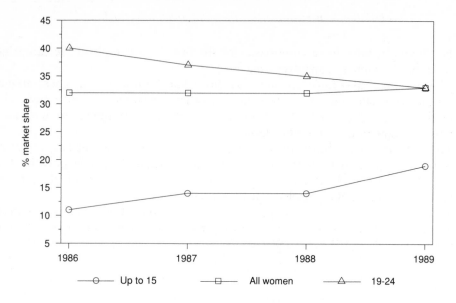

Figure 1. *Pre and post advertising effect amongst core*
*Source:* AGB

## WAS THE ADVERTISING A GOOD INVESTMENT?

We have argued that there is enormous loyalty in this market which is formed early in a woman's menstrual life. This argument formed the basis of a strategy which assumes that the most cost effective way to gain new users (Lil-lets' only hope of growth) is to recruit them in their youth. The benefit to the brand does not lie in the increased volume of the advertised Mini variant. It will be found in the future volume and profit gained from loyal usership formed through the recruitment campaign. We have examined two methods by which the expenditure on advertising can be justified.

Profitability information is not available. Therefore in our calculations, we are assuming, for argument, three *example* levels of profitability: 10%, 20% and 30%.

### Method 1 – Trial Gain

In 1988 free samples were sent to 132,999 girls. If we subtract the average of the samples sent out in the preceding years, 18,486, from this number we could say that 114,513 extra responses were generated by advertising.

Assume that 114,513 respondents might not have tried the brand and now try it. Conversion levels of 44% (1987 U&A) are applied to this number.

> 114,513 x 44% = 50,386 incremental users

The average consumer uses 16 tampons per period and has 13 periods a year, so she uses 208 tampons a year or 10.4 packs of 20 (Smith & Nephew).

> 50,386 x 10.4 = 524,014 incremental packs of 20 a year

The price for 20 Lil-lets Regular is £1.49.

524,014 x £1.49 = £780,781 incremental turnover per year at constant price
The advertising spend in 1988 was £453,000.

TABLE 21: EXAMPLE PROFIT CALCULATIONS

| Assumed profit | At 10% | At 20% | At 30% |
|---|---|---|---|
| Expenditure | 453,000 | 453,000 | 453,000 |
| Profit | 78,078 | 156,156 | 234,234 |
| Payback period | 5.8 yrs | 2.9 yrs | 1.9 yrs |
| Period of profit (assumes 38 yrs of menstruation) | 32.2 yrs | 35.1 yrs | 36.1 yrs |
| Total incremental profit from one year's incremental recruits | £2,514,112 | £5,481,076 | £8,459,096 |

## Method 2 – Share Gain

1989 AGB/TCPI data shows Lil-lets share amongst the under fifteens at 19%, an increase of 5% over the previous two years (for reasons already discussed).

There are 1,000,019 girls aged twelve to fourteen. We will use this as a base to calculate the effect of a 5% share gain in the tampon market.

First we must subtract one third of this number; one third of all women who use sanpro do not use tampons, so we can only assume that two thirds will enter our market.

1,000,019 x 66% = 660,013 potential tampon users

660,013 x 5% = 33,001 incremental users

The average consumer uses 16 tampons per period and has 13 periods a year. So she uses 208 tampons a year or 10.4 packs of 20 (Smith and Nephew).

33,001 x 10.4 = 343,210 incremental packs of 20 a year

The price for 20 Lil-lets Regular is £1.49.

342,210 x £1.49 = £509,893 incremental turnover per year at constant prices

The advertising spend was £453,000.

TABLE 22: EXAMPLE PROFIT CALCULATIONS

| Assumed profit | At 10% | At 20% | At 30% |
|---|---|---|---|
| Expenditure | 453,000 | 453,000 | 453,000 |
| Profit | 50,989 | 101,979 | 152,968 |
| Payback period | 8.9 yrs | 4.4 yrs | 3.0 yrs |
| Period of profit (assumes 38 yrs of menstruation) | 29.2 yrs | 33.6 yrs | 35.0 yrs |
| Total incremental profit from one year's incremental recruits | £1,488,879 | £3,426,494 | £5,353,880 |

In both instances, even at the lower level of assumed profit, the incremental users (if they behave typically) will more than cover the cost of the advertising. This does not, of course, take into account changing market forces which would have to be addressed if and when they arose. However, this shows that the advertising has been a good investment in terms of return against outlay.

## SUMMARY

To summarise, we would argue that the Lil-lets campaign was an unprecedented success in gaining trial for the brand amongst young girls. This is demonstrated by the very high levels of direct response. Our U & A shows that awareness and usage of the brand in our target group rose and that the brand's image improved. The advertising was seen, and the competitive proposition understood and remembered.

There was a large distribution gain for Mini and an ex-factory volume gain consequent on it. The sales force found advertising instrumental in their success in gaining shelf space for an established, but low volume variant.

AGB/TCPI, when re-purchased, showed a 5% share gain for Lil-lets Mini in the under fifteen age range by the end of 1989. We claim this as an advertising result.

Lastly we have argued that the long-term incremental profit will far outweigh the advertising cost.

# 15

# The Relaunch of Choosy Catfood or a Dog Called Tiddles

## INTRODUCTION

This paper is about the relaunch of Choosy, one of Spillers four catfood brands, which took place during autumn 1989. The relaunch was judged by Spillers to have been very successful, exceeding volume targets set for the brand. In December 1989, two months after the end of the relaunch advertising campaign, the brand was running at volume sales levels 31% higher than the same period the previous year in a market which was up only 1% over the same period. This was in spite of a price rise relative to the market which took place in November. The aim of this paper is to demonstrate that advertising played an important role within the total relaunch package in causing a significant increase in the product's rate of sale. Additionally, the success of the campaign relieved trade pressure on Choosy's distribution levels in what is an intensely competitive market with over 20 brands and more than 125 different varieties. That all this was achieved on a budget of only £300,000 which was equivalent to a 1.5% share of voice, and using posters in a market where the norm is heavy use of TV, makes this achievement all the more noteworthy.

## THE TINNED CATFOOD MARKET IN THE UK

The tinned catfood market in this country has been growing steadily over the last few years. Not only are people buying more catfood (because there are more cats), but the catfood they are buying is of a better quality, hence more expensive.

The market represents one of the few grocery areas where own label products have been unable to take significant share – in December 1989 own label accounted for only 6.7% of volume in the market on a MAT basis. In part this is due to the retailers' inability, thus far at least, to persuade consumers that they are really offering products of sufficient quality to do justice to the delicate palates of their pets; parallels are often drawn with the babyfood market – where you don't consume the product yourself you are more likely to depend on the reassurance offered by a brand. It is, however, also true that over the years the major manufacturers in the market have invested considerable sums of money in persuading consumers that for the owner who really loves his or, more often, her cat there is just no substitute for one or other of their brands.

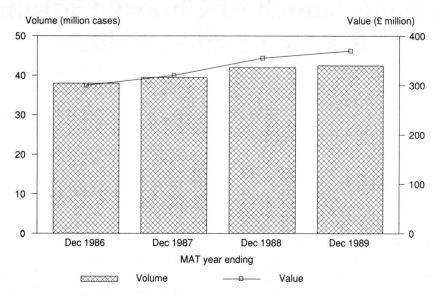

Figure 1. *Total catfood market*
*Source:* Nielsen

In particular, during 1989 Pedigree invested in advertising to the tune of over £14m, £8.6m of which was spent behind Whiskas (see Table 1).

TABLE 1:  CATFOOD ADVERTISING SPEND:
FOURTH QUARTER MATS 1986 – 89 (£000s)

| | 1986 | 1987 | 1988 | 1989 | 1989 Share of voice (%) |
|---|---|---|---|---|---|
| Whiskas | 9,191 | 12,009 | 12,425 | 8,630 | 44.3 |
| Kit-e-Kat | 4,529 | 3,531 | 3,145 | 1,206 | 6.2 |
| Katkins Premium | 1,040 | — | 992 | 862 | 4.4 |
| Sheba | — | 1,303 | 2,451 | 3,489 | 18.0 |
| *Total Pedigree* | *14,760* | *16,843* | *19,013* | *14,187* | *73.1* |
| Kattomeat | — | 3,038 | 2,612 | 1,972 | 10.2 |
| Choosy | — | — | — | 300 | 1.5 |
| *Total Spillers* | — | *3,038* | *2,612* | *2,272* | *11.7* |
| Felix | — | — | — | 310 | 1.6 |
| Others | 2,370 | 1,607 | 2,793 | 2,634 | 13.6 |
| *Total* | *17,130* | *21,487* | *24,418* | *19,403* | *100* |

Source:   MEAL; Own sources for Choosy's poster spend

Whiskas' domination of advertising activity is reflected in its domination of the market. Although the brand has come under pressure over the last year or so and has seen some loss of share, it nevertheless had in August 1989 a 46% share of the market on a MAT basis. Whiskas is far from being seen by Spillers as a direct competitor to Choosy, but it is nonetheless important to set what follows in the context of a market very much dominated by one company and indeed, to a large extent, one brand.

As shown in Table 2, the market has traditionally been divided by manufacturers and the trade into Premium, Sub-Premium and Economy brands. The delineation between these sectors is based primarily on 'palatability' levels. Palatability in the catfood market refers to a precise measurement which is the amount of product a cat will eat in a given time in controlled conditions. Essentially it is a measurement of a product's cat acceptability. One of the most interesting developments in the last few years has been the development of the Super Premium sector, evidencing pet owners' desire to buy better quality food for their animals. This has implications for brands further down the scale in that it puts increased pressure on shelf-space in major retailers in an already intensely competitive market.

TABLE 2:   VOLUME BRAND SHARES – MAT AUGUST 1989

|  | % |
| --- | --- |
| *Super Premium* | |
| Sheba (Pedigree) | 1.1 |
| Purrfect (Spillers) | 0.1 |
| Go Cat Gourmet/à la carte (Nestlé) | 1.4 |
| *Premium* | |
| Whiskas (Pedigree) | 46.2 |
| Kattomeat (Spillers) | 12.8 |
| *Sub-premium* | |
| Choosy (Spillers) | 5.0 |
| Felix (Quaker) | 6.5 |
| Katkins Premium and Mariner (Pedigree) | 4.9 |
| Kit-e-Kat (Pedigree) | 10.7 |
| *Economy* | |
| Savour (Spillers) | 1.0 |
| Katkins (Pedigree) | 1.0 |
| Own Label | 6.7 |
| Other | 2.6 |

Source:   Nielsen

In summary, therefore, the catfood market in 1989 was highly competitive, heavily advertised and dominated by Pedigree.

## THE CHOOSY BRAND

Choosy was initially launched in the late 1960s. As can be seen from Table 2, it is Spillers' second string brand and the company's representative in the Sub-Premium sector. It occupies the position between Kattomeat in the Premium sector and Savour which is Spillers brand in the Economy sector. Choosy's major competitors are seen by the trade and Spillers themselves to be the other Sub-Premium brands – Felix, Katkins Premium and Kit-e-Kat. Consumers tended to see Choosy as a fairly good quality, good value brand.

Choosy had been relaunched in February 1987 with a new recipe and new packaging and in the two years since that time had shown significant increases in distribution and sales.

However, by the end of 1988 the brand was again starting to come under pressure. While distribution was holding up, rate of sale was beginning to cause concern and sales share seemed to be plateauing or even falling back slightly.

Spillers attributed this to two reasons. Firstly, the price differential between Choosy and its major competitors had closed (see Table 3).

TABLE 3:   CHOOSY PRICE DIFFERENTIALS

|            | 1987/88 | 1988/89 |
|------------|---------|---------|
| Vs Kit-e-Kat | –3p   | –2p     |
| Vs Katkins   | —     | +2p     |
| Vs Felix     | –1.5p | –1p     |

Source:   Spillers

Secondly, all of the three major competitors had been relaunched with strong support.

At the same time, the overall competitive environment within the catfood market was getting tougher, with the launch of the new brands at the Super Premium end of the market and the continuing desire of retailers to increase their own label share of the market putting ever increasing pressure on the allocation of shelf-space.

So, with a background of strong competitive pressure, a somewhat lacklustre performance from the brand itself and an increasing threat of a trade delisting, it was decided that Choosy required a major relaunch, to take place in September 1989.

## THE RELAUNCH

There were four main elements to the relaunch, namely 'Reformulation', 'Repackaging', 'New Varieties' and 'Advertising', and each of these will be looked at in turn.

### Reformulation

Catfood products from the major manufacturers have regularly been reformulated to improve quality and increase 'cat palatability'. Cats are notoriously fussy animals and will show a distinct preference for food of higher quality. Since repertoire purchasing is very common within the catfood market and owners are, in general, very sensitive to any sign from their cat that they are not impressed by the food they are being offered, a fall in 'cat palatability' of one product relative to its competitors is likely to be picked up fairly quickly by both consumers (cats) and customers (humans).

Reformulation was an element of the relaunches of both Kit-e-Kat and Katkins, and Spillers decided that it was necessary to do the same with Choosy. They therefore tested different recipes and came up with a new formulation that substantially improved Choosy's palatability relative to both Kit-e-Kat and Katkins.

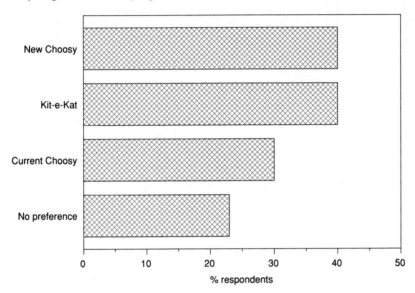

Figure 2. *Blind home placement test results (Q. Which product did your cat prefer overall?)*
*Source:* Independent Market Research
*Sample:* 483 Sub-Premium catfood servers

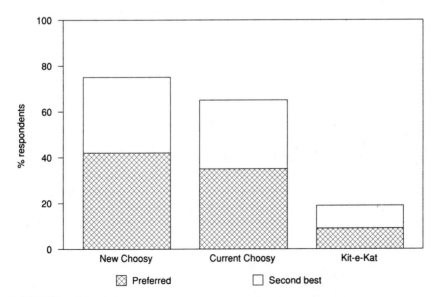

Figure 3. *Blind hall test results*
*Source:* Independent Market Research
*Sample:* 511 Sub-Premium catfood servers

They were confident that this improvement would be noticed both by the cats, who would tend to eat more of the product more quickly, and by the owners who would appreciate the sight of their contented cat licking the empty bowl! (see Figure 2). Additionally, the new product had an improved appearance which quantitative research suggested would be remarked upon by owners (see Figure 3).

### New Varieties

Variety is very important to cat owners, far more so in fact than it is to the cat. Most owners feel that it is important to give their animals a range of different flavours, to add interest to what they subjectively feel might otherwise become a very boring diet for their pet.

In the past few years, the range of different flavours available has become much wider and more exotic, and in particular dual varieties, such as 'Ocean White Fish with Prawns', have been introduced. Research shows that these are perceived as slightly more exotic and are usually offered by the more expensive Premium brands. It was therefore decided that the inclusion of some dual varieties within the Choosy range would be an important quality signal. Three new varieties were introduced – 'Tuna and Pilchard', 'Sardine' and 'Beef and Kidney'. Two less popular varieties, 'Beef' and 'Liver', were phased out, leaving a total of seven varieties in the range.

### Repackaging

This represented a significant change to the existing packaging. Each variety now had a different colour background but featured the same cat's face. This made it much easier to tell one from the other and gave the range greater coherency so that the on-shelf impact was considerably improved. In research, the new packaging was found to be both very appealing and to increase quality ratings of the product. Reformulation was clearly signalled on the pack with a 'New Recipe' flash.

The final major element of the relaunch was advertising.

## THE ADVERTISING CAMPAIGN

### Background

Prior to September 1989 Choosy had not benefited from any above-the-line activity since 1984.

The most recent activity had been in the form of a poster campaign which, both because it was essentially an attractive pack shot and also because it happened so long ago, did not give us much to build on in terms of a brand personality. Existing consumer perceptions of the brand, which were derived mainly from the pack, pricing and product experience, positioned Choosy as a fairly good quality, value for money brand.

### Advertising Objectives and the Target Market

The catfood market is characterised by a considerable amount of repertoire buying and experimentation and although only 15% of cat owners claimed to buy Choosy regularly nowadays, 44% had bought the brand at some point in the past. From research we knew that a large number of these lapsed users no longer used the brand because they thought of it as 'sloppy', 'mushy' and generally of lower quality.

Research suggested that the other elements of the marketing mix, namely the repackaging, the new recipe and the new varieties, would work hard to increase the appeal and the likelihood of purchase of the brand. It also suggested that this was true amongst non-users as well as current users of Choosy. Given this fact it was decided that the main objective of the advertising must be to stimulate reconsideration of the brand amongst those who might not otherwise notice the changes at the point-of-sale because they did not currently buy Choosy. The primary target market for the advertising was defined as 'lapsed users' since these cat owners had shown themselves willing to buy Choosy in the past. Cat owners who were non-users of Choosy but who were buying another Sub-Premium brand were also a target. Those cat owners who didn't buy any Sub-Premium brands, it was decided, were a much tougher proposition and beyond the scope of this advertising.

It was agreed that the most motivating claim we could make to lapsed users was that of 'new tastier recipe'. In many markets the 'new improved' claim or varieties thereof is often met with considerable scepticism. However, the experience of cat owners is that claims of new improved formulation in this market are generally accompanied by a perceptible product improvement, and the barrier of cynicism is therefore not so hard to overcome.

Given the brand's position in the market, it was tempting in some ways to play to perceptions of Choosy as a good value, no-nonsense brand. However, all the research available to us suggested that all cat owners want to feel and believe that they are doing the best for their cat. Cats are unlike dogs in that it is much harder to coax overt displays of affection from them. Feeding time is one of the key occasions for the giving and receiving of love (even if there is a suspicion, buried not too far below the surface, that it is love of the cupboard variety!) and owners would not therefore wish to give their cats anything that they might reject because it would be tantamount to a rejection of them. If we even suggested that Choosy might be the catfood for people who didn't want to spend so much money on their cats, we would run the risk of alienating many potential users.

We therefore decided that, as well as communicating clearly that the Choosy recipe had been improved, we should make a strong overall quality statement about the brand. Choosy should confidently claim to be the connoisseur's catfood, even though the price might tell a slightly different story. In some markets taking up what is essentially a Premium position with a Sub-Premium brand might be considered foolhardy. In this market we decided it was exactly the confident stance that was required. We described this on the brief as the 'After 8' tone of voice.

## Media

Choosy is a national brand with almost 100% distribution in the major retailers. The relaunch was taking place nationally, and it was also very important for the brand's stature for it to be seen by the trade to be a national advertiser. In an environment as competitive as the catfood market, any suspicion that a product is other than a 'must stock' brand quickly leads to pressure on distribution.

The available media budget was only £300,000. Although the catfood market overall is a very high value market with correspondingly high media budgets, Choosy itself had in August 1989 a MAT value share of only 4.1% – £300,000 was all that Spillers felt they could responsibly justify for a brand of this size.

It was decided that this precluded a national TV campaign at an effective weight, but it remained necessary to reach a wide target audience of cat-owning housewives with a high level of frequency in order to make Choosy top-of-mind and establish recognition of the new packaging.

A poster campaign using a combination of Superlites, backlit sites permitting strong visibility and impact, and four sheets was selected as the best option. Given the relatively low weight of the campaign, it was decided that we could maximise the opportunity by buying sites which were close to major retailer outlets. In this way, the possibility of the advertising being seen by housewives immediately prior to them doing the shopping would be increased, so enabling it to have a more immediate effect on purchasing behaviour. It was impossible to buy every site to be close to a major retailer, and not everyone who saw the advertising outside a retail outlet would be about to do the shopping; clearly the advertising would have to work even harder in these situations. Nevertheless, given the limited budget every effort that could be made to increase the campaign's efficiency would be key. The advertising was to run for six weeks from the middle of September until the end of October (see Figure 4).

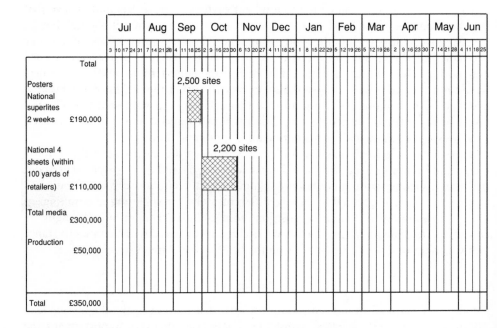

Figure 4. *Media Plan*

'CAT'

"**The last thing I wanted to be was a cat till I heard about new tastier recipe Choosy.**"

FOR REALLY CHOOSY CATS.

## THE EXECUTIONS

Two executions were produced to the creative brief. Even a cursory glance reveals that they break a long-established convention of catfood advertising – they do not show a cat! Nonetheless, qualitative research conducted at the concept stage concluded that both executions performed extremely well against the brief of prompting reconsideration of the brand amongst lapsed users. Specifically the executions clearly communicated the fact that the recipe had been improved and, interestingly, the use of the dog implied to some respondents that the texture of the product had changed, countering perceptions of Choosy as a somewhat sloppy, mushy brand.

Perhaps most importantly in a market where advertising spend is so high and Choosy's share of voice would be so small, the posters were widely seen by respondents to be both amusing and different. These points are made clearly in the comments below.

'They've made it tastier'.

'It's an improved recipe – it's going to be tastier'.

'It's changed, it's improved'.

'Not sloppy – not so much jelly – they don't actually say that'.

'It's through the dog. Dog food tends to be chunkier'.

'Makes a change from general catfood adverts – the fact that it is different'.

'I liked the humour in it. Fancy a dog wanting to be a cat. The humour appeals to me'.

'A witty way to advertise catfood' (Source: Liz Hauck Research).

The advertising appeared to have the potential to begin to establish a distinct personality for Choosy which, although new and different, was quite in keeping with what cat owners could believe to be true of the brand. The tone of voice of the advertising suggested that Choosy was a brand of quality catfood which nonetheless did not take itself too seriously.

It was decided that both 'Cat' and 'Tiddles' should be included in the campaign.

The relaunch went ahead as planned at the beginning of September. All research evidence pointed to the fact that each element of the relaunch package should perform well. The advertising was brave and unconventional with an unusual media strategy designed to achieve national coverage on a very limited budget. Nonetheless could we really expect to have much effect with a spend of only £300,000 in a market where this represented only a 1.5% share of voice?

'TIDDLES'

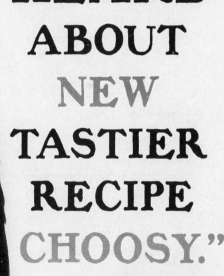

# "I CHANGED MY NAME TO TIDDLES WHEN I HEARD ABOUT NEW TASTIER RECIPE CHOOSY."

FOR REALLY CHOOSY CATS.

## THE RESULTS

The increase in sales was marked and rapid. In September, October and November 1989 Nielsen reported the highest brand shares for over four years for Choosy, with each month higher than the last (see Figure 5). Sales remained high in December in spite of the fact that a decision was taken by Spillers to increase the brand's price in November, in order to further improve profitability. The absolute increases in volume compared with the same periods in the previous year are shown in Figure 6.

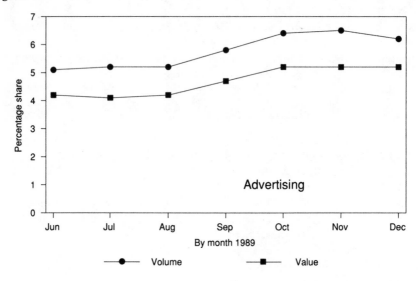

Figure 5. *Choosy national share*
*Source:* Nielsen

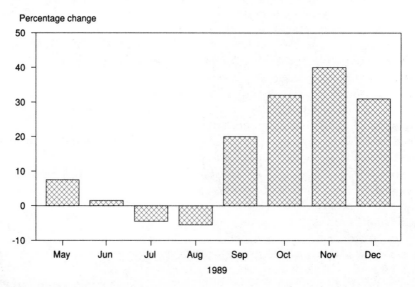

Figure 6. *Choosy total sales*
*Source:* Nielsen

## ISOLATING THE ADVERTISING EFFECT

Having chronicled in considerable detail the various elements of the marketing mix that were put in place for the relaunch we shall not now claim that the whole of this sales increase was due to the effect of the advertising. The repackaging, reformulation and new varieties clearly played a very considerable role in the success.

The task is to separate out the effect of the advertising from the impact of the other elements of the relaunch, and indeed from any other factors which may have been contributory to the success.

Clearly there were elements which complicated this task. The campaign was national and the new packs and varieties were available everywhere so there was no control region or store group. Distribution of the new product in the top end of the trade was achieved by the beginning of September over a very short period: Nielsen figures show that only about six days worth of stock is held in a major retailer outlet so a speedy changeover can be achieved relatively painlessly compared with many other products. However, advertising, timed to coincide with the relaunch, also broke in September so we would have no baseline data showing the sales of the new product without advertising support.

However, by revisiting the rationale for the media choice, that with posters we had the opportunity to reach housewives on the way to doing their shopping, a way forward became apparent. Although the campaign had been bought to tie in closely with retail outlet location, on a budget of £300,000 it was not possible to achieve coverage of every outlet. There were therefore two groups of stores – those that had had poster sites close by and those that had not. If we could separate one from the other and look at the sales patterns in each, then it would be possible to isolate those sales increases which were directly attributable to the advertising.

In the days when deliveries from the manufacturers went direct to the store, this might have been possible using Spillers ex-factory sales data. However, almost all the major retailers now take deliveries into central warehouses for onward distribution to individual stores. The only other measure of sales available was Nielsen data. This was used to look at the two groups of stores separately, those with and those without posters.

Postcodes were assigned to all the poster sites used in the campaign and to retail outlets. Obviously locating the postcode of every retail outlet in the country that sold Choosy was not feasible, so the list was restricted to those store groups for which reliable and up-to-date information was available, namely the 'Top 5' (as defined by Nielsen) store groups – Asda, Gateway, Safeway/Presto, Sainsbury and Tesco. In fact, these outlets alone account for over 60% of catfood sales through the grocery trade and almost exactly the same percentage of Choosy's volume. Additionally, using these stores as the base meant that we eliminated from the analysis the independent sector where distribution gains made since the beginning of 1989 had contributed to the sales growth.

The information was then collated in the form of a list of stores with a poster site in the same postcode area and a list of those stores which had no poster site nearby, and passed on to Nielsen who compared the lists with their store panel comprising audited stores. These sample stores, chosen to represent the grocery universe, could then be split into two groups on the same basis. Five months data covering the period from August to December 1989 were considered. An increased sales volume and brand share as shown in the national picture can be achieved in two ways – increased distribution or an increased rate of sale. Choosy's distribution in the 'Top 5' sector was at almost 100% before the relaunch, so it was the rate of sale that would be key.

Figures were indexed on August which was an entirely normal month for Choosy in terms of brand share (as shown in Figure 5) and rate-of-sale in the 'Top 5' sector of the trade.

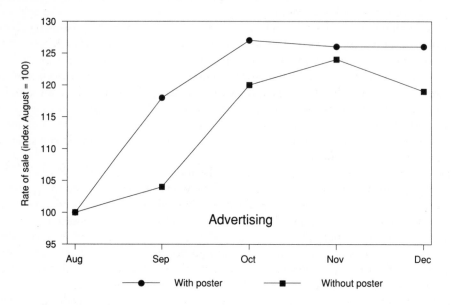

Figure 7. *Choosy 'Top 5' grocers*
*Source:* Nielsen Insight

Figure 7 showing the rate of sale in the two groups of stores clearly demonstrates a difference in both the pattern and level of rate of sale increases. Clearly those stores which had one or more posters in the immediate vicinity showed an uplift in sales which was more rapid and attained, and maintained a higher level. We knew from research that the strength of the non-advertising elements of the relaunch package would work hard once they were actually seen on the shelf. The difference in the rate of sale increases for the two groups of stores in September suggests that the advertising was successful in achieving the objective of attracting people who would not otherwise have seen the changes, ie lapsed and non-users.

The group of stores without posters close by showed a similar increase in sales in October, a month later, not in September when the new product was first available. Although impossible to prove, it would seem to suggest that the advertising had an effect even in those stores which did not have a poster in the immediate vicinity. Over the period of the six week campaign, estimated coverage was 75% of housewives at an average 30 OTS so that many of those housewives not shopping in our sample of 'stores with posters' would see the advertising, although not generally at times when it could be expected to have an immediate effect on behaviour. We would hypothesise that in this way the advertising had a more indirect effect in the 'stores without posters' causing the lag effect. That an increased rate of sale is observed in those stores without posters, albeit with a timing lag, argues strongly for the impact and memorability of the executions.

It is not possible to give a figure for the total extra profit generated by the relaunch in general and the advertising in particular. In such a competitive market place it is clearly impossible to give any information which would reveal Spillers gross margin on the Choosy product.

What is indisputable from the evidence is that the advertising had a marked effect on rate of sale. In addition, its importance in maintaining increasingly threatened distribution levels can only be guessed at since no distribution has been lost. Spillers themselves clearly consider the campaign to have been profitable; they are re-running the advertising this year at a higher weight.

Clearly it is not sufficient merely to demonstrate that those stores with posters in the immediate vicinity showed a greater and more rapid increase in sales than those without posters. The possibility that the two samples were significantly different in other respects which may also have affected sales must also be ruled out. The two sub-samples were matched as far as possible in terms of store characteristics by Nielsen. Details are given in the Appendix. Other possible factors are examined below.

### Distribution

Did those stores with posters outside for some reason experience an uplift in Choosy distribution over the period of the campaign?

As mentioned briefly, distribution of the Choosy brand in the 'Top 5' sector was almost 100%, and remained so throughout the period of the campaign in both groups of stores.

TABLE 4:  STERLING DISTRIBUTION

|                        | Aug % | Sep % | Oct % | Nov % | Dec % |
|------------------------|-------|-------|-------|-------|-------|
| Stores with posters    | 97    | 97    | 97    | 98    | 97    |
| Stores without posters | 98    | 98    | 98    | 98    | 98    |

Source:  Nielsen Analysis

### Share of Forward Stocks

Did Choosy have a higher share of forward stocks in one group of stores compared with the other?

Shares did vary somewhat over the period of analysis. However, it is certainly not true to say that Choosy was better faced in those stores with posters. In fact, in November and December at least, the opposite was the case.

TABLE 5:  SHARE OF FORWARD STOCKS

|                       | Aug % | Sep % | Oct % | Nov % | Dec % |
|-----------------------|-------|-------|-------|-------|-------|
| Stores with posters   | 3.7   | 3.6   | 4.1   | 3.9   | 3.8   |
| Stores without posters| 3.7   | 3.6   | 4.1   | 4.3   | 4.5   |

Source:  Nielsen Analysis

### Out of Stock Levels

Perhaps there was a higher level of out of stock in those stores without posters?

There was almost no reported out of stock over this period, although the level in the group of stores without posters was very slightly higher than for the group of stores with posters.

TABLE 6:  OUT OF STOCK LEVELS

|                          | Aug % | Sep % | Oct % | Nov % | Dec % |
|--------------------------|-------|-------|-------|-------|-------|
| Stores with posters      |       |       |       |       |       |
| – out of forward stock   | 0     | 0     | 0     | 1     | 0     |
| – out of all stock       | 0     | 0     | 0     | 1     | 0     |
| Stores without posters   |       |       |       |       |       |
| – out of forward stock   | 1     | 2     | 2     | 1     | 1     |
| – out of all stock       | 1     | 2     | 2     | 1     | 1     |

Source:  Nielsen Analysis

The 1% increase in out of stocks for stores without posters, when comparing September with August, goes nowhere close to explaining the shortfall in the rate of sale of this group of stores compared with the stores with posters.

### Pricing

Was there a different pricing policy operating in the two groups of stores?

Absolute pricing levels were very closely matched in the two groups, although Choosy was actually marginally more expensive in the group of stores with posters. As mentioned earlier, Choosy's price was increased throughout the trade in November, but rate of sale held up well in November and December, particularly in those stores that had had posters nearby.

TABLE 7:  PRICING IN PENCE

|                       | Aug % | Sep % | Oct % | Nov % | Dec % |
|-----------------------|-------|-------|-------|-------|-------|
| Stores with posters   | 29.5  | 29.3  | 29.5  | 30.2  | 30.9  |
| Stores without posters| 29.2  | 29.3  | 29.4  | 30.0  | 30.5  |

Source:  Nielsen Analysis

Choosy's price relative to the competition increased in both groups of stores in November. Apart from this, relative pricing was very consistent. Overall, relative price does appear to have been slightly higher in 'stores without posters', but if one looks at, for example, September compared to August, since August was taken as the base level for rate of sale, then the stores with posters experienced a relative increase in price whereas stores without posters experienced a relative decrease.

TABLE 8:   PRICE AS A PERCENTAGE OF AVERAGE CATFOOD PRICE

|                        | Aug % | Sep % | Oct % | Nov % | Dec % |
|------------------------|-------|-------|-------|-------|-------|
| Stores with posters    | 86.3  | 86.4  | 86.0  | 89.3  | 89.6  |
| Stores without posters | 86.6  | 86.5  | 86.5  | 89.0  | 90.2  |

Source:   Nielsen Analysis

In conclusion, therefore, distribution levels were the same in both panels of stores, forward stock shares were slightly higher in the group of stores without posters, out of stock levels do not appear to have had a significant influence, absolute prices were slightly higher in the stores with posters, and relative pricing does not seem to have been a contributory factor. Overall, only advertising can satisfactorily explain the differential pattern in the uplift in Choosy's rate of sale.

## FURTHER BACK-UP

Understandably, given the small budget, and the notorious problems involved in measuring the effects of a poster campaign where it is very difficult to get a true idea of even basic awareness, Spillers were keen to avoid spending large sums on research. However, in addition to the piece of qualitative research to which reference has already been made, a small piece of quantitative research was also set up. This was carried out by an independent research company in three stages – the first before the campaign started, the second at the beginning of October (ie after two weeks of the campaign), and the third at the end of the campaign. The results suggested that spontaneous brand awareness amongst cat-owning housewives had increased.

TABLE 9:   SPONTANEOUS BRAND AWARENESS

|                             | Pre (252) % | Mid (255) % | Post (259) % |
|-----------------------------|-------------|-------------|--------------|
| Spontaneous brand awareness | 25          | 31          | 31           |

Prompted brand awareness, as would be expected for a long-established brand, was already at 93% and unsurprisingly showed no movement. It was clearly saliency of Choosy which improved rather than overall awareness of the brand.

Prompted advertising awareness and aided recognition, however, both showed shifts over the period of the campaign.

TABLE 10:  PROMPTED BRAND AWARENESS

|                                | Pre (252) % | Mid (255) % | Post (259) % |
|--------------------------------|:-----------:|:-----------:|:------------:|
| Prompted advertising awareness | 6           | 8           | 13           |
| Aided recognition              | 4           | 24          | 34           |

   One of the most encouraging findings of the qualitative research referred to earlier was the degree to which the campaign was seen to be both amusing and likeable and also very different from other advertising in the market. Some further evidence for this was found in the quantitative study, shown in the following table.

TABLE 11:  PARTICULARLY CHOOSE TO AGREE WITH

|                                   | 'Cat' (255) % | 'Tiddles' (259) % |
|-----------------------------------|:-------------:|:-----------------:|
| It's amusing                      | 40            | 36                |
| It's different from other posters | 22            | 24                |
| It's eye catching and stands out  | 21            | 29                |
| It's dull and uninteresting       | 4             | 6                 |

Overall, although limited in scope, the quantitative study provided further evidence to support our belief in the campaign.

## CONCLUSION

The Choosy relaunch is judged by Spillers to have been a great success. All elements of the relaunch package contributed to a very substantial increase in sales and the highest volume brand share for over four years. It has been argued in this paper that, as well as protecting threatened distribution, the advertising campaign significantly increased the rate of sale and, by carrying out an analysis where all other factors remained the same, the magnitude of this effect has been measured. It is a very simple assertion that is being made here: those stores which had Choosy posters nearby showed a greater and more sustained uplift in the brand's rate of sale than those stores which had no such poster. This simplicity should in no way detract from the campaign's achievement. The media spend was £300,000 which is equivalent to a 1.5% share of voice in the catfood market in 1989 according to MEAL figures. In addition, it was spent in a medium where it is notoriously difficult to directly attribute sales effect to media spend. We would argue that the fact that on this occasion we have been able to demonstrate just such an effect says much for the creative strength of the campaign, as borne out by respondents' comments in research, as well as for the astute use of a limited budget in terms of the media strategy.

The clearest demonstration of the success of the advertising is that this year Spillers are re-running the campaign with an additional execution and a significant increase in the media budget.

## APPENDIX

### Major Data Sources

1.  Qualitative research looking at the two proposed poster executions of 'Cat' and 'Tiddles'. Conducted during July 1989 by Liz Hauck Research Agency.

    6 group discussions          2 with current regular buyers of Choosy.
                                 4 with non-buyers or lapsed buyers currently
                                   buying other sub-Premium brands.

2.  Quantitative advertising awareness study conducted in three stages:

    Pre – 14th/15th September 1989
    Sample size 252
    Mid – 2nd/3rd October 1989
    Sample size 255
    Post – 30th/31st October 1989
    Sample size 259

All respondents 'buyers of catfood nowadays'. Research carried out by The Oxford Research Agency.

3.  Nielsen Insight Analysis
    *Raw Data* – Full list of poster sites used in campaign supplied by Portland Outdoor Advertising.
    Full list of 'Top 5' (Asda, Safeway/Presto, Gateway, Tesco, Sainsbury) outlets supplied by Spillers National Account Team.
    Postcoding of poster sites and retail outlets carried out by SPA. All coding done to full postcode (ie to street level) where possible from address (88% of cases) and at least to digit of second element, eg SK3 9.
    *Insight Analysis* – matching of samples – all stores drawn from Nielsen panel of audited stores in 'Top 5' multiple groups.

    Number of stores in panels
    Stores with posters = 56
    Stores without posters = 126

Two sub-samples matched for mix of store groups, ie equivalent proportions of Tesco's, Sainsbury's etc.

Stores were also matched for size, ie the average size of store in each of the two samples was roughly equivalent in terms of total catfood sales. There was a small remaining difference.

|  | Stores with posters | Stores without posters |
|---|---|---|
| Average monthly sales/store | 12,000 standard units | 13,000 standard units |

Any effect this may have had was eliminated by indexing rate of sale on the pre-launch level for each group.

VOLUME BRAND SHARE IN AUGUST 1989

|  | Stores with posters % | Stores without posters % | Index |
|---|---|---|---|
| Choosy | 3.9 | 4.1 | 95 |
| Kattomeat | 12.5 | 12.4 | 101 |
| Total Spillers | 18.4 | 18.6 | 99 |
| Whiskas | 43.2 | 43.7 | 99 |
| Kit-e-Kat | 7.4 | 7.9 | 94 |
| Katkins Premium/Mariner | 4.2 | 4.2 | 100 |
| Total Pedigree | 59.0 | 60.7 | 97 |
| Felix | 7.9 | 8.2 | 96 |

The table above shows that brand shares of all brands were very closely matched in both groups of stores.

# 16

# Hogsheads Revisited:

## *How Advertising Helped Accelerate the Development of Aberlour Malt Whisky*

### INTRODUCTION

It is normally very difficult to assess the effectiveness of advertising for malt whisky until it has been running for some years.

The typical malt drinker only buys three bottles a year, is middle aged, rather conservative and not easily influenced. Retailers would normally take time to be convinced to accept a newcomer from among dozens of malts seeking distribution.

Consequently traditional advertising campaigns for malt whisky have concentrated on small spaces in specialised publications. These are run for years to gradually build awareness and an image for the brand.

Aberlour was another typical small malt whisky which had never been advertised before in the UK.

Yet its advertising campaign consisted of full colour pages in national quality daily newspapers. The advertising invited consumers to invest in a unique promotion: a hogshead (360 bottles) of Aberlour which would mature at the turn of the millennium, in 1999.

The results more than justified such a bold strategy.

175 hogsheads have been sold to date. This is the equivalent of almost three years' retail sales of Aberlour in the UK. Advertising contributed to all of the sales, and analysis indicates that its contribution was profitable.

Even more significantly the advertising helped Aberlour leapfrog over other unsupported malt whiskies in gaining distribution in major retailers such as Tesco. These listings gains mean that Aberlour's year on year retail sales since the advertising took effect have increased by 129%. The impact of the advertising has been so strong that it will now run in Holland and the USA.

This paper will aim to describe how advertising contributed to this rapid acceleration in the brand development of an obscure malt whisky.

## THE UK WHISKY MARKET

The size of the whisky market in the UK in 1989 was 12.3 million cases. Most of this consumption was of household names such as Bells and Teachers, commonly known as scotches. These are the sort of whiskies which are to be found on optics in the on trade. However, growth in the market in recent years has come from whiskies which appeal to more tightly defined consumer segments. Bourbon, or US whiskey, has been a particularly buoyant sector during the 1980s as has Irish whiskey.

Another healthy sector has been that of single malts, the produce of just one distillery. They tend to be smoother to taste than ordinary scotch whisky – and more expensive to buy.

TABLE 1:   THE UK WHISKY MARKET 1989

| Type | Examples | Consumption Profile |
|---|---|---|
| **SCOTCH** | | |
| 'Mainstream' | Bells<br>Teachers<br>Grants | Drunk by men lacking in confidence or too indifferent to choose any other |
| 'Premium' | Chivas Regal<br>Johnnie Walker<br>  Black Label | Often given as gifts, or offered at dinner parties by men who enjoy playing the generous host |
| Own Labels | Sainsbury<br>Tesco | A 'pick me up' for men (and women) at home |
| **IRISH** | Jamesons<br>Black Bush | Often the choice of those introduced to Irish whiskey by Irish friends or connections |
| **BOURBONS** | Jack Daniels<br>Jim Beam<br>Wild Turkey | 'Trendy' whiskies drunk mainly by men in their twenties attracted to bourbon's American image. |
| **MALTS** | | |
| 'First Tier' | Glenfiddich<br>Glenmorangie | Drunk by men over 35 attracted to the discerning image of malts but lacking the time or inclination to explore the rest of the sector |
| 'Second Tier' | Macallan<br>Laphroaig | Post 'First Tier' men attracted by the idea of a relatively obscure malt in reasonable distribution. Small scale advertising campaigns will have stimulated awareness |
| 'Third Tier' | Edradour<br>Glengarrioch<br>Tullibardine | Hundreds of malts exist which are unheard of outside a small band of devotees |

## ABERLOUR MALT WHISKY

Aberlour is a malt whisky from Speyside in Scotland. It is described by the authoritative Michael Jackson in his book on whisky as having 'a full rich aroma; a rounded, fruity palate; and a clean finish'. It was very much a 'third tier' malt. Prior to advertising, annual retail sales of Aberlour stood at 1,800 cases. This gave Aberlour an estimated share of the UK malt sector of 0.38%.

The whisky has a colourful background. At the turn of the century the villagers of Charlestown of Aberlour changed the name of their birthplace simply to Aberlour in honour of the whisky which they distilled. Other stories abound. Kenny, the chief brewer, for instance, attributes the drink's flavour to his bagpipes. On his rounds of the ageing cellars he plays wistful airs to sooth the whisky during its ten year maturation.

## THE ORIGINAL SUPPORT PLAN

Despite being the sixth biggest selling malt whisky in the world, Aberlour had never previously been supported in the UK. In 1989 Campbells decided to support the brand here for the first time.

Drawing on previous experience in handling such whiskies, it was assumed by Campbells that the brand development process for Aberlour could not be rushed. Consumers in this marketplace seemed to need time to accept the credentials of a 'new' brand into an 'establishment' category. Opportunities for large distribution gains appeared to be limited. A realistic figure of £60,000 was allocated for the 1989 advertising budget. The marketing objective was simply to raise awareness among both consumers and in the trade.

As we shall see, this initial thinking was eventually rejected as over-cautious.

BMP DDB Needham, who were working on other brands with Campbells, were appointed as the advertising agency.

## BACKGROUND TO THE ADVERTISING

Before developing an advertising plan, a qualitative research project was carried out by BMP DDB Needham. Since budgets were small it was intended to aid understanding in the development of other Campbells brands as well, but some time was taken within each of the eight extended groups to discuss Aberlour. All of the groups were conducted among ABC1 males (except one female group) ranging from 20 to 55 in age, in Scotland and in the South East of England. Three of the groups were among 'second tier' malt drinkers; one among 'first tier' malt drinkers, three among premium scotch and bourbon drinkers; one among Irish whiskey drinkers.

The qualitative work yielded four important findings concerning Aberlour:

— Confirmation that awareness of Aberlour was extremely low. During the project not one respondent claimed to have heard of it, or recognised the bottle when shown. This was not surprising in the case of scotch, bourbon and Irish whiskey drinkers, but more surprising in the case of 'second tier' malt drinkers.

— A sharper definition of the likely Aberlour consumer was developed. In addition to being male, rather upmarket and over 35, he exhibited other traits. He tended to be rather conservative in outlook and not easily influenced by new trends in society. He was interested in malt whisky, and although admitting to ignorance about Aberlour in particular, relished the idea of introducing an obscure malt whisky to friends and acquaintances who fancied themselves as connoisseurs. The fact that Macallan, for example, is matured in sherry casks to give it its distinctive taste provided him with exactly the sort of rationale he required to justify his recommendation. All in all he tended to be a good-natured sort of chap – in short a sociable would-be malt buff.

— The bulk of whisky advertising across all sectors when exposed during discussion was condemned as dull, samey and unadventurous.

— Reaction to the Macallan campaign however was markedly different. It seemed to be appealing for two reasons. The 'quirky' look of the campaign, black and white in small spaces with gently humorous copy, set it apart from other malt whisky advertising. And the media choice – many respondents recalled seeing executions in *Private Eye* – seemed to flatter the intellectual aspirations of these drinkers.

## THE 'MILLENNIUM' OFFER

It was now possible to develop an advertising strategy. At this stage, however, a fresh turn to the story occurred which completely changed the communication package plan for 1989.

Campbells had developed a unique promotion. Customers would be invited to invest in a hogshead (360 bottles) of Aberlour which would mature in the year 1999. The cost would be £1,350 payable on order. Duty, shipping and VAT (if applicable in 1999) would be due on delivery.

The inspiration for the promotion came from two sources.

For many years Bordeaux wines and ports had been sold in this way – 'en primeur' as it is called. Purchase and payment are made prior to bottling and bottles are then laid down in one's own name or in the name of sons, grandchildren, godchildren, friends or business colleagues.

Secondly, celebrations were being planned for the millennium, which was a mere ten years away, and were already receiving publicity in the media. London's Ritz was receiving bookings for the New Year's Ball 1999. A table for the evening had been booked at a New York restaurant yet to be built. Concorde had been booked to allow revellers to toast the millennium not once but twice.

Strategically this felt like a very appropriate promotion for Aberlour. Potentially it could invest the brand by association with a similar prestigious stature to fine wines and ports. It was topical. And it was unique – the first time that a malt whisky had been offered 'en primeur'.

But most importantly it had radical implications for the brand development plan on Aberlour.

## A CHANGE OF STRATEGY

A unique opportunity seemed to be offered by this promotion. Perhaps it could be used to speed up the lengthy process of developing an obscure malt whisky. Aberlour's support programme was re-examined. The original marketing objectives and strategy were redefined.

### Marketing Objectives

*Overall*: To accelerate the development of Aberlour.
*Specifically*:
1. To increase consumer share of the retail product in the UK malt sector.
2. To gain trade acceptance and distribution of the retail product.

The marketing strategy for 1989 would be tactical.

### Marketing Strategy

1. To use the promotion and its support package to help gain acceptance in the trade, and consequently increase consumer exposure to the brand.
2. To sell as many hogsheads of Aberlour as possible.

Advertising would be the main element of the support package.

The priority was to stimulate enquiries about the offer – after all, 60 hogsheads represented total sales of Aberlour for a whole year.

But a bold and impactful advertisement for the promotion might also offer proof to the trade that Campbells was serious in its intentions for this brand. It would position Aberlour to them as a genuinely differentiated malt whisky. This was vitally important considering the dozens of malt whiskies with a similar share of the sector to Aberlour seeking distribution.

### Advertising Objectives

1. To stimulate inquiries about the 'Millennium' offer.
2. To help convince retailers that they should stock Aberlour.

### Advertising Strategy

By positioning Aberlour as a significant contender within the UK malt sector through investing the brand with the credentials and status of an authentic yet distinctive malt.

### The Advertising Brief

Several key elements featured in the advertising brief.

— We did not simply want Aberlour to be promoted from 'third tier' to 'second tier' status. Macallan, seemingly the most successfully advertised malt of recent years, was perceived in a different light from other 'second tier' malts.

It had a highly distinctive personality. Research indicated that a campaign which had equally different tonal qualities was also required for Aberlour in order to stand out from the unimaginative mass of whisky advertising; and that an inventive media solution would support this uniqueness.

— The offer would *not* be positioned as an astute financial investment. Astute speculators would be able to find investments which were likely to be more profitable. And we were probably talking to astute financial speculators.

— Advertising would need to feature a direct response mechanism to allow interested readers to send off for further information.


## THE ADVERTISING


A short while later the concept was presented. Ian Mitchell, the distillery manager, would appear with wings in front of a hogshead of Aberlour as a 'Guardian Angel'. This was a reference to the 'angel's share', or the alcohol which evaporates into the atmosphere during maturation. Copy would run to over 1,000 words expressed in olde worlde phraseology and featuring the stories which have attached themselves to Aberlour over the years. 18th century typography would reflect these traditional values. There would be a coupon but it would blend into the overall tonal approach. The end line would be 'There are more hours in Aberlour'. There would be only one execution – full page and in colour to appear in the national quality dailies.

In the malt whisky sector, only 'first tier' malts such as Glenfiddich and Glenmorangie ever use full page advertising. This was a unique approach for such a small malt which seemed to reflect the values of our target audience.

The length of copy allowed anecdotes space to breathe. The 'onerous existence of a distillery manager' is described at length. There is conjecture that St. Dunstan, who founded the first settlement at Aberlour and went on to become Archbishop of Canterbury, may have welcomed in the previous millennium with 'a spot of private bibulation'. This was all ammunition for the 'second tier' malt drinker badly needing information so he could 'outconnoisseur' other connoisseurs.

The trade could now be provided with the evidence when they asked if Campbells were serious about putting funding behind developing Aberlour.


## PR


Campbells were delighted with the advertising. They decided to use it as the basis for their PR campaign. Support material was developed, and together with a copy of the advertisement, sent to a variety of national and regional publications, and to TV and radio stations.

The PR campaign would not have been as comprehensive nor would it have been developed in this way without the advertising to support it. In particular, Campbells would not have committed to support material.

## THE MEDIA PLAN

The creative treatment had already encompassed the strategic requirement for an unusual media solution. In the event, within the confines of the budget, the size of the ad and the profile of the target audience, choice was severely limited. Among quality daily newspapers ones with the best coverage of malt drinkers (apart from Glenfiddich – not the choice of the would-be buff) were chosen.

TABLE 2:   MEDIA PLAN

| Publication | Insertion Date | Position | Booked cost |
|---|---|---|---|
| The Times | 21 October | Outside back cover (second section) | £13,500 |
| | 25 November | Outside back cover (second section) | £13,500 |
| The Independent | 11 November | Right hand page in food and drink | £14,700 |

The Independent insertion was in a prime site for those interested in specialised food and drink. The Times had an alternative position within their arts section, but all things being equal, it was judged that the effective back cover of the paper would gain more impact.

Analysis indicates that this total spend of £41,700 achieved a share of voice of the whisky sector of 1.8% in the period over which the advertising ran, and a total sector share of voice for 1989 of 0.4%.

It can be seen how loudly Aberlour had to 'shout' to be 'heard'.

## RESULTS

Funds were not available to carry out any quantitative or further qualitative research. However, the analysis we can do is remarkably encouraging.

### Sales of Hogsheads

The number of purchases of the 'Millennium' offer far outstripped expectations. Response was sluggish initially and by Christmas only a handful of customers had actually committed to purchase. In the next few weeks however rate of purchase considerably increased. At the time of writing (end May 1990) it has declined to one or two a week. 175 hogsheads have been ordered. This figure represents the minimum level of response. More purchasers may be left.

175 hogsheads are equivalent to 5,250 case sales. Therefore the promotion has sold almost three years' UK retail case sales of Aberlour.

### Distribution

Subsequent to the advertising running two major retailers have now stocked Aberlour again who had not stocked it for 12 months. Morrisons took 90 cases and

Vauxhall Vintners 40 cases. Most significantly, however, Tesco agreed to take Aberlour into their top 200 stores for the first time. 240 cases have been sold since March 1990. Aberlour has been listed ahead of other unsupported malts with a larger share of the UK malt whisky sector, and consequently beyond the brand's expectations prior to advertising. To put this in context, Morrisons, Vauxhall Vintners and Tesco have accounted for 48% of ex-distillery sales of the retail product in 1990 to date, Tesco alone for 31%. Many other smaller retailers also listed Aberlour for the first time after the advertising ran.

Just as encouraging is Tesco's decision to *carry on* stocking Aberlour. To date they have ordered 110 cases in March, 20 cases in April and 110 cases in May. This in turn suggests consumer demand for the brand. This is particularly heartening since it justifies the decision to employ such bold marketing and advertising tactics so early on in the brand development process.

### Retail Sales

These distribution gains have naturally had an effect on ex-distillery sales of Aberlour.

It seems fairest to look at the figures from the first week of January to the latest figures available (last week April). The data then begins at the first point when listings gains could reasonably be a function of advertising rather than stock ordered for the traditional pre-Christmas peak in malt whisky sales.

This analysis shows that Aberlour's year on year retail sales have increased by 129%, from 335 to 767 case sales.

### Other Effects

The advertising produced some unexpected effects.

A number of rival companies magnanimously rang the marketing director on seeing the advertising and, in addition to acknowledging that Campbells had pipped them to the post by running the promotion, commented very favourably on the unique qualities of the ad itself.

At an international Aberlour conference involving marketing departments worldwide held in March 1990, it rapidly became clear that the UK had emerged as the force to be reckoned with. Both the promotion and the advertising received widespread commendation and as proof of their impact, it is now intended to run the promotion and the advertising in as many countries as possible. It is about to run in Holland and in the USA, in publications such as *The New York Times* and *The Wall Street Journal*. The idea is being adapted for use in France.

The style and content of the advertisement, but without the promotion, has also been adapted for use in magazines for international businessmen such as in flight and duty free publications.

# ABERLOUR Single Malt Whisky takes ten years to mature † (Or so our head taster, Mr. Mitchell, would have us believe.) ⚘ ⚘ ⚘

the atmosphere.

While a rather larger portion finds its way into Mr. Mitchell.

And there's surely not a man in Scotland with a sharper nose or keener palate.

Mr. Mitchell has been steeped in malt whisky since he was but a tot.

Born in a nearby distillery, he is now a mellow sixty-year-old himself, having spent forty years at Aberlour, twenty or more as distillery manager.

Overseeing the entire process.

The first stage involves hand-picking the best Scottish ⚘ barleys from as far afield as the Black Isle, Moray Coast and the milder Border region.

Once malted, the barley is dried over local Aberdeenshire peat, which gives it a *unique*, smoky aroma.

Then the barley is mashed and, using the unique waters of Aberlour's own secret spring, distilled, in stills with a shape, reminiscent, some say, of a rising swan, or perhaps, more prosaically, of a prize-winning onion.

In truth, though, it's hard to determine what exactly makes Aberlour so distinctive.

Perhaps it's to do with its location in the centre of the great malt whisky-producing region along the banks of the Spey, which seems to spawn almost as many distilleries as it does salmon.

More significantly, Aberlour is held in such high esteem in the Highlands that the inhabitants of the little settlement which is the distillery's home actually renamed the town in honour of their favourite malt.

And the reason for their regard, at least, is clear.

Because, when you buy a bottle of Aberlour Single Speyside Malt, you can be sure of its quality.

*After all*, Mr. Mitchell has been drinking it for ten years.

DURING ten years of maturation, Aberlour Single Speyside Malt Whisky is kept in two quite distinct kinds of container.

One is a stout oak bourbon or sherry cask. The other is Mr. Ian Mitchell, Aberlour's taster-in-chief and distillery manager *par excellence*.

Over this period, a small amount of the heavenly nectar (commonly known as the "angel's share") naturally evaporates into

THE EXCEPTIONAL MALT FROM THE HEART OF SPEYSIDE.

## ISOLATING THE CONTRIBUTION OF ADVERTISING

### Sales of Hogsheads

64 purchases were accredited to people who applied via the coupon at the bottom of the ad. It seems reasonable to infer that advertising was the major influence on their decision to purchase.

In an effort to find out more about how the advertising worked we contacted a small sample of purchasers by telephone. Among those who had enquired about the offer from the advertising, most agreed that it was very clever and arresting. One was even able to quote large chunks of copy.

The other methods of finding out about the offer were being approached directly by an employee of Campbells or from the PR effort. One salesman contributed five purchasers, while the marketing department within the company persuaded eight of their friends to invest. Campbells also bought one hogshead.

The marketing department certainly made use of the advertising when selling to their acquaintances. The comments of the salesman who sold the hogsheads directly to his customers are interesting:

'There is no question the ad helped. It was a talking point. I loved the ad, I wished I had got more. It was a very funny piece. Some customers had, of course, seen the ad in the paper, but weren't interested in investing in a hogshead. I got the ad put up in some of the bars locally'.

Of the remaining 97, it seems likely that PR was the primary reason for the majority of purchases. The salient point here is that it was the advertising which provided the catalyst for the PR campaign. The coverage (see Table 3) could not have been achieved without advertising.

TABLE 3: PR COVERAGE

| Media | Items | Impacts |
|---|---|---|
| National | 15 | 16,640,000 |
| Regional | 33 | 2,147,000 |
| Radio | 7 | 650,000 |
| TV | 1 | 915,000 |
| Trade | 9 | 151,000 |
| Financial | 2 | 77,000 |
| Total | 67 | 20,580,000 |

### Distribution

Proof of commitment to support in the form of a national full page advertisement in quality dailies combined with the promise of more advertising support to come, we believe are more likely to have formed a persuasive argument for listing Aberlour than a tactical promotion or its publicity drive. Advertising, promotion and PR were the only variables in the marketing mix operating over this period of fresh trade listings.

The gain of Tesco does not coincide with the normal peak for distribution gains. That comes before Christmas when the trade is stocking up, and first sales into

Tesco were not until March. Hence advertising seems to have been a causal factor in gaining distribution in, for example, Tesco.

### The Other Elements of the Marketing Mix

There had been no change in Aberlour's packaging for years. No other advertising ran during 1989 or during the first four months of 1990. There was no change in pricing strategy and, although distribution data from audit sources is not available, no major gains or losses of listings prior to the advertising.

## PROFIT

In assessing the overall return on Campbells' advertising investment, there are various angles to consider, some easily quantifiable, some much less so.

The first way to analyse profit is to assess the gross profit generated by sales of the hogsheads. The profit per hogshead is £800 and there were 175 purchases. Hence gross profit is £140,000. All sales of hogsheads included some advertising contribution.

It is more realistic however to consider what would have happened to the Aberlour whisky had it not found its way into the hogsheads. The answer is that it would probably have been sold off for use in blended whiskies for less profit. Hence the minimum profit generated by the sale of the hogsheads is the difference between the profit on whisky sold in the promotion and the profit on the same volume of whisky had it been sold for use in blends. This figure is £745 per hogshead. Hence when multiplied by 175 this gives an incremental profit figure for the promotion of at least £130,375.

If we consider the 64 direct response purchases which are wholly attributable to advertising, then advertising's bare minimum contribution to profit is £47,680. This figure is 14% higher than media costs (which seems the fairest measure since production costs will be amortised by using the execution outside the UK in the future).

At the very minimum, therefore, advertising was more than self-liquidating.

A true evaluation should take into account the spin off effects from the success of the offer. As we have seen, advertising played a major role in gaining distribution which in turn greatly boosted year on year sales.

However, there are also profit implications in being paid now for whisky which will not be delivered until 1999.

Campbells could always invest in their own business with the help of this 'interest free loan'.

The advantage of such a loan could, of course, be severely reduced if real whisky prices were likely to increase faster than real interest rates. But, in fact, over the last ten years, real interest rates have been on average 5.7% higher than the percentage change in whisky prices (see Figures 1 and 2). There is little evidence to show that this differential will vary significantly over the next ten years.

As an academic exercise, it should also be noted that the revenue could be invested where it is likely to yield an even higher rate of return than real interest rates. Campbells could plough this money into a relatively low risk investment, such as government bonds. Were they to perform in line with the last ten years (see Appendix), then the additional profit generated through this mechanism by advertising would be at least £115,540, based on the revenue from sales of hogsheads to date of £236,250.

To sum up, advertising more than paid for itself via the direct response to the offer, then contributed to profit gained from PR sales of hogsheads, from gains in distribution and from retail sales.

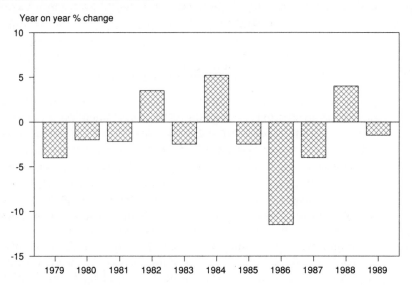

Figure 1.  *Year on year percentage change in real whisky price*
*Note:*    Price excludes duty and VAT

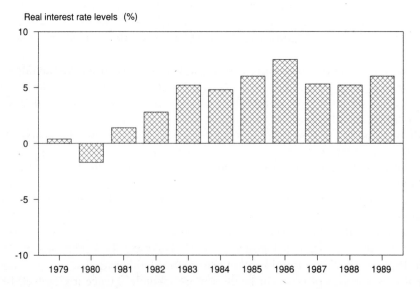

Figure 2.  *Real interest rate levels*
*Source:* CSO

## COULD THE PROMOTION HAVE BEEN COMMUNICATED AS EFFECTIVELY WITHOUT ADVERTISING?

The promotion might simply have been communicated via PR. But it was advertising which originally stimulated such a successful PR campaign.

The only other realistic way of running the promotion would be on the bottle itself. But it would have been impossible to reach the same numbers of people since Aberlour was in such patchy distribution. With case sales of 1,800 a year, since there are 12 bottles in a case, only 21,600 impacts for the promotion could have been achieved with a resulting penetration of awareness for the offer of considerably less. And a piece of stiff card around the neck of the bottle could not have projected a prestigious image which the promotion demanded.

## COULD THE PROMOTION HAVE BEEN COMMUNICATED AS EFFECTIVELY IN DIFFERENT MEDIA?

The justification for larger spaces rather than smaller spaces in more magazines has already been argued. Posters cannot incorporate a direct response mechanism and such a mechanism seems justified by the results. TV does not allow whisky advertising. There is a gentlemen's agreement that it should not be transmitted on radio.

Although Macallan has recently been on cinema, theirs is a rather special case. They seem now to be attempting to broaden their franchise, having established their heartland credentials over a number of years. Significantly they did not use cinema in their early years since its target audience is younger than 'second tier' malt drinkers. Moreover the production costs of communicating such a prestigious offer would have ruled cinema out as an option.

## WILL SALES BE DEPRESSED IN TEN YEARS TIME?

A theory might be advanced that in ten years time sales of Aberlour will fall heavily when the hogsheads are distributed. However, the number of purchasers is 175. At 1989 levels of 1,800 UK case sales a year, and assuming the average drinker buys about three bottles a year, the introduction of hogsheads into the market would result in sales being depressed by less than 3%. It is true that consumption of purchasers is likely to be above average, and that they are also likely to give bottles to their friends. But it is also true that the brand is likely to be consistently supported over the next ten years. Hence annual retail sales in 2000 are likely to be considerably more than 1,800. Overall, then, a future depression in sales is unlikely to be a major concern.

Moreover qualitative research indicates that 'second tier' malt whisky drinkers particularly enjoy introducing their friends to new malts. TGI analysis suggests that malt drinkers are 22% more likely to entertain than other adults. It is possible that investors in such an offer might be even more sociable. Hence it may well be that during the next ten years purchasers will want to tell their friends about the offer they have invested in and encourage them to try Aberlour (quite apart from continuing to drink it themselves). In fact it seems quite possible that the shortfall in sales occurring in ten years time will be compensated for by fresh purchasers generated over the previous ten years by word of mouth.

We like to think that the Guardian Angel in the ad now has a loyal band of disciples, eager to spread the good word.

## CONCLUSION

Successful advertising achieved the immediate objective of generating sales of hogsheads for Aberlour, and in so doing more than paid for itself. It then went on to help Aberlour gain distribution in major retailers and hence greatly increase retail sales of the brand. The advertising is now helping Aberlour's marketing effort in other countries.

We hope to have demonstrated that by reversing traditional marketing and advertising thinking in the malt whisky market, Aberlour has achieved in six months what might otherwise have taken years to accomplish.

## APPENDIX

TABLE 4: REAL AVERAGE RETURN ON GOVERNMENT BONDS

|      | Short-term | Medium-term | Long-term |
|------|------------|-------------|-----------|
| 1980 | −4.16      | −4.09       | −4.22     |
| 1981 | 2.75       | 2.98        | 2.84      |
| 1982 | 4.19       | 4.49        | 4.28      |
| 1983 | 6.59       | 6.67        | 6.20      |
| 1984 | 6.29       | 6.27        | 5.69      |
| 1985 | 5.03       | 4.96        | 4.52      |
| 1986 | 6.61       | 6.65        | 6.47      |
| 1987 | 5.16       | 5.37        | 5.27      |
| 1988 | 4.76       | 4.77        | 4.46      |
| 1989 | 2.91       | 2.38        | 1.77      |

Source:  CSO Financial Statistics (adjusted for retail price inflation)

# Section Five

*Special*

# 17

# Alliance & Leicester
# First Time Buyer Mortgages

## INTRODUCTION

During a boom year in 1988, clouds were growing on the horizon of the mortgage market. All forecasts pointed towards a tough 1989 with mortgage supply far outstripping demand. Profitability was seriously threatened.

This case study attempts to demonstrate an unusual use of advertising; namely, to change the purchasing process for a particular product. In this case, first time buyer mortgages.

In essence, it shows how an understanding of the basic needs of a market enabled the Alliance & Leicester and BMP to develop advertising that, through altering the purchase process, fundamentally changed the structure and profitability of the Alliance & Leicester's first time buyer business.

## BACKGROUND TO THE MORTGAGE MARKET

The mortgage market showed steady growth during the 1980s. In particular, this growth was driven by:

1. Abolition of the Bank of England 'corset' controls allowing entry into the market of the clearing banks.
2. The consequent increase in competition leading to mortgage suppliers having to court demand rather than vice versa.
3. The reduction in the base rate of tax from 33% to 25% and the highest rate from 83% to 40%.
4. The consequent increasing demand fuelling steady house price inflation that, like many other asset markets, was self-sustaining (at least short-term). Average house prices rose by over 80% between 1981 and 1987. In real terms, this represented an increase of nearly 30%.

In 1986 and 1987, the mortgage interest rate began to fall and, as with the stock market, property became seen as an investment that couldn't lose. In 1988, house buying fever continued. Multiple tax relief* was abolished (in the budget in April) for purchases after August. At the same time, the mortgage interest rate dropped to 9.5% (its lowest level since 1978). Demand was such that the average house price rose by nearly 25% across the first eight months of the year. And then, over three months, the mortgage interest rate rose by 34% to 12.75%. In combination with the sudden drop in demand post-August caused by the pulling forward of around 50,000 loans (Bank of England estimate) to beat multiple tax relief abolition, the bubble seemed about to burst (cf Stock Market crash 1987). Indeed, October 1988 saw the first reduction in absolute average house prices for almost a decade.

Forecasters were predicting a gloomy future:

'We would now argue forcefully that this heady atmosphere of euphoria and complete confidence in the housing market has been replaced savagely with an atmosphere of uncertainty and even fear as the severe turns of the screw...take effect.

The current consensus is that turnover will be down 50% on 1988 in the coming year. This unprecedentedly severe depression in the housing market is going to have grave consequences for the strategies and profitability of financial service companies' (PA Consulting Group).

## BUILDING SOCIETIES IN THE MORTGAGE MARKET

The sudden emergence of strong competition in the mortgage market caused major problems for all building societies. In particular, the varying cost of wholesale funding versus retail funding**(building societies almost wholly depend on retail funding) sent the share of mortgage lending accounted for by building societies plunging from the 'traditional' 80%+ to 50% by 1987. The building societies fought back through competitive rates and new products. Deferred interest, capped, fixed rate and discount mortgages appeared.

By 1988, they had clawed back to around 60% share of the market. Despite this loss of share during the 1980s, the overall market growth more than compensated in terms of volume. In 1980, building societies lent c£9 billion. In 1988, this had risen to c£41 billion.

Amidst the doom and gloom of the 1989 forecasts, there was one sign of hope. The sudden huge rises in the bank base rate gave the building societies the chance to lag the increase in their interest rate on retail investments and thereby profitably undercut bank mortgage rates on the basis of cheap retail funding. Even if the market as a whole was about to plunge, at least the building societies would get a larger share of whatever was around (A & L, DoE).

* Tax relief on the first £30,000 of a mortgage had historically been granted per person rather than per property (except for married couples). Hence, two people getting a joint mortgage on a single house were entitled to tax relief on £60,000. In the 1988 budget, the Chancellor announced that from August, the £30,000 would apply per property rather than per person. This removed the tax advantage for multiple purchasers and made many change their plans so that they would beat the August deadline.
** Wholesale funding basically involves funding lending activity using money from the international finance markets. Retail funding involves funding lending activity with your customers' savings. The relative price of money from these two sources (ie the interest rate the bank/building society has to pay in order to get it) varies according to the domestic and foreign economic climate. During the mid 1980s, wholesale funding tended to be cheaper, favouring the banks over the building societies.

## TYPES OF BORROWERS

Borrowers in the mortgage market fall into two sectors – owner occupiers (ie people who already have a mortgage) and first time buyers (FTBs).

Each year, these two sectors are of roughly equal size, each accounting for 50% ±2% of the total market.

In all other respects they differ enormously.

Owner occupiers are an extremely heterogeneous group, ranging from a couple with a new baby who need an extra bedroom to a 65 year old retiring to a bungalow by the sea. They tend to be reasonably confident about mortgages since they have been through it all before and hence tend to be either highly price conscious or highly inert (ie stick with the lender they are already with). They are generally quite unprofitable lending targets since they will already have an endowment policy (ie little commission to be made).

In contrast, FTBs are a fairly homogeneous group. The vast majority (c80%) are aged 20 – 40 and in social classes C1 C2 (c70%). In terms of lifestage, they are almost all either young independents, nearly-weds or newly-weds.

The idea of borrowing, what is to them an enormous sum of money, is quite daunting and they are consequently less likely to be purely price sensitive. They are also a potentially more profitable group through commission earnings on new endowment policies.

For these reasons, the Alliance & Leicester chose to focus their 1989 mortgage activity on FTBs (J Levin, *House Purchase Decision*, A & L, DoE).

## DIRECT VERSUS INDIRECT

In addition to the owner occupier/FTB segmentation, borrowers can be classified according to whether they come to you direct (ie via a branch) or indirect (ie via an intermediary/broker).

A direct FTB is by far the most profitable borrower of all. Almost always, a direct FTB will arrange not only the loan but also his endowment policy and household insurance policy with the building society, resulting in the building society getting all the commission. Consequently, a direct FTB is over twice as profitable as an indirect FTB (or any owner occupier borrower).

In addition to being highly profitable, direct FTBs are believed to be of further value since they tend to be more loyal and more susceptible to cross-selling of other products.

'You get a better rapport since you chat to them about their whole situation and they trust you more' (Alliance & Leicester Branch Manager).

In the light of these attractions and the forecast decline in volume (and hence profit) in the market, the Alliance & Leicester chose to concentrate specifically on attracting FTBs to them *direct*.

'With the forecast cooling of demand in 1989, direct FTBs will be very important – not only from the insurance commission that can be won but because they become our 'existing borrowers' for the future' (A & L Marketing Plan 1988).

It was felt that a new product targeted purely at FTBs would be needed as a vehicle to attract FTBs to the branches. (Once in the branch, it was up to the branch staff to offer them the mortgage most suited to their individual circumstances from the Alliance & Leicester's portfolio of mortgages and this might well not be the new product).

## DEVELOPING THE PRODUCT

Extensive qualitative research was carried out amongst potential and recent FTBs. The research showed:

— All borrowers describe the process of buying a house as a major, traumatic event.
— The whole experience is frightening since it is unknown territory.
— FTBs find their main problem is not knowing where to find guidance.
— Overall, they simply seek reassurance. (BMP, *Mortgage Concept Research; IMR, Large Mortgage Research;* J Levin, House Purchase Decision).

Based on this research and the requirement to attract FTBs direct, the Alliance & Leicester developed a product that was reasonably price competitive, gave a physical manifestation of help and advice and was only available through branches.
Specifically, the Smarter Starter mortgage offered FTBs:

— 0.5% off the mortgage rate for the first year.
— 100% mortgage if necessary.
— A filofax filled with useful advice – 'The Homebuyer's Planner'.
— A mortgage guarantee card – ie a card confirming their mortgage offer.

The product was made available in branch in January 1989 and was planned to run until December 1989.

## BUSINESS OBJECTIVE

To maximise profitability of the Alliance & Leicester first time buyer mortgage business.

## MARKETING OBJECTIVES

1. To secure at least asset share of the FTB mortgage market.*
2. To significantly improve the proportion of FTB business that is direct.

## THE ADVERTISING STRATEGY

Existing qualitative research suggested that the basic need of the FTB was not centred simply on the cheapest deal possible but rather on reassurance/help and advice.

The research on the product itself suggested that Smarter Starter was not seen as *significantly* better than the competitive offerings. Consequently, it seemed unlikely that the product points alone would be sufficient support for the product followed simply by a statement 'only available from Alliance & Leicester branches'.

The key objective of attracting people direct to branches suggested that we should take a closer look at the way in which FTBs went about choosing the source of their mortgage. Further qualitative research was undertaken to gain an understanding of the FTB mortgage purchase process.

In summary, the research showed that, in general, FTBs got their mortgage from one of three sources:

1. The estate agent in-house broker.
2. The building society with which they already have a relationship.
3. The default option of Halifax or Abbey National, ie FTBs who had no good reason to go to any particular society tended to end up with the one they had heard of most and hence trusted most. Eventually, the majority ended up going to the 'Big 2'.

In addition, there were three key findings of the qualitative research that proved to be the inspiration for the advertising strategy. These were:

1. There was an overwhelming belief amongst FTBs that 'First you find the house you want then you get a mortgage'.
2. Almost every FTB accepted the first mortgage he/she was offered. Indeed, the first 'father figure' they came across tended to make the sale.

> 'Most respondents appeared not to have gone through the formalities of seeing a building society manager before looking at property. Once they'd found a property they were then very susceptible to an estate agent offering to sort out the details of a mortgage. Most respondents were very happy to take the line of least resistance, which could well mean taking a mortgage from the first person to offer them one' (Pegram Walters Associates).

---

* Asset share is defined on the basis of the Alliance & Leicester's share of the total fixed assets of all building societies. In effect, it represents the Alliance & Leicester's 'expected share' of any building society market. Asset share is an extremely slow-moving variable. Across the time period of this paper it can be treated as static. The Alliance & Leicester's asset share is 6.6%.

3. Their major worries as far as mortgages were concerned were quite simplistic:

— Will anyone give me a mortgage?
— If yes, how much will they lend me?

Desk research confirmed most of the qualitative findings. Firstly, that a growing number of FTBs were indeed being snapped up by the increasing number of estate agents with brokers in-house:

TABLE 1

| Mortgage arranged | % FTB mortgages arranged through estate agent/broker |
|---|---|
| Pre April 1986 | 11 |
| Apr 1986 – Sep 1987 | 19 |
| Oct 1987 – Oct 1988 | 24 |

Source:   A & L

Secondly, the fact that most societies have always performed close to asset share in the FTBs market suggested that there was a proportion of FTBs that tended to use the society with whom they already had an investment relationship.

Thirdly, the 'default option' conclusion was confirmed by the disproportionate number of direct FTBs at both Halifax and Abbey National. Indeed, the data below on the UK's top five building societies tend to support the hypothesis that, in general, the bigger the society is, the better it does amongst these 'floating' buyers.

TABLE 2:   FTB MORTGAGES OPENED OCTOBER 1987 – OCTOBER 1988

| | % who came direct | % asset share |
|---|---|---|
| Halifax | 61 | 28 |
| Abbey National | 73 | 22 |
| Nationwide Anglia | 48 | 17 |
| Woolwich | 36 | 8 |
| Alliance & Leicester | 34 | 7 |
| Total market | 51 | 100 |

Source:   Financial Research Survey/DoE

(NB The remaining 25% of FTBs (who didn't go direct or to estate agent/brokers) sourced their loans from independent advisors, their local authority or claimed not to remember what the source was.

The FTBs going through independent advisors represents the more sophisticated/confident end of the FTB market. They were not likely to be influenced by advertising since they went to the advisor precisely to let him/her find them the best deal. Those going to the local authority were buying their council house. Neither group were part of our target market.

The 'don't knows' we can only speculate about).

From the research, we constructed a simplified model of the FTB mortgage purchase process:

From this, we decided that ideally, the advertising should get people to come direct to the Alliance & Leicester by:

— Giving a good reason not to use the estate agent/broker.
— Giving a good reason to come to the Alliance & Leicester rather than your existing building society.
— Giving a good reason to come to the Alliance & Leicester rather than default.

The only way we could do this was to get the Alliance & Leicester into the flow chart above the estate agent. In other words, make the Alliance & Leicester the first 'father figure' FTBs came across.

When we put together all the key findings, the solution became clear:

1. FTBs need reassurance.
2. The key things they want reassurance on are:

    — Will anyone give me a mortgage?
    — How much will they lend me?

3. *They believe (wrongly) that before you can get an answer to these questions you have to find a home.*
4. They tend to accept the first mortgage they are offered.
5. We want them to come to us first.

↓

'Get your mortgage sorted out before you find a house'.

What we had arrived at was a positioning that we hoped would turn the purchase process on its head by inverting the key attitude that caused it ie:

Furthermore, we were inverting the purchase process by offering FTBs exactly what they needed. The worries of buying their first home were weighing heavily on their shoulders. The Alliance & Leicester were offering to remove some of those worries and, what is more, were offering to remove them *now*, before they'd found a home.

It is worth noting that the idea of 'sorting your mortgage out first' is *not* a product specific feature of the Smarter Starter mortgage. In other words, we believed we had found a proposition for the Alliance & Leicester itself rather than simply a product specific proposition.

## THE CREATIVE BRIEF

### Advertising Objectives

— To attract FTBs to come to the Alliance & Leicester direct.
— To continue to build awareness of the Alliance & Leicester.

### Strategy

By communicating that at the Alliance & Leicester you can get your first mortgage sorted out before you find a house.

### Target Market

FTBs, 20 – 40, C1C2. Unconfident; frightened about the whole process of buying their first house.

*Proposition*

It's never too early to get your first mortgage.

*Support*

You can do it before you find your house.
Product points:

— 0.5% off.
— 100% mortgages.
— Home buyers' planner.

*Guidelines*

This ad must change the way FTBs believe you have to go about getting a mortgage. Currently, they think they have to have found a house and had an offer of £x accepted before they can go and try to borrow £x from a lender. We need to convince them that they can get their mortgage worries out of the way *before* they start the traumatic process of house buying. The product points are additional 'sweeteners' and should be dealt with as such. They must not be allowed to cloud the main thrust of the ad.

## THE AD

The ad had to attract FTBs direct whilst fitting into the campaign using Stephen Fry and Hugh Laurie that had been running since 1987.

The creative team took the proposition literally and wrote a script that involved using 12 year old boy lookalikes for Fry and Laurie with Fry and Laurie's real voices dubbed on. The ad was called 'Young Ones'.

## THE MEDIA STRATEGY

The ambitious nature of the marketing and advertising objectives together with the requirement to build awareness quickly so as to maximise response in a tough year meant that TV was the natural medium.

We targeted C1C2 adults aged 20 – 40 and aimed for programmes that maximised their conversion versus all adults.

The advertising was deployed in two bursts.

Burst 1:  6/2/89 – 19/3/89; 579 60 second Adult TVRs; £1.8m.
Burst 2:  22/5/89 – 30/6/89; 311 60 second Adult TVRs; £1.2m.

*Client:* Alliance & Leicester      *Title:* Young Ones

| VISION | SOUND |
|---|---|
| In the sitting room of a country house two boys of about twelve years of age sit in large chairs having an earnest discussion. | |
| One of them bears an uncanny resemblance to Hugh Laurie, the other is an exact twelve year old replica of Stephen Fry. | |
| The young Fry puts down a frothy drink with a curly straw sticking out of it and leans forward in his chair. | **Boy Fry:** So Mostyn, you've decided to start thinking about your first mortgage.<br>**Boy Laurie:** Yes, well actually I've already got one.<br>**Boy Fry:** Have you? Bit quick off the mark aren't we?<br>**Boy Laurie:** Yes, well at the Alliance & Leicester you can get your mortgage sorted out before you've found a home. |
| The young Fry lifts his glass and the straw sticks up his nose. | **Boy Fry:** Really.<br>**Boy Laurie:** Yes, saves wasting time once |
| Young Laurie stands up casually, takes something out of his inside pocket and hands it to the young Fry. | you have found a place, and they give half percent off your first year's repayments, they'll even give you one of these.<br>**Boy Fry:** Big Ears Goes Fishing? |
| He realises his mistake and hands him a Smarter Starter pack from another pocket. | **Boy Laurie:** What? Oh, here.<br>Its got everything you need to know about buying a house. |
| Young Fry flicks through the filofax. | **Boy Fry:** Hmm! You don't think you're a bit young to start worrying about mortgages do you? |
| Young Laurie paces the room as he speaks. | **Boy Laurie:** Well I think there comes a time in a man's life when he has to leave behind his wild, reckless years and face up to his responsibilities like a mature and sensible adult. |
| He walks up to a built-in bar and picks up a cocktail shaker. | Another milkshake?<br>**Boy Fry:** Oh don't mind if I do.<br>**Boy Laurie:** Choccy topping?<br>**Boy Fry:** Oh I don't know.<br>**Boy Laurie:** Go on!<br>**Boy Fry:** No I couldn't.<br>**Boy Laurie:** Course you can.<br>**Boy Fry:** Oh well perhaps just a little bit.<br>**Boy Laurie:** (Fades) That's what I like to hear. |
| Cut to Alliance & Leicester logo.<br>Super: Building Society.<br>Freephone 100 | **MVO:** Get your mortgage before you've found your house and be a smarter investor with the Alliance & Leicester. |

# 'YOUNG ONES'

## RESULTS

### Background*

The basic market picture has already been dealt with. The actual figures are listed in Table 3.

TABLE 3:  NUMBER OF LOANS ADVANCED (000s)

|                    | 1985  | 1986  | 1987  | 1988  |
|--------------------|-------|-------|-------|-------|
| Market total       | 1,450 | 1,620 | 2,000 | 2,100 |
| Building Societies  | 1,090 | 1,230 | 1,047 | 1,230 |

Source:  DoE

* The Alliance Building Society and the Leicester Building Society merged at the end of 1985. A single computer system/data base was not fully operational until towards the end of 1986. The specific data we required for this case study (ie FTB/owner occupier splits; direct/indirect splits) are therefore only available for 1987 onwards. Hence, we will in general be dealing only with the period 1987 – 1989 (inclusive).

An added complication is that monthly data was unavailable for 1987 and 1988 (apparently, getting hold of it would involve about a week of mainframe computer time) hence, econometric modelling was not feasible since we would only have 12 data points. We hope that (as you will see), there are a sufficient number of clear indications of the advertising effect without it.

Against FTBs, The Alliance & Leicester had a particularly successful year in 1988 (see Table 4). This strong performance was largely caused by two factors:

1.  The abolition of multiple mortgage tax relief. This pulled purchases forward particularly in the Midlands and the South where house prices dictated that FTB purchases were very often based on more than one income. The Alliance & Leicester are particularly strong in the Midlands and the South (the Alliance originated in Hove, the Leicester (obviously) in Leicester).
2.  In 1988, the Alliance & Leicester was the only building society offering a 1% discount on a FTB product through intermediaries. This was an effective short-term way to buy market share. In both 1987 and 1989 the Alliance & Leicester was offering products through intermediaries at price parity with other major societies. (As we shall see later, increased discounting in the market in 1989 meant Smarter Starter was actually *more expensive* than its competitors).

TABLE 4:  NUMBER OF FTB LOANS ADVANCED (000s)

|                    | 1987  | 1988  |
|--------------------|-------|-------|
| Building Societies | 505   | 580   |
| A & L              | 27.05 | 40.20 |
| A & L share (%)    | 5.36  | 6.93  |

Source:  DoE, A&L

However, in both 1987 and 1988 the profitability of this FTB business was strongly affected by the proportion who came from indirect sources. Although the Alliance & Leicester's performance here looks poor versus the market average, we have already seen that compared with societies of similar size, this performance is quite normal.

The 1988 figure for both the market and the Alliance & Leicester illustrates the effect estate agents were having on direct business compared with 1987.

TABLE 5:  PERCENTAGE OF FTB ADVANCES DIRECT

|                    | 1987 | 1988 |
|--------------------|------|------|
| Building Societies | 55   | 51   |
| A & L              | 39   | 34   |

Source:  FRS, A&L

As predicted, the overall market plummeted from 2,100,000 advances in 1988 to 1,300,000 in 1989, a drop of 38%. However, the retail versus wholesale funding advantage mentioned earlier meant that the building societies were less badly hit. Even so, the total number of advances through building societies dropped by 23% from 1,230,000 in 1988 to 950,000 in 1989.

Within the FTB market, the Alliance & Leicester managed to achieve their first marketing objective of gaining at least asset share, despite the backlash swing of business away from their areas of strength due to the pulling forward of multiple purchases from 1989 into 1988.

TABLE 6:  NUMBER OF FTB LOANS ADVANCED (000s)

|                    | 1987  | 1988  | 1989  |
|--------------------|-------|-------|-------|
| Building Societies | 505   | 580   | 498   |
| A & L              | 27.05 | 40.20 | 34.80 |
| A & L share (%)    | 5.36  | 6.93  | 7.00  |

Source:  DoE, A&L

What is more exciting is the Alliance & Leicester's performance against direct FTBs.

TABLE 7:  NUMBER OF DIRECT FTB LOANS ADVANCED (000s)

|                    | 1987 | | 1988 | | 1989 | |
|                    | No | Index | No | Index | No | Index |
|--------------------|------|-------|------|-------|------|-------|
| Building Societies | 278  | 100   | 296  | 107   | 259  | 93    |
| A & L              | 10.55| 100   | 13.67| 130   | 18.00| 171   |

Source:  DoE, A&L

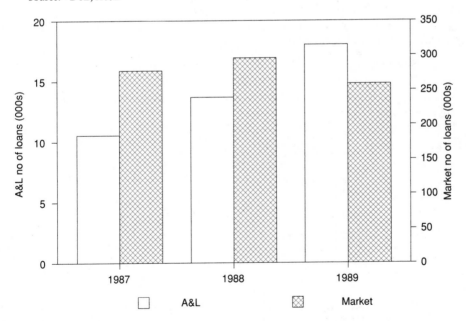

Figure 1.  *Alliance & Leicester direct FTB business 1987 – 1989*
*Source:*  A&L, DoE and FRS

What was also clear was the enormous swing in favour of direct business within the Alliance & Leicester in 1989 compared with 1988 or 1987.

TABLE 8: PERCENTAGE OF FTB LOANS WHICH WERE ADVANCED DIRECT

|                      | 1987 | 1988 | 1989 |
| -------------------- | ---- | ---- | ---- |
| Building Societies   | 55   | 51   | 52   |
| A & L                | 39   | 34   | 52   |

Source: FRS, A&L

It was quite clear that the marketing objectives (and, as we shall see later, the business objective) had been achieved. The rest of this case study deals with the evidence that supports the role the advertising played in causing this structural change in the Alliance & Leicester FTB business.

## THE PERFORMANCE OF SMARTER STARTER AND OTHER SIGNS OF ADVERTISING EFFECT

### Rate of Application for Smarter Starter Mortgages

Applications for Smarter Starter were made at the rate of 28.5 per day during January when the product was available with branch window support but not advertising. From February to December, applications were made at the rate of 67.7 per day. Between February and July (ie during the advertising) the rate of application was 76.5 per day (Figure 2). The poor performance of Smarter Starter in January is due only in small part to seasonality. The main reason is that direct applications were still accounting for only 33% of all applications.*

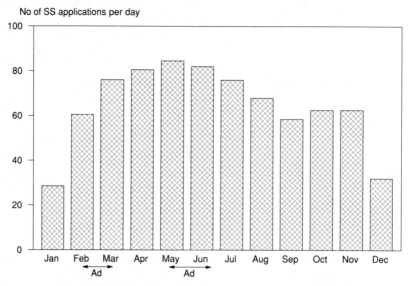

Figure 2. *Smarter Starter daily applications 1989*
*Source:* A&L

* The drop-off in December is due partly to seasonality and partly to the fact that the Smarter Starter advances officially terminated in December, hence branch staff were reluctant to allow applications. This is clarified by Figure 3 showing Smarter Starter advances by month.

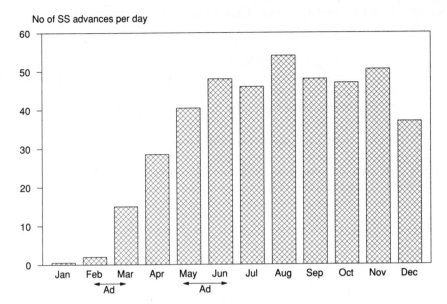

Figure 3. *Smarter Starter daily advances 1989*
*Source:* A&L

TABLE 9:  FTB APPLICATIONS PER DAY 1989

|  | Jan | | Feb – Dec | |
|---|---|---|---|---|
|  | No | % | No | % |
| Total | 120.9 | 100 | 157.4 | 100 |
| All direct | 40.3 | 33 | 91.9 | 58 |
| Smarter Starter | 28.5 | 23 | 67.7 | 43 |

It should be strongly noted that the increased demand for Smarter Starter is just a by-product of the true advertising effect which was to attract more FTBs to the branches.

### Proportion of Direct Business Accounted for by Smarter Starter

Smarter Starter accounted for 73% of all Alliance & Leicester's direct FTB applications in 1989. It also accounted for 60% of all direct FTB advances. However, bearing in mind the time that elapses between applications and advances*, we can see that Smarter Starter advances were only coming through in large numbers from April onwards.

During April – December 1989, Smarter Starter accounted for 69% of all Alliance & Leicester's direct FTB advances. The remaining 30% of advances were accounted for by the Alliance & Leicester's other mortgage products (eg Professional Mortgage Plan, Fixed Rate etc). It was up to the branch staff to offer the 'right' product to the customer. Interestingly, Smarter Starter accounted

---

* An application is counted as a customer 'applying' to the society to be considered for a mortgage (ie filling in an application form). An advance happens when the mortgage loan is actually 'advanced' to the vendors solicitor on completion of the house purchase.

for c70% of direct applications in January as well as across the rest of the year (Figure 4) demonstrating quite clearly

1.  Out of the portfolio of mortgages the branch staff could offer FTBs, Smarter Starter was the 'right' product for around three quarters of them whether there was advertising or not.
2.  The additional FTBs attracted to the branches following the advertising were a reasonably representative sample of all FTBs, ie Smarter Starter was the 'right' product for around three quarters of them too.

It seems clear that the change in performance of the Alliance & Leicester's direct FTB business was advertising rather than product related.

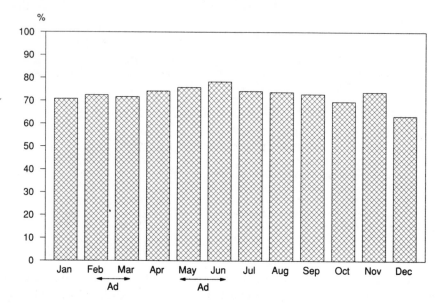

Figure 4. *Smarter Starter applications as percentage of all direct FTB applications 1989*
Source: A&L

## Lag Time from Application to Advance

On average, the gap between applying for a mortgage (direct or indirect) and the advance being issued is seven weeks. For Smarter Starter (which represented 69% of direct FTB advances post the advertising), this average gap was 13 weeks. This gives the first indication that the mortgage was indeed being 'sorted out' (ie applied for) much earlier in the purchase process. The advertising seemed to be changing behaviour exactly as we had hoped it would.

## The Change in Profile of Alliance & Leicester FTB Business 1987 – 1989.

Figures 5 and 6 show the huge shift towards direct FTB business that occurred when we ran the advertising. The direct/indirect profile has been almost reversed versus 1987 and 1988. (NB Due to the lack of monthly data, we have assumed

1987 and 1988 were constant throughout. There is no reason we know of to suggest that this isn't a very fair approximation to the truth).

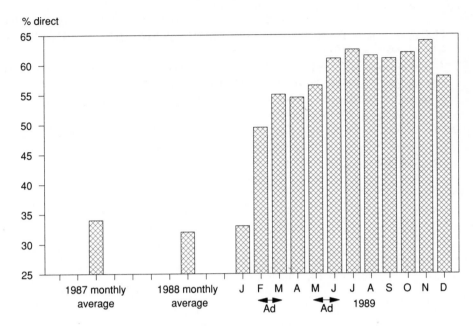

Figure 5. *Alliance & Leicester profile of FTB business, number of applications*
*Source:* A&L

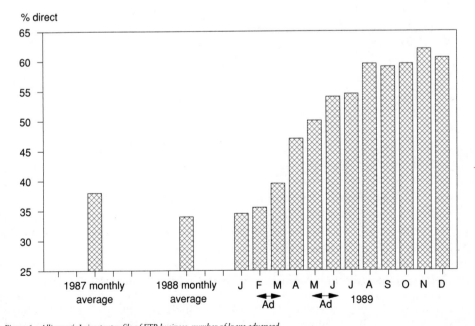

Figure 6. *Alliance & Leicester profile of FTB business, number of loans advanced*
*Source:* A&L

### The Change in Profile of Alliance & Leicester Business in 1989

Figure 7 demonstrates a number of points quite clearly:

1. The proportion of *applications* that came direct increased immediately the advertising was on air.
2. The proportion of *advances* that came direct lagged well behind applications and didn't catch up until after April. It seems clear that the increasing proportion of direct advances is precisely as a result of the increasing proportion of direct applications that began in February.
3. Once the effect of the increasing proportion of direct applications is allowed to fully materialise (ie May onwards), the proportion of direct advances reaches 58% (cf 1987 39%; 1988 34%; market in 1989 52%).

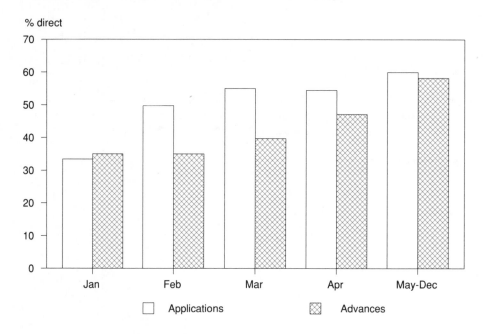

Figure 7.  *Alliance & Leicester profile of FTB business, applications versus advances, 1989*
*Source:* A&L

### The Increasing Number of Direct FTB Applications in 1989

Figure 8 shows the number of direct FTB applications made by month to the Alliance & Leicester between 1987 and 1989. The increase, starting in February 1989, is quite dramatic. If we assume that the total number of applications in the market would behave in a similar way to the total number of advances in the market then Figure 9 illustrates the change that began in February 1989 even more clearly by allowing for market growth of 6.5% in 1988 and decline of 12.5% in 1989.

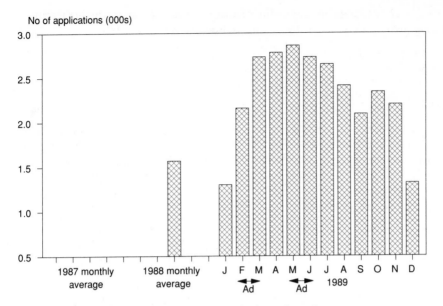

Figure 8.  *Alliance & Leicester direct FTB business 1987 – 1989, number of applications by month*
*Source:* A&L

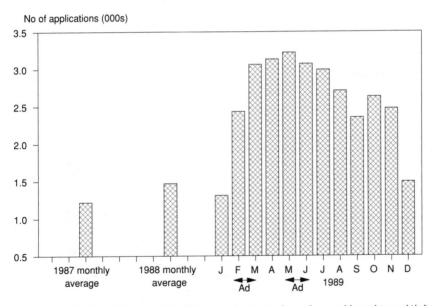

Figure 9.  *Alliance & Leicester direct FTB business 1987 – 1989, number of applications by month corrected for market growth/decline*
*Source:* A&L

## *The Increasing Number of Direct FTB Advances in 1989*

Figure 10 shows the number of direct FTB advances made monthly by the Alliance & Leicester between 1987 and 1989. The dramatic increase in 1989 is clear.

Figure 11 attempts to show this change even more clearly by correcting for the market growth of 6.5% in 1988 and decline of 12.5% in 1989.

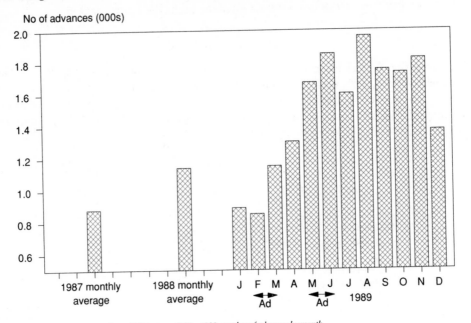

Figure 10. *Alliance & Leicester direct FTB business 1987 – 1989, number of advances by month*
*Source:* A&L

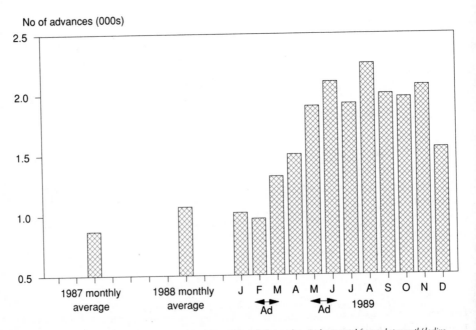

Figure 11. *Alliance & Leicester direct FTB business 1987 – 1989, number of advances by month corrected for market growth/decline*
*Source:* A&L

(NB Once again, the lack of monthly data has necessitated a simple averaging of the annual figures for 1987 and 1988. Whilst seasonality would serve to alter the 'shape' of 1987 and 1988 it would not alter the point the figures make).

## Quantitative Post Test

The Alliance & Leicester conducted a quantitative post test of all its ads in November 1989. This was five months after 'Young Ones' had been on air.

The test was conducted in halls and involved showing each ad to a separate sample (of ABC1C2D adults, aged 18 – 65, men and women) followed by a battery of questions. Table 10 shows the results for 'Young Ones'.

TABLE 10

|  | Total sample % | 18 – 44 year olds % |
|---|---|---|
| (Base | 105 | 66) |
| **Main message (unprompted)** |  |  |
| Apply for a mortgage early/ before you find a house | 45 | 55 |
| Easy to get a mortgage/ quick decision | 21 | 18 |
| **Opinion of ad** |  |  |
| Original | 82 | 85 |
| Memorable | 58 | 56 |
| Amusing | 85 | 91 |
| Confusing | 13 | 14 |
| **Seen advert before?** |  |  |
| Yes | 89 | 92 |
| **Willing to see again?** |  |  |
| Yes | 64 | 65 |

Source:   Sample Surveys

All measures appeared encouragingly high. It is gratifying that advertising awareness (albeit highly prompted) is at c90% so long after the ad ran. It is also particularly pleasing that unprompted main message communication was so clear in an ad that was also so enjoyable and entertaining.

## Survey Amongst Smarter Starter Purchasers

The Alliance & Leicester conducted a telephone survey in January 1990 amongst 30 people who had taken up a Smarter Starter mortgage. Whilst the base is small, the signs are still extremely positive regarding the effects of the advertising.

TABLE 11

|  | % |
|---|---|
| Did you get your mortgage sorted out before you started looking for a home? | |
| Yes | 93 |
| No | 7 |
| | |
| Were you surprised that you could do this? | |
| Yes | 73 |
| No | 27 |

These two results are particularly enlightening since the advertising was the only part of the promotional mix suggesting that they sort their mortgage out first.

Respondents were then asked why Smarter Starter had appealed to them. There were five possible answers and respondents could choose as many or as few as they liked.

TABLE 12

|  | % |
|---|---|
| Smarter Starter appealed to me because... | |
| It made the whole process of buying a house easier | 73 |
| It offered me help and advice | 47 |
| It gave me half % off | 23 |
| It gave a homebuyers planner | 3 |
| It gave me a mortgage guarantee card | 0 |

There were clear signs that we were meeting the basic need of the bulk of FTBs. Next we asked them about the advertising.

TABLE 13

|  | % |
|---|---|
| Did you see any advertising for the Smarter Starter Mortgage? | |
| Yes | 97 |
| No | 3 |
| | |
| Did you like it? | |
| Yes | 93 |
| No | 3 |
| Don't know | 3 |

Despite the fact that the ad had been off air for seven months, the respondents were asked unprompted open-ended questions about main message. Their answers when taken in conjunction with their previous responses certainly suggest that the ad was influential in shaping their purchasing behaviour. Below are some representative responses.

### What was the ad trying to put over?

'Never too early to go there'.

'Get your mortgage arranged before you go looking for a house' (x5).

'Start planning before you get your home'.

'Start early. It's never too early to get a mortgage'.

'Friendly and helpful. If you go there they take the hassle out'.

'Help you a lot better'.

'Simple and easy. Even a school kid could do it'.

'You feel about five years old when you start buying a house. You don't have to worry – they know everything. Do it in one fell swoop. This is the simple package'.

'Their mortgages are so simple even two kids could understand it'.

Finally, respondents were asked how they felt when they first decided to buy their first home. Again, some representative quotes:

'I had no idea. It put me off looking to begin with'.

'Frightened. Terrified'.

'I didn't understand much'.

'Not confident'.

'I didn't know what to do' (1989 Smarter Starter User Survey).

It seemed that, at least for this sample, the advertising had worked precisely as hoped. They were nervous and unconfident. They needed reassurance and help. The advertising offered it to them and they took it.

### Survey Amongst Branch Managers

One of the roles of the advertising is to engender support amongst branch staff. Particularly in this case where potential customers were coming into the branch looking for an arm around their shoulder, it was important that the staff were motivated about the product and about selling it.

We conducted a telephone survey of ten area branch managers who between them were responsible for over 30 branches. The results are summarised below.*

All had seen the advertising on TV.

All agreed that 'it had worked'.

All agreed that more FTBs came into branches compared with 1988.

All agreed that more FTBs came to get a mortgage before they started looking for a house.

All agreed that through this they had significantly improved their endowment and household insurance business.

### Did customers talk about the advertising at all?

'They never stopped. They joke and then they relax'.

'Yes, all the time'.

'Yes, we got jokes like, excuse me, do you sell milkshakes?'.

'Yes, we got lots of people going on about it'.

'Many would say something like, we saw the ad and we liked it'.

### What did you think of the ad?

'Very proud. Lots of comment from people who had seen it'.

'I got excellent feedback. It gave a good modern image. Shows we're interested in young people'.

'We feel it's well thought out. The advertising generally has done a hell of a lot for improving our name and awareness. Smarter Starter gave a professional image – a professional society giving good advice'.

'Good. Not too staid and stuffy. A sense of humour. Not just throwing figures at you which blinds you and cheapens it'.

### How do you feel the advertising worked?

'It brought the FTBs in and gave us the chance to quote to them'.

'It really helped awareness'.

'The advertising meant we got a lot more enquiries from FTBs who hadn't bought their house yet'.

'It helps you get a banter with the customers'.

'Specifically, it got people to arrange their mortgage before they got a house'.

*Three points to note: (1) We represented ourselves as a research company working for the A & L, *not* the ad agency, (2) We told the respondents that they had been randomly selected and their names would not be recorded, (3) Branch managers are not slow to complain when they are unhappy!

These levels of support and enthusiasm were a vital component of the success of the advertising. If the customer had come in looking for reassurance and help and had found instead uninspired and uninterested staff, we feel sure the results in this case study would look significantly less impressive than they in fact do.

## ELIMINATING OTHER VARIABLES

### Distribution

Distribution in this market changes very little over time as it is directly related to number of branches. Hence, neither the Alliance & Leicester not the competitors' distribution altered to any significant degree in 1989.

### Price

The 0.5% discount offered for the first year was in fact less than many competitors were offering FTBs. In 1989, FTBs were being offered a 1% discount by building societies who between them accounted for c70% of the market. Much of the major building societies mortgage advertising was focused solely on these discounts. The Smarter Starter interest rate was 0.23% *higher* than the average for the top 14 building societies.

We would argue from this, that if anything, the product's price should have had a negative influence on its success.

### Branch Window Activity

Branch window activity started in January when Smarter Starter was available without advertising support. The window material did not include any mention of 'sort your mortgage out first'. The lag time of 13 weeks between application and advance compared to the more normal 7 weeks suggests that this *was* being communicated by something. It can only have been the advertising. In addition, the window material did not appear to increase the proportion or number of applications coming direct. This did not increase until February when advertising broke.

### Other Advertising

*Alliance & Leicester* – The Alliance & Leicester ran only one other TV ad in 1989. It was a general investment ad and received 310 TVRs in July.

The Alliance & Leicester runs press advertising sporadically throughout every year concentrating mainly on investment interest rates.

We see no reason why this would affect the direct/indirect profile of FTBs.

*Competitive* – The total media spend by all building societies was up by 27% in 1989 versus 1988 and the Alliance & Leicester's share of voice dropped from 9.5% in 1988 to 7.4% in 1989.

In addition MEAL suggests that Halifax, Abbey National, Nationwide Anglia, The Woolwich, The Leeds and National & Provincial were all advertising mortgages on TV in 1989 with comparable spends to the Alliance & Leicester.

If anything, the competitive advertising environment in 1989 was even tougher than in 1988.

In summary, it seems reasonable, on the basis of the evidence, to suggest that much of the Smarter Starter mortgages success and, far more importantly, *all* of the credit for the structural change in the Alliance & Leicester FTB direct/indirect profile lies with the advertising.

## PROFITABILITY

What follows is a gross profit calculation for the Alliance & Leicester's FTB business in 1989. At the end of it we will take into account the advertising cost.

The average FTB loan in 1989 was £33,000. After taking into account all administration costs, discounts and, of course the cost of funding the loan, the Alliance & Leicester make a gross profit of £990 on a *direct* loan of £33,000 and £440 on an *indirect* loan of £33,000 in the first year. The difference between these two profit figures is largely accounted for by commission earnings on the endowment policy and household insurance policy.*

After the first year, the gross profits on direct and indirect loans become more similar since endowment commission earnings are a one-off commission. The annual gross profit after year one is £490 *indirect*, £540 *direct* (on a £33,000 loan).

The average FTB loan has a life of five years. However, the majority of loans are replaced immediately by a new loan for the FTBs second property. The majority of second loans are taken out with the same lender as supplied the first loan. Hence, a FTB new to the Alliance & Leicester continues to generate profit for them, on average, for well over five years. For the purposes of profit calculation, we will look at first year and five year profits only.

In 1989, the Alliance & Leicester made a first year gross profit of £25.2m from new FTBs. Taking into account the average five year lifespan of a FTB mortgage, the Alliance & Leicester will make a total profit of £97m from FTBs who came to them in 1989.

There are a number of ways in which one could forecast what would have happened in 1989 without the advertising. One route is to suggest an extremely optimistic view and extremely pessimistic view and to assume that what really would have happened in 1989 if there had been no advertising would lie between these two extremes.

In both the optimistic and pessimistic scenarios, we shall assume that the direct/indirect profile would have been 35%/65%. This is justified, we believe, by the following points:

1.   The market profile of direct/indirect remained at roughly 50%/50% in 1989.

---

*The vast majority(c85%) of direct FTBs took out an endowment policy and household policy at the same time as arranging their mortgage. The profit figures take into account the c15% who took out a repayment mortgage rather than an endowment mortgage.

2.  The Alliance & Leicester profile of direct/indirect was 33%/67% in January 1989 (and 34%/66% in 1988).
3.  The profile of the society closest in size to the Alliance & Leicester (ie The Woolwich) was c35%/65% in 1988 and remained there in 1989.

### Optimistic View of 1989 without Advertising

Same number of loans (ie 34,800) but split 35%/65%. In this case, first year profit would have been £22.0m. Five year profit would have been £92.7m.

### Pessimistic View of 1989 without Advertising

Same number of loans indirect (ie 16,800) but a split of 35%/65% giving only 9,050 direct loans. In this case, first year profit would have been £16.4m. Five year profit would have been £68.8m. Hence, the additional first year profit generated by the advertising lies between £3.2m and £8.8m. Over five years, the advertising generated additional profit of between £4.3m and £28.2m. The midpoint between the optimistic and pessimistic view may give the best estimate of what really would have happened. If this is the case, then the advertising generated £6.0m of additional gross profit in the first year and will generate £16.25m additional profit over five years.

With an advertising cost of £3m, 'Young Ones' was clearly a good investment for the Alliance & Leicester in terms of mortgage profit. What should also not be ignored are the additional benefits in terms of increased customer loyalty through so many extra new branch/customer relationships.

An additional point to note is that, because of the change in direct/indirect profile, the average first year profit per FTB loan from the Alliance & Leicester was £565 in 1988 and £725 in 1989. In other words the average FTB was 28% more valuable to the Alliance & Leicester in 1989 than he/she was in 1988 despite the average size of the loan being almost identical.

## SUMMARY

There were two needs to be met here. One was the FTBs need for reassurance – the removal of worries. The other was the Alliance & Leicester's need to maximise profitability in a market forecast to be significantly depressed versus the year before.

By offering to sort out the mortgage first, before you've found your house, we were able to meet both.

The FTB was worried about his mortgage *now*, the Alliance & Leicester would remove those worries *now*.

The Alliance & Leicester's need was met by the influence of this offering on the purchase process. By effectively inverting the purchase process, the advertising generated a disproportionate number of doubly profitable and far more loyal customers.

The Alliance & Leicester's FTB business generated more gross profit in 1989 than in 1988 (£25.2m versus £22.7m) despite the forecasts for the market proving to be true.

Even taking the most optimistic view of what would have happened to the Alliance & Leicester's FTB business if there had been no advertising, calculations show that the advertising was an investment that paid back within one year and will continue to generate additional profits for the Alliance & Leicester for over five years into the future. Furthermore, the 18,000 direct FTBs the society attracted in 1989 count for more than just increased mortgage profits. They represent 18,000 additional customers who have a relationship with a specific branch. The value of this in future cross-selling of investment products, further mortgages and other loans cannot even be estimated.

## CONCLUSION

The magnitude of the task we set the advertising should not be underestimated. Basic logic has always suggested to FTBs that the first step they have to take in buying their first home is finding it. Only then, when they can tell the lender what it is they want to buy, would the lender tell them whether or not he/she would loan the money.

We were telling FTBs, through our advertising, that their basic logic was flawed. We were telling them that the Alliance & Leicester would sort their mortgage out now, even though they didn't yet know what they were going to buy. No wonder c75% of 'Smarter Starters' were 'surprised that they could do this'.

We needed advertising that had to fundamentally change the way they went about purchasing their first home. To do this it had to have a powerful proposition and an impactful execution. We believe the advertising we developed had both. The results certainly seem to suggest we are right.

For the Alliance & Leicester, 1989 proved to be a remarkable year. In a market that was panicking, discounted mortgages and pure interest rate advertising were the normal reactions. They, however, developed a sensible product and we promoted it in a way that made the Alliance & Leicester the society that met the true needs of the market – not necessarily the lowest rate but lots of help, lots of advice and lots of reassurance. Looking at their first year and five year profit in 1989 (higher not only than in 1988, but their highest *ever*) the Alliance & Leicester certainly think we got it right.

# 18

# Adding a Little Magic to Lea & Perrins' Worcestershire Sauce

## INTRODUCTION

This paper tells the story of how TV advertising has begun to restore the fortunes of one of Britain's oldest and best-loved brands: Lea & Perrins' Worcestershire Sauce.

It is a story of rediscovering the heart of a brand's core values, understanding the consumers' relationship with it, decoding the complex usage patterns associated with it, and developing a new research methodology to measure directly the effects of the advertising on people's behaviour.

Although press advertising played its part, particularly in the construction of the final strategy, it is on the TV activity that the case for advertising effectiveness relies.

## HISTORY OF THE BRAND

The history of the brand is full of incident and anecdote – a mixture as complex as the product itself.

It was in 1837, the year William IV died and Victoria acceded to the throne of England, that Lea & Perrins' Worcestershire Sauce was first sold commercially, but it was fourteen years earlier in 1823 that the story really begins when John Wheeley Lea and William Perrins went into partnership as pharmacists in their shop at 68 Broad Street, Worcester. They soon earned a reputation for obtaining rare herbs and spices so when Lord Sandys, the governor of Bengal, returned to England in 1835 he approached them with a recipe for an Indian sauce he'd grown fond of and asked them to make some up for him. This they did, making a few gallons extra for themselves.

On tasting it they thought it was horrible and, so the story goes, consigned it to their cellar only to rediscover it a year or so later and found that it had matured and tasted superb. The product hasn't really altered since.

Exports to the United States began in 1849, and labels were used for the first time in the 1870s to distinguish the then glass-stoppered bottle from the competition.

It is known that a bottle reached the New Zealand city of Te Wairoa before it was destroyed by a volcano in 1886 because excavations in the 1970s produced the evidence. But even more extraordinary was when in 1903 Colonel Younghusband became the first European to enter the forbidden city of Lhasa in Tibet and was astonished to find a bottle of Lea & Perrins had beaten him to it.

The following year in 1904, a royal warrant was granted by Edward VII and in 1906 following a decisive High Court battle, it was declared that only Lea & Perrins can be described as the 'Original and Genuine' Worcestershire Sauce.

Other items in the company archives in the factory in Worcester include an account of how the sauce went by sleigh to the mining camps of Alaska, by caravan across Arabia and by pack train over the Andes and Himalayas. There is also a tale of a tribal chief in Borneo who had the magical words 'Lea & Perrins' tattooed on his arm, and a 1919 advertisement declaring, next to a drawing of a steamship and sailing ship, 'Steam takes the place of sail, but no sauce has superseded Lea & Perrins, the original and genuine Worcestershire. A wonderful liquid tonic that makes your hair grow beautiful'.

Today Lea & Perrins is sold in over 130 countries worldwide.


## MARKET BACKGROUND


Lea & Perrins' Worcestershire Sauce is a unique blend of natural ingredients (some of which have to be matured for up to three years) still made to the same secret recipe as was used when it was first produced over 150 years ago.

It has a spicy, piquant flavour and can be used either *on* food as a condiment or *in* cooking (as an ingredient to bring out the flavour of the food) as well as mixed in tomato juice and Bloody Marys.

The brand dominates the market it invented – the competition being small and fragmented by comparison. So in essence Lea & Perrins *is* the market.

After years of steady if unspectacular growth the market and hence Lea & Perrins' sales began to falter in 1987, even though its brand share was improving.

TABLE 1:   HISTORIC MARKET GROWTH AND LEA & PERRINS' BRAND SHARE

|                          | 1984 | 1985 | 1986 | 1987 | 1988 |
|--------------------------|------|------|------|------|------|
| Tonnes (indexed)         | 100  | 106  | 107  | 99   | 96   |
| % change                 | +1.9 | +6.0 | +0.5 | −7.9 | −2.9 |
| Lea & Perrins' share (%) | 79.8 | 78.8 | 79.8 | 84.3 | 85.7 |

Source:   NMRA

Various hypotheses were examined which might explain this.

*Could It Be Price?*

TABLE 2

|  | 1985 | 1986 | 1987 | 1988 |
|---|---|---|---|---|
| 5 fl. oz bottle | 43p | 48p | 54p | 59p |
| Increase (%) | — | +11.0 | +12.5 | +9.3 |

Although the total increase in price from 1985 to 1988 was 37% (ahead of inflation) there was ample evidence in group discussions about price perceptions which revealed that consumers either over-estimated the price (and so were pleased when told the actual price) or they got the price about right and said they would be prepared to pay more if the price went up.

They justified this attitude on the basis of 'one bottle goes a long way'. The fact that the product is a relatively low-frequency purchase supports the notions of price insensitivity and price level misconceptions.

### Could It Be Competitive Activity?

There was no noticeable advertising or promotional or price-cutting activity by the handful of small competitors known to exist at this time; besides, Lea & Perrins' brand share was actually increasing at the time (even though its volume was actually falling).

### So Where Was the Volume Going?

Tracking data and TGI pointed to the same conclusion: users were *lapsing*. They would finally come to the end of a bottle that had been in the kitchen cupboard for a very long time and simply not replace it.

*Clearly then the key to reversing the brand's faltering sales was to find out why people were lapsing.*

Initial exploratory qualitative research and desk research soon pointed us in the right direction.

On the one hand there seemed to be a hard core of 'frequent' consumers of the product who tended to be slightly older and more downmarket than the norm and who were apparently happy splashing it on practically all their meals and in practically all their cooking.

On the other hand, however, there were 'infrequent' consumers who tended to be younger and more upmarket using the product much more 'in' cooking than 'on' food. And when they did use it in cooking it was only on an irregular basis when a particular recipe specified it or in recipes handed down from one generation to the next. There appeared to be little or no experimentation with the product amongst these 'infrequent' users compared with the 'frequents' and nearly all the Lea & Perrins' dishes in their collectively infrequent repertoire tended to be more traditional recipes involving beef, lamb, mince, ie red meat dishes.

Tables 3 and 4 show the broad trend away from red meat consumption towards white meat; and an example of the growth of snacking.

TABLE 3:   FOOD CONSUMPTION TRENDS (KG PER HEAD PER ANNUM)

|  | 1980 | 1985 | 1986 | 1987 | 1988 |
|---|---|---|---|---|---|
| Beef (bone in) | 20.9 | 19.0 | 19.4 | 20.3 | 18.9 |
| Lamb | 7.9 | 6.9 | 6.4 | 6.4 | 6.5 |
| Poultry | 13.4 | 16.0 | 17.2 | 18.0 | 19.5 |
| Fish (fresh/ frozen/cured) | 5.6 | 5.3 | 5.7 | 6.2 | 6.4 |

Source:   Advertising Association

TABLE 4:   TREND FOR LUNCH TO BE A 'SNACK' MEAL RATHER THAN A 'MAIN' MEAL

|  | 1981 | 1983 | 1985 | 1989 |
|---|---|---|---|---|
| Lunch |  |  |  |  |
| Snack meal | 31 | 30 | 32 | 43 |
| Main meal | 69 | 70 | 68 | 57 |

Source:   Taylor Nelson Family Food Panel

The underlying trend became apparent. In a matter of years Lea & Perrins' Worcestershire Sauce *could*:

—   With its red meat associations be left in a kind of 'red meat ghetto' as the move to white meat continues.
—   Be dropped from housewives' meal repertoires as a result of this and the trend away from cooked meals towards snacking.
—   Be left with an ageing hard core of users that would diminish over time and not be replenished.

Overall the brand was becoming out of touch with modern eating habits. The prospects looked bleak.

## THE OPPORTUNITY

Before we could sensibly examine the opportunity, we needed to quantify some of the dynamics in the market place. To simplify things, a decision was taken to ignore for the time being tomato juice usage given its perceived limited growth potential and to focus instead upon the 'in' and 'on' usage question – which was more important? And among frequent and infrequent users, what proportions of the product's total consumption did these types of usage account for?

It proved to be an arduous process.

### Measuring Consumer Behaviour

The first attempt was a usage and attitude study. However, such was the goodwill towards the brand (we discovered later) that a substantial amount of overclaim crept in to responses to the interviewers, so substantial in fact that on scaling up the results to give a national picture, the UK was consuming *eight times* the Worcester factory's annual output!

Any further attempt therefore had to be approached with considerable caution.

After much deliberation, finally, we decided on an in-home placement of calibrated bottles of the product with self-completion diaries covering 'in' and 'on' usage, and 'frequent' and 'infrequent' users. 350 housewives were recruited on the basis of self-perception of frequency.

The 'infrequents' were left with bottles for a longer time period compared with the 'frequents'. A 'hiatus' period of about four weeks at the beginning of the measurement process was observed in the cases of both sets of respondents prior to a more 'steady-state' pattern emerging so data collected during this period was not included in the final analysis.

Nevertheless, respondents were bound to be more aware of the product than usual given that the bottle and a diary had been placed with them.

To try and counteract this, calibrated bottles and diaries for a different product were also placed in-home to dilute the attention being given to the Worcestershire Sauce. There was a slight 'diary fatigue' effect towards the end of the fieldwork for both sets of respondents.

After collection the data was normalised to account for the different time periods allowed for the 'frequents' and 'infrequents', and finally the data was weighted in line with omnibus data to take into account the different proportions and sociodemographics of 'frequents' and 'infrequents' in the population.

To our knowledge this kind of research technique had never been attempted before.

*Consumer Behaviour Measurement Results*

Whilst 24% of housewives in the UK (TGI 1988) 'claimed to use' Lea & Perrins' Worcestershire Sauce nowadays, the omnibus survey (carried out in October 1989 prior to the TV test and which asked housewives actually to *check* their kitchen cupboards) produced a more encouraging national figure of 37%. The difference in the two figures in probably due to bottles being in cupboards and either not being used or simply having been forgotten.

What became known as the 'In and On' research thankfully confirmed what we had suspected.

Firstly, that 'in' usage was far more prevalent than 'on' usage in terms of not only meal occasions but also volume consumption in a proportion of roughly 2:1.

Secondly, that the amount of product used 'in' cooking on a per occasion basis by 'frequents' and 'infrequents' was fairly consistent. And similarly for usage 'on' food on a per person per meal basis.

Thirdly, that frequent 'in' users had a much wider repertoire of usage for the product compared to the 'infrequents' who tended to repeat old favourites.

Thus the immediate advertising task – converting 'in' usage 'infrequents' into 'frequents' – became plain.

## STRATEGY CONSTRUCTION

In all, four waves of research comprising a total of seventeen group discussions were carried out covering strategy and advertising development.

Initially eighteen different concepts had been prepared and explored qualitatively in research. The three key concepts emerging (opposite) revealed several important things:

— The *product* leverage was its sheer *versatility* – it could be used with white meat and fish, not just red meat.
— The *brand* leverage was its *persona* – an upmarket blend of potency and exotic mystique related to its sub-continent origins.
— The consumers' relationship with the brand was that they didn't want to know what the product contained – that would undermine its mystery. Instead they viewed the product as 'adding a touch of magic' to cooking by enhancing the natural flavour of the food. Infrequent users in particular felt a kind of 'guilt' about not using the product as much as they perhaps used to. They imagined the brand as a favourite uncle that they were sadly losing touch with and they were looking for good reasons to keep in contact.
— Overall, the brand needed shaking up.

But one element of our initial hypothesis did have to change and that concerned the selection of dishes to be featured in the advertising.

We originally felt that by focusing exclusively on 'new' usages such as white meat and fish it would be possible to secure a reassessment of the brand as being not just for red meat dishes.

However, it became clear in research that whilst these suggestions would be acceptable to the 'frequents' who were attuned to experimentation, a rather more cautious approach was needed for the 'infrequents' for whom the suggestion that Lea & Perrins could be added to gravy or used in spaghetti bolognese came as a revelation.

The policy was developed then that initially at least the serving suggestions featured in the advertising should broaden the repertoire of the 'infrequents' in very *basic* ways by focusing on simple, everyday recipes.

## FORMAL STATEMENT OF STRATEGY

### Advertising Objectives

1. To increase sales by increasing the frequency of 'in cooking' usage.
2. Longer term: to position the brand as eminently suitable for white meat, fish and vegetables as well as red meat.

## Target Audience

*Primary*: Existing infrequent 'in cooking' users. They tend to be 25 – 35 BC1, currently using the product on just a few old favourites. *Secondary*: All other users of the brand.

## Single-minded Proposition

Lea & Perrins' Worcestershire Sauce adds a touch of magic to everyday meals.

## Support

In cooking, the product enhances the natural flavour of the food.

## Tone of Voice

Confident but with a touch of mystery consonant with the brand's persona.

## Executional Guideline

To demonstrate versatility, feature several dishes per execution.

## THE ADVERTISING

The campaign that emerged from the creative brief first found expression as colour press.

The reason for this was that national presence was required because the campaign was to start in the spring of 1989, and the brand had not been supported anywhere in the country since the middle of 1988.

The press executions shown in the second illustration were developed and produced, and they ran in women's monthly magazines in June and July 1989.

The campaign line 'Add a little Worcester Saucery' worked for several reasons:

— The saucery pun directly reflected the consumer's perception of the brand's potency and mystique and 'adding a touch of magic'.
— If the product was magical, it was nevertheless the housewife who was in control of it.
— The line is an injunction, a call to action and yet it's not hectoring in any way.

We nevertheless felt from the beginning that the brand really needed TV if it was to get the shake-up it really deserved.

The size of the brand (around £6 – 7 million at RSP) argued against the use of TV, but the client was brave enough to accept that, whatever the cost, TV had to be tested, so an execution was developed and produced for a regional TV test. There was also a 10 second cutdown that featured just the cheese on toast suggestion.

## PRESS EXECUTIONS

**'ADD A LITTLE WORCESTER SAUCERY' STILLS**

## THE TEST MARKET

The region chosen for the TV test market was the Midlands because it was a large area and because in sales terms it was an exactly average area. An added bonus was the availability of Central TV's 'Adlab' facility which made useful contributions to our reading of the test with pre- and post-advertising measures.

In our approach to the measurement of advertising success, we were mindful of the immediate advertising objective to increase the frequency of 'in' usage amongst infrequent users of the brand. Accordingly we decided not to rely *just* on retail audit sales data but to return to the research technique pioneered for the 'In and On' research and measure consumer response to the advertising directly. After all, people might respond to the advertising by using the product more often, but might not necessarily finish the bottle and buy another one within the time frame of the test.

Given the issue of awareness being generated in test households by the placement of the product itself as well as by the advertising, it was decided to place a calibrated bottle and self-completion diary in 300 homes in the test area, and have another 300 homes in the rest of the UK to act as a control sample.

Thus the effect of the advertising could be calculated simply as the *difference* between the two samples because any defects in the measuring technique in absolute terms would be cancelled out.

Clearly no other element in the market mix such as price or trade distribution would be playing any part.

The test samples were sub-divided as shown in Table 5.

TABLE 5:  TEST SAMPLES

|  | Midlands | Rest of UK |
|---|---|---|
| Frequent users (at least once a week) | 100 | 100 |
| Infrequent users (once a month or less often) | 200 | 200 |

All respondents taking part were ABC1C2D housewives aged 25 – 55, and all had an ITV-receiving TV set in the home.

The placements were made four weeks prior to the advertising starting in order to avoid the initial 'hiatus' associated with the research technique and, as with the 'In and On' research, a second calibrated bottle and self-completion questionnaire for a different product was placed at the same time to dilute the attention given to the Worcester Sauce and also to ensure the results were directly comparable with the 'In and On' research results.

The campaign ran in the Central TV area from 9th October to 3rd December 1989. The TVRs (housewives) achieved were as follows:

30 second version (three usage suggestions): 467 TVRs
10 second version (cheese on toast suggestion): 215 TVRs

The media cost was less than £150,000.

## RESULTS AND EVALUATION

The effect of the advertising was in the final analysis examined in four different ways:

1. *Direct measurement* using the calibrated bottles and self-completion diaries.
2. *Recall interviews* conducted amongst the participants of (1) after the test was completed.
3. *Retail sales data.*
4. *Adlab pre- and post-advertising measures.*

### Direct Measurements

The results achieved were very positive indeed and had an unexpected side to them as well.

For although the advertising had been tailored to increasing the frequency of 'in' usage, the impact on 'on' usage was also significant with the greatest effects being observed amongst the *infrequent* users of the brand.

The most important measure was the total volume consumed as monitored on the calibrated bottle at the start and finish of the test because it was not dependent on accurate diary keeping nor on respondents' claimed usage but on the *actual* measurement down the calibrated bottle.

The source of the data in this section and for the recall interviews is PHD Research.

TABLE 6: VOLUME INCREASES

|  | Rest of UK | Midlands |
|---|---|---|
| Total | 100 | 132 |
| Frequent ABC1 | 100 | 150 |
| Frequent C2D | 100 | 129 |
| Frequent 25–34 | 100 | 159 |
| Frequent 35–55 | 100 | 127 |
| Total frequents | 100 | 139 |
| Infrequent ABC1 | 100 | 137 |
| Infrequent C2D | 100 | 114 |
| Infrequent 25–34 | 100 | 132 |
| Infrequent 35–55 | 100 | 121 |
| Total infrequents | 100 | 130 |

Source: PHD Research

The dramatic differences clearly indicate a statistically significant advertising effect, but were the increases due to people using the same amounts but more frequently, or simply using more of the product but with the same regularity?

Analysis showed that the average volume used per 'in' occasion (ie the amount splashed *in* the spaghetti bolognese) was essentially *unaffected* by the advertising and was broadly in line with the original 'In and On' research. There was a slight increase in the average volume used by an individual per 'on' occasion (ie the amount splashed *on* the meal by a person) but this cannot account for the total volume increases shown in Table 6.

Which means the *frequency* of usage has increased.

### Frequency of Usage

In fact most of the increases in frequency came from the *infrequent* users:

TABLE 7: FREQUENCY OF USAGE

|  | Rest of UK | Midlands |
| --- | --- | --- |
| **Frequents:** | | |
| 'In' cooking | 100 | 113 |
| 'On' food | 100 | 92 |
| **Infrequents:** | | |
| 'In' cooking | 100 | 115 |
| 'On' food | 100 | 119 |
| **Significant sub-groups:** | | |
| Infrequent 'in' ABC1 | 100 | 135 |
| Infrequent 'on' C2D | 100 | 133 |

### Broadened Repertoires

The most significant increase in the case of the items featured in the TV commercial was for cheese on toast – not surprising, given that this was the focus of the 10 second cutdown which supplemented the 30 second version.

In the Midlands, 20% of the households had used the product at least once in this way during the six week test period compared with 6% for the rest of the UK.

Amongst those who claimed to have seen the TV commercial, usage of the product with cheese on toast was even higher compared with the rest of the UK.

TABLE 8: BROADENED REPERTOIRES

| | |
| --- | --- |
| All frequent users | 23% |
| Frequent users and seeing the TV ad | 25% |
| All infrequent users | 27% |
| Infrequent and seeing the TV ad | 32% |
| Infrequent and seeing the TV ad at least 3 times | 34% |

The other featured items in the TV ad, namely spaghetti bolognese and stir fry, also showed increases in usage although not to the same extent as cheese on toast.

### Recall Interviews

Prompted awareness of the TV campaign reached 57% in the test area.

Amongst the key target audience of infrequent users aged 25 – 34, this figure rose to 73%.

Versatility was regarded as the main message coming across from the advertising.

24% of the test area users claimed that they were more likely to use more of the product in the future than in the past. This figure was 11% for the rest of the UK, and for infrequent users in the test area who claimed to have seen the advertising on three or more occasions, the 24% figure rose to 42% – further evidence of an advertising effect.

### Retail Sales Data

As can be seen from Figures 1 and 2, the timing of the uplifts in sales and rate of sale in the Midlands test area coincide with the timing of the TV campaign.

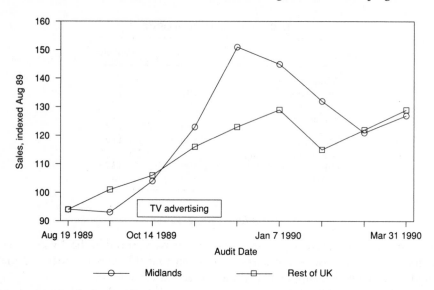

Figure 1.  *Lea & Perrins sales volume*
*Source:* NMRA

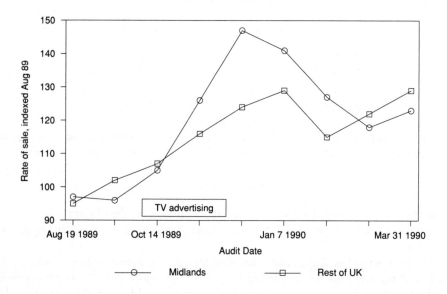

Figure 2.  *Lea & Perrins rate of sale*
*Source:* NMRA

And although the last day of the campaign was 3rd December, the effect of the advertising had a long 'tail' which endured until early March 1990. During this period there was no price promoting nor were there any significant changes in distribution.

### Adlab Pre- and Post-Advertising Measures

The data here were obtained from Central TV's Adlab facility which provides research support for advertisers in that area.

Although the principal objective of the advertising was to increase the frequency amongst existing users rather than gain new users of the brand, the figures below do suggest that approximately 3% extra penetration was achieved.

Pre-stage (4th – 6th September 1989) household penetration: 36.6%
Post-stage (27th – 29th November 1989) household penetration: 39.4%

The sample size was 979 and the interviewers on both occasions actually saw the bottle brought from the kitchen, so the figures are based on *actual* not claimed possession.

## CONCLUSIONS

All the evidence points to the advertising being responsible for increasing the consumption of the product.

The direct measurement evidence which could not have been influenced by price or distribution and which does not rely on claimed usage but on *actual consumption* points to a 32% volume consumption uplift during the test period.

And if this technique was unequivocal in demonstrating the *scale* of the advertising effect, then the *durability* of the advertising effect was clearly indicated by the NMRA data which in fact *are themselves unequivocal* in demonstrating an advertising effect given that distribution did not change significantly, price did not change at all and there was not, to our knowledge, any significant competitive activity to affect Lea & Perrins' sales.

The Adlab penetration data, although on the edge of being statistically significant, nevertheless suggest that the TV advertising exceeded its brief and either brought in new users to the brand or brought back lapsed users.

Overall then, we believe this constitutes a convincing case for advertising effectiveness.

At the time of writing, the final calculations over whether or not the test was self-liquidating have not yet been completed. But since the criterion for success was not based around self-liquidation but on changing consumer attitudes and securing a substantial volume uplift, the test *has* been deemed a resounding success by Lea & Perrins and their commitment to further TV advertising as the prime means of restoring the fortunes of the brand is now unshakeable, and justifiably so.

Table 1, repeated below and updated with 1989 data, completes the story of the level of impact that the *regional* advertising test has had on the *national* market figures overall and the brand's UK share.

SPECIAL

TABLE 9: MARKET SHARE

|  | 1984 | 1985 | 1986 | 1987 | 1988 | 1989 |
|---|---|---|---|---|---|---|
| Market size (tonnes, indexed) | 100 | 106 | 107 | 99 | 96 | 103 |
| % change | +1.9 | +6.0 | +0.5 | −7.9 | −2.9 | +7.8 |
| Lea & Perrins' share (%) | 79.8 | 78.8 | 79.8 | 84.3 | 85.7 | 86.4 |

Source: NMRA

## THE FUTURE

Plans are now in hand for the TV advertising to roll out into new regions in 1990. Given the effect that the cheese on toast suggestion has had, it's planned to create a new commercial for next year which will take the 'Add a little Worcester Saucery' theme on with the usage suggestions emphasising snacking, thus cementing the brand's association with modern food trends. Press will also continue to have a role in giving the brand a national presence whilst emphasising the product's versatility with white meat and fish as well as with red meat dishes.

# 19

# Low Cost Gas Central Heating

*How a Shift in Media and Copy Strategy
Helped British Gas to Consolidate its
Position in the Market*

## INTRODUCTION

This case history deals with the national launch of a new, low cost product in the central heating market, by British Gas, and details the contribution of a national press advertising campaign to the success of the launch.

The new product was first promoted nationally in autumn 1987, supported by a television campaign (October – November 1987) and from September 1988 onwards by a press campaign which ran until the end of 1989.

Analysis of the results of the first campaign suggested that the product was not realising its full potential, and this paper seeks to demonstrate how a shift in both media and copy strategy helped address this and launch the new low cost product into the central heating market successfully.

## BUSINESS BACKGROUND

The sale and supply of gas in the UK forms the core of British Gas business; the majority of company turnover derives from the sale of gas itself rather than from retail sales, service operations or any other area. This being the case British Gas are primarily concerned to maximise the penetration and usage of gas generally in the UK.

The total UK energy market (excluding transport) is currently around 40 billion therms (and has been so throughout the 1980s) and divides into three sectors: the domestic sector (42%), the industrial sector (40%) and the commercial sector (19%).

British Gas has increased its share of energy sales to the domestic sector from a 40% market share in 1975 to 61% at the present time. Just over half of all gas sold by British Gas now goes to the domestic sector; maintaining, or preferably improving share of energy sales in this market is very important to long-term profitability.

Within the domestic market, as is shown in Figure 1, usage of central heating is the key to building sales of gas – central heating systems which provide both heating and hot water account for 70% of domestic gas usage.

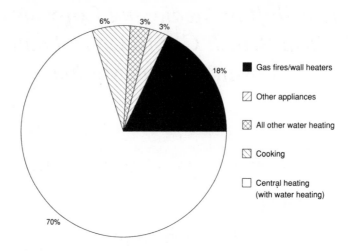

Figure 1. *Domestic gas usage by appliance*
*Source:* British Gas analysis of domestic gas usage 1989

## THE CENTRAL HEATING MARKET

British gas use two main data sources to monitor their performance in the central heating market:

1.  The National Domestic Equipment Survey* to measure size and structure.
2.  The AGB Home Audit to measure new purchases.

Looking at this data, a difference between the two sources needs to be recognised.

Gas is not universally available in the UK. Currently a gas supply is available to 18.1 million homes, or 86% of all households in the UK. This is known as the Gas Supply Area (GSA) and is growing at a rate of approximately 250,000 homes per year.

Because of the unavailability of gas outside this area, the National Domestic Equipment Survey (NDES) looks at the size and structure of the market within the GSA whereas the AGB data on purchases, being an external data source, looks at the national picture.

---

* The National Domestic Equipment Survey is a stratified random sample of 40,000 households, commissioned exclusively by British Gas on a biannual basis. It was last conducted in 1988 – fieldwork for the 1990 survey is currently in the field.

However, both sources show that the central heating market in the UK is a mature, but steadily growing market, with approximately one million households buying a new central heating system each year, with just over half being first time purchases, and the remainder replacement systems (AGB).

In 1986, 70% of households in the Gas Supply Area had central heating of some kind, with gas having the dominant share of market (see Table 1).

TABLE 1:  OWNERSHIP OF CENTRAL HEATING BY FUEL

|  | 1980 17m % | 1982 17.2m % | 1984 17.5m % | 1986 18.1m % |
|---|---|---|---|---|
| Gas | 42 | 48 | 53 | 57 |
| Electricity | 8 | 7 | 7 | 6 |
| Solid Fuel | 5 | 4 | 5 | 4 |
| Oil | 2 | 1 | 1 | 1 |
| No central heating | 42 | 39 | 34 | 30 |

Source:  National Domestic Equipment Survey, British Gas 1986.
Base:  All households in the gas supply area (million households)

However, because of the relatively small number of new purchases each year (and the growth of the Gas Supply Area), changes in the composition of new purchases do not show through clearly in ownership data.

In fact, by 1986, AGB data shows that changes in the balance of the share of purchases going to each of the four key fuels (gas, electricity, solid fuel and oil) were well underway (see Table 2).

TABLE 2:  FUEL SHARES OF CENTRAL HEATING ACQUISITIONS

|  | 1980 692 % | 1981 759 % | 1982 864 % | 1983 1,019 % | 1984 973 % | 1985 1,054 % | 1986 1,007 % |
|---|---|---|---|---|---|---|---|
| Gas | 78 | 79 | 77 | 74 | 71 | 72 | 71 |
| Electricity | 7 | 7 | 9 | 13 | 17 | 19 | 19 |
| Solid Fuel | 13 | 11 | 11 | 11 | 10 | 6 | 7 |
| Oil | 2 | 2 | 1 | 2 | 2 | 3 | 3 |

Source:  AGB Home Audit/Acquisition Data.
Base:  All acquisitions of central heating (000s)

Gas had long held the lion's share of the acquisitions market too, but in the early 1980s, electricity significantly improved its share of new central heating purchases, largely at the expense of gas.

The combination of electricity's updated Electric Storage Radiator product in combination with the Economy 7 price offer allowed electricity to do two things:

1.   To build sales outside the GSA in new private housing (Medallion Homes)*

* Medallion Homes are new houses built to be heated and powered entirely by electricity. In order to be as efficient as possible in their use of electricity, they are insulated to a very high standard.

2.   To compete effectively against gas at the margin of the market.

Whilst the first issue could not be addressed directly, the second certainly could.

Gas central heating is recognised by consumers as the best form of home heating available – in qualitative research, householders consistently describe gas central heating as 'the gold standard' in the market, 'the best you can get' (British Gas Qualitative Research 1986/1987).

This being the case, why should people increasingly choose an electric system?

*The answer seemed to lie in a simple economic trade-off: price versus quality.*

The outlay for a full gas central heating system is commonly £1,500 –£2,000 for an average, 3-bedroomed, semi-detached or terraced house. This is a high capital cost, compared to the electric product: three electric storage radiators could be installed and working in 1986 for £600 – £700. Additionally, the nature of the electric product is more piecemeal than the gas system, being able to be purchased in individual units and 'built-up' into a full system bit by bit, rather than needing to be purchased and installed as a whole. It seemed likely that people were simply trading off 'the quality' of the gas product for the lower initial cost of the electric system, despite the lower running cost with gas.

TABLE 3:   PROFILE OF HOUSEHOLDS WITH NO CENTRAL HEATING

|  | All homes in GSA 18.05m % | Non-central heating owners 5.2m % |
|---|---|---|
| ABC1 | 39 | 22 |
| C2DE | 61 | 78 |
| 15–34 | 26 | 25 |
| 35–44 | 19 | 13 |
| 45–64 | 30 | 28 |
| 65+ | 24 | 33 |
| Owner-occupier | 64 | 46 |
| Local authority | 27 | 37 |
| Private rented | 9 | 17 |
| Detached house | 12 | 2 |
| Semi-detached house | 31 | 29 |
| Terraced house | 30 | 42 |
| Bungalow | 8 | 3 |
| Flat/maisonette | 18 | 24 |

Source:   NDES, 1986.
Base:   All homes in the GSA (18.05 million).

Analysis of the demographic profile of households with no central heating supported this view (see Table 3) – being clearly biased to the lower social class groups, the elderly and people living in rented accommodation.

Discounting the last group reduced the numerical opportunity to 2.4 million owner-occupiers, still biased to the economically constrained social groups. The challenge to British Gas was to develop a product within their means.

### The New Product

The new low cost product package which was developed was based on a simple premise: it would need to be directly competitive with the electricity offer, in terms of price.

The new product was launched initially under the name 'Budget Central Heating' and consisted of two product options:

1.  A wall-hung boiler plus three radiators.
2.  A radiant gas fire with back boiler plus two radiators.

This package was priced for advertising purposes at £778 and £748 respectively, and was available through all regional showrooms from September 1987 onwards. It was supported by a national television commercial.

## LAUNCH: YEAR 1

### The Role of Advertising

On the basis that perceived cost represented the major barrier to purchase, we defined the role for advertising as being to communicate the availability of a low cost central heating product from British Gas. We felt that people would want more information about this and the advertising therefore contained an injunction to visit a gas showroom, for more details.

### Target Audience

This we defined very broadly as all owner-occupier households within the Gas Supply Area, who did not have any central heating.

### The Creative Work

One commercial 'Book' was aired in autumn 1987 with a budget of £1.08 million and, creatively, was designed to fit the new product into the theme of mainstream gas advertising (a storyboard for the commercial is shown overleaf).

### Response To the Launch

Sales response to the launch of the new product was disappointing. Throughout the winter of 1987/88 British Gas sold less than 1,000 units of the new product in total. It was not immediately possible to isolate whether this was due to the product itself or to a lack of response to the advertising, as for practical reasons, we were unable to monitor the level of enquiries in showrooms. In spring 1988, we therefore set about finding out what had really happened.

British Gas conducted an in-depth piece of qualitative research amongst the target audience to help understand why response had been low.

## 'BOOK'

·THE COVER STORY·

I'm not going in there.

·THE GOOD REVIEW·

When the weather takes a turn for the worse...

...from as little as £748 you can have a real gas central heating system.

You can get details on budget gas central heating at your local gas showroom

...right now...

·THE HEAT OF THE MOMENT·

...because gas is the heat of the moment.

·NOW FROM ONLY £748·

**British Gas**
*ENERGY IS OUR BUSINESS*

It emerged from the research that there were a number of problems:

1. Although we had thought that the 'economically constrained' status of non-central heating owners would mean that price was the key barrier to purchase, the research identified, additionally, an attitudinal segmentation which also had a major influence on likelihood of buying.

   Attitudinally, the research indicated, the broad target group could be divided into three groups, described as 'Drifters/Laggards', 'Procrastinators' and 'Self-Improvers' and indicated that the split between the three groups was roughly a third each.

   *'Drifters/Laggards'* emerged as people who were not interested in home improvements and would be unlikely to recognise a need for central heating.

   *'Procrastinators'* on the other hand did recognise the need for central heating but simply never got around to doing anything about it. These were people who would complain during a cold winter, but when summer arrived, put the decision off for another year.

   *'Self-Improvers'* seemed more likely to act, the problem being available funds. Many included installing central heating on their future home improvement programme, as and when funds became available. (The Qualitative Consultancy, June 1988).

   So, 'drifters and laggards' would probably never act, 'procrastinators' would be a tough nut to crack and 'self-improvers' should be the most responsive to the new product in the short-term.

2. Secondly, the research indicated that a number of non-rational factors were at work, contributing to an inertia amongst a large proportion of non-central heating owners.

   Some of the people in the target group had become so used to their current heating arrangements, that they claimed they did not need central heating, despite saying they were dissatisfied with current heating performance. Thus they tended not to do anything.

   Others claimed that central heating is often the root cause of many modern health problems, eg colds – again a reason not to act.

3. Finally, the research indicated a flaw in the composition of the product package. The package had been developed in the belief that people were simply trading off quality against price at the bottom of the market (and on this basis, no product test was conducted before the launch). However, the qualitative research indicated that the trade-off was not that simple.

   For most people, 'real' central heating meant heating in every room of the house, *even* warmth *everywhere*. To constitute 'real' central heating, the product needed to comprise a boiler plus four or five radiators (with automatic control) to ensure a properly heated home – and home owners claimed that they were prepared to pay more (£750 plus) to secure this.

*The Advertising Revisited*

Putting all this data together we concluded that the advertising had not worked quite as intended in two important respects:

1. We had incorporated the low cost message into the main theme of gas advertising and so 'Book' conformed to the advertising 'rules' of the category: it clearly depicted the generic benefits of central heating in an amusing, but typical way. It achieved a 4.5% share of voice (of all heating TV activity, October/November 1987, MEAL) and as such was just one of a wide variety of heating advertising messages on air during the autumn of 1987. We concluded that the conformity of advertising style allowed those people who recognised the need for central heating, but didn't do anything about it, largely to ignore the call to action. The style of the advertising met their expectations and previous experience of heating advertising – and as such they were able to 'shut off' from the message, and continue to procrastinate about purchase.
2. In addition, the results from the advertising post-test conducted by British Gas showed that the message being taken out of the advertising was primarily a generic one about the benefits of central heating rather than the availability of a low cost product (see Table 4).

TABLE 4: PROMPTED COMMUNICATION OF 'BOOK' TV COMMERCIAL

|  | % |
|---|---|
| Gas central heating warms up your home quickly | 58 |
| Gas central heating is economical | 40 |
| Gas is the best fuel for central heating | 34 |
| Now you can get gas central heating at a low price | 28 |
| Gas is reliable | 23 |
| Gas is popular | 21 |
| For details of gas central heating go to your British Gas showroom | 20 |
| Gas central heating is easy to install | 18 |

Source: Roberts Research (for British Gas), October 1987.
Base: All seeing advertisement (378).

We concluded that we needed to communicate the core proposition in a more motivating way, and to adopt a more focused approach in targeting and stylistic terms to address 'resistors'.

## YEAR 2: THE NEW PACKAGE

*The Revised Product Package*

With the new learning, British Gas revisited the basic product concept, and came up with a core package consisting of five radiators and a boiler with full automatic time and temperature control for £1,060, ie offering quality at a reasonable price (although recognising that some people would be put off by this higher price).

A qualitative research study among 1,100 target consumers conducted by British Gas in the summer of 1988 confirmed this to be the most relevant product option: 32% of this sample stated that they would *never* buy central heating (Drifters/Laggards) – tying in with the proportional split suggested by the qualitative work – but 41% said that a package offering five radiators was the ideal compared with just 15% who said four, and 12% who said three.

The price level also appeared to be acceptable: over half (53%) of those wanting five radiators said that they would be very or fairly likely to pay £1,060 for the system.

The package was renamed Low Cost Central Heating (rather than 'Budget') on the basis of consumer feedback and was ready for the key autumn sales period.

## The Target Audience

The additional information gained in spring 1988 led us to agree with British Gas to define the target audience much more tightly on both a demographic and attitudinal basis:

1.  *Primary target audience*: 25 – 44 year old owner-occupiers, probably with young families, household income £11,000 pa or above, living in terraced or semi-detached housing. We estimated that this group numbered approximately 600,000 – 700,000 households. We believed that a majority of this group were likely to be 'self-improvers', and the remainder 'procrastinators'.
2.  *Secondary target audience*: owner-occupiers aged 45+ years, living in terraced/semi-detached housing, again with an income level above £11,000. We felt that 'self-improvers' would be in the minority in this group, with 'procrastinators' and 'drifters/laggards' forming the majority.

## The Advertising Strategy Revisited

For new advertising, we now understood the need for a completely fresh approach in order to 'break' the inertia in the market.

The new campaign needed to differ from the previous one in two important respects:

1.  It needed to communicate clearly the availability of a low cost central heating package to the target group without straying into either specific product detail or the well-trodden ground of the generic benefits of central heating (the research having suggested that this should be sufficient to prompt action amongst 'self-improvers').
2.  The advertising needed to be clearly differentiated from mainstream gas and general heating advertising to push the more resistant sectors of the target group into action.

We agreed that the basic communication objective of the advertising should remain unchanged, but reviewed the way in which people might respond to the advertising.

We decided to include a direct response mechanism in the advertising to make it easier for those people who were less likely to visit a showroom to get more information about the product.

### The Creative Brief and the Ads

The desired take-out from the advertising was simply:

> 'Now, there is a real central heating system, which I can afford, available from British Gas (I want to know more about it!)'.

Beyond the simple economic barrier to purchase, the brief detailed the less rational attitudes of non-central heating owners and so included an injunction to 'break the mould' of gas advertising and not conform to expected stereotypes.

The creative idea which emerged drew on two of the institutions of British life – British 'Seaside Humour' as depicted in seaside picture postcards, and the Page 3 pin-up.

In the first burst of advertising, five different executions ran.

Qualitative pre-testing of the campaign by British Gas indicated that the advertising would do a very good job in terms of attracting attention, and was generally felt to be amusing and a 'refreshing change'. Most people readily understood the campaign style (Low Cost Central Heating Pre-Test, Roberts Research Ltd, July 1988).

### Media Strategy

Research led us to suggest a radical departure from accepted media norms to fulfil the new advertising strategy. We took the decision, early in the summer of 1988, to shift media from TV into press. This would differentiate the campaign from other heating activity, help with more precise targeting and help achieve greater coverage of the target group.

Sunday newspapers supplemented by the daily tabloids best fulfilled these criteria.

We recommended two bursts of activity during the winter of 1988/1989 in September/October then January/February.

Subsequently the campaign was extended by two bursts of additional activity in 1989, in May/June and September/October (see Figure 2).

### Response to the Campaign: the First Burst

Although our target audience was still large in numerical terms, response in 1987/88 to the product proposition had been low (less than 1,000 units). With this in mind, British Gas set a target of 5,000 unit sales for autumn/winter period (September 1988 – March 1989); although conservative in relation to the absolute size of the target audience, this nevertheless looked realistic given actual sales performance the previous year.

£1,000*

Gas Central Heating is the hottest deal in the puniverse!

'Fat chance of central heating, I used to say. But then my Uncle Willie of Warminster told me it only costs a puny amount.

'So I called Free-fone British Gas Heating to get the low-down. In no time five radiators and a boiler were in the pipeline. All for just £1,060!

'British Gas saved a broker from going broke, that's for sure. Now the only thing cool about me is my boxer shorts!'

*Full price including VAT £1,060.

GAS THE HEAT OF THE MOMENT

To take advantage of this offer, dial 100 and ask for FREEFONE BRITISH GAS HEATING. Alternatively, fill in the coupon, or visit your local British Gas Showroom.

Title_____ Initial_____

Surname_____

Full address_____

_____

_____Postcode_____

Tel. no._____

My home has ☐ bedrooms. Please arrange an appointment for me. ☐ Send me further information ☐

Post to: British Gas plc, FREEPOST, PO Box 61, London NW1 1YH.

British Gas
ENERGY IS OUR BUSINESS

Picture: CHRIS HOLLAND

| Publication | No ins | 1988 Sep Oct Nov Dec | 1989 Jan Feb Mar Apr | May Jun Jul Aug | Sep Oct Nov | Total |
|---|---|---|---|---|---|---|
| Daily Mirror | 9 | | | | | £203,555 |
| Daily Record | 11 | | | | | £76,424 |
| Star | 10 | | | | | £44,100 |
| Sun | 13 | | | | | £297,652 |
| Today | 12 | | | | | £56,343 |
| Mail on Sunday | 16 | | | | | £233,000 |
| News of the World | 15 | | | | | £368,090 |
| Sunday Express | 5 | | | | | £76,000 |
| Sunday Mirror | 14 | | | | | £279,773 |
| People | 11 | | | | | £210,800 |
| Sunday Post | 6 | | | | | £40,830 |
| Sunday Magazine | 1 | | | | | £20,000 |
| Radio Times | 1 | | | | | £17,000 |
| TV Times | 2 | | | | | £29,000 |
| Regional papers | 101 | | | | | £229,277 |
| **Total** | **227** | **£611,037** | **£614,571** | **£397,751** | **£558,486** | **£2,181,844** |

Figure 2. *British Gas low cost central heating media plan*

Response to the first burst of activity was swift:

The new campaign broke in the middle of September 1988, and during the first week, 2,350 requests for additional information were received by the agency handling the direct response. Requests for further information had risen to 6,600 four weeks into the campaign and to 8,300 by the end of December.

As is shown in Figure 3, sales of the low cost product climbed steadily throughout the autumn of 1988, reaching the sales target of 5,000 units by early November; by the end of December 1988 sales had reached a total of 6,174 units, well in excess of the agreed sales target for the whole winter period (up to March 1989).

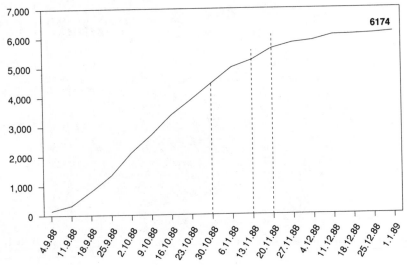

Figure 3. *Cumulative sales of low cost gas central heating (September – December 1988)*
Source: BG Sales Data

## SO WHAT MADE THE DIFFERENCE?

We were immediately able to discount distribution as a contributory factor: in both 1987 and 1988 the low cost package was available, nationally, through all British Gas showrooms.

In moving the price of the new package from £748/£778 in the autumn of 1987 to £1,060 in the autumn of 1988 we had increased it by about 40%, still out-performing the sales targets and validating the research evidence that consumer purchase would be made on a balance between price and quality, rather than price alone. So price, too, could be discounted as a contributory factor.

However and more fundamentally, the basic product offer *had* changed to a more acceptable proposition – boiler plus five radiators. Could this product change have been sufficient to generate the much greater levels of consumer take-up which occurred in autumn 1988?

We believe that although the change in the nature of the product proposition undoubtedly helped convert general interest into actual sales once in the showroom, it was not, in itself, responsible for the much greater levels of interest shown by consumers in the low cost offer second time around, and that it was principally the advertising which generated this interest.

In both the autumn of 1987 and 1988 the advertising communication objective had remained constant: to communicate the availability of a low cost central heating package from British Gas and to generate interest in it – in neither instance did we mention the detailed composition of the product itself in the advertising. We believe that the much greater levels of interest shown in 1988 were driven by response to a campaign which broke the established norms of the category in a relevant and impactful way. The campaign achieved this in two ways:

1. It communicated the availability of a low cost product to 'self-improvers' more effectively, and prompted them to visit a British Gas showroom.
2. It included a direct response mechanism, so the more resistant sector of the target audience ('Procrastinators') were given the option to find out more with very little effort. British Gas provided regional showrooms with the names and addresses of people who used the direct response mechanism, so they could be followed up. Subsequent research amongst a sample of 1,100 people who used this mechanism in autumn 1988 showed a conversion rate of just over a third; 34% of those people who responded to the advertising went on to purchase a gas central heating system. The experience of Wunderman, the direct response company within the Y&R Group, indicates that this is a good conversion rate for consumer durables.

British Gas monitored consumer response to the press campaign via two advertising checks conducted during, and at the end of, the campaign, and these checks confirmed our hypothesis that the campaign was working as intended (see Table 5).

TABLE 5: CONSUMER RESPONSE TO PRESS CAMPAIGNS, AUTUMN 1988

|  | Mid campaign (Sept) % | End campaign (Oct) % |
|---|---|---|
| Campaign awareness | 44 | 37 |
| **Communication** | | |
| Gas c/h not as expensive as may have thought | 30 | 31 |
| British Gas now offering real c/h for only £1,000 | 20 | 27 |
| Gas c/h will turn your cold house into a warm house | 26 | 35 |
| **Reactions to the advertising** | | |
| Interesting | 52 | 31 |
| Funny | 53 | 56 |
| Appealing | 48 | 38 |
| Believable | 47 | 52 |
| Informative | 63 | 53 |

Source:  Roberts Research Adchecks Sept/Oct 1988.
Base:  All C2D adults who saw the advertisement with no c/h but gas in home.
Note:  Awareness scores are based on total campaign. All other figures represent average score across 5 press executions.

For practical cost reasons, it was not possible to replicate the primary target exactly in research, however, awareness of the campaign amongst C2D adults, with no central heating but gas in home, was 44% at the end of September. The data also indicated that the communication objectives were being met and beyond this, the advertising was perceived to be interesting, informative, believable, appealing and funny (see Table 5).

Interestingly, consumer response to the press campaign compared favourably with response to the preceding year's TV activity. Although we recognise that comparisons between press and TV campaigns are difficult given people's propensity to mention TV rather than other media in tracking studies, we were nevertheless heartened to see that prompted awareness of the press campaign at 44% was at much the same level achieved by the 'Book' commercial in 1987 (38%), as measured using comparable methodology.

At the end of 1988 we concluded that the new campaign had fulfilled its objectives by creating awareness of and genuine interest in the new product, in an amusing but impactful way, helping break the considerable consumer apathy in the category, and by consolidating gas's hold on the central heating market. The advertising to appliance sales ratio for the first burst of activity was just 8% – we believe this to be a highly acceptable figure for a new product launch.

## Extending the Campaign Through 1989

With such a favourable response, British Gas decided to continue advertising support throughout 1989. Thus, low cost gas central heating was advertised in January/February 1989 (£640,000), in May/June 1989 (£398,000) and again, in the key autumn sales period, September/October 1989 (£558,500). As the research had also suggested there was no problem with wear-out of the core campaign, we continued to use the same core idea, refreshing it with one or two new 'characters' in May/June and again in September/October.

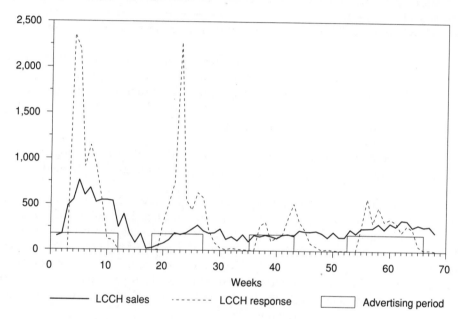

Figure 4. *Low cost central heating response and sales, September 1988 to November 1989*
Source: BG Sales Data

Direct response and sales response throughout 1989 are shown in Figure 4 Response to the campaign in 1989 was at a lower level than response to the first burst of activity.

TABLE 6

|  | LCCH sales | Direct response enquiries |
|---|---|---|
| Sep–Dec 1988 | 6,174 | 8,311 |
| Jan–Mar 1989 | 2,123 | 6,358 |
| Apr–Aug 1989 | 3,677 | 2,630 |
| Sep–Dec 1989 | 4,272 | 3,421 |
| Total | 16,246 | 20,720 |

So why did response to the advertising activity fall during 1989?

We believe that a number of factors account for the lower response levels:

1. The winters of 1988/89 and 1989/90 were exceptionally warm. British Gas data shows a clear correlation between snaps of cold weather and increases in sales. The warmer than average temperatures in January/March 1989 and again in the autumn probably allowed some 'procrastinators' to put off (again) doing anything about their heating arrangements.
2. Central heating sales are seasonal, with the 'heating sales season' traditionally peaking in the autumn – a lower rate of sales outside of the autumn period would be expected.
3. Throughout 1989 the economic situation became increasingly difficult:

   — By the summer, the deliberate government policy of using high interest rates to cut consumer spending was clearly beginning to bite.
   — Joint mortgage relief was also abolished after August, which would clearly have adversely affected the disposable income levels of 'young marrieds' in particular, part of our target group.

   In a difficult economic environment, household durables tend to be one of the first categories affected, purchase of them being more easily postponed.

Both British Gas estimates and AGB home audit data suggest a fall in the total size of the central heating acquisitions market during 1989 of 50,000 – 60,000 units indicating that the market as a whole was suffering. We believe the lower levels of response during 1989 were probably the result of an increasingly difficult environment generally (particularly given the constrained nature of the target group) rather than to reduced effectiveness of the advertising in particular. Indeed, British Gas advertising tracking data continued to show a positive consumer response to the campaign throughout 1989.

Our calculations suggest that, to date, we have grown penetration by 5% – 6% amongst the core target audience. Operating in a mature market, we believe this is a very positive result.

Finally, AGB acquisition data does show that the growth in electricity's share of new central heating acquisitions has levelled off (see Table 7).

TABLE 7: CENTRAL HEATING FUEL TRENDS

|  | 1982 | 1983 | 1984 | 1985 | 1986 | 1987 | 1988 | 1989 |
|---|---|---|---|---|---|---|---|---|
|  | 864 | 1,019 | 973 | 1,054 | 1,007 | 1,149 | 1,147 | 1,095 |
|  | % | % | % | % | % | % | % | % |
| Gas | 77 | 74 | 71 | 72 | 71 | 74* | 73 | 73 |
| Electricity | 9 | 13 | 17 | 19 | 19 | 18 | 20 | 20 |
| Solid fuel | 11 | 11 | 10 | 6 | 7 | 6 | 4 | 4 |
| Oil | 1 | 2 | 2 | 3 | 3 | 2 | 3 | 3 |

Source: AGB Home Audit.
Base: All acquirers (000s)
Note: *We believe that the increase in gas share of new purchases in 1987 is largely attributable to the significantly increased activity and media coverage surrounding the company at the time of privatisation at the end of 1986.

## CONCLUSIONS

By the end of 1989, the low cost gas central heating press campaign had generated a total of over 22,000 direct responses and British Gas had sold over 16,000 units of the low cost central heating product, equating to a revenue of over £17 million.

Over the whole period, we estimate that the level of advertising investment was 12% of total income – a highly acceptable level for the launch of a new durable product.

We believe that the advertising attracted 'self-improvers' directly to the showrooms and provided the tougher attitudinal sectors of the broader target group with easy access to more information. The direct response mechanism facilitated the purchase procedure for 'procrastinators' and the conversion from direct leads to sales was good.

In conclusion we have sought to demonstrate that, by focusing our strategy, adopting an unusual and impactful approach creatively, and shifting media, British Gas were able to penetrate the tough end of the central heating market with this new product, achieving the right balance between price and product specification. This will continue to contribute to the consolidation of the position of gas in the domestic fuel market.

# 20

# 'Vote Valley'
# Changing the Agenda in a Local
# Government Election

## INTRODUCTION

This paper seeks to demonstrate the central role that advertising played in the success of one particular political party, which stood in one London borough in the 1990 local elections. The story it tells is unique for two reasons: one because it is the first time a large scale campaign has been launched by a body formed specifically to contest a local election; and two, because of the nature of the 'Client'. The 'Client' was the Valley Party and it was standing on the single issue of Charlton Athletic Football Club's proposed return to its home ground in the London Borough of Greenwich.

To explain the role of advertising in this highly unusual arena, it is necessary to explain the background to the formation of the Valley Party.

## THE EXILE OF A TRIBE

In September 1985, Charlton Athletic had started their Second Division season well – on the pitch. Behind the scenes, however, the Club faced problems. Following near liquidation in 1984, it no longer owned its ground – The Valley – which now faced major renovation costs. The then directors decided that it would make financial sense to leave The Valley and share Selhurst Park, the home of Crystal Palace FC. The supporters were outraged.

Most Charlton supporters were people with local (ie Greenwich and Bexley) roots. To drive ten miles across London on a winter Saturday to see a home game was, to them, anathema.

There were demonstrations after the final game at The Valley, banners of protest were unfurled at subsequent games to general applause, and the refrain 'we should have stayed at The Valley' was heard at virtually every game for two years afterwards.

Despite the coincidence of the Club's return to the First Division in that season the move was a commercial disaster. Gates were poor*, 'the supporters' discontent was palpable and the Club felt very much like the 'tenants' they were at Selhurst Park. Greenwich Council, which opposed the move, withdrew its financial aid to the Club.

In 1987, new directors realised that the Club had to return to its home area. They re-purchased The Valley, but their original intention was to build a brand new ground at a different site in the area funded by development of The Valley. Emotionally most supporters preferred a return to The Valley. However, no new site was forthcoming. Thus, in March 1989, the Club announced to a packed meeting in Woolwich Town Hall that it was coming home to The Valley.

The Leader of the Council was at the meeting and endorsed the announcement, but a month later he was no longer leader. He lost the position in an internal upheaval. A new Chair of Planning was also installed. Meetings between Club and Council became fractious. The Club's application to make The Valley a modern all-seater stadium was not the planning formality that it had assumed.

On 31 January 1990, the Council's Planning Committee held a meeting in public to consider the application. It was rejected by ten votes to two. The issue was the scale of commercial development needed to make the plan viable. Football alone could not provide the revenue, but the Council's Borough Plan forbade all but the smallest of developments at the site.

Supporters felt that the Council were behaving duplicitously. It had maintained that it wished to see the Club's return; the Leader of the Council had endorsed the initial announcement; and it conceded user rights to play football at The Valley. Yet it blocked any scheme which would make the Club commercially viable.

Most supporters felt frustrated but impotent. One group was prepared to fight the Council.

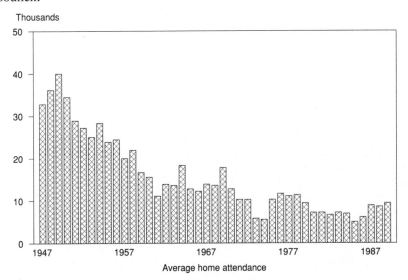

Figure 1. *Charlton attendance record*
*Note:* Average league attendances have been in steep decline since the early fifties, when the Valley sometimes saw crowds in excess of 70,000

* Charlton's average for the season of 6,028 was 22% below the divisional average. A team winning promotion would normally expect to have gates above the divisional average.

This group reasoned that with the exception of residents around the ground few people in the Borough opposed the return, since the Club had an excellent record for crowd behaviour (see Table 1) and it had many lapsed supporters from its fifties heyday (see Figure 1). Since the Council's behaviour appeared to be unfair and against majority wishes the supporters' group decided to take the ultimate democratic course; to place the issue before the public at the ballot box. The Valley Party made the ambitious pledge to contest all 36 Greenwich seats at the May 1990 local elections.

TABLE 1: LEAGUE GROUNDS ARRESTS 1987 – 88

**First Division**

| | Attendance | Arrests |
|---|---|---|
| Portsmouth | 324,780 | 282 |
| Chelsea | 408,538 | 271 |
| Southampton | 290,617 | 208 |
| Coventry City | 350,165 | 194 |
| Arsenal | 598,059 | 153 |
| Newcastle United | 419,742 | 149 |
| West Ham United | 396,473 | 149 |
| Nottingham Forest | 384,648 | 130 |
| Oxford United | 218,632 | 105 |
| Queen's Park Rangers | 265,813 | 91 |
| Sheffield Wednesday | 395,519 | 90 |
| Derby County | 343,107 | 86 |
| Tottenham Hotspur | 517,970 | 74 |
| Wimbledon | 159,691 | 49 |
| Watford | 291,464 | 43 |
| Manchester United | 783,099 | 38 |
| Liverpool | 791,977 | 33 |
| Norwich City | 313,904 | 32 |
| Everton | 555,692 | 24 |
| Charlton Athletic | 173,629 | 14 |
| Luton Town | 161,884 | 1 |

**Second Division**

| | Attendance | Arrests |
|---|---|---|
| Aston Villa | 403,838 | 308 |
| Bradford City | 285,509 | 197 |
| Leeds United | 443,094 | 184 |
| Bournemouth | 168,757 | 149 |
| West Bromwich Albion | 222,261 | 132 |
| Huddersfield Town | 150,334 | 126 |
| Middlesbrough | 321,219 | 110 |
| Birmingham City | 188,722 | 101 |
| Ipswich Town | 258,037 | 99 |
| Leicester City | 223,049 | 81 |
| Blackburn Rovers | 211,120 | 79 |
| Crystal Palace | 215,496 | 78 |
| Shrewsbury Town | 108,202 | 68 |
| Swindon Town | 209,800 | 67 |
| Sheffield United | 223,960 | 60 |
| Stoke City | 211,234 | 57 |
| Barnsley | 168,339 | 55 |
| Millwall | 185,165 | 44 |
| Hull City | 157,507 | 38 |
| Manchester City | 428,655 | 35 |
| Plymouth Argyll | 226,152 | 29 |
| Reading | 150,352 | 20 |
| Oldham Athletic | 147,995 | 19 |

**Third Division**

| | Attendance | Arrests |
|---|---|---|
| Fulham | 116,454 | 99 |
| Sunderland | 400,760 | 80 |
| Brentford | 105,430 | 72 |
| Grimsby Town | 76,641 | 66 |
| York City | 62,902 | 62 |
| Notts County | 144,624 | 50 |
| Rotherham United | 84,107 | 47 |
| Walsall | 128,153 | 47 |
| Aldershot | 70,642 | 39 |
| Blackpool | 96,935 | 36 |
| Brighton | 205,263 | 34 |
| Gillingham | 106,260 | 32 |
| Doncaster Rovers | 43,223 | 28 |
| Chester City | 58,967 | 22 |
| Port Vale | 88,126 | 22 |
| Bristol City | 225,861 | 21 |
| Chesterfield | 61,239 | 21 |
| Mansfield Town | 90,894 | 21 |
| Preston North End | 139,998 | 20 |
| Bristol Rovers | 84,753 | 18 |
| Northampton Town | 126,578 | 11 |
| Bury | 58,997 | 5 |
| Wigan Athletic | 86,776 | 4 |
| Southend United | 79,320 | 3 |

**Fourth Division**

| | Attendance | Arrests |
|---|---|---|
| Scarborough | 70,504 | 145 |
| Wolverhampton Wdrs | 226,964 | 132 |
| Burnley | 144,770 | 90 |
| Exeter City | 58,264 | 83 |
| Tranmere Rovers | 76,847 | 53 |
| Scunthorpe United | 74,405 | 46 |
| Cardiff City | 101,752 | 43 |
| Halifax Town | 39,358 | 38 |
| Newport County | 40,261 | 35 |
| Rochdale | 44,903 | 32 |
| Cambridge United | 52,896 | 29 |
| Hereford United | 50,712 | 28 |
| Carlisle United | 51,282 | 27 |
| Bolton Wanderers | 114,778 | 21 |
| Crewe Alexandra | 51,828 | 21 |
| Torquay United | 67,434 | 21 |
| Stockport County | 52,154 | 17 |
| Wrexham | 51,539 | 17 |
| Peterborough United | 71,881 | 15 |
| Hartlepool | 48,972 | 12 |
| Swansea City | 100,957 | 10 |
| Leyton Orient | 90,322 | 8 |
| Darlington | 50,374 | 5 |
| Colchester United | 40,607 | 0 |

This league table received widespread publicity when the minister of Sport published it in connection with the football ID card debate. The only First Division club suffering less arrests at matches than Charlton was Luton who had banned away supporters.

## OBJECTIVES AND STRATEGY OF THE VALLEY PARTY

Having committed itself to an election campaign, the Valley Party evaluated exactly what could be achieved, and how. The Party's objective emerged as:

'To bring political pressure on the Council so that it becomes politically desirable to reach an agreement on The Valley application which is acceptable to the Club'.

The strategy was defined as:

'To run a campaign which is credible, responsible and high profile; thus generating continuing favourable media attention on the issue'.

Initially the Party hoped that the political pressure would generate a softer attitude from the Council well before Election day. In the event this did not happen, and the Party was required to fight a full-scale campaign, and to make a significant impression at the ballot box.

## THE ELECTION PLATFORM

Agency planners volunteered advice on strategy. It was important that the Party did not over-claim the importance of its case to the electorate. The Party should present the Council's actions as unfair and undemocratic; but it should ask only for sympathy for the cause and acknowledge that people might vote on wider issues. It was calculated that this approach would in fact trigger votes. It would also prevent the opposition from using the size of the vote as a measure of support for the Club's return, were the vote to be unimpressive.

Stress would be laid on Charlton's reputation as a family club and how a football club helps to maintain a sense of community in an increasingly anonymous city. The Party would have to combat negative perceptions of professional football generated by stories of hooliganism and the Government's response to it*.

No other policies would be addressed but it would be suggested that as local people the candidates could be relied upon to represent the people with honesty and integrity; the implication being that the Council could not be trusted, given their behaviour towards Charlton.

The reader will note that the election strategy could have been implemented without the support of advertising. It is thus a good point at which to consider what the Party's prospects would have been without advertising.

In order to generate media attention sufficient to concern the Council it would be necessary to get coverage from the broadcast media and national newspapers. The main local newspaper – *The Greenwich and Eltham Mercury* – was already

---

* According to TGI, 22% of the working population pay to watch football at least once a year. The Party assumed that most of the other 78% would be prone to negative perceptions and would need to be carefully addressed.

covering the issue and largely in a vein sympathetic to the Club and supporters; but it was clear the paper did not wield sufficient editorial influence to concern the Council.

It could be argued that the Valley Party's effective canvassing and leaflets might have achieved good results. However, this route on its own would not have been likely to attract the same level of media attention. The media would need evidence of a high-profile, *interesting* campaign. Door-to-door work in one small area would have been unlikely to attract media attention on its own.

The political calibre of the Party itself should now be considered. It was decided to try and field candidates in every ward, so that everyone in the Borough had the chance to consider the issue. This required 60 candidates and ten signatures for each candidate. Six candidates had previous political experience. Most of the rest had never remotely considered such activity for themselves before. This paper will contend that the advertising played a significant role in drawing in candidates, giving them the confidence and morale to stand, and to go out and campaign in the streets.


## THE ADVERTISING CAMPAIGN

Volunteers at BMP DDB Needham investigated the feasibility of a campaign. Supporters were able to commit no more than £3,500 to the campaign, and did not wish to approach the Club for funds. A process of elimination determined the media strategy:


—   Television was patently outside financial practicality.
—   Radio was uneconomic. Greenwich constitutes less than 5% of Capital Radio's and LBC's audience area.
—   Local press was seen as superfluous. The principal paper, the *Mercury*, was deemed to be actively supportive of the campaign already.


Posters were a clear choice. They could be bought within the confines of the Borough, and are now an established medium for political and issue advertising.

The agency bought sites for a minimal rate by taking advantage of a soft market and the sympathy the campaign evoked. Twenty-eight 48-sheet and seven 16-sheet sites were eventually obtained, most for the month of April, immediately before the election (Figure 2). This represented a good medium-weight campaign within the local area.

But what would go on the posters? What was the Valley Party's creative strategy to be?

The advertising campaign's objectives were straightforward:

1.   To attract non-local media attention to the Valley Party.
2.   To motivate candidates and supporters.
3.   Ultimately to encourage people to 'Vote Valley'.

**IF YOU DON'T SUPPORT US, WHO IS HE GOING TO SUPPORT?**

VOTE VALLEY MAY 3RD

**IF THE COUNCIL HAS ITS WAY, WE'LL NEVER SEE THIS SORT OF TRAFFIC PROBLEM AGAIN.**

VOTE VALLEY MAY 3RD

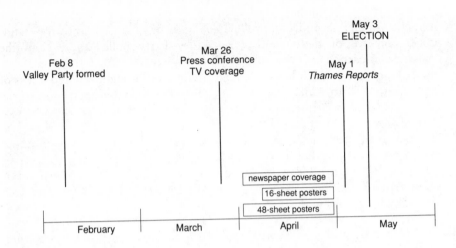

Figure 2. *Campaign timing plan*

Objective three may seem to be modestly placed in the order of priorities. But this is the correct order since it was hoped that the appearance of the campaign would force the Council to modify its stance before election day. This did not happen. Anecdotal evidence suggests that the Council did not believe the campaign would generate votes.

The strategy was thus:

1. Focus on the emotional appeal of the club as a symbol of local pride.
2. Adopt a recognised 'political advertising' style in the art direction.

The copywriter – a Mancunian football fan – met with supporters in a local restaurant in order to research his brief. The developing creative work was shown at weekly Valley Party meetings, but the advertising was not mentioned to the press, pending a launch press conference of the Party on 26th March.

## ELECTION RESULTS

The eventual size of the Valley Party's vote was considered to be a remarkable success by the Party itself and by members of rival parties' organisations.

The main highlights of the result were:

1. Total votes cast for the Valley Party were 14,838.
2. This constituted 10.8% share of the vote.
3. Valley votes came from the big three parties. All three suffered a loss of share of vote compared with 1986.

4. There are 36 wards and in 31 of them the Valley Party faced opposition from all three of the established parties. In 13 of these wards, the Valley Party finished in either second or third place, ahead of at least one of the major parties. In five of these wards, the Valley Party polled more than the Conservative party.

5. The Labour Party, which has a big majority in the Borough, suffered a loss of share from 47% to 42%. The two Council officers whose opposition to the Valley plan had been most public suffered particularly badly. The Chair of Planning lost his seat to the SDP.

6. The Leader of the Council also suffered. In other wards, where two Labour candidates stood together in a ward, the difference between the two in votes polled averaged 8%. But in his ward, the Leader polled 22% less than his junior Labour colleague. No other reason than the 'Valley factor' has been offered by politicians in the borough for this large shortfall.

The other parties professed amazement at the large number of Valley votes. Subjectively it must be surprising that a party standing on a relatively obscure single issue, where only six of its 60 candidates had any previous political involvement, could poll so many votes. Can the figures be put in more objective context?

The Club estimate that the 'base level' of active supporters (those who regularly attend matches at Selhurst Park) is between 6,000 – 7,000. Of these, it can reasonably be stated that many live outside the London Borough of Greenwich\*. In the final full season at The Valley the average attendance was 5,039. The figure is 34% of votes cast for the Valley Party. Clearly the Valley vote consisted of far more than just Charlton football supporters.

In Greenwich the Green Party polled a total of 4,697 votes giving them 3% share of the Borough vote although they contested 24 seats. The Greens beat the Valley Party in only three of the 24 wards. A typical result was for the Valley Party to poll three times as many votes as the Greens. The reader will recall that in the last year the Green Party has benefited from a television Party Political Broadcast as well as continuous media exposure of issues related to their manifesto.

The Green Party did better in some Boroughs. It achieved 16% in Islington and in Hackney. But its average across London was 9%. No other 'independent' party came anywhere near the Valley Party's share of vote in London\*\*.

This paper's contention is that the advertising was the driving force behind all the factors which persuaded people to Vote Valley. Figure 3 shows our hypothesis on the interaction between these factors. The advertising had a direct effect. But it also drove the media coverage, and inspired the candidates, as we shall describe later.

Do we, though, have evidence that the advertising message and content was a positive factor in people's voting activity? Ideally a telephone poll of voters would have tried to answer the question. The cost prohibited this. However, at a Valley Party meeting on 14th May, after the election, the agency distributed a questionnaire to candidates. All 26 candidates at the meeting completed it. It sheds light on the effect of the advertising:

\* For example, of the 12 who attended the original Party meeting only 8 lived in the borough.
\*\* The agency has been unable to confirm whether the Valley Party's vote was in fact the largest share of vote in one Borough for a Party outside the established group (Conservative, Labour, SDP, Lib. Dem. and Green).

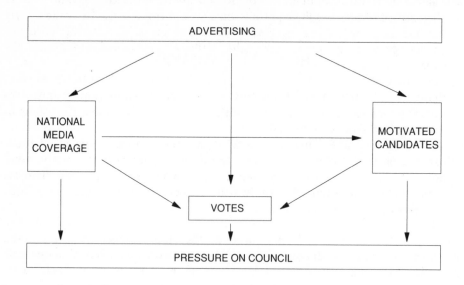

Figure 3.

Q: During your campaign work, can you remember whether people mentioned the advertising campaign to you?

Yes:                          100%
No:                           —
Can't Remember                —

Q: Could you estimate about how many people mentioned the advertising campaign?

Nearly Everybody:             31%
Over Half:                    19%
About Half:                   31%
Less Than Half:               12%
Hardly Any:                   7%

Q: In your words, could you sum up what the *main* comments about the advertising campaign were?

'Clear surprise that a 'small' party could organise such a professional and impressive campaign. The size and quality lifted the Valley Party to the status of the national parties in Greenwich'.

'...the posters and leaflets were instrumental in focusing peoples' minds on the issue'.

It is impossible to offer an accurate analysis of how many extra votes were generated in this way. However, an intriguing 'control' area does exist which can shed some light on the figures. For in the West Midlands, supporters of Wolverhampton Wanderers FC had followed a similar route to the ballot box.

## THE WOLVES CAMPAIGN

The following information was provided to the agency by the supporters of Wolves who initiated their campaign.

Wolves famous ground is owned by the Borough Council. Two sides of it are disused for safety reasons. This restricts the capacity, and restrains the atmosphere. Wolves fans felt the Council were prevaricating. The Council did not wish to spend money on the necessary repairs. Neither though would they sell to Club directors who would make those repairs. The fans therefore decided to stand, in the hope that this would force the Council to address the issue.

The fans hoped that they would field candidates in all 20 seats. In the event they were able to field only two. In both seats the candidates polled 3% each of the vote. Total votes cast for the candidates were 284, constituting 0.3% of the vote throughout Wolverhampton.

The supporters we spoke to told us that they were unaware of the Charlton initiative when they decided to fight an election. They expressed disappointment that they could not field more than two candidates, and had found the effort of distributing one leaflet to be most arduous.

Analysis of the Wolves effort must start with acknowledgement that their argument with the Council was probably not perhaps as bitter as Charlton's. They were at least able to play at their ground. On the other hand Wolves benefit from a large loyal support. During the season just finished, Wolves, a Second Division club, had an average home attendance of 17,044. First Division Charlton's average was 37% lower at 10,755. It is interesting to express votes cast as a percentage of these attendance figures:

| | |
|---|---|
| Charlton | 138.0% |
| Wolves | 1.4% |

In summary here was a similar campaign, but without the benefit of advertising. In terms of the objectives set for Charlton's advertising campaign, the Wolves campaign achieved modest results:

1. No non-local media coverage, other than two lines in the *Guardian* sports page.
2. Candidates in only 10% of the seats, compared with the Valley Party's 100%.
3. Only one leaflet distributed, compared with the Valley Party's three.
4. Only 0.3% of the vote, compared with the Valley Party's 10.8%.

## MEDIA COVERAGE

The Valley Party realised that coverage of such a local issue in national media would increase credibility of the Valley Party in Greenwich, and suggest a political issue that was running out of the Council's control. This paper will contend that, without advertising, the Valley Party could have expected no more than an initial announcement to the effect that 60 football supporters were contesting the Greenwich elections to try and get their club back to its ground. This announcement would have come six weeks before the election. It is difficult to see how non-local journalists would have justified further coverage until after the votes were counted.

The approach to the media for the launch conference had to be carefully planned. It was essential to demonstrate that far from being just 60 football fans, the Valley Party was highly organised and capable of delivering a high profile campaign. So the invitations went out on BMP DDB Needham notepaper, and were designed to hint at the involvement of a large advertising agency in the campaign.

Before the press conference was called there had been just one article in the press outside the Greenwich area. Tables 2, 3 and 4 show the extensive TV, radio and national press coverage following the launch.

TABLE 2: SUMMARY OF TELEVISION COVERAGE OF VALLEY PARTY FOLLOWING PRESS CONFERENCE

| Date | Programme | Time | Feature length | Advertising exposure |
|------|-----------|------|----------------|----------------------|
| 26 March | BBC Newsroom South East | 18.30 | 3 minutes | Showed posters at printers plus proofs |
| 26 March | Thames News | 18.30 | 2 minutes | Showed proofs |
| 26 March | Thames News | 22.30 | 1 minute | Mentioned ad agency |
| 1 May | Thames Reports | 19.30 | 10.5 minutes | Posters in situ. Partly filmed in agency |
| 3/4 May | BBC Newsnight Election Special | 23.00 | — | — |

TABLE 3: RADIO COVERAGE OF VALLEY PARTY FOLLOWING PRESS CONFERENCE

| Date | Programme | Time | Feature length | Advertising mentioned |
|------|-----------|------|----------------|------------------------|
| 27 March | LBC Talkback | 15.00 | 2 minutes | Yes |
| 28 March | Capital Gold Sport | 21.15 | 3 minutes | Yes |
| 4 May | Capital Gold Sport | 20.20 | 3 minutes | No |

The most valuable coverage was considered to be:

1. The TV programmes, because of the instant coverage of the Borough they conferred together with the perceived level of credibility.
2. The *Guardian* and *Time Out* articles. They were perceived by the Agency as 'serious' publications in political terms. Further it was understood by the Valley Party that many councillors read both titles.

TABLE 4: SUMMARY OF PRESS COVERAGE OF VALLEY PARTY FOLLOWING PRESS CONFERENCE
(excluding local South London titles)

| Date | Publication | Position | Size | Comments |
|---|---|---|---|---|
| 7 March | Daily Telegraph | Sport | ½ page | Mentioned advertising role |
| 22 March | Evening Standard | Sport | ½ page | Derided formation of Valley Party |
| 27 March | Evening Standard | Advertising column | 4 paras | Headline 'BMP gets stuck in'. |
| 27 March | Daily Mirror | Sport, back page | 2 paras | |
| 27 March | Guardian | Back page | ⅓ page lead | Photo; advertising a major element |
| 27 March | Times | Sport | 2 paras | |
| 29 March | Campaign | Diary | ½ column | |
| 29 March | Evening Standard | Sport | ⅓ page | Letters rebutting previous article |
| 31 March | Guardian | Sport | ⅓ page | Written by Michael Grade Photos of ads |
| 19 April | Evening Standard | Sport | ⅓ page | Acknowledged fans organisation |
| 22 April | Sunday Times London magazine | Cover story | Cover plus page | Lead article on South London football |
| 25 April | Time Out | Editorial | 1½ pages | Featured advertising; suggested 'Wards could fall' |
| 29 April | Sunday Express | Page 8 | ¼ page | Photo, plus report. Local elect. cover |
| 29 April | Sunday Times | Politics | ⅛ page | Focus on candidate. Mentioned ads |
| 1 May | Daily Mail | Politics (p 16) | ¼ page | Local elect. coverage. Significant cover of ads |
| 4 May | Guardian | Sport | ⅓ page lead | 'The Valley Party makes its point' |
| 4 May | Evening Standard | Page 2 | ½ column | 'Fans cheer as Valley Party rattles rulers' |

The agency has since asked the reporters of the articles and programmes concerned to comment on the role of advertising in their coverage of the story. Specifically they were asked 'Was the advertising an important reason for your initial interest? Was it important in gaining for the story the amounts of time/space achieved?'

Marcus Powell was the reporter who produced the ten minute film on the Valley Party for *Thames Report*, a weekly current affairs programme covering London issues in an investigative style. It goes out at the 'peak' time of 7.30 pm on Tuesdays.

He stated that the advertising was a 'significant element' in the decision to investigate the story. 'The advertising was certainly a fascinating phenomenon in its own right. It made the issue sufficiently interesting to run a story about a political party formed around football'.

The advertising helped him sell the story to his editor. It was something he could focus on. It was significant and serious. It demonstrated that there was professionalism behind the politics.

Mr Powell felt that although without the advertising the story might have run, there was 'every chance it would have been less interesting. With the advertising the story carried a lot more weight than if it had been just the Valley Party. The story needed something like advertising as an ingredient'.

Paul Arnott wrote the two page *Time Out* report which led the magazine's preview of the local elections. In his view the advertising was 'clearly the most interesting thing about The Valley story. In the first instance there is a story about a new party, but interest can die away in a few days. The launch of the advertising sustained the whole thing'. Mr Arnott would have liked an even bigger feature which addressed the pros and cons of a large-scale advertising campaign in a local election.

Michael Herd is Sports Editor of the *Evening Standard*. This paper's stance on the Valley Party shifted from deep scepticism (22 March) to praise for the achievement in the poll (4 May). Mr Herd admits that initially 'I underestimated the influence that the media attention would have on the voters. The involvement of the advertising agency was the initial point of interest because (the campaign) was clearly being done by professional people'.

## MOTIVATION OF CANDIDATES AND SUPPORTERS

Even amongst the organisers, political experience was minimal, and the task of getting 60 candidates, each backed by ten proposers was seen as daunting.

Initially it was not expected that every candidate should actively campaign. In the event the Valley Party believes it was able to deploy a bigger campaign force than all the other parties. The evidence is:

1.  Figure 4 shows attendances at The Valley Party's weekly meetings. Ex-Labour Party activists in the Valley Party state that no more than about 20 people attend pre-local election planning meetings of Greenwich Labour Party. The first Valley Party meeting attracted 12 people. The final one before the election attracted over 300 people who answered an appeal for volunteers to leaflet and canvass. Over 120 stayed for the whole meeting (see Figure 4).
2.  The Valley Party was advised by a political activist that it should aim to deliver three leaflets to the whole Borough, the last one day before the election. The Party set about this task with trepidation. Three drops each to 85,000 homes was an awesome task. In the event it delivered all three leaflets. It turned out that the other parties only delivered one leaflet each on a Borough wide basis*.

This paper contends that the advertising motivated candidates to participate in this way. It is proposed that the advertising persuaded the candidates and supporters that they were part of a big credible campaign, and that the sight of the posters was a continuous morale booster. Without this morale booster, it is

* Some candidates of other parties delivered their own personalised leaflet, as did one Valley Party candidate.

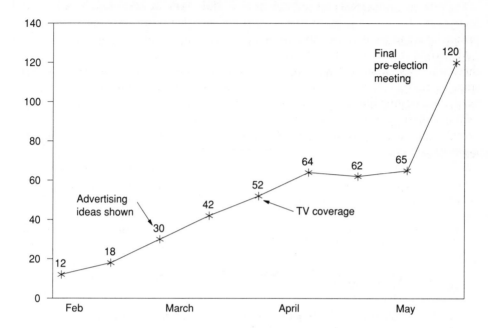

Figure 4. *Attendances at Valley Party's weekly meetings*

proposed that the effective distribution of even one leaflet would have been difficult (NB the Wolves experience).

The questionnaire distributed to candidates on 14 May demonstrates the effect. In the questionnaire the candidates were asked how useful the advertising was to them in their own campaign. Answers to the specific question were:

| | |
|---|---|
| Very useful | 92% |
| Quite useful | 8% |
| Not useful | — |

An open-ended question asked them to explain *how* it helped:

'Personally it helped to convince me to commit time to the campaign. I was not prepared to commit to an amateurish effort which may well have acted to our detriment. The advertising was the factor which pointed us towards a professional campaign'.

'The posters were our standard bearer, providing confidence in the cause and organisation'.

It is perhaps not frivolous to ask how many large companies' sales forces endorse their companies' advertising so comprehensively. One comment also illustrates the practical help the posters provided:

'It was particularly useful whilst canvassing door to door because everybody had heard of the Valley Party and knew what we stood for'.

## CONSUMER APPEAL OF THE ADVERTISING

There is evidence that the advertisements were very well liked by people in the Borough.

At the suggestions of candidates mini-proofs of the posters were made available for sale by the Supporters Club. 'Marketing' was confined to two small references in the Football Club's matchday programme. The proofs went on sale in mid-April. To date, 939 have been sold.

The candidates' questionnaire also replays some very positive comments from consumers:

'The main comment was that people thought the advertising was extremely effective, and they too were proud to either come from Charlton or support Charlton'.

'Because the advertising was so effective and prominent within the Borough, people began to ask about the Valley Party and the issue at stake'.

'It certainly caught the imagination of people, particularly people who remembered the like of Sam Bartram and Don Welsh'.

'Noticeable that electors were drawn to a particular poster, from 'Sam Bartram' for the older group to the 'Boy' appealing to the young family'.

## COST EFFECTIVENESS

This is not obviously a campaign which lends itself to normal measures of cost-effectiveness. This is because its objectives were not essentially commercial. Because the campaign ran so recently, the end result itself is still in doubt. To the client – the Valley Party – the right end result is literally priceless.

The Football Club stands to benefit financially. The reader must assume that since the Club's directors are not multi-millionaires the Club is better off financially playing football at The Valley rather than elsewhere. It is assumed that gates for a given game will always be higher at The Valley than if the same game is played at Selhurst Park or any other shared ground*.

Specifically if planning permission is given this summer, the campaign will have enabled the Club to return to The Valley at least one year earlier than would otherwise have been the case. The Club already owns The Valley ground. At Selhurst Park they are paying a rental of £200,000 per year. By bringing forward the return to The Valley by one year, £200,000 is saved, in addition to any revenue gained from increased gates.

But the Club was not the client. It put in no money to the campaign, although it offered to**.

---

* No market research exists to aid prediction. The Club's view is that 95% of Charlton supporters who attend Selhurst Park would prefer and find it easier to attend The Valley. Virtually no new support around Selhurst Park has been picked up. Conversely 'several thousand' stopped attending when the club moved to Selhurst Park.

** The Valley Party wished to be independent of the Club, since it was feared that opponents might exploit the financial links between Party and Club.

The client was the Valley Party, and it may find that irrespective of the 'final result' all their advertising costs are recovered. This is by virtue of the profit on the sale of mini-proofs of the advertisements.

The cost of the campaign cannot be detailed for commercial reasons but will be no higher than £3,500. The Party purchased 2,500 mini-proofs at a cost of £500. To date 939 have been sold, with very little additional marketing effort, generating profit of nearly £700. The Party are confident that all the rest will be sold at the Club's Open Day in August this year, an annual event attracting around 4,000 visitors. If this is achieved the profit generated will be £3,000. A steady trickle of sales is expected thereafter. It is therefore likely that the advertising will have paid for itself by the end of 1990 in this very direct manner.

## CONCLUSION

The objective of the electoral campaign was to put political pressure on the Council so that it becomes politically desirable to reach an agreement on the Valley application which is acceptable to the Club. The advertising, it has been argued, was at the heart of an effective campaign. It was the advertising which generated powerful media coverage and helped to recruit 60 citizens who in the space of a couple of months became a potent political force in their Borough. That much has already been demonstrated, and forms the main contention of this paper. However, the ultimate test of effectiveness of the advertising is the fulfilment of the electoral campaign objective. What evidence is there that the objective will be achieved?

This paper was prepared three weeks after the election. Already the signs are most encouraging.

At midnight on 3rd May, as the count progressed, a Valley Party official was congratulated by the Chair of the Planning Committee for running 'the best campaign, with the best advertising'. Three hours later the Chair of Planning had lost his seat. At 5 am, the Leader of the Council acknowledged for the first time in public that the supporters could take their place in the discussion. He told the radio station Capital Gold Sport:

'The supporters and the Council I hope are going to work together and we both want the Directors to also join us so that we can get forward a planning application which fits in with Borough wide policies on planning'.

Whilst this was not quite a U-turn, the statement was most encouraging in its acknowledgement of the central role of the supporters. Previously the Council had specifically rejected the involvement of 'third parties' in the planning process.

However, as the political implications of the vote sunk in, the *Mercury* reported a new conciliatory approach emanating from the Council*.

On 21 May, the *Guardian* reporter Martin Thorpe, who had followed the Party's progress from the day of the press launch filed a report that the Council were

---

* Its 17 May edition ran a story on the back page, headed 'Fresh Hope', which reported the new Planning Committee chairman as saying 'I think the Council really wants to resolve the issue. We recognise the legitimate needs of the Club and its supporters...'

making conciliatory noises prior to a meeting with Charlton chairman Roger Alwen on 30th May*.

On 31st May, the agency spoke to Roger Alwen who confirmed that the Council's attitude had markedly softened, that the Leader had confirmed his wish to see Charlton back at The Valley – as opposed to just Greenwich – and that the Council had agreed to a timescale involving a decision by the end of June 1990.

Mr Alwen highlighted three benefits to the Club emanating from the campaign.

1. The publicity generated by the advertising hurt the Council. In particular the *Thames Reports* programme was a major upset for them.
2. The campaign gave a lift to those involved at the Club during April and of course on election night.
3. The publicity generated by the advertising attracted the attention of members of the Shadow Cabinet, who, Mr Alwen said, are concerned that the Greenwich attitude to football should not be repeated by any other Labour controlled Council.

So although it is too early to record victory, the signs are encouraging that The Valley will once again echo to the sounds of its lost tribe next year. It will be an emotional moment for thousands. For the 60 candidates, it will be a moment when they reflect that it was all down to their remarkable decision to turn football into a political issue, and to run an advertising campaign. It can safely be forecast that they will have had no regrets about their investment.

* Mr Thorpe's report said: '...after the local election success of the Valley Party, who are campaigning for Charlton's return to the Valley ground, Greenwich Council is making conciliatory noises over the club's planned development of the site with a new stadium, plus offices and a banqueting suite to help finance the projects. The Council turned down the Club's original plan because some buildings were deemed too large for a residential area. Now Charlton's chairman, Roger Alwen, is to submit three revised plans to the council on May 30, one of which proposes turning the pitch 90 degrees so that the offending buildings can be sited well away from residential streets'.

## APPENDIX

### *Candidates Record of Quotes from Electorate on the Advertising*

'Amazement that a local election could produce firstly posters of such quality backed by leaflets that made such a broad appeal based on a single issue'.

'Most people were extremely impressed by the professionalism of the campaign'.

'Some people also commented...that they couldn't drive too far in the Borough without seeing one of our posters'.

'It was run really professionally, and many people congratulated the Party'.

'The advertising campaign had a significant effect on the result...I feel my 18.5% was partly due to the poster campaign'.

'Some people even said they would vote for me because of it'.

'Made the other parties' PR look like a Tom and Jerry cartoon'.

### *Candidates' Comments on Usefulness of the Advertising to Them*

'...indicated to the public that the Valley Party campaign was being run in a serious and committed way by people not on the lunatic fringe'.

'At a time when football supporters have a poor reputation national, (sic), this enabled us to rise above it. It was crucial in launching the new Party'.

'The advertisements were able to develop a sense of pride among the workers/supporters which helped give them/us the confidence and self belief to go out and do what we did achieve at the ballot box'.

## ADDENDUM

On 2 April 1991 Greenwich Council approved a revised planning application from Charlton Athletic. The Club expect to return to play football at The Valley in August 1991.

# Index